Recent Advances in Educational Robotics

Recent Advances in Educational Robotics

Editors

Savvas A. Chatzichristofis
Zinon Zinonos

MDPI • Basel • Beijing • Wuhan • Barcelona • Belgrade • Manchester • Tokyo • Cluj • Tianjin

Editors
Savvas A. Chatzichristofis
Neapolis University Pafos
Cyprus

Zinon Zinonos
Neapolis University
Cyprus

Editorial Office
MDPI
St. Alban-Anlage 66
4052 Basel, Switzerland

This is a reprint of articles from the Special Issue published online in the open access journal *Electronics* (ISSN 2079-9292) (available at: https://www.mdpi.com/journal/electronics/special_issues/educational_robotics).

For citation purposes, cite each article independently as indicated on the article page online and as indicated below:

LastName, A.A.; LastName, B.B.; LastName, C.C. Article Title. *Journal Name* **Year**, *Volume Number*, Page Range.

ISBN 978-3-0365-7052-5 (Hbk)
ISBN 978-3-0365-7053-2 (PDF)

© 2023 by the authors. Articles in this book are Open Access and distributed under the Creative Commons Attribution (CC BY) license, which allows users to download, copy and build upon published articles, as long as the author and publisher are properly credited, which ensures maximum dissemination and a wider impact of our publications.

The book as a whole is distributed by MDPI under the terms and conditions of the Creative Commons license CC BY-NC-ND.

Contents

About the Editors vii

Savvas A. Chatzichristofis
Recent Advances in Educational Robotics
Reprinted from: Electronics 2023, 12, 925, doi:10.3390/electronics12040925 1

Ricardo J. Ruiz, Jorge L. Saravia, Víctor H. Andaluz and Jorge S. Sánchez
Virtual Training System for Unmanned Aerial Vehicle Control Teaching–Learning Processes
Reprinted from: Electronics 2022, 11, 2613, doi:10.3390/electronics11162613 7

Christos Chronis and Iraklis Varlamis
FOSSBot: An Open Source and Open Design Educational Robot
Reprinted from: Electronics 2022, 11, 2606, doi:10.3390/electronics11162606 27

Majd Kassawat, Enric Cervera and Angel P. del Pobil
An Omnidirectional Platform for Education and Research in Cooperative Robotics
Reprinted from: Electronics 2022, 11, 499, doi:10.3390/electronics11030499 41

Sandra Cano
A Methodological Approach to the Teaching STEM Skills in Latin America through Educational Robotics for School Teachers
Reprinted from: Electronics 2022, 11, 395, doi:10.3390/electronics11030395 53

Andres El-Fakdi and Xavier Cufí
An Innovative Low Cost Educational Underwater Robotics Platform for Promoting Engineering Interest among Secondary School Students
Reprinted from: Electronics 2022, 11, 373, doi:10.3390/electronics11030373 75

Georgios Tsalmpouris, George Tsinarakis, Nikolaos Gertsakis, Savvas A. Chatzichristofis and Lefteris Doitsidis
HYDRA: Introducing a Low-Cost Framework for STEM Education Using Open Tools
Reprinted from: Electronics 2021, 10, 3056, doi:10.3390/electronics10243056 91

Dimitris Ziouzios, Dimitrios Rammos, Tharrenos Bratitsis and Minas Dasygenis
Utilizing Educational Robotics for Environmental Empathy Cultivation in Primary Schools
Reprinted from: Electronics 2021, 10, 2389, doi:10.3390/electronics10192389 111

Deepti Mishra, Karen Parish, Ricardo Gregorio Lugo and Hao Wang
A Framework for Using Humanoid Robots in the School Learning Environment
Reprinted from: Electronics 2021, 10, 756, doi:10.3390/electronics10060756 127

Vivien Lin, Hui-Chin Yeh and Nian-Shing Chen
A Systematic Review on Oral Interactions in Robot-Assisted Language Learning
Reprinted from: Electronics 2022, 11, 290, doi:10.3390/electronics11020290 139

George A. Papakostas, George K. Sidiropoulos, Cristina I. Papadopoulou, Eleni Vrochidou, Vassilis G. Kaburlasos, Maria T. Papadopoulou, et al.
Social Robots in Special Education: A Systematic Review
Reprinted from: Electronics 2021, 10, 1398, doi:10.3390/electronics10121398 177

Aphrodite Sophokleous, Panayiotis Christodoulou, Lefteris Doitsidis and Savvas A. Chatzichristofis
Computer Vision Meets Educational Robotics
Reprinted from: Electronics 2021, 10, 730, doi:10.3390/electronics10060730 213

Jesús López-Belmonte, Adrián Segura-Robles, Antonio-José Moreno-Guerrero and María-Elena Parra-González
Robotics in Education: A Scientific Mapping of the Literature in Web of Science
Reprinted from: *Electronics* **2021**, *10*, 291, doi:10.3390/electronics10030291 . . . . **237**

About the Editors

Savvas A. Chatzichristofis

Professor of Artificial Intelligence, Neapolis University Pafos, Cyprus. Savvas A. Chatzichristofis pursued a diploma and Ph.D. degree (with honors) from the Department of Electrical and Computer Engineering, Democritus University of Thrace, Greece. Today, he serves as Vice Rector for Research and Innovation and a Professor of AI at the Department of Computer Science of the Neapolis University Pafos in Cyprus. His research endeavors center on the exciting intersection of Artificial Intelligence, Computer Vision, and Robotics. In recent years, he has served as Adjunct Lecturer at Cyprus University of Technology (CUT), as well as a senior researcher at the Centre for Research and Technology Hellas (CE.R.T.H.), Information Technologies Institute (I.T.I.). Moreover, he has served as a Visiting Professor for teaching and research cooperation at Institute for Information Technology (ITEC) at Klagenfurt University in Austria.

Zinon Zinonos

Assistant Professor of IoT, Neapolis University Pafos, Cyprus. Dr. Zinon Zinonos received a diploma in Computer Engineering from the Computer Engineering and Informatics Department (CEID) of the University of Patras, Greece, in 2005, and M.Sc and Ph.D degrees from Computer Science Department, University of Cyprus, in 2008 and 2013, respectively, in computer science. In recent years, he has served as as a Postdoctoral Researcher at KIOS Center of Intelligent Systems and Networks and a Visiting Lecturer at Neapolis University. He has served as a reviewer for scientific journals in the area of Internet of Things, Sensor Networks, Wireless, AdHoc and Mobile Networks, and Mobile Computing. He has published articles in journals and presented his work at several conferences organized by the computer science and communication networks community.

Editorial

Recent Advances in Educational Robotics

Savvas A. Chatzichristofis

Intelligent Systems Laboratory, Department of Computer Science, Neapolis University Pafos, Pafos 8042, Cyprus; s.chatzichristofis@nup.ac.cy

Abstract: The widespread use of artificial intelligence and robotics contributes, among other things, to create a new scientific field that aims to modernize and disrupt education. The term 'educational robotics' is being introduced as a learning tool and definitively transforming young people's education. At the same time, however, it is helping to create a fast-growing new industry that produces educational robots and tools. Companies with a long tradition, either in the creation of robotic equipment or in the production and distribution of toys, are setting up appropriate divisions and supplying the market with electronic devices for educational robotics. This new market is overgrowing and is rapidly becoming an investment attraction. According to MarketsandMarkets research, the educational robotics market is projected to grow from USD 1.3 billion in 2021 to USD 2.6 billion by 2026. Notably, the educational robotics market is expected to grow at a Compound Annual Growth Rate (CAGR) of 16.1% from 2021 to 2026. At the same time, however, the field is attracting many startups securing independent funding for equipment design and implementation and independent efforts competing for funding from crowdfunding platforms. More than 2000 ideas have recently secured funding to build and distribute educational robotics tools through Kickstarter-type platforms. However, what is educational robotics, and how is it expected to transform how the next generation is educated?

Keywords: educational robotics; computer vision; educational tool

Citation: Chatzichristofis, S.A. Recent Advances in Educational Robotics. *Electronics* **2023**, *12*, 925. https://doi.org/10.3390/electronics12040925

Received: 7 February 2023
Accepted: 10 February 2023
Published: 12 February 2023

Copyright: © 2023 by the authors. Licensee MDPI, Basel, Switzerland. This article is an open access article distributed under the terms and conditions of the Creative Commons Attribution (CC BY) license (https://creativecommons.org/licenses/by/4.0/).

1. Introduction

Although the term educational robotics has been introduced into our everyday life in recent years, the research and development of tools dating back to 1969, Seymour Papert was the first to design and implement the Turtle robot, which allows students, by programming in Logo programming language, to move it. His effort is recorded as the maiden attempt at an alternative way of teaching algorithmic thinking and programming. At the same time, however, it is also a source of inspiration for the toy manufacturer Lego. With the expiry of the patent rights on the blocks that are the building blocks for the development of its products, Lego is in a difficult financial situation and is looking for alternatives. The Turtle robot forms the foundation for the company's new product, dynamic and programmable blocks. Lego introduces a product to the market that provides consumers with the possibility of programming in addition to the traditional option of building. Static constructions that helped develop many skills are evolving into animated units. Children, through play, are taught programming principles, expanding their knowledge base with skills that are likely to become the cornerstone of the demands of the modern age. At the same time, however, the market is welcoming a new product, and the commercial use of the term educational robotics is becoming widely known. In the years that followed, many companies presented similar solutions, developing the subject in a multidimensional way. Companies such as Robolink, Hanson Robotics, Modular Robotics, Primo Toys, and Engino develop excellent tools that transform the way of teaching. At the same time, research institutions and universities, with scientists from different research fields (computer science, engineering, psychology, and teaching sciences), are joining forces and presenting teaching methods and techniques that target specific expected educational outcomes.

Given the increased interest of researchers [1] and considering the new findings in the field [2,3], we found it valuable to design a Special Issue on recent advances in educational robotics. The subject of educational robotics focuses on the intersection of robotics and the education sciences. Unfortunately, the absence in the literature of journals focused on this field limits researchers from publishing their work. Therefore, the Special Issue published 12 papers, of which 4 were review articles. By observing the articles, one can easily observe that the Special Issue involves five academic institutions from Greece, four from Spain, three from Taiwan, two from Norway, one from Cyprus, one from Ecuador, and one from Chile. (kindly refer to Figure 1) The following section analyses the findings from these articles.

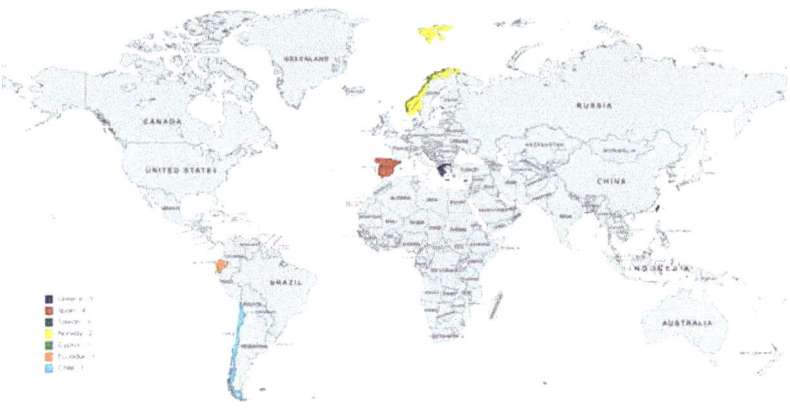

Figure 1. Geographical distribution of academic institutions participating in the Special Issue.

2. Analysis of the Articles

Toma et al. [4] developed a virtual unmanned aerial vehicle control training system in their work. It uses the mathematical models of kinematics and dynamics to visualize the behavior of uncrewed aerial vehicles. The new system can be used for educational processes without purchasing a physical robot. Furthermore, researchers proved the stability and robustness of the controller by implementing the advanced control algorithm for autonomous trajectory tracking tasks, both in the virtual training system and in the test performed experimentally with the hexacopter.

In another work [5], researchers introduce FOSSBot, a new educational solution that can cover multiple learning needs and can be adopted by different ages and programming skill levels. The proposed robot is 3D-printable and features a flexible software stack that supports four operating modes, such as block-based or text-based programming. The paper provides a detailed list of electronics and printable parts and their assembly instructions. The open nature of FOSSBot makes it a unique tool for educators who can teach several subjects, such as programming, sciences, and arts, at all educational levels.

A new robotic platform suitable for research and education in cooperative robotics is also presented in Kassawat et al. work [6]. The researchers introduce a novel concept for cooperatively lifting, manipulating, and transporting an object through the new robot platform. The proposed robot consists of three omnidirectional wheels with two additional traction wheels, making multi-robot object manipulation possible. To validate the new system, researchers conducted three experiments using a setup with one robot and one target object.

Using the Arduino platform, Cano, in her recent work [7], developed a methodological approach for teaching STEM skills with a genre focus. The proposed method includes a learning model called 5E (Engage, Explore, Explain, Elaborate, and Evaluate). It aimed to design a set of workshops for introducing concepts in electronics and programming.

Researchers conducted workshops in virtual mode through the Zoom platform with teachers from Latin American schools. It was confirmed that Arduino, its components, and the workshop increase students' creativity, attitude, and motivation.

El-Fakdi et al. in [8] present an educational robotics project specially designed for university students. Participants can create an underwater device using low-cost materials based on the proposed project. The Underwater Robotics Workshop project has been held for more than 13 years at the University of Girona, explaining the research in underwater robotics that is carried out there. The project aimed to promote physics, engineering, electronics, programming, and robotics. The authors presented positive feedback from participating students and teachers as concerned about students' satisfaction and learning objectives.

Another educational system driven by the need for low-cost solutions is proposed in [9]. The proposed method is called HYDRA and addresses elementary and secondary educational needs. The new system provides an expandable, modular design of low complexity for students without previous experience in programming and robotics. However, its most important feature is its slight learning curve. The researchers evaluated HYDRA using flow theory in three different grades of a Greek elementary school and found a high adoption rate among the participants.

A different use of educational robotics is presented in Ziouzios et al. [10] work. More precisely, researchers aimed to measure the development of children's empathy through the proposed educational scenario. In this project, a robot gives the students a message from the future, warning them about climate change and encouraging them to change their thinking and attitudes. A pilot study including 50 students in a sixth-grade class proved that the development of children's empathy and the effectiveness of programming on the robot were complemented and enriched with the pre-existing knowledge of teachers. Moreover, using a robot to convey the message increased students' interest and participation.

As concerns humanoid robots, Mishra et al. [11] proposed a multidisciplinary framework for using humanoid robots in an educational environment. The proposed framework has four aspects: technological, pedagogical, the efficacy of humanoid robots, and a consideration of the ethical implications of using humanoid robots. Moreover, the authors proposed a way to apply and evaluate the framework and a case study. Lin et al. [12] conducted a systematic review of 22 empirical studies published between 2010 and 2020 to study their interactive designs of oral tasks by evaluating the teaching methods, the types of oral tasks, the role played by the robots and the facilitators, and their effectiveness as a tool for improving oral competence. Researchers concluded that robot-assisted language learning instructional design employs communicative language teaching and storytelling as the most dominant language learning methods, and audiolingual and total physical response methods often complement these two methods.

The use of humanoid robots in special education is described by Papacostas et al. [13] in a systematic review of the period 2008 to 2020. The research focused on the investigation of the degree of integration of social robots in the training of special education individuals, the assessment of the scope of application of social robots in different impairments, the search for different types of social robots and their appropriateness by category of impairments and the emergence of challenges that need to be addressed for social robots to make a significant contribution to the social integration of people with impairments. The review presented various robots that target very different skills and children with diverse special education needs. However, it is pointed out that most of them were designed for something other than the specific needs of special education individuals.

Sophokleous et al. [14], in their review, focused on the studies that show how computer vision supports educational robotics. Using a systematic mapping process, they analyzed 21 primary articles from the recent literature. More precisely, they investigated computer vision's role, benefits, and efficiency in educational robots in K-12 education. The study showed that computer vision in educational robots has a high potential for teaching assistance. It is also shown that students' interest and satisfaction increase when computer vision is used in educational robotics projects. At the same time, they learn the concepts they are taught more efficiently and complete their work in less time.

Finally, Belmonte et al. [15] analyzed 926 scientific papers related to the "robotics" concept in the educational field from the Web of Science database. The authors discussed several topics: educational research, education of scientific disciplines, engineering, interdisciplinary computer science, and applications. More than half of investigated papers appeared in conference proceedings. Based on the focus of the scientific publication, this work found three different periods: in 1975–2012, physics engineering issues of robots, and basic concepts of education were the most prominent subjects; in 2013–2016, the most important topics were "programming" and "computational thinking" and in 2017–2019 subjects such as technologies supporting training and simulation techniques were the most discussed topics.

3. Conclusions

Conversely, educational robotics is a powerful and flexible learning tool that supports learners and instructors in many learning environments. Educational robotics is primarily suitable for teaching science, mathematics, technology, and computing. However, it can also be applied to other fields, such as literature, theatre, and the arts. As an educational tool, the robot can offer practical yet fun activities. It helps to create an enjoyable and participatory environment that keeps students interested and engaged. In addition, the play aspect involved in robots is an essential factor of positive motivation. Through hands-on robotics activities, students cease to be passive recipients of knowledge and take an active role. The activities allow them to deepen and 'master' more meaningful knowledge about their study subjects. In addition to acquiring new knowledge, the hands-on involvement offered by robotics has been shown to lead to the development and improvement of skills needed in the 21st century, such as problem-solving, critical thinking, and cooperation.

Acknowledgments: We thank all researchers who submitted articles to this Special Issue for their excellent contributions. We are also grateful to all reviewers who helped evaluate the manuscripts and made valuable suggestions to improve the quality of their contributions. We want to acknowledge the editorial board of *Electronics*, who invited us to guest edit this Special Issue. We are also grateful to the *Electronics* Editorial Office staff, who worked thoroughly to maintain the rigorous peer-review schedule and timely publication.

Conflicts of Interest: The authors declare no conflict of interest.

References

1. Evripidou, S.; Georgiou, K.; Doitsidis, L.; Amanatiadis, A.A.; Zinonos, Z.; Chatzichristofis, S.A. Educational robotics: Platforms, competitions and expected learning outcomes. *IEEE Access* **2020**, *8*, 219534–219562. [CrossRef]
2. Evripidou, S.; Amanatiadis, A.; Christodoulou, K.; Chatzichristofis, S.A. Introducing Algorithmic Thinking and Sequencing Using Tangible Robots. *IEEE Trans. Learn. Technol.* **2021**, *14*, 93–105. [CrossRef]
3. Evripidou, S.; Doitsidis, L.; Tsinarakis, G.J.; Zinonos, Z.; Chatzichristofis, S.A. Selecting a Robotic Platform for Education. In Proceedings of the IEEE International Conference on Consumer Electronics, ICCE 2022, Las Vegas, NV, USA, 7–9 January 2022; pp. 1–6. [CrossRef]
4. Toma, C.; Popa, M.; Iancu, B.; Doinea, M.; Pascu, A.; Ioan-Dutescu, F. Edge Machine Learning for the Automated Decision and Visual Computing of the Robots, IoT Embedded Devices or UAV-Drones. *Electronics* **2022**, *11*, 3507. [CrossRef]
5. Chronis, C.; Varlamis, I. FOSSBot: An Open Source and Open Design Educational Robot. *Electronics* **2022**, *11*, 2606. [CrossRef]
6. Kassawat, M.; Cervera, E.; del Pobil, A.P. An omnidirectional platform for education and research in cooperative robotics. *Electronics* **2022**, *11*, 499. [CrossRef]
7. Cano, S. A methodological approach to the teaching stem skills in Latin America through educational robotics for School Teachers. *Electronics* **2022**, *11*, 395. [CrossRef]
8. El-Fakdi, A.; Cufí, X. An Innovative Low Cost Educational Underwater Robotics Platform for Promoting Engineering Interest among Secondary School Students. *Electronics* **2022**, *11*, 373. [CrossRef]
9. Tsalmpouris, G.; Tsinarakis, G.; Gertsakis, N.; Chatzichristofis, S.A.; Doitsidis, L. HYDRA: Introducing a low-cost framework for STEM education using open tools. *Electronics* **2021**, *10*, 3056. [CrossRef]
10. Ziouzios, D.; Rammos, D.; Bratitsis, T.; Dasygenis, M. Utilizing educational robotics for environmental empathy cultivation in primary schools. *Electronics* **2021**, *10*, 2389. [CrossRef]

11. Mishra, D.; Parish, K.; Lugo, R.G.; Wang, H. A framework for using humanoid robots in the school learning environment. *Electronics* **2021**, *10*, 756. [CrossRef]
12. Lin, V.; Yeh, H.C.; Chen, N.S. A systematic review on oral interactions in robot-assisted language learning. *Electronics* **2022**, *11*, 290. [CrossRef]
13. Papakostas, G.A.; Sidiropoulos, G.K.; Papadopoulou, C.I.; Vrochidou, E.; Kaburlasos, V.G.; Papadopoulou, M.T.; Holeva, V.; Nikopoulou, V.A.; Dalivigkas, N. Social robots in special education: A systematic review. *Electronics* **2021**, *10*, 1398. [CrossRef]
14. Sophokleous, A.; Christodoulou, P.; Doitsidis, L.; Chatzichristofis, S.A. Computer vision meets educational robotics. *Electronics* **2021**, *10*, 730. [CrossRef]
15. López-Belmonte, J.; Segura-Robles, A.; Moreno-Guerrero, A.J.; Parra-González, M.E. Robotics in education: A scientific mapping of the literature in Web of Science. *Electronics* **2021**, *10*, 291. [CrossRef]

Disclaimer/Publisher's Note: The statements, opinions and data contained in all publications are solely those of the individual author(s) and contributor(s) and not of MDPI and/or the editor(s). MDPI and/or the editor(s) disclaim responsibility for any injury to people or property resulting from any ideas, methods, instructions or products referred to in the content.

Article

Virtual Training System for Unmanned Aerial Vehicle Control Teaching–Learning Processes

Ricardo J. Ruiz *, Jorge L. Saravia *, Víctor H. Andaluz * and Jorge S. Sánchez *

Departamento de Eléctrica y Electrónica, Universidad de las Fuerzas Armadas ESPE, Sangolquí 171103, Ecuador
* Correspondence: rjruiz3@espe.edu.ec (R.J.R.); jlsaravia@espe.edu.ec (J.L.S.); vhandaluz1@espe.edu.ec (V.H.A.); jssanchez@espe.edu.ec (J.S.S.); Tel.: +593-958-779-578 (V.H.A.)

Abstract: The present work is focused on the development of a Virtual Environment as a test system for new advanced control algorithms for an Unmanned Aerial Vehicles. The virtualized environment allows us to visualize the behavior of the UAV by including the mathematical model of it. The mathematical structure of the kinematic and dynamic models is represented in a matrix form in order to be used in different control algorithms proposals. For the dynamic model, the constants are obtained experimentally, using a DJI Matrice 600 Pro UAV. All of this is conducted with the purpose of using the virtualized environment in educational processes in which, due to the excessive cost of the materials, it is not possible to acquire physical equipment; moreover, is it desired to avoid damaging them. Finally, the stability and robustness of the proposed controllers are determined to ensure analytically the compliance with the control criteria and its correct operation.

Keywords: UAV; autonomous control; hexacopter; dynamic compensation; dynamic model

Citation: Ruiz, R.J.; Saravia, J.L.; Andaluz, V.H.; Sánchez, J.S. Virtual Training System for Unmanned Aerial Vehicle Control Teaching–Learning Processes. *Electronics* **2022**, *11*, 2613. https://doi.org/10.3390/electronics11162613

Academic Editors: Savvas A. Chatzichristofis and Zinon Zinonos

Received: 29 June 2022
Accepted: 2 August 2022
Published: 20 August 2022

Publisher's Note: MDPI stays neutral with regard to jurisdictional claims in published maps and institutional affiliations.

Copyright: © 2022 by the authors. Licensee MDPI, Basel, Switzerland. This article is an open access article distributed under the terms and conditions of the Creative Commons Attribution (CC BY) license (https://creativecommons.org/licenses/by/4.0/).

1. Introduction

With each generation for the last couple of decades, the rate at which technologic innovations are changing society has been accelerating. The way we communicate, interact, and conduct our daily work is vastly different compared to previous generations [1]. Due to this, many working areas had to adapt to this new and fast changes, being the educational sector one of the most salient. This is because education is one of the most influential factors in the progress and growth of people and societies [2,3], in which the learning and teaching process in superior education institutes is a key point for that advance. In addition to contribute with theorical knowledge, this institute offers a great reinforcement in the practical application of this concepts [4], achieving a better performance in the future generations of professionals, who can specialize in any branch of knowledge, such as medicine, construction, industrial automatization, and robotics, among others.

Robotics and automation play an important role in industries across the world. Recent technological advances have enabled robots to excel in industrial automation, gaining advantages, e.g., in improving quality and increasing production [5]. Nowadays, robots are no longer restricted only to the industrial sector; they have gradually spread to different applications in non-industrial environments and are called service robots. These can perform a variety of tasks for the entertainment or assistance in the daily life of a person [6]. Among the service robots that attract most attention in the scientific community are Unmanned Aerial Vehicles (UAVs), by virtue of the fact that they can perform completely autonomous tasks in unstructured spaces [7]. The applications of UAVs include navigation and localization [8], bridge and building inspection [9], extreme sports videography [10], autonomous detection of damage to steel surfaces by capturing panoramic images [11], and so on. Most of these areas share the same purpose to track a desired trajectory [12].

Unfortunately, the COVID-19 pandemic had an unprecedented impact on education. Classrooms were emptied and lockdowns were imposed [13]. Universities, professors, and students were expected to adapt to the new circumstances and continue to achieve their educational goals. This forced education systems around the world to quickly switch to an emergency remote education. This mean that the institution and its users could communicate at a distance during the crisis, making greater use of Information and Communication Technologies (ICT). These are tools that transfer, process, and store information digitally [14], thus turning classrooms into virtual ones and increasing the popularity of immersive virtual environments [15].

What is sought with the virtualization of a process or scenario is to provide the user with a sense of immersion and interactivity to capture their attention. There are several ways to develop virtual environments, as detailed in [16], using different modeling languages and software, but the one that has a greater interest for its technological development is Virtual Reality (VR) in three-dimensional environments. VR is focused on stimulating a person's visual and auditory senses to replicate the experience of a real situation through a computer simulation [17]. This is a benefit when it is necessary to recreate events that may be costly or difficult to carry out in the real world. In addition, it is a great tool for training new skills remotely [18], as can be seen in the following examples. In the instrumentation area, the work presented by [19] presents a VR training system for the industrial maintenance of hydraulic pumps. For the automotive area [20] shows a low-cost VR system to simulate vehicle prototypes quickly. In the mechatronics area, ref. [21] proposes a VR environment to simulate control algorithms in simulation tasks of a wheelchair as robotic assistance and [22] also presents a unicycle robot training control in environments with hardware in the loop.

This work considers the constructivist pedagogical model, which allows students or users to contribute to their own learning process [23]. Therefore, the development of immersive and interactive virtual reality environments with users allows to simulate environments that resemble reality in different areas of knowledge, without the need for a high economic investment, or endangering the user, among other advantages [24]. Thus, nowadays, there are different strategies to capture the attention of users, for example, gamification strategies oriented to education through the development of serious games [25].

The purpose of these games is that they serve to test and explore multiple solutions to problems posed in real situations, and discover the information and knowledge that would help to intervene without fear of making mistakes [26]. Therefore, this work presents an interactive and immersive virtual training system that allows the implementation and evaluation of advanced control algorithms for the autonomous and teleoperated navigation of a UAV. The virtual system is intended to serve as a learning tool in the engineering area, specifically in the robotics area. The virtual environment is developed in the Unity3D graphics engine (Unity Software Inc., San Francisco, CA, USA). In addition, the kinematic and dynamic modeling of the UAV is incorporated with the purpose of generating greater realism in the flight animation. The mathematical models are obtained through the heuristic method and experimentally validated with the DJI Matrice 600 Pro hexacopter (DJI, Nashan District, Shenzen, China). The control scheme implements a cascade controller, which consists of a kinematic controller and another one with dynamic compensation, for which the mathematical model requires as input control signals the maneuvering velocities of the UAV. For the implementation of the advanced control algorithms the mathematical software MatLab (the MathWorks Inc., Natick, MA, USA) is considered. Therefore, a real time communication between Unity and MatLab software is considered through shared memories developed by the authors. Finally, the results obtained through the 3D virtual simulator and validated by experimental tests are presented. In addition, the usability results are presented in order to evaluate the acceptance of the developed virtual system.

The following document consists of six sections. Section 2 describes the structure of the virtual environment and the methodology that relates the teaching–learning process. Section 3 describes the UAV used, including its mathematical modeling. Section 4 explains the control scheme together with a kinematic and a dynamically compensated controller. Section 5 presents the results obtained from experimentation and simulation, as well as the percentage of usability of the virtual training system. Finally, Section 6 contains the conclusions of the application of the virtual environment.

2. Methodology and Digitalization

Reality Virtual (VR) has become a broad topic of research in recent years, as an innovative solution to the problem facing higher education in times of pandemic. For the development of the work, different techniques of 3D digitization, modeling, controller design are used, including a process of experimentation.

2.1. Methodology

The methodology used was based on the scheme shown in Figure 1, which shows several stages of development that allow the implementation of a 3D virtual simulator.

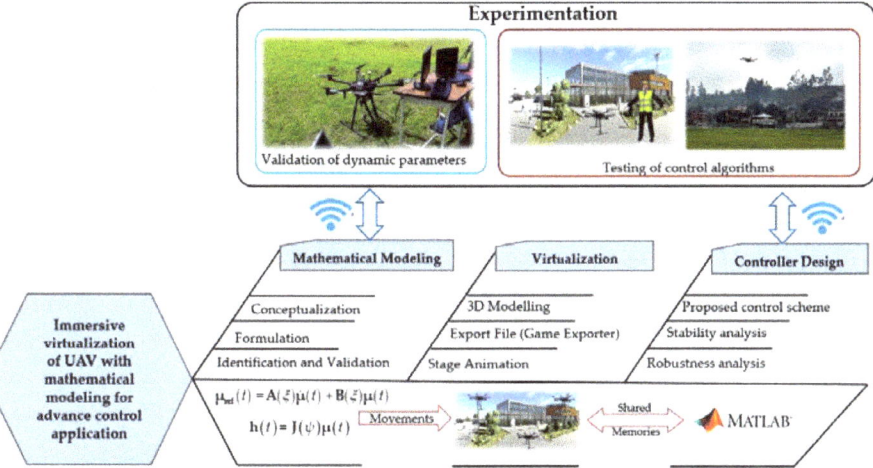

Figure 1. Methodology for the control and virtualization of UAVs.

The scheme proposed in Figure 1 is composed of three main stages, validated through experimental tests: (i) Mathematical Modeling is performed in order to simulate the UAV behavior in the virtual environment. Therefore, a kinematic model representing the navigation characteristics and restrictions is considered; and a dynamic model representing the dynamic behavior of the UAV-environment interaction. In addition, the identification and validation of the dynamic parameters is considered through experimental tests with the UAV Matrice 600 pro; (ii) Virtualization, both the UAV and the elements of the virtual environment are modeled using CAD tools, considering their real shapes. In addition, elements that allow simulating disturbances and different weather conditions that affect the navigation of the UAV when executing a defined task are considered. Then, by means of the 3DS Max software (Autodesk, San Francisco, CA, USA), we exported the files compatible with the Unity 3D software; (iii) Controller Design, the virtualized environment being focused for teaching–learning processes allows the testing of different proposals of advanced control algorithms, in the case of the present research the proposal is a cascade system; a controller based on the kinematic model for the tracking of the assigned trajectory considering that the robot manages to adapt perfectly to the control speeds; and a compensator based on the dynamic model, since for reasons of dynamics, reference speeds are needed to achieve the control speeds in the UAV. Then, these control speeds are communicated with the Unity 3D platform through the use of DLL libraries. Therefore, the closed control loop implemented between Unity3D and MatLab software is used at a sampling time of 100 [ms].

Finally, the tests are performed both in the real UAV Matrice 600 and in the virtualized UAV, which allows checking the operation of the proposed control algorithms and comparing with the tests in the virtual environment developed. With the purpose of validating the use of virtual environments in teaching–learning processes as test systems for new proposals of advanced control algorithms.

2.2. Virtual Environment

Virtual environments focused on the teaching–learning process must have real life scenes present, allowing robot–human interaction, ensuring educability. Next, the implementation of a virtual simulator that allows interaction with the virtualized hexacopter for future proposals of advanced control algorithms is detailed. In addition, the environment has elements and sounds that simulate rural and urban scenarios to increase immersion in the virtual environment. The process carried out for the Virtual Simulator was based on the scheme shown in Figure 2, where the developed sections are described.

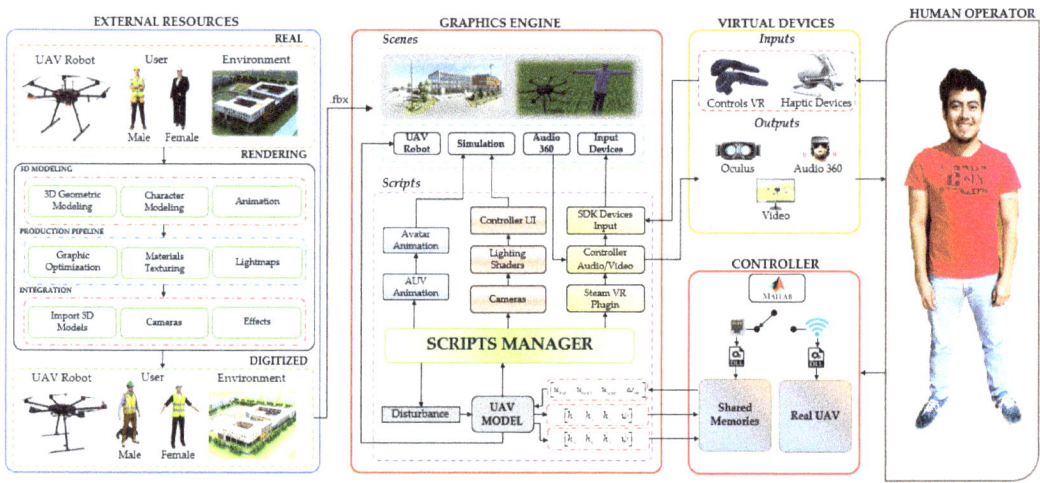

Figure 2. Proposed outline of the virtual simulator.

For the development of the virtual environment, the diagram in Figure 2, is made up of the following phases: (i) External Resources, includes all the elements immersed in the virtual environment, these elements can be organized mainly into three groups: (a) virtualized scenario, referred to urban, rural, and educational environments, as close to reality as possible in order to achieve learning in the environment itself for the implementation of the different advanced control algorithms for UAV trajectory tracking; (b) Virtualized UAV, the DJI Matrice 600 Pro hexacopter is digitized based on its physical characteristics and real dimensions; (c) Avatar represents the user who will use the simulator, for the digitization the anthropomorphic aspect of a human, male and female, is taken into account. The role that the avatar can play can be changed and this affects the clothing of the digital model. To perform the digitization process of these resources, CAD tools are used to model the elements, then using software such as 3DS Max and SketchUp, among others. In addition, layers are added to the elements to increase their realism, finally, the files are exported in .fbx compatible with Unity software; (ii) Graphics Engine, Unity is defined as a graphics development platform, available for Microsoft Windows, Mac OS, and Linux [27]. The development process of the virtual environment in Unity is organized in two groups:

(a) The Virtual Scenario, conformed by all the external resources digitized in .fbx format, audios, and other elements that allow the user's senses to be deceived. On the other hand, the virtual scenario is equipped with a user interface (UI), which facilitates the user's interaction with the simulator by modifying desired tasks, physical characteristics of the environment, avatar gender selection, among others. It is also worth mentioning that this virtual scenario has implemented a real-time graphic representation system, where the evolution of each of the control errors can be observed; and (b) Programming Scripts, are one of the most relevant features when developing a 3D virtual simulator, since they allow emulating the real behavior of an Unmanned Aerial Vehicle. These movements are given by means of mathematical models both kinematic and dynamic of the UAV, considering climatic disturbances (wind speed). On the other hand, there are several scripts that have the necessary codes for the correct operation of the 3D virtual simulator. One group of these scripts allows the management of the libraries (SDK-Software Development Kit) focused on the virtual input devices, which make possible the interaction and communication between them. The remaining group of scripts manage the other components involved in the virtual scenario, such as: the UAV model, the user interface (UI), the lighting, the camera selection, the audio control, and the weather disturbances (wind speed). Together, these two groups make it possible for the virtual simulator to be interactive and immersive. (iii) Controller allows to implement advanced control algorithms capable of governing the UAV to perform trajectory tracking tasks. For this case study, the implemented scheme is based on a cascade system, with a kinematic controller and a dynamic compensation, determined through the mathematical model of the UAV. Shared memories are used as a means of communication between the Virtual Simulator developed in the Unity 3D Graphics Engine and the controller implemented in the MatLab mathematical software; on the other hand, wireless communication is used to link the controller implemented in the MatLab mathematical software, with the DJI Matrice 600 Pro UAV. Finally, (iv) Human Operator, through the virtual interface, is in charge of modifying the different parameters for the simulation, such as reference signals and disturbance data, among others, and observing the behavior of the control errors.

3. UAV Robot

This section describes the modelling of the UAV in order to virtualize the behavior of it for the 3D simulated scenes proposed in this work. The UAV used for this research is the DJI Matrice 600 Pro hexacopter. This work considers the kinematic modeling of the UAV, as well as the dynamic model of the robotic system.

The literature covering the mathematical modeling of UAVs is quite extensive. In recent years, much research has been based on obtaining the kinematic and dynamic models of these aerial vehicles. The purposes for which these models are used vary according to each author, but it can be agreed that in almost all cases, the mathematical model of a UAV is given as explained in the following cases [28–30]. In addition, other authors choose to represent the behavior of UAVs in a more simplified way, both for their kinematics and dynamics, some examples are [31,32]. In the following, this paper makes use of these simplified mathematical models to represent a non-linear model for the kinematics and a linear one for the dynamics.

3.1. Kinematic Model

The DJI Matrice 600 Pro drone is going to perform monitoring or inspection tasks, so it will track a trajectory set by the user. In this way, it will require low speeds and low value limits for the pitch angle θ and roll angle ϕ [33]. Therefore, the autopilot integrated in the UAV assumes that these values are negligible, although generating velocities in the front l and lateral directions m of the mobile reference frame $\{R_D\}$ [31]. The mathematical analysis is based on the scheme represented in Figure 3.

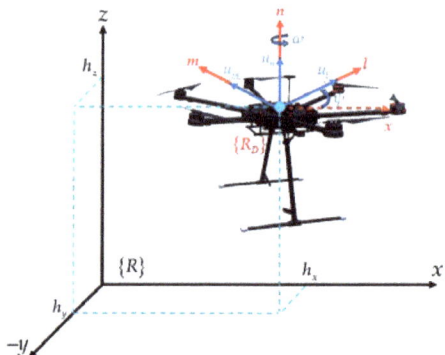

Figure 3. Diagram of the aerial robot.

In the mobile reference frame $\{R_D\}$ located at the center of mass of the hexacopter, the velocities are defined as follows: u_l as front velocity, u_m as lateral velocity, u_n as elevation velocity, and the angular velocity as ω, which describes the rotation of the UAV counterclockwise to the reference frame $\{R_D\}$ with respect to the axis z. Thus, defining the movement of the hexacopter as seen from the reference frame $\{R\}$ as follows:

$$\begin{bmatrix} \dot{h}_x \\ \dot{h}_y \\ \dot{h}_z \\ \dot{\psi} \end{bmatrix} = \begin{bmatrix} \cos\psi & -\sin\psi & 0 & 0 \\ \sin\psi & \cos\psi & 0 & 0 \\ 0 & 0 & 1 & 0 \\ 0 & 0 & 0 & 1 \end{bmatrix} \begin{bmatrix} u_l \\ u_m \\ u_n \\ \omega \end{bmatrix} \tag{1}$$

$$\dot{\mathbf{h}}(t) = \mathbf{J}(\psi)\boldsymbol{\mu}(t)$$

where $\dot{\mathbf{h}}(t) \in \mathbb{R}^m$ with $m = 4$ represents the vector of velocities of the hexacopter with respect to the reference frame $\{R\}$; $\mathbf{J}(\psi) \in \mathbb{R}^{m \times n}$ with $n = 4$ is a non-singular matrix representing the behavior of the UAV in motion, and $\boldsymbol{\mu}(t) \in \mathbb{R}^n$ represents the vector of maneuverability velocities of the UAV.

3.2. Dynamic Model

The dynamic model of the hexacopter is obtained by considering the UAV as a rigid body in space, which depends on the force acting on it and the torques generated by the propellers of its rotors. Thus, by using the Euler–Lagrange or Newton–Euler equations, expressions governing the translational and rotational motion of the system are obtained. However, as mentioned in [31,32], it is not necessary to develop all the dynamics of the hexacopter, simplifying it in an approximate linear model:

$$\begin{cases} \dot{u}_l = \zeta_1 u_{lref} - \zeta_2 u_l \\ \dot{u}_m = \zeta_3 u_{mref} - \zeta_4 u_m \\ \dot{u}_n = \zeta_5 u_{nref} - \zeta_6 u_n \\ \dot{\omega} = \zeta_7 \omega_{ref} - \zeta_8 \omega \end{cases} \tag{2}$$

Regrouping terms of Equation (2) in order to have a compact structure for controller design, it can be expressed as follows:

$$\begin{bmatrix} u_{lref} \\ u_{mref} \\ u_{nref} \\ \omega_{ref} \end{bmatrix} = \begin{bmatrix} \frac{1}{\zeta_1} & 0 & 0 & 0 \\ 0 & \frac{1}{\zeta_3} & 0 & 0 \\ 0 & 0 & \frac{1}{\zeta_5} & 0 \\ 0 & 0 & 0 & \frac{1}{\zeta_7} \end{bmatrix} \begin{bmatrix} \dot{u}_l \\ \dot{u}_m \\ \dot{u}_n \\ \dot{\omega} \end{bmatrix} + \begin{bmatrix} \frac{\zeta_2}{\zeta_1} & 0 & 0 & 0 \\ 0 & \frac{\zeta_4}{\zeta_3} & 0 & 0 \\ 0 & 0 & \frac{\zeta_6}{\zeta_5} & 0 \\ 0 & 0 & 0 & \frac{\zeta_8}{\zeta_7} \end{bmatrix} \begin{bmatrix} u_l \\ u_m \\ u_n \\ \omega \end{bmatrix}$$

$$\boldsymbol{\mu}_{\mathbf{ref}}(t) = \mathbf{A}(\zeta)\dot{\boldsymbol{\mu}}(t) + \mathbf{B}(\zeta)\boldsymbol{\mu}(t) \qquad (3)$$

where, $\dot{\boldsymbol{\mu}}(t) = \begin{bmatrix} \dot{u}_l & \dot{u}_m & \dot{u}_n & \dot{\omega} \end{bmatrix}^T \in \mathbb{R}^m$ with $m = 4$ represents the vector of accelerations of the aerial robot with respect to the reference frame.$\{R_D\}$. $\mathbf{A}(\boldsymbol{\xi}) = diag\left(\frac{1}{\xi_1}, \frac{1}{\xi_3}, \frac{1}{\xi_5}, \frac{1}{\xi_7}\right) \in \mathbb{R}^{m \times m}$ represents the inertia matrix of the aerial robot system. $\mathbf{B}(\boldsymbol{\xi}) = diag\left(\frac{\xi_2}{\xi_1}, \frac{\xi_4}{\xi_3}, \frac{\xi_6}{\xi_5}, \frac{\xi_8}{\xi_7}\right) \in \mathbb{R}^{m \times m}$ represents the matrix of centripetal forces acting on the aerial robot. $\boldsymbol{\mu}_{ref}(t) = \begin{bmatrix} u_{lref} & u_{mref} & u_{nref} & \omega_{ref} \end{bmatrix}^T \in \mathbb{R}^m$ represents the vector of standardized control commands of the UAV between $[-1, +1]$. Finally, we have $\zeta = \begin{bmatrix} \zeta_1 & \zeta_2 & \cdots & \zeta_l \end{bmatrix}^T \in \mathbb{R}^l$ with $l = 8$ which represents the vector containing the dynamic parameters of the aerial robot.

3.3. Identification and Validation

For the identification and validation process of the model, experimental tests were performed with the DJI Matrice 600 Pro hexacopter, then the data obtained were entered into the identification algorithm, which allowed finding the dynamic parameters of the model through an algorithm based on optimization and validation through the comparison of the hexacopter and the mathematical model.

This process consists of the following stages: (i) Excitation of the Hexacopter, the objective of this stage is to know the value of the output velocities before a predetermined excitation value, the difference between these signals indicates the dynamics of the hexacopter; (ii) Identification Algorithm, in this stage the dynamic parameters of the model are identified based on the data taken in the previous phase, as shown in Figure 4a. For which an algorithm based on optimization was implemented, which reduces the error resulting from comparing the values of the hexacopter with the values obtained from the mathematical model. Finally, when the error is considered negligible, the estimated dynamic parameters approximate the values of the hexacopter. Figure 4b shows the behavioral signals of the real UAV velocities $\boldsymbol{\mu}_{\mathbf{r}}(t) = \begin{bmatrix} \mu_{lr} & \mu_{mr} & \mu_{nr} & \omega_r \end{bmatrix}^T$ with respect to the excitation or reference signals $\boldsymbol{\mu}_{\mathbf{ref}}(t) = \begin{bmatrix} u_{lref} & u_{mref} & u_{nref} & \omega_{ref} \end{bmatrix}^T$ injected into the UAV.

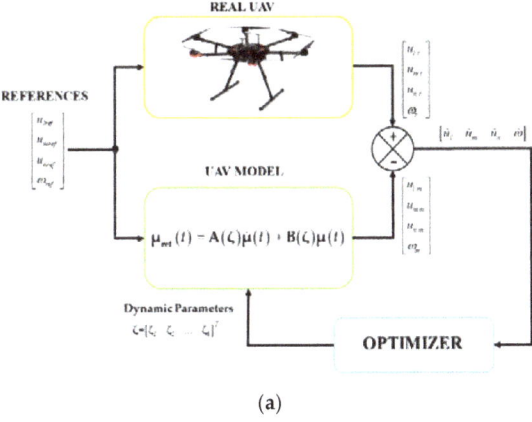

(a)

Figure 4. *Cont.*

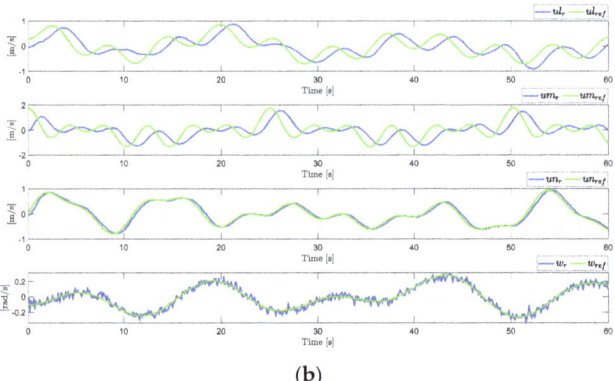

(b)

Figure 4. Identification of dynamic parameters. (**a**) Identification scheme; (**b**) Identification data signals.

(iii) Validation, the final stage allows us to evaluate whether the dynamic model with the obtained parameters represents the behavior of the hexacopter as it is seen in Figure 5a by using reference signals other than those used in the dynamic parameter identification process. The values for the dynamic parameters can be seen in Appendix A.

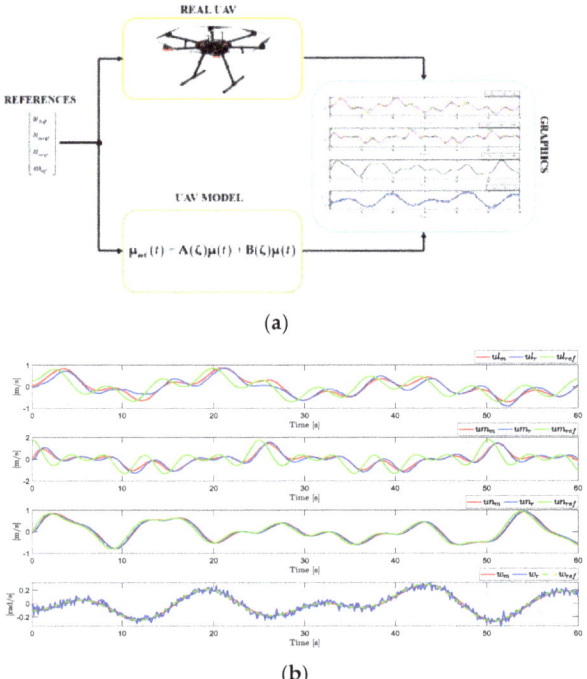

Figure 5. Velocities obtained from the dynamic model of the DJI Matrice 600 Pro, with the previously identified dynamic parameters, closely resemble the real UAV velocities behavior during its experimentation. (**a**) Validation scheme; (**b**) Velocity signals comparison.

4. Control Scheme

The proposed control scheme for the fulfillment of trajectory tracking tasks is shown in Figure 6. This scheme is based on the design in two main stages. The first stage where both kinematic and dynamic compensation controllers are developed based on the structure of their models, respectively; on the other hand, it should be mentioned that this stage is hosted in a mathematical software in our case Matlab. Moreover, in the second stage, called virtual reality, the mathematical models are housed which allow to describe the real movements of a UAV within the 3D simulator; furthermore, this simulator is equipped with an interactive menu for the user allowing the change of the desired task as the disturbance of the process.

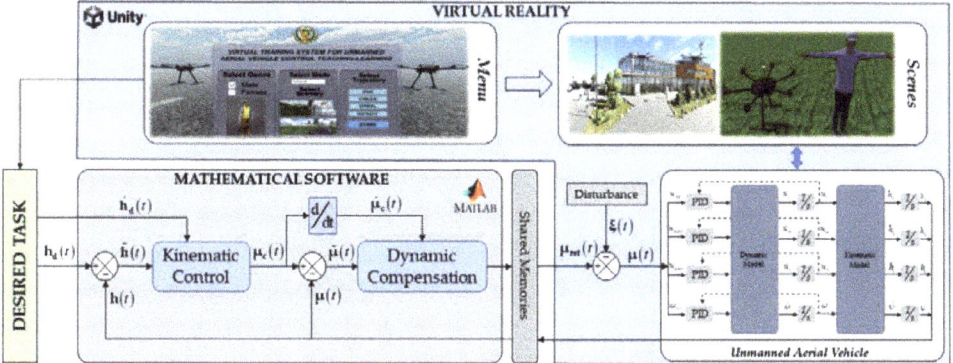

Figure 6. Proposed control scheme.

4.1. Kinematic Controller

The control errors of the UAV positions are calculated in each sampling period and are used to guide the UAV in the direction that decreases these errors. This controller is based on the kinematic model found previously in Equation (1) and is represented as follows:

$$\boldsymbol{\mu_c}(t) = \mathbf{J}^{-1}\left(\dot{\mathbf{h}}_\mathbf{d}(t) + \mathbf{K}_{\tilde{h}} tanh\left(\tilde{\mathbf{h}}(t)\right)\right) \quad (4)$$

where $\mathbf{J}^{-1}(\psi)$ represents the inverse matrix of the aerial robot kinematics $\mathbf{J}(\psi)$; $\dot{\mathbf{h}}_\mathbf{d}(t) = \begin{bmatrix} h_{dx} & h_{dy} & h_{dz} & \psi_d \end{bmatrix}^T$ represents the vector of desired velocities for the chosen trajectory; $\tilde{\mathbf{h}}(t) = \begin{bmatrix} \tilde{h}_x & \tilde{h}_y & \tilde{h}_z & \tilde{\psi} \end{bmatrix}^T$ represents the vector of control errors; while $\mathbf{K}_{\tilde{h}}$ represents a diagonal matrix of positive gain; finally an analytical saturation $tanh(.)$ is included which limits the control error $\tilde{\mathbf{h}}(t)$.

For the kinematic controller, the behavior of the position control errors $\tilde{\mathbf{h}}(t) = \mathbf{h}_\mathbf{d}(t) - \mathbf{h}(t)$ are analyzed by considering a velocity tracking under ideal conditions, that is $\boldsymbol{\mu}(t) \equiv \boldsymbol{\mu_c}(t)$. Replacing Equation (4) in (1) we obtain the closed-loop equation $\dot{\tilde{\mathbf{h}}}(t) = -\mathbf{K}_{\tilde{h}} tanh\left(\tilde{\mathbf{h}}(t)\right)$. For the stability analysis we consider a candidate Lyapunov function defined negative $V\left(\tilde{\mathbf{h}}(t)\right) = \frac{1}{2}\tilde{\mathbf{h}}^T(t)\tilde{\mathbf{h}}(t) < 0$. Finally, by considering the time derivative of the candidate function $\dot{V}\left(\tilde{\mathbf{h}}(t)\right) = \tilde{\mathbf{h}}^T(t)\dot{\tilde{\mathbf{h}}}(t)$ and replacing it in the closed-loop equation, we obtain:

$$\dot{V}\left(\tilde{\mathbf{h}}(t)\right) = -\tilde{\mathbf{h}}^T(t)\mathbf{K}_{\tilde{h}} tanh\left(\tilde{\mathbf{h}}(t)\right) < 0 \quad (5)$$

thus, guaranteeing the stability of the proposed control law, when $\mathbf{K}_{\tilde{h}} > 0$, and ensuring that $\tilde{\mathbf{h}}(t) \to 0$ it is asymptotically stable when $t \to \infty$.

4.2. Dynamic Compensation

The objective of the dynamic compensator is to balance the dynamics of the hexacopter in order to reduce the velocity tracking error $\tilde{\boldsymbol{\mu}}(t) = \boldsymbol{\mu_c}(t) - \boldsymbol{\mu}(t)$, which is generated by the non-perfect velocity tracking, that is $\boldsymbol{\mu}(t) \neq \boldsymbol{\mu_c}(t)$. That is why the following control law is proposed, which is based on the dynamic model (3) of the aerial robot:

$$\boldsymbol{\mu}_{ref}(t) = \mathbf{A}\left(\dot{\boldsymbol{\mu}}_c(t) + \mathbf{K}_{\tilde{\boldsymbol{\mu}}} tanh\left(\tilde{\boldsymbol{\mu}}(t)\right)\right) + \mathbf{B}\boldsymbol{\mu}(t) \tag{6}$$

where, the control actions provided by the proposed controller are represented by $\boldsymbol{\mu}_{ref}(t) = \begin{bmatrix} u_{lref} & u_{mref} & u_{nref} & \omega_{ref} \end{bmatrix}^T$; $\dot{\boldsymbol{\mu}}_c(t) = \begin{bmatrix} \dot{u}_{lc} & \dot{u}_{mc} & \dot{u}_{nc} & \dot{\omega}_c \end{bmatrix}^T$ represents the derivative of the kinematic controller velocities; $\boldsymbol{\mu}(t) = \begin{bmatrix} u_l & u_m & u_n & \omega \end{bmatrix}^T$ represents the UAV velocities; the gain matrix to compensate for the velocity errors $\mathbf{K}_{\tilde{\boldsymbol{\mu}}}$; finally an analytical saturation $tanh(.)$ is included which limits the error $\tilde{\boldsymbol{\mu}}(t)$.

In the same way that we work with the kinematic controller, for the stability analysis of the dynamic compensator, we propose a negative candidate Lyapunov function $\mathbf{V}\left(\tilde{\boldsymbol{\mu}}(t)\right) = \frac{1}{2}\tilde{\boldsymbol{\mu}}^T(t)\tilde{\boldsymbol{\mu}}(t) < 0$; and its time derivative $\dot{\mathbf{V}}\left(\tilde{\boldsymbol{\mu}}(t)\right) = \tilde{\boldsymbol{\mu}}^T(t)\dot{\tilde{\boldsymbol{\mu}}}(t)$. Then we replace the control laws Equation (6) and (3) in the time derivative of the Lyapunov candidate function, we obtain:

$$\dot{\mathbf{V}}\left(\tilde{\boldsymbol{\mu}}(t)\right) = -\tilde{\boldsymbol{\mu}}^T(t)\mathbf{K}_{\tilde{\boldsymbol{\mu}}} tanh\left(\tilde{\boldsymbol{\mu}}(t)\right) < 0 \tag{7}$$

thus, guaranteeing the stability of the proposed control law, when $\mathbf{K}_{\tilde{\boldsymbol{\mu}}} > 0$, and ensuring that $\tilde{\boldsymbol{\mu}}(t) \to 0$ it is asymptotically stable when $t \to \infty$.

4.3. Robustness Analysis

On the other hand, the robustness analysis is focused on the kinematic controller; specifically, the behavior of the control error in the center of mass of the hexacopter, considering that the velocity tracking is not perfect $\boldsymbol{\mu}_{ref}(t) \neq \boldsymbol{\mu}(t)$ [34]. This error in the velocity can be caused by disturbances, which is why it is defined as a Lyapunov candidate function $\mathbf{V}\left(\tilde{\mathbf{h}}\right) = \frac{1}{2}\tilde{\mathbf{h}}^T\tilde{\mathbf{h}}$, with its respective time derivative $\dot{\mathbf{V}}\left(\tilde{\mathbf{h}}\right) = \tilde{\mathbf{h}}^T\dot{\tilde{\mathbf{h}}}$. Now, considering $\boldsymbol{\mu}(t) = \boldsymbol{\mu}_{ref}(t) + \boldsymbol{\xi}(t)$ where $\boldsymbol{\xi}(t)$ represents disturbances due to climatic conditions, such as wind force, Equation (4) is substituted in (1) resulting in $\dot{\mathbf{h}}(t) = \mathbf{J}\mathbf{J}^{-1}\left(\dot{\mathbf{h}}_\mathbf{d}(t) + \mathbf{K}tanh\left(\tilde{\mathbf{h}}(t)\right)\right) + \mathbf{J}\boldsymbol{\xi}(t)$. In addition, considering that $\dot{\tilde{\mathbf{h}}}(t) = \dot{\mathbf{h}}_\mathbf{d}(t) - \dot{\mathbf{h}}(t)$, we obtain the closed loop equation expressed as:

$$\dot{\tilde{\mathbf{h}}}(t) = -\mathbf{K}_{\tilde{\mathbf{h}}} tanh\left(\tilde{\mathbf{h}}(t)\right) - \mathbf{J}\boldsymbol{\xi}(t) \tag{8}$$

Replacing Equation (8) in the time derivative of the Lyapunov candidate function yields the expression:

$$\dot{\mathbf{V}}\left(\tilde{\mathbf{h}}\right) = -\tilde{\mathbf{h}}^T \mathbf{K}_{\tilde{\mathbf{h}}} tanh\left(\tilde{\mathbf{h}}(t)\right) - \dot{\tilde{\mathbf{h}}}^T \mathbf{J}\boldsymbol{\xi}(t) \tag{9}$$

The necessary condition to fulfill that Equation (9) is negative definite is $\left|\tilde{\mathbf{h}}^T \mathbf{K}_{\tilde{h}} tanh\left(\tilde{\mathbf{h}}(t)\right)\right| > \left|\tilde{\mathbf{h}}^T \mathbf{J}\boldsymbol{\varepsilon}(t)\right|$. For large values of $\tilde{\mathbf{h}}(t)$, it can be considered that $\mathbf{K}_{\tilde{h}} tanh\left(\tilde{\mathbf{h}}(t)\right) \approx \mathbf{K}_{\tilde{h}}$. With such consideration results Equation (10) as follows:

$$\|\mathbf{K}_{\tilde{h}}\| > \|\tilde{\mathbf{h}}^T \mathbf{J}\boldsymbol{\varepsilon}(t)\| \tag{10}$$

thus, making the errors decrease. For small values of $\tilde{\mathbf{h}}(t)$, it is considered that $\mathbf{K}_{\tilde{h}} tanh\left(\tilde{\mathbf{h}}(t)\right) \approx \mathbf{K}_{\tilde{h}}\tilde{\mathbf{h}}$, so Equation (11) can be written as:

$$\|\tilde{\mathbf{h}}\| > \frac{\|\mathbf{J}\boldsymbol{\varepsilon}(t)\|}{\lambda_{\min}(\mathbf{K}_{\tilde{h}})} \tag{11}$$

Therefore, the error $\tilde{\mathbf{h}}(t)$ is expressed as follows:

$$\|\tilde{\mathbf{h}}(t)\| \leq \frac{\|\mathbf{J}\boldsymbol{\varepsilon}(t)\|}{\lambda_{\min}(\mathbf{K}_{\tilde{h}})} \tag{12}$$

5. Experimental Analysis and Results

This section presents the virtual training system developed, as well as the implemented control scheme. This section presents the virtual training system, with its highly interactive main window that allows the modification of the different parameters immersed in the controller, as well as the configuration of the virtual environment. We also present the results obtained with the implementation of the advanced control algorithm for autonomous trajectory tracking tasks, both in the virtual training system and in the tests performed experimentally with the hexacopter.

5.1. Virtual Training System

For the design of the user interface within the virtual environment, the ISO 25010 standard was used as reference, which deals specifically with the usability of a software product [35]. Usability is defined as the ability of the product to be understood, learned, used, and attractive [36]. For the development of the HMI (Human Machine Interface), the double diamond model [37] was considered, for which it was needed that the virtual training system should be realistic and easy to interact with for the simulation of autonomous navigation tasks of UAVs. Likewise, the environment had to be simple enough to operate, error-free and eye-catching.

Figure 7 shows the main window of the virtual training system where the avatar's gender can be configured, allowing to choose and visualize the avatar's appearance, between male and female gender. It is also possible to select the operation mode and the scenarios, where there are two operation modes: (i) operator, which has several within the virtual simulator such as: modify the controller gains, set new trajectories, set new disturbance parameters, scenario selection, among others. (ii) observer, has several restrictions on the tasks that the operator can perform, where he can only select the trajectories set in the virtual simulator and the scenario selection. In addition, the main window allows the selection of the virtual scenario among various.

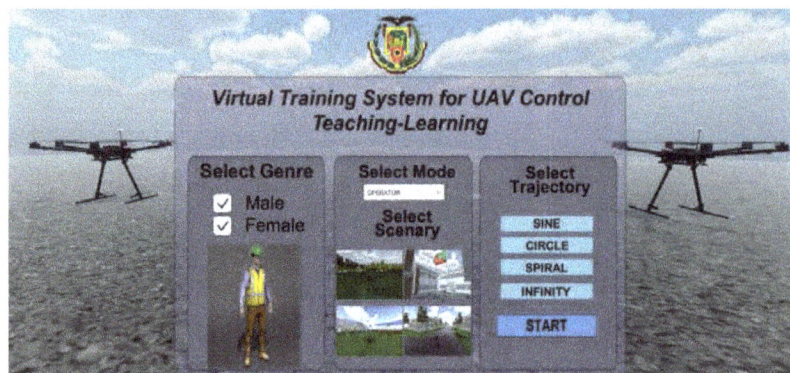

Figure 7. Main window of the virtual interface of the training system.

For this research, four different scenarios were developed, as shown in Figure 8. These scenarios can be classified as: (a) Park, an open place where there is abundant vegetation, such as grass, trees, and shrubs; we also find elements typical of a park, such as sidewalks and a water fountain. (b) Educational Center, there is a classroom building; it is a site with many constructions which would be obstacles for the navigation of the UAV, which has courtyards and parking lots. (c) Sports area, an open place where there is a diversity of sports venues, such as soccer stadiums, volleyball courts, tennis courts, and others, where there is a diversity of soils, such as sand, concrete, and grass, and has a little vegetation which are mostly palm trees. (d) Industrial Complex, shows a set of factories considering a moderate place in terms of space available for the execution of the task, has structures that resemble an industrial complex, and with spaces of vegetation, where trees and grass predominate.

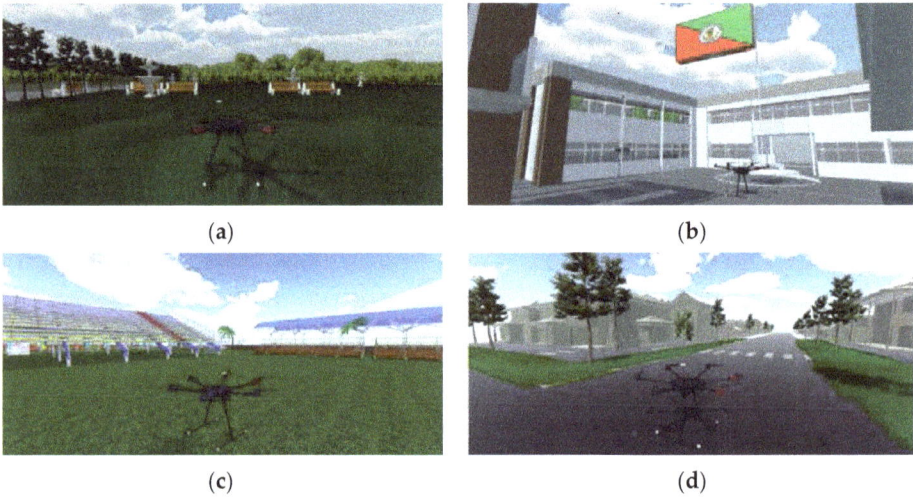

Figure 8. Virtual scenarios developed for the execution of trajectory tracking tasks, all related to real life. (**a**) Park Scenario; (**b**) Educational Center Scenario; (**c**) Stadium Scenario; (**d**) Neighborhood Scenario.

5.2. Implemented Control Scheme

This subsection presents the results of the experimentation in real life, as well as the simulation in a 3D virtual environment of the behavior of an hexacopter under the control scheme implemented for this work.

For the experimentation, the DJI Matrice 600 Pro was used as this UAV is designed for different industrial applications. It has six rotating propellers, which drive the movement of the hexacopter. It has a transmission range of 5 km and a capacity to move loads of up to 6 kg, and its 6 LiPo 6S batteries of 22.8 volts and 5700 mAh [38]. They allow it to have a flight autonomy of 38 min [39]. In addition to the standard software and hardware offered by this UAV, an Intel Nuc computer is integrated, which allows the execution of the control algorithms (see Figure 9). This modification makes it possible for control signals to be sent to the flight control board by running a Matlab script, which communicates wirelessly a remote station with the Intel board in the UAV.

Figure 9. DJI Matrice 600 Pro UAV provided by the ARSI research group.

To implement the control algorithms, feedback from the positioning data obtained by the UAV's sensors, such as the D-RTK GNSS (Global Navigation Satellite System) antennas, is used. These three antennas connected to DJI's own A3 flight controller allow the UAV a vertical navigation accuracy of 0.5 m and a horizontal navigation accuracy of 1.5 m [40].

For the simulation process, the implemented control scheme is detailed in Section 2.2. The controller also runs in a Matlab script and it is in cascade form, consisting of two phases. The first one is a kinematics-based controller and the second one is a dynamic compensator, as described in Section 4. This cascade controller was based on the mathematical model of the hexacopter through the identification of the dynamic parameters based on optimization for which tests were carried out experimentally with the DJI Ma-trice 600 Pro. In this way the virtual training system becomes immersive as it best reflects the actual behavior of this UAV.

To test the performance of the advanced control scheme, an experiment is developed with the parameters described in Table 1.

Table 1. Desired references for the UAV.

Coordinates	Desired Function	Initial Conditions
h_x	$8\cos(0.2t)\,[m]$	$4\,[m]$
h_y	$7\sin(0.4t)\,[m]$	$1\,[m]$
h_z	$0.35\sin(t) + 7\,[m]$	$3\,[m]$
ψ	$\tan^{-1}\left(\frac{h_y}{h_x}\right)\,[rad]$	$0.5\,[rad]$

For this experiment, a displacement of the hexacopter is performed with respect to the plane x, y and z of the global reference frame. Figure 10 shows the trajectory of the desired task, which tends to an infinite symbol trajectory with variations in the height for the z axis. To analyze the performance of the implemented control scheme, the results obtained from the experimentation (see Figure 10a) are compared with those obtained from the simulation (see Figure 10b). Flight reconstruction is performed with the actual data obtained from the UAV.

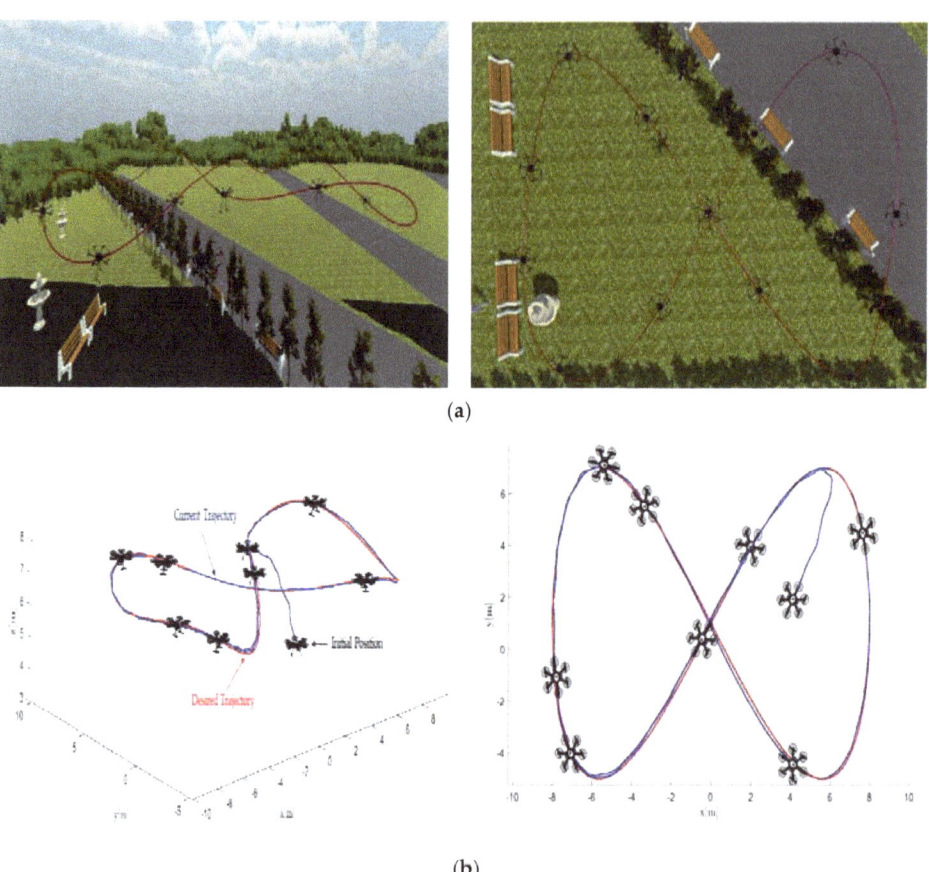

Figure 10. Stroboscopic movement of the UAV. (**a**) UAV stroboscopic flight based on simulated data; (**b**) UAV stroboscopic flight based on real experimental data.

In the Figure 11 show, the control errors $\tilde{\mathbf{h}}(t) = \begin{bmatrix} \tilde{h}_x & \tilde{h}_y & \tilde{h}_z & \tilde{\psi} \end{bmatrix}^T \in \mathbb{R}^4$ tend to zero asymptotically when time tends to infinity, as well as errors in the experimentation process as in the simulation process. On the other hand, velocity errors are non-zero, as shown in Figure 12. The velocity errors are not equal to zero due to the various disturbances found in the environment where the tests were performed such as the wind force that pushes the UAV in different directions. In this way, the wind speed had a top value of 6.5 mph during the experimentation with the UAV [41]. Figure 13 shows the wind speeds during the day of experimentation. The value of the wind speed was used to accurately represent the behavior of the real UAV, as it was implemented in the simulation model.

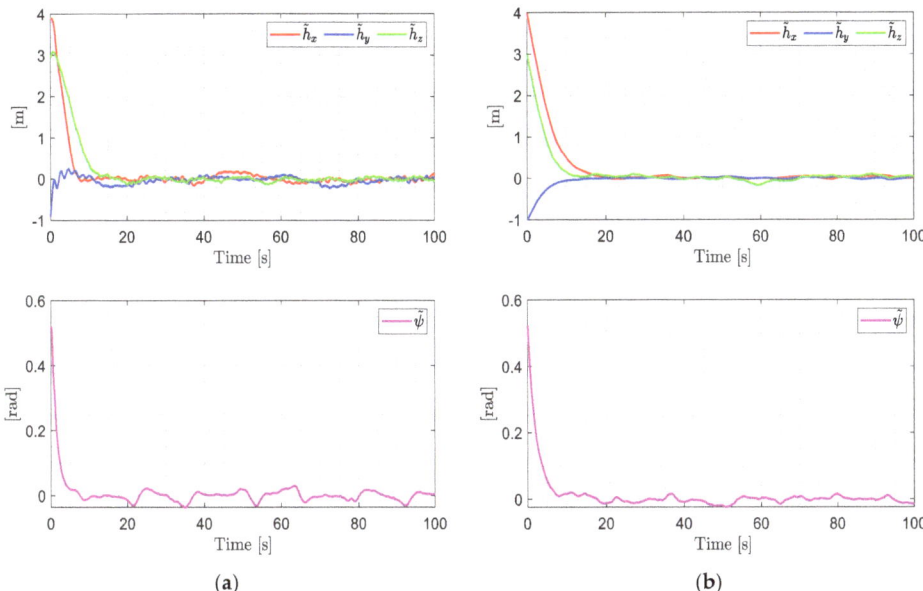

Figure 11. Position errors $\tilde{\mathbf{h}} = \left(\tilde{h}_x, \tilde{h}_y, \tilde{h}_z\right)$ and angle errors $\tilde{\psi}$. (**a**) Real control errors; (**b**) Simulation control errors.

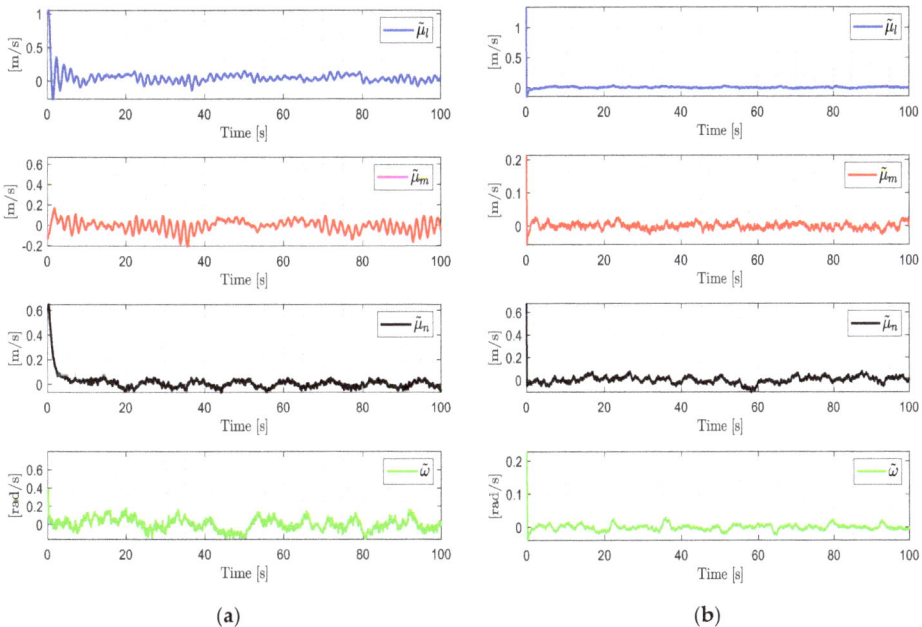

Figure 12. Velocity errors behavior $\tilde{\boldsymbol{\mu}} = \left(\tilde{u}_l, \tilde{u}_m, \tilde{u}_n, \tilde{\omega}\right)$. (**a**) Real velocity errors; (**b**) Simulation velocity errors.

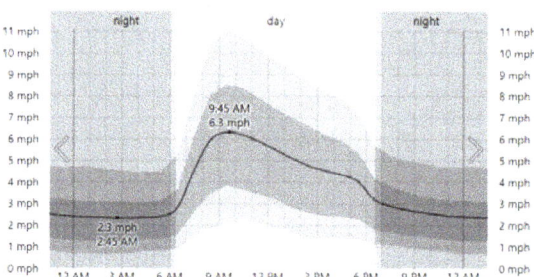

Figure 13. Wind speed on 2 February in Ambato. The average of mean hourly wind speeds (dark gray line), with 25th to 75th and 10th to 90th percentile bands. Civil twilight and night are indicated by shaded overlays.

Figure 14 shows the control actions applied to the hexacopter during the experiment.

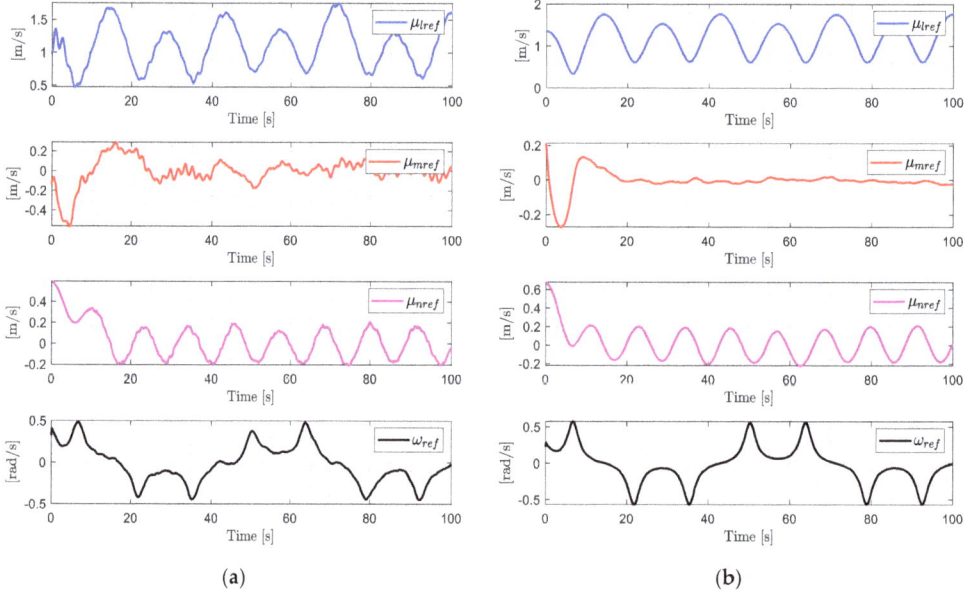

Figure 14. Evolution of UAV control inputs $\mu_{ref} = \left(u_{lref}, u_{mref}, u_{nref}, \omega_{ref}\right)$. (**a**) Real input velocities; (**b**) Simulation input velocities.

Finally, it can be evidenced in the results presented that the signals: control errors, speed errors and control actions of both the experimental and validation processes have a similar behavior under the same case study, differentiating one from the other by the action of climatic conditions in the experimental process; therefore, the virtual system is a suitable environment for the implementation of various control algorithms.

5.3. Usability

To measure the degree of usability of the developed application, we used the System Usability Scale (SUS), which serves as a fast and reliable tool for measuring the usability attitude of a system [42]. It is a survey that gives positive results with a small sample size; in this case, we count with the help of a group of 20 people with knowledge in the area of robotics. Before the experiments, all participants were trained to navigate in VR environments. In the training, no autonomous control tasks were considered for UAV trajectory tracking. After finishing the experiments, the group completed a usability test to measure the level of acceptance of the system's features. The total average SUS score obtained was 85,375%, which indicates a good degree of usability for our virtual environment.

6. Conclusions

The implementation of a virtual training system for unmanned aerial vehicle control teaching–learning processes has demonstrated its capacity to simulate a scenario similar to reality. This allows future research around this application to develop a diversity of advanced controllers, observing their behavior through the evolution of control errors in diverse urban and rural scenarios. The mathematical models of kinematics and dynamics have allowed corroborating the performance of the virtual training system considering the dynamics of the UAV. This was achieved through the dynamic parameters obtained with the identification process based on optimization, for which tests were carried out experimentally with the DJI Matrice 600 Pro. The controller implemented makes possible the correction of external disturbances produced by air currents, which determines that the proposed controller is stable and robust, both in the virtual training system and in the tests carried out experimentally with the hexacopter.

Author Contributions: Conceptualization V.H.A., R.J.R. and J.L.S.; methodology V.H.A., R.J.R. and J.L.S.; software J.S.S., R.J.R. and J.L.S.; validation V.H.A., R.J.R. and J.L.S.; formal analysis J.S.S. and V.H.A.; investigation V.H.A., R.J.R. and J.L.S.; resources J.S.S., R.J.R. and J.L.S.; data curation R.J.R. and J.L.S.; writing—original draft preparation V.H.A., R.J.R. and J.L.S.; writing—review and editing V.H.A., J.S.S., R.J.R. and J.L.S.; visualization V.H.A., R.J.R. and J.L.S.; supervision V.H.A. and J.S.S.; project administration V.H.A.; funding acquisition V.H.A., R.J.R. and J.L.S. All authors have read and agreed to the published version of the manuscript.

Funding: This research received no external funding.

Institutional Review Board Statement: Not applicable.

Informed Consent Statement: Informed consent was obtained from all subjects involved in the study.

Acknowledgments: The authors would like to thank the Universidad de las Fuerzas Armadas ESPE for their contribution to innovation, especially in the research project "Advanced Control of Unmanned Aerial Vehicles", as well as the ARSI Research Group for their support in developing this work.

Conflicts of Interest: The authors declare no conflict of interest.

Appendix A

Dynamic parameters of the DJI Matrice 600 Pro UAV.

$\zeta_1 = 0.8681$; $\zeta_2 = 0.6487$; $\zeta_3 = 0.8491$; $\zeta_4 = 0.6436$; $\zeta_5 = 2.5824$; $\zeta_6 = 2.5153$; $\zeta_7 = 4.2899$; $\zeta_8 = 4.3033$.

References

1. Musić, J.; Bonković, M.; Kružić, S.; Marasović, T.; Papić, V.; Kostova, S.; Dimitrova, M.; Saeva, S.; Zamfirov, M.; Kaburlasos, V.; et al. Robotics and information technologies in education: Four countries from Alpe-Adria-Danube Region survey. *Int. J. Technol. Des. Educ.* **2022**, *32*, 749–771. [CrossRef]
2. Zeng, W. An empirical research on China's policy for ICT integration in Basic Education from 1988 to 2021. *Educ. Technol. Res. Dev.* **2022**, *70*, 1059–1082. [CrossRef]
3. Morales-Doyle, D. There is no equity in a vacuum: On the importance of historical, political, and moral considerations in science education. *Cult. Stud. Sci. Educ.* **2019**, *14*, 485–491. [CrossRef]
4. Morin, É. On the importance of the relationship to knowledge in science education. *Cult. Stud. Sci. Educ.* **2018**, *14*, 621–625. [CrossRef]
5. Sharma, A.; Zanotti, P.; Musunur, L.P. Enabling the Electric Future of Mobility: Robotic Automation for Electric Vehicle Battery Assembly. *IEEE Access* **2019**, *7*, 170961–170991. [CrossRef]

6. Samarakoon, B.; Sirithunge, C.; Muthugala, V.; Jayasekara, B. Proxemics and Approach Evaluation by Service Robot Based on User Behavior in Domestic Environment. In Proceedings of the International Conference on Intelligent Robots and Systems (IROS), Madrid, Spain, 1–5 October 2018; pp. 8192–8199.
7. Koch, W.; Mancuso, R.; West, R.; Bestavros, A. Reinforcement learning for UAV attitude control. *ACM Trans. Cyber-Phys. Syst.* **2019**, *3*, 1–21. [CrossRef]
8. Pham, H.X.; La, H.M.; Feil-Seifer, D.; Nguyen, L.V. Autonomous UAV Navigation Using Reinforcement Learning. January 2018. Available online: http://arxiv.org/abs/1801.05086 (accessed on 27 April 2022).
9. Chen, S.; Laefer, D.F.; Asce, M.; Mangina, E.; Zolanvari, S.M.I.; Byrne, J. UAV Bridge Inspection through Evaluated 3D Reconstructions. *J. Bridge Eng.* **2019**, *24*, 5019001. [CrossRef]
10. Mademlis, I.; Mygdalis, V.; Nikolaidis, N.; Montagnuolo, M.; Negro, F.; Messina, A.; Pitas, I. High-Level Multiple-UAV Cinematography Tools for Covering Outdoor Events. *IEEE Trans. Broadcast.* **2019**, *65*, 627–635. [CrossRef]
11. Luo, C.; Yu, L.; Yan, J.; Li, Z.; Ren, P.; Bai, X.; Yang, E.; Liu, Y. Autonomous detection of damage to multiple steel surfaces from 360° panoramas using deep neural networks. *Comput. Civ. Infrastruct. Eng.* **2021**, *36*, 1585–1599. [CrossRef]
12. Mueller, M.; Smith, N.; Ghanem, B. *A Benchmark and Simulator for UAV Tracking*; Springer International Publishing: Cham, Switzerland, 2017; Volume 9905. [CrossRef]
13. Slavkovic, M.; Vrgovi, P.; Peki, J.; Mirkovi, M.; Anderla, A.; Lekovi, B. Prolonged Emergency Remote Teaching: Sustainable E-Learning or Human Capital Stuck in Online Limbo? *Sustainability* **2022**, *14*, 4584. [CrossRef]
14. Al-Azawi, R.; Shakkah, M.S. Embedding Augmented and Virtual Reality in Educational Learning Method: Present and Future. In Proceedings of the 2018 9th International Conference on Information and Communication Systems (ICICS), Irbid, Jordan, 3–5 April 2018.
15. Guillén-Gámez, F.D.; Cabero-Almenara, J.; Llorente-Cejudo, C.; Palacios-Rodríguez, A. Differential Analysis of the Years of Experience of Higher Education Teachers, their Digital Competence and use of Digital Resources: Comparative Research Methods. *Technol. Knowl. Learn.* **2021**, *1*, 21. [CrossRef]
16. Wang, S.; Chen, J.; Zhang, Z.; Wang, G.; Tan, Y.; Zheng, Y. Construction of a virtual reality platform for UAV deep learning. In Proceedings of the 2017 Chinese Automation Congress CAC 2017, Jinan, China, 20–22 October 2017; pp. 3912–3916. [CrossRef]
17. Burova, A.; Mäkelä, J.; Hakulinen, J.; Keskinen, T.; Heinonen, H.; Siltanen, S.; Turunen, M. Utilizing VR and Gaze Tracking to Develop AR Solutions for Industrial Maintenance. In Proceedings of the CHI Conference on Human Factors in Computing Systems, Honolulu, HI, USA, 25–30 April 2020. [CrossRef]
18. Lai, N.Y.G.; Wong, K.H.; Yu, L.J.; Kang, H.S. Virtual reality (VR) in engineering education and training: A bibliometric analysis. In Proceedings of the 2020 2nd World Symposium on Software Engineering, Chengdu, China, 25–27 September 2020; pp. 161–165. [CrossRef]
19. Winther, F.; Ravindran, L.; Svendsen, K.P.; Feuchtner, T. Design and evaluation of a VR training simulation for pump maintenance. In Proceedings of the 2020 CHI Conference on Human Factors in Computing Systems Proceedings, Honolulu, HI, USA, 25–30 April 2020. [CrossRef]
20. Schroeter, R.; Gerber, M.A. A low-cost VR-based automated driving simulator for rapid automotive UI prototyping. In Proceedings of the 10th International Conference on Automotive User Interfaces and Interactive Vehicular Applications, Toronto, ON, USA, 23–25 September 2018; pp. 248–251. [CrossRef]
21. Ortiz, J.S.; Palacios-Navarro, G.; Andaluz, V.H.; Guevara, B.S. Virtual reality-based framework to simulate control algorithms for robotic assistance and rehabilitation tasks through a standing wheelchair. *Sensors* **2021**, *21*, 5083. [CrossRef]
22. Quispe, M.A.; Molina, M.C.; Ortiz, J.S.; Andaluz, V.H. Unicycle Mobile Robot Formation Control in Hardware in the Loop Environments. In *Applied Technologies: Second International Conference (ICAT 2020)*; Springer Nature: Berlin, Germany, 2021; Volume 1388, pp. 1–14. [CrossRef]
23. Zajda, J. Effective constructivist pedagogy for quality learning in schools. *Educ. Pract. Theory* **2018**, *40*, 67–80. [CrossRef]
24. Abulrub, A.G.; Attridge, A.N.; Williams, M.A. Virtual reality in engineering education: The future of creative learning. In Proceedings of the 2011 IEEE Global Engineering Education Conference (EDUCON), Amman, Jordan, 4–6 April 2011; pp. 751–757. [CrossRef]
25. Santana-Mancilla, P.C.; Rodriguez-Ortiz, M.A.; Garcia-Ruiz, M.A.; Gaytan-Lugo, L.S.; Fajardo-Flores, S.B.; Contreras-Castillo, J. Teaching HCI skills in higher education through game design: A study of students' perceptions. *Informatics* **2019**, *6*, 22. [CrossRef]
26. López Raventós, C. The video game as an educational tool. Possibilities and problems about Serious Games. *Apertura* **2016**, *8*, 00010.
27. Andaluz, V.H.; Chicaiza, F.A.; Gallardo, C.; Quevedo, W.X.; Varela, J.; Sánchez, J.S.; Arteaga, O. Unity3D-MATLAB simulator in real time for robotics applications. In *International Conference on Augmented Reality, Virtual Reality and Computer Graphics*; Lecture Notes in Computer Science; Springer: Cham, Switzerland, 2016; Volume 9768, pp. 246–263. [CrossRef]
28. Kose, O.; Oktay, T. Simultaneous quadrotor autopilot system and collective morphing system design. *Aircr. Eng. Aerosp. Technol.* **2020**, *92*, 1093–1100. [CrossRef]
29. Oktay, T.; Kose, O. Hexarotor Longitudinal Flight Control with Deep Neural Network, PID Algorithm and Morphing. *Eur. J. Sci. Technol.* **2021**, *21*, 115–124. [CrossRef]
30. Gardecki, S.; Giernacki, W.; Goslinski, J.; Kasinki, A. An adequate mathematical model of four-rotor flying robot in the context of control simulations. *J. Autom. Mob. Robot. Intell. Syst.* **2015**, *17*, 1–23. [CrossRef]

31. Santos, M.C.P.; Rosales, C.D.; Sarapura, J.A.; Sarcinelli-Filho, M.; Carelli, R. An Adaptive Dynamic Controller for Quadrotor to Perform Trajectory Tracking Tasks. *J. Intell. Robot. Syst. Theory Appl.* **2019**, *93*, 5–16. [CrossRef]
32. Jaramillo, J.G.; Vaca, F.A. Implementación de un Sistema de Control Robusto Para Seguimiento de Trayectoria de Tres Cuadricópteros en Formación. Master's Thesis, Escuela Politécnica Nacional, Quito, Ecuador, 2018.
33. Yuan, D.; Wang, Y. Data driven model-free adaptive control method for quadrotor formation trajectory tracking based on rise and ISMC algorithm. *Sensors* **2021**, *21*, 1289. [CrossRef]
34. Andaluz, V.; Roberti, F.; Toibero, J.M.; Carelli, R. Adaptive unified motion control of mobile manipulators. *Control Eng. Pract.* **2012**, *20*, 1337–1352. [CrossRef]
35. ISO. ISO/IEC 25010:2011—Systems and Software Engineering—Systems and Software Quality Requirements and Evaluation (SQuaRE)—System and Software Quality Models. 2011. Available online: https://www.iso.org/standard/35733.html (accessed on 27 July 2022).
36. Hornbæk, K. Current practice in measuring usability: Challenges to usability studies and research. *Int. J. Hum. Comput. Stud.* **2006**, *64*, 79–102. [CrossRef]
37. Quan, Q. Design Process for a Photography Service Application: The Application of Double Diamond to UX/UI Design Process. Title of Publication Design Process for a Photography Service Application. 2022. Available online: https://www.theseus.fi/handle/10024/755313 (accessed on 27 April 2022).
38. DJI. DJI Matrice 600 Pro. 2022. Available online: https://www.dji.com/matrice600-pro (accessed on 27 April 2022).
39. El Vuelo Del Drone. Drone DJI Matrice 600 Pro. 2020. Available online: https://elvuelodeldrone.com/drones-profesionales/drones-industriales/drone-dji-matrice-600-pro/ (accessed on 27 April 2022).
40. DJI. A3 Flight Control. 2022. Available online: https://www.dji.com/a3/info (accessed on 27 July 2022).
41. Historic Weather in Ambato on 2 February 2022 (Ecuador)—Weather Spark. 2022. Available online: https://weatherspark.com/h/d/20027/2022/2/2/Historical-Weather-on-Wednesday-February-2-2022-in-Ambato-Ecuador#Figures-Temperature (accessed on 6 June 2022).
42. Sauro, J.; Lewis, J.R. When Designing Usability Questionnaires, Does It Hurt to Be Positive? In Proceedings of the SIGCHI Conference on Human Factors in Computing Systems, Vancouver, BC, Canada, 7–12 May 2011; p. 2215.

Article

FOSSBot: An Open Source and Open Design Educational Robot

Christos Chronis [†] and Iraklis Varlamis [*,†]

Department of Informatics and Telematics, Harokopio University of Athens, Omirou 9, 17778 Athens, Greece; chronis@hua.gr
* Correspondence: varlamis@hua.gr; Tel.: +30-210-9549405
† Current address: Omirou 9, 17778 Athens, Greece.

Citation: Chronis, C.; Varlamis, I. FOSSBot: An Open Source and Open Design Educational Robot. *Electronics* 2022, *11*, 2606. https://doi.org/10.3390/electronics11162606

Academic Editor: Ahmad Taher Azar

Received: 25 July 2022
Accepted: 19 August 2022
Published: 20 August 2022

Publisher's Note: MDPI stays neutral with regard to jurisdictional claims in published maps and institutional affiliations.

Copyright: © 2022 by the authors. Licensee MDPI, Basel, Switzerland. This article is an open access article distributed under the terms and conditions of the Creative Commons Attribution (CC BY) license (https://creativecommons.org/licenses/by/4.0/).

Abstract: In the last few years, the interest in the use of robots in STEM education has risen. However, their main drawback is the high cost, which makes it almost impossible for schools to have one robot per student. Another drawback is the proprietary nature of commercial solutions, which limits the ability to expand or adapt the robot to educational needs. Different robot kit versions, which have different electronics and programming interfaces and target different age groups, make the decision of educators on which robot to use in STEM education even more complicated. In this work, we propose a new low-cost 3D-printable and unified software-based solution that can cover the needs of all age groups, from kindergarten children to university students. The solution is driven by open source and open hardware ideas, with which, we believe we will help educators in their work. We provide detail on the 3D-printable robot parts and its list of electronics that allow for a wide range of educational activities to be supported, and explain its flexible software stack that supports four different operating modes. The modes cover the needs of users that do not know or want to program the robot, users that prefer block-based programming and less or more experienced programmers who want to take full control of the robot. The robot implements the principles of continuous integration and deployment and allows for easy updates to the latest software version through its web-based administration panel. Though, in its first steps of development and testing, the proposed robot has a huge potential, due to its open nature and the community of students, researchers and educators, that potential has kept growing. A pilot at selected schools, a performance evaluation of various technical aspects and a comparison with state-of-the-art platforms will soon follow.

Keywords: STEM; educational robotics; 3D-printable robot; Blockly; open design; open software

1. Introduction

The use of science, technology, engineering and mathematics (STEM) tools has proven to be valuable for both teachers and students in various educational contexts. Robotics has a big impact on STEM education, since it offers a constructive learning environment that is ideal for explaining, simulating and teaching both scientific and non-scientific subjects [1]. It can be particularly helpful in educating STEM students because it allows engineering and technology principles to be applied in real world cases, reducing the abstractness of science and mathematics. In this direction, numerous robotics-related activities enhance students' understanding of science, technology, engineering and/or mathematics, and stimulate the interest of students in other non-scientific fields, such as art, history or literature [2–4].

Studies of the usage of STEM in early childhood [5] and on the status and trends in STEM education research [6] summarize the majority of the latest publications in this field and discuss a number of issues concerning its increased popularity. Based on the aforementioned publications, STEM tools are considered to be important and innovative and can shape education from kindergarten to university in a wide variety of fields [7,8].

The core idea behind STEM is the constructionism learning theory developed by Papert [9]. Based on this theory, the students interact with tools and materials, use previous knowledge and experiences and construct new information [2]. The STEM tools offer these means and provide the opportunity to students to solve real-world problems and, at the same time, to expand their personal experiences, as they become active learners [2,3,7,10]. The interaction with physical devices can transform the procedure of learning into a fun activity, and can keep the students' interest in learning at a high level [11]. Through this process, students have the opportunity to improve their critical thinking and problem-solving skills [12,13]. Many studies also report that it can also improve collaboration, social and communication skills, cognitive, meta-cognitive and social responsibilities [12,14] through the improvement of self-confidence and self-direction [7,12,13,15]. Finally, the exposure to the use of the STEM tools can also give students the needed inspiration for their future careers, as was highlighted in [16].

Nowadays, the skills of algorithmic thought and programming are becoming fundamental knowledge blocks, since almost all of the science fields require such competencies. Especially in the last decade, the continued rise of machine learning (ML) and artificial intelligence (AI) applications has put AI-based systems in the front line of most companies. The programming, aside from the potential benefits of a future job in education, can be used to teach computational thinking and problem-solving competence. There have been many approaches to teaching programming [17] but, for many students, it still remains a difficult and, in some cases, boring task to perform [4,17]. That difficulty is due to the fact that a student has to understand the theory of algorithms thought abstract concepts, or to learn the syntax and the commands of a programming language by memorizing or testing them in a virtual scenario. An additional barrier is raised for students that do not speak English as their native language, since most of the programming languages use English keywords to represent syntactic and semantic rules. All of the previous reasons and difficulties can lead the students to adopt a negative attitude towards programming [18].

Much research has been carried out in order to determine how the STEM tools (robotic kits) can positively affect the education procedure [19,20]. The usage of educational robots is a good practice for an educator in order to tackle the previous problems. A robot allows learners to establish new and creative ways to solve real-world problems, to test their ideas and to experiment. A unique ability provided by robotic systems is the direct execution of a solution and the direct feedback from a decision, either right or wrong. Furthermore, it is more interactive and tangible than a simulation environment [21]. This interaction between the robot and the student creates a unique feeling to a student that accomplishes a task, and forms an excellent playground for testing and building his/her puzzle-solving skills [4,18,19].

At the same time, a real-life object can give the needed motivation to a student to utilize any previous knowledge and try to find optimal solutions that can transform a boring procedure into a game. An educator selecting the correct robot for their students can reach students of different ages, different intellectual backgrounds or with learning disorders in order to access learning [22–24]. In addition, many researchers suggested that the usage of a game with fantasy or strategy and some goals can transform a game into an educational tool [19,25,26].

A very important role of the acceptance of a robotic system in education is the user interface or, more precisely, the way that a student can interact with it and transfer their solution into the robot commands. The user interface has been widely studied with different robotics kits in many group ages [4].

In this article, we present the Free and Open Source Software Bot (FOSSBot (https://github.com/eellak/fossbot (accessed on 10 August 2022)) for short), an open source and open design robot that can be used for educational purposes at all levels of the educational system, supporting many different activities and teaching scenarios. The unique features of FOSSBot can be summarized in the following:

- The designs of the robot are open and can be modified accordingly in order to support more scenarios.
- The plastic parts of the robot can be printed in a 3D-printer at a very low cost. Any worn plastic parts can be easily 3D-printed again

- FOSSBot comprises a list of electronics that can be easily found in the market at a low cost. All parts can be assembled following the assembly instructions, which are also publicly available. Any faulty electronic parts can be easily replaced.
- The software stack, which is written in Python, is modular and containerized, and thus can be easily expanded with more functionalities, allowing the robot users to update to the latest version at the click of a button.
- The robot is self-sustained and remote-operated, which means that anyone can connect to it through a laptop, smartphone or tablet, or it can connect to the local network via WiFi.
- The programming of the robot can be carried out in a multitude of ways, which makes it accessible and usable by different ages and in different contexts: (i) directly in Python at the lowest level, (ii) using interactive notebooks (Python Jupyter) at the middle level, (iii) using a no-code interface (Google Blockly) or (iv) using a button-based UI that executes pre-defined code scripts.

Section 2. which follows, surveys the main work in the field. Section 3 introduces FOSSBot and provides details on its main hardware features, whereas Section 4 explains FOSSBot's software stack and its main operation modes. Section 5 briefly presents how FOSSBot is designed to fit the educational scenarios at different age levels and Section 6 concludes the paper with our next steps on improving the robot functionalities and on exploiting FOSSBot in various educational activities.

2. Related Work

In the last two decades, tangible programming has seen a great development. From the Logo language that was designed in the 1970s by Feurzeig and Lukas for teaching mathematics [27] and AlgoBlock [28] that was introduced in the 1990s by Suzuki and Kato for teaching algorithms, using a programming language with interlocking blocks to represent commands, we have moved to the Tangible Programming Bricks of McNerney in the 2000s [29], which support the use of parameters and variables.

However, the real boost to robot programming has come from LEGO during the last decade. The Bricks interface was used by LEGO bricks combined with embedded electronics through the Logo Block and LEGO Mindstorms [4,18,20]. More specifically, LEGO Mindstorms combined hardware blocks with the graphical representation of the code that operates them, thus giving a boost to tangible programming and converting it into a game-like activity. Every LEGO kit includes a big brick with a microprocessor inside and, around it, everyone can attach different kind of bricks, such as motor bricks and modular sensors. In addition, besides the hardware, LEGO provides a graphical programming interface. In that interface, a user has the opportunity to create complicated programming using a graphical representation of the bricks, and can then manipulate the robot [10].

The popularity of Mindstorms gave rise to more programming interfaces, such as FlowBlock [25]. FlowBlock used an arrows-to-blocks and a branches-based visual representation of the programming flows with real-time value updates. Similarly, authors in [30] proposed graphical representations of commands and, in [31], the authors introduced Electronic Blocks, which are tangible programming elements for preschoolers that allowed students to build and program a robot. Finally, authors in [32,33] proposed the Quetzal and Tern languages, which emphasize the use of cheap and durable components that do not contain any electronics but can be used offline to compile a program. The blocks are scanned and the resulting program is compiled accordingly in a smartphone or tablet.

Moving from components that can be assembled to programmable robots, we still find several interesting approaches. The great acceptance from educators and students of the robotic kits in education led to the release of even more robot kits [7]. In the commercial domain, the dominant robotic kit in education is the LEGO Education with the Mindstorm and Wedo series, followed by the Engino Robotics, Bee-Bot and Arduino-based kits. Some of these systems use a graphical representation of commands or low-level code [34,35].

As far as it concerns research works, authors in [36] introduced Hydra, a new low-cost educational framework with a custom printed circuit board (PCB) and modular electronic connections. Hydra is based on the Arduino micro-controller and also supports block-based coding through ArduBlockly. Its list of sensors is much smaller than that of FOSSBot. However, the authors of Hydra introduce a methodology for monitoring the progress of the educational process using the Petri Nets model, which can be very useful in future educational scenarios with robots.

FOSSBot has its origins in another open source and open design robot, which we designed in 2019 as part of the Google Summer of Code project. That robot, called Proteas (https://github.com/eellak/gsoc2019-diyrobot (accessed on 10 August 2022)), was a do-it-yourself robot, with 3D-printable parts and a modular design.

Although all of the previous solutions are suitable for specific ages or groups, students and their teachers often seek for a solution that can cover multiple learning needs and can be adopted by different ages and programming skill levels. Most of the commercial solutions do not offer that capability and limit the user to a specific range of capabilities. This limitation, in most cases, is part of the marketing strategy of the companies, which offer different version of their products to different age groups, each with its own, but limited capabilities. On the opposite side, FOSSBot is suitable for all ages due to its ability to boot different operation modes that cover the needs of different age groups, from kindergarten children to students. The closed structure of FOSSBot (shown in Figure 1), which protects all electronic devices and mechanical parts inside and does not leave anything exposed, makes it very safe for children of ages younger than 4 years old. However, the minimum child age that we target is 4 years, and the use of FOSSBot must always be under the supervision of an adult (parent or educator).

Figure 1. A front top view of the FOSSBot.

An open source and open design robot with low-cost electronics and printable parts that supports popular coding environments can be the basis for designing and delivering a wide range of educational solutions. It can support various STEM activities and help students and their educators to play, experiment and learn.

3. Proposed System

From the hardware point of view, FOSSBot is a complete end-to-end robot that employs easy-to-find, low-cost commercial electronics, and easy-to-print-and-assemble plastic parts. It has been designed to work on Raspberry Pi Zero, which provides internet connectivity, supports a wide range of sensors and allows the running of complex operations, such as robot control and computer vision tasks, on its micro-processor. Running on Raspberry Pi's operating system, the software stack of FOSSBot was developed using the latest trends in software development, such as micro-services logic, dockerization and continuous integration (CI).

3.1. 3D-Printable Parts

Every plastic part of the robot, apart from the wheels, is 3D-printable and was designed from scratch in such a way that every sensitive electronic component or sensor is housed inside the robot in special sockets or specially designed containers. For example, a special container was designed for each wheel motor, which allows it to be quickly and steadily mounted to the main body of the robot. The same container has a special position to mount the odometer. The total time needed to print all of the plastic robot parts in a commercial 3D printer (e.g., Wanhao Duplicator 9) is approximately 36 h.

We employed PETG filament for our prints. PETG stands for polyethylene terephthalate glycol and is resistant to heat, impact and solvents. However, any other #D print filament alternative (ABS, ASA or PLA) can be employed, given that it provides strength to the printed parts.

The main body is the biggest part of the robot and was designed to ease the assembly of the different parts. In its interior there are predefined spaces for every electronic part. The external surface has printed symbols that indicate the position of every sensor. The symbols can be very useful to educators, since they provide an easy way to track every sensor and other electronic parts (e.g., speaker, charging plot, etc.). The front and upper side of the robot have printed grids that assist the cooling of the electronic parts. The charging port is located in the back side of the robot, along with the On/Off switch and a special loop that allows the towing of small items. Another purpose of this loop is to protect the robot from minor crashes. The second purpose is for courses that demand the robot to pull small objects. The main body also contains a vertical tube that runs from top to bottom and allows a pencil or marker to be attached to the robot. This allows the drawing of shapes in the ground by moving FOSSBot over a paper-covered area. Two spoilers were printed to the left and right of the robot in order to protect the wheels from side crashes and to add to the aesthetic design of FOSSBot.

The top surface of the robot is made up of two parts. The first part is a cover with special clips that is attached to the main body. The cover has a big circular cut in the middle with small rectangular cuts, which allow the main cover to be attached, using a place-and-rotate move, and lock. This main cover is easily detachable in order to provide access to the interior of the robot and, at the same time, can bear a LEGO bricks basis, allowing for more bricks to be attached on top of the robot. This option allows educators in the lower grades to use FOSSBot along with other LEGO activities, and can help in extending FOSSBot with more detachable electronic components that will be designed and developed in the future.

3.2. Electronics

The choice of suitable electronic parts for FOSSBot is not an easy task. It is important to use electronics that are common in the market, low-cost and compatible with Raspberry Pi. The list of electronics, as shown in Figure 2, comprises the following parts: gyroscope, accelerometer, two odometers, two motors for the wheels (the third standing point is a ball caster), RGB LED, rechargeable battery system, photo resistor, battery sensor to measure the power of the rechargeable batteries, ultrasonic distance sensor, speaker and, finally, gap/distance infrared sensor. The use of low cost and easy to find electronics gives the opportunity to everyone to buy and assemble FOSSBot with less than USD 200, and also maximizes the ability to repair the robot by replacing the defective part or by printing the worn plastic part. The different sensors and actuators can give the educators the ability to create numerous courses and activities that cover a wide range of disciplines.

One of the biggest challenges was to choose a suitable processor for FOSSBot that can support all sensors and provide an expandable platform for hosting our software stack and developing various educational activities [37]. Our programming language was Python and the most promising platform choices were Raspberry Pi (Zero or 4), Arduino MKR and ESP32, which support Wi-Fi connectivity and are frequently used by robot software developers. Although Arduino MKR and ESP32 are frequently used in automation and robotics educational projects, they use a mobile version of Python programming language, which limits the ability to easily develop a composite software stack. Choosing Raspberry Pi Zero allows for the use of the full version of Python programming language, combined with a series of stable and handy libraries. Finally, the operating system of Raspberry Pi (Raspbian) supports software tools, such as Docker, which are very useful in the continuous integration and updates of the software stack.

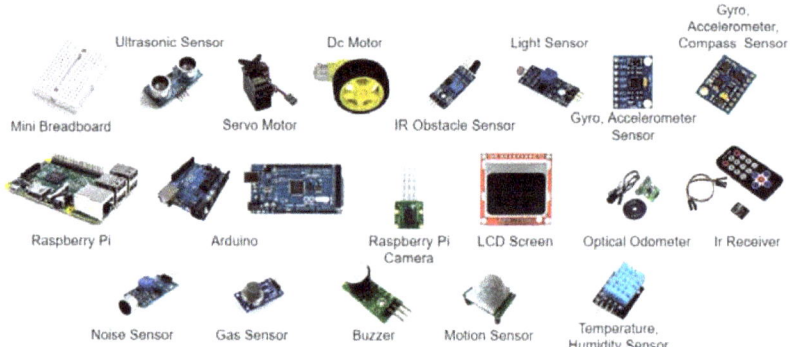

Figure 2. The suite of FOSSBot electronics.

4. The Software Stack of FOSSBot

FOSSBot is based on a modular software stack, which is illustrated in Figure 3, that allows for (i) the implementation of various operation/programming modes, (ii) the orchestration of everything through its administration GUI and (iii) the controlling of the hardware in an easy way through a software library that plays the role of the FOSSBot operating system

Figure 3. The software stack.

The software stack of FOSSBot comprises the following interconnected components: Google Blockly (https://developers.google.com/blockly (accessed on 10 August 2022)), Python Jupyter (https://jupyter.org/ (accessed on 10 August 2022)), Python Flask (https://flask.palletsprojects.com/en/2.1.x/ (accessed on 10 August 2022)), which hosts the administration/supervisor GUI of FOSSBot, the core FOSSBot library written in Python that controls the robot hardware, and, finally, the manual operation mode UI, which provides a friendly interface for users to control the robot without any knowledge of programming.

The core code of FOSSBot is written in Python and allows us to control the main actions of the robot (i.e. movement, sensors, actuators, sanity checks). The core library of the robot uses a high level of abstraction and offers an easy way to command the electronic parts of the robot. The core library is accessible by all other operation/programming modules of the robot.

The administration/supervisor container is responsible for ensuring the normal operation of the robot and provides the end user a way to modify default parameters and maintain them from the software aspect of the system.

The operation/programming modules are further detailed in the following sections.

A major open source project and community that develops robotic software is the Robot Operating System (ROS (https://www.ros.org/ (accessed on 10 August 2022))). ROS also adopts a modular architecture that organizes code in packages for basic operations, movement, sensors and data analysis, etc. It also defines a middleware interface between ROS and any specific middleware implementation. The current list of FOSSBot's sensors and electronics mostly supports the movement of the robot in 2D and some basic sensor data collection activities. Respectively, the OS of FOSSBot mainly wraps up basic movement functions (move forward/backward and turn) and sensor interfaces for collecting data. More advanced packages, such as path planning, computer vision, etc., are still not supported by the FOSSBot OS. We are currently developing packages for logging and diagnostics in order to support testing and quality assurance. The core FOSSBot OS library is also called by a middleware interface in the case of the no-coding and block-based coding modes, which wraps the main functionalities in REST API calls. The management interface also interacts with the robot through the same middleware interface.

4.1. Operation Modes

Through the administration panel, the users can choose to use the robot in one of the three following modes: (i) the no-coding UI, which is suitable for pre-school children and mainly demonstrates the robot's abilities, (ii) the block-based coding UI, which targets primary school students, and (iii) the notebook coding mode, which can be used to teach high school students the basics of programming (e.g., loops, conditions, events, etc.) in Python. In addition to these three modes, it is possible for more experienced users to write Python scripts directly on the FOSSBot programming shell, thus achieving a low-level control of the robot and its electronics. We call this mode the Python programming mode.

4.1.1. No-Coding Mode

This mode is addressed to users with little or no coding experience. The robot can be operated using buttons that appear in the main robot control screen. The screen contains, by default, four buttons that can move the robot forward and backward and turn the robot clockwise and anti-clockwise. The length of a forward of backward step and the degrees of the rotation are defined through the administration panel, but the default is 10 cm and 90 degrees, respectively.

This mode also allows for the addition of more buttons with pre-defined or newly coded functionality, as shown in Figure 4. For example, the educator can add more buttons that implement steps of different length, play a sound or turn on the LED light of the robot. The buttons can also be connected with more complex scripts, coded using the block-based coding UI. For example, the educator can prepare a follow-the-line script in the block-based coding UI, save it and link it to a button using FOSSBot's administration panel.

The ability to expand the basic set of buttons with more specially crafted buttons can keep the interest of students high, with new scenarios and activities. It also allows for the complexity of the course and activities to be easily adjusted based on the students' level and learning pace.

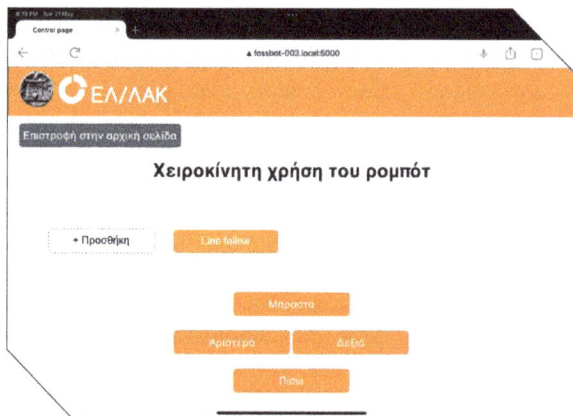

Figure 4. No-coding UI preview.

4.1.2. Block-Based Coding Mode

The block-based coding interface follows the successful paradigm of Scratch software (https://scratch.mit.edu/ (accessed on 10 August 2022)) in education. However, FOSSBot's UI is based on the open source Google Blockly software.

In the block-based coding mode, the user can create full operational programs using coding blocks, as shown in Figure 5. Every block corresponds to a command, which can also be parametrized, take one or more inputs and provide output and have a special role in the program, and can be connected or embedded in other blocks like pieces of a puzzle. The proper combination and arrangement of coding blocks builds the coding script.

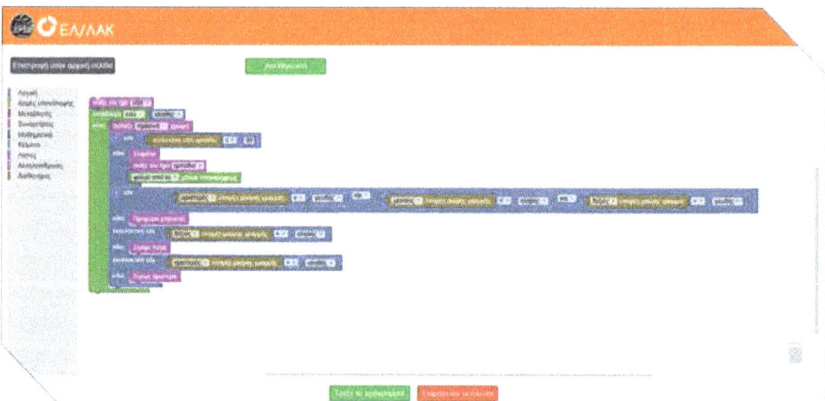

Figure 5. Block-based coding UI preview.

All of the block-based scripts can be stored in the robot's memory storage (i.e., an SD memory card) and retrieved at any time. They can be opened, modified and executed. They can also be linked to buttons in the no-coding mode. When the user decides to create a new script, a new screen with the Blockly UI appears that contains an empty script-construction area on the right and a sidebar on the left that groups all of the available commands in categories (e.g., loops, conditions, functions, etc.). The block categories comprise buttons commonly used in coding and mathematics.

What is unique here is a group of Blockly blocks that map directly to FOSSBot commands. These blocks are programmed in Python and call methods of the core FOSSBot library that control the sensors or the movement of the robot. More specifically, blocks in the Movement category control the movement and rotation of the robot (e.g., keep moving forever, or move for a certain distance) and blocks in the Sensor category allow for the interaction with the sensors (e.g., to measure the distance from an obstacle). Finally, a third category of Interaction blocks controls how FOSSBot interacts and communicates with the user by blinking or changing the color of the RGB LED or by recording and playing an audio message from the speaker.

Developing a script using the block-based UI is a straightforward process of connecting the building blocks. The execution of the script is performed directly on the robot. Behind the scenes, the Blockly compiler module converts the block-based script to an executable Python script, which is executed in FOSSBot's backend.

4.1.3. Notebook Programming Mode

In this mode, FOSSBot can be transformed from an educational toy robot to an advanced educational tool that can support various activities, with emphasis on Python programming. The robot can be programmed using the Python programming language, which is combined with the high-level abstraction of the robot, as defined in the core FOSSBot library. Using the notebook mode, a Jupyter notebook opens that allows for the combining of Python commands that are executed directly on FOSSBot, with their output and with notes that describe and explain the whole process. Additional data management and visualisation commands provided by the popular Python libraries of Pandas and Matplotlib allow it to collect data from the sensors, analyze them and create a visual plot for the users. The final result looks like what is depicted in Figure 6, where an introductory paragraph about the human brain reaction time is followed by a script that runs on FOSSBot, prompts the way the user responds to a visual signal and records his/her reaction time.

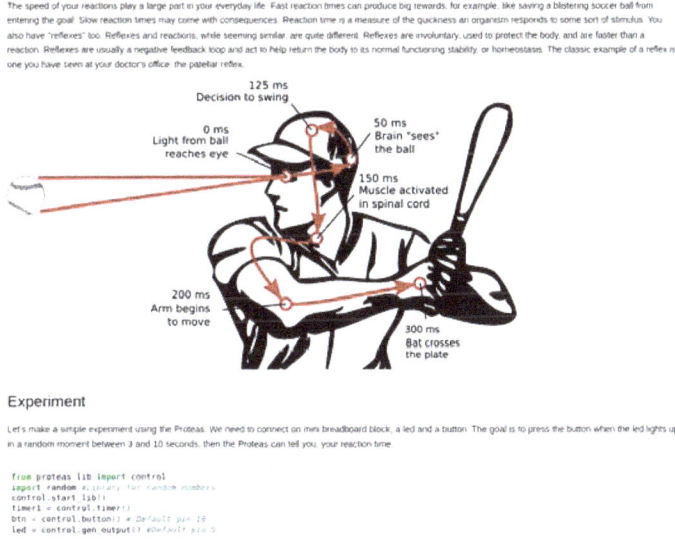

Figure 6. Notebook coding mode example.

The Jupyter notebook is a tool that is commonly used by data scientist and educators because of it browser-based UI and its ability to execute Python commands and directly display their output. FOSSBot's notebook IDE runs directly on the robot and can be accessed by any device (i.e., laptop or PC) that is connected in the same network as FOSSBot. The interactive nature of the notebook coding mode can be very appealing for students, who have an unlimited number of ways to use FOSSBot's sensors, capture and analyze their data and set up their own experiments.

4.1.4. Python Programming Mode

The fourth and more advanced operation mode is by directly accessing the operating system of the robot. This can be achieved by directly connecting to FOSSBot's shell using an SSH connection. Then, the user can launch the Python environment and start writing Python scripts that are executed directly on FOSSBot. This mode is suitable for experienced users or researchers who wish to extend the capabilities of the robot by adding to its core library, or who simply want to have direct access to all sensors and electronics. This is the same mode used by the development team of FOSSBot for developing new functionalities or for adding new options to the administration module, to the Blockly-based programming mode, etc. A screenshot of the code behind the core robot library is depicted in Figure 7.

```
class motor():

    """
    The motor class creates new motor objects. For every motor you should create a new object
    e.g. left_motor = motor(pwm_pin,pin a,pin b) also you can insert the frequence as freq of pwm
    and duty cycle as dc. The dc parameter controls the speed of the motor and accepts values 0 - 100
    by default the constructor set the frequence at 1000 Hz and the duty cycle to 50
    """

    def __init__(self,speed_pin,terma_pin,termb_pin,freq=1000,dc=50):
        GPIO.setup(speed_pin,GPIO.OUT)
        GPIO.setup(terma_pin,GPIO.OUT)
        GPIO.setup(termb_pin,GPIO.OUT)
        self.terma_pin = terma_pin
        self.termb_pin = termb_pin
        self.mot = GPIO.PWM(speed_pin,freq)
        self.freq = freq
        self.dc = dc
        self.dir_control("forward")
        self.mot.start(0)
    def control_speed(self,speed):
        self.mot.ChangeDutyCycle(speed)
    def set_speed(self,speed):
        self.dc = speed
    def dir_control(self,direction):
        if direction == "forward":
            GPIO.output(self.terma_pin,GPIO.HIGH)
            GPIO.output(self.termb_pin,GPIO.LOW)
        elif direction == "reverse":
            GPIO.output(self.terma_pin,GPIO.LOW)
            GPIO.output(self.termb_pin,GPIO.HIGH)
        else:
            print("Motor accepts only forward and reverse values")
    def move(self,direction ="forward"):
        self.dir_control(direction)
        self.mot.ChangeDutyCycle(self.dc)
    def stop(self):
        self.mot.ChangeDutyCycle(0)
```

Figure 7. Real coding mode example.

4.2. Continuous Software Development and Updates

FOSSBot adopts a modern system architecture that has each one of the stack components in a separate dockerized image, which allows for the fast deployment and continuous integration of software updates.

The whole architecture is based on the continuous integration (CI) concept and, for that reason, the GitHub code repository is employed for staging our code. GitHub is a great code repository with several code management and collaboration capabilities. In addition, it offers a special tool, the GitHub Actions, which offers the ability to the developers to trigger a sequence of actions after a successful commit and merge in their code. In the case of FOSSBot, these actions handle the update of the container files of the FOSSBot software for various processor architectures (ARMv7, ARMv6, ARM64), which are immediately published as new images in the Docker Hub (https://hub.docker.com/repository/docker/chronis10/fossbot_basic (accessed on 10 August 2022)). The latter is a publicly available repository of software images that allows everyone from everywhere to pull a software image and deploy it in his/her system without the need for further installation or configuration steps. This flow offers a great way to push updates to any FOSSBot around the world, and allows FOSSBot users to retrieve software updates at the click of a button. Figure 8 illustrates the aforementioned process.

The use of GitHub also allows the open source community developers to safely contribute to the robot's code and, at the same time, allows end-users to raise issues in the Open Issues section.

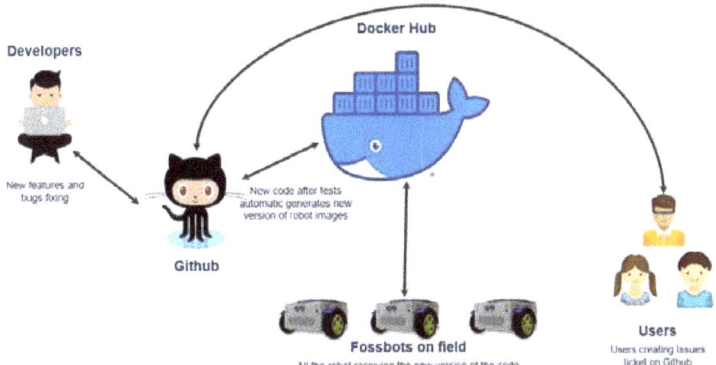

Figure 8. The software stack with the flow between robots, users and developers.

5. FOSSBot Pilot

As detailed in the previous sections, FOSSBot offers a multitude of ways to create educational activities for children and students of all ages. The different operation/programming modes and the variety of its sensors, electronics and other gadgets allow educators to use FOSSBot in various scenarios and teach various subjects, from programming and sciences to history or arts, through proper educational activities.

FOSSBot is currently supported by the Greek Free Open Source Software Society (GFOSS (https://eellak.ellak.gr/ (accessed on 10 August 2022))) and a huge effort has been made to assemble and distribute 100 robots to teachers in Greece, spanning all levels of education, in order to pilot FOSSBot. In close collaboration with a specialized team of STEM educators from GFOSS, the development team of FOSSBot carefully designs code blocks, extends the core library with functionality and continuously improves the administration UI in order to support the emerging educational needs and ideas. The experience of the educators with similar educational robots and kits provides valuable feedback for the design of the robot and new ideas for improving its integration into educational activities.

At the time of writing, the educators' team is working on the development of the FOSSBot usage manual and the educational material that will support courses for nursery schools and primary and secondary schools, as well as vocational training schools that will be trained on printing and assembling the robot. The nursery school material comprises courses and activities that use the no-coding mode and a special floor carpet with rectangles that teaches children how to navigate the robot, but also teaches them multiple topics by connecting the rectangles with domain specific concepts. Respectively, the primary school activities are simple, game-like activities designed on the Blockly mode, and so on. All of the educational material will be pre-loaded to the robot, and an additional external repository is under development, which will allow any educator that used FOSSBot to share his/her educational material with the community.

6. Conclusions and Next Steps

This work introduces FOSSBot, a new open source software and open design robot with a long list of sensors and several features that make it a powerful tool for educators who want to teach programming, sciences, arts and more topics at all educational levels.

In its first steps, FOSSBot has already found the support of open source communities and initiatives, such as the Greek FOSS society and the Onassis' foundation, which funded the assembly of the first 100 FOSSBots, the Google Summer of Code program, which funded the first rounds of development, and, of course, the students and professors from Greek universities that embraced our effort. However, there is still space for improvement in order to make FOSSBot competitive to commercial solutions. Our main goal is to solve any issues related to the software of FOSSBot in order to simplify its assembly. In this direction, the next steps comprise the development of the educational material and the piloting of the robot, and the design of a board that will integrate most of the electronics' connections and will reduce the complexity of assembling the robot.

The development team is in close communication with educators, with the open source software and open hardware communities and FabLabs in Greece, in order to create a competitive and real useful tool for educators, students and robot enthusiasts. At the same time, we are currently working on porting FOSSBot to a robot simulation program (e.g., Gazebo or CoppeliaSim) so that anyone can use the same software stack and experiment with a virtual FOSSBot at no cost.

Last, but most importantly, we are currently working on optimizing all of the performance parameters of FOSSBot. As part of our next steps in this project, we plan an experimental evaluation in terms of computing efficiency, communication speed, control accuracy and other factors that require the careful design of the tasks and challenges, and a comparison with state-of-the-art solutions from the market and research.

Author Contributions: Conceptualization, I.V. and C.C.; software, C.C.; validation, I.V. and C.C.; writing—original draft preparation, C.C.; writing—review and editing, I.V.; supervision, I.V. All authors have read and agreed to the published version of the manuscript.

Funding: This research received no external funding.

Data Availability Statement: All of the code, data and material can be found at https://github.com/eellak/fossbot (accessed on 10 August 2022).

Acknowledgments: The authors would like to thank the students from Harokopio University of Athens who supported the development and assembly of FOSSBot so far: Eleftheria Papageorgiou, Thanassis Apostolidis, Dimitris Charitos, Giorgos Kazazis. In addition, the students from National Technical University of Athens who contributed with code during GSOC: George Yiannakoulias, Danai Brilli. Last but not least, the people from GFOSS and especially Thodoros Karounos who believed in FOSSBot and support our effort from its conception.

Conflicts of Interest: The authors declare no conflict of interest.

References

1. Evripidou, S.; Georgiou, K.; Doitsidis, L.; Amanatiadis, A.A.; Zinonos, Z.; Chatzichristofis, S.A. Educational robotics: Platforms, competitions and expected learning outcomes. *IEEE Access* **2020**, *8*, 219534–219562. [CrossRef]
2. Papert, S.; Harel, I. Situating constructionism. *Constructionism* **1991**, *36*, 1–11.
3. Benitti, F.B.V. Exploring the educational potential of robotics in schools: A systematic review. *Comput. Educ.* **2012**, *58*, 978–988. [CrossRef]
4. Kwon, D.Y.; Kim, H.S.; Shim, J.K.; Lee, W.G. Algorithmic bricks: A tangible robot programming tool for elementary school students. *IEEE Trans. Educ.* **2012**, *55*, 474–479. [CrossRef]
5. Wan, Z.H.; Jiang, Y.; Zhan, Y. STEM education in early childhood: A review of empirical studies. *Early Educ. Dev.* **2021**, *32*, 940–962. [CrossRef]
6. Li, Y.; Wang, K.; Xiao, Y.; Froyd, J.E. Research and trends in STEM education: A systematic review of journal publications. *Int. J. Stem Educ.* **2020**, *7*, 1–16. [CrossRef]
7. Alimisis, D. Educational robotics: Open questions and new challenges. *Themes Sci. Technol. Educ.* **2013**, *6*, 63–71.
8. Shen, V.R.; Yang, C.Y.; Wang, Y.Y.; Lin, Y.H. Application of high-level fuzzy Petri nets to educational grading system. *Expert Syst. Appl.* **2012**, *39*, 12935–12946. [CrossRef]
9. Stager, G. A constructionist approach to teaching with robotics. In Proceedings of the Constructionism and Creativity Conference, Paris, France, 16–20 August 2010; pp. 16–20.
10. Miglino, O.; Lund, H.H.; Cardaci, M. Robotics as an educational tool. *J. Interact. Learn. Res.* **1999**, *10*, 25–47.
11. Eguchi, A.; Shen, J. Student learning experience through CoSpace educational robotics. In *Proceedings of the Society for Information Technology & Teacher Education International Conference*; Association for the Advancement of Computing in Education (AACE): Asheville, NC, USA, 2012; pp. 19–24.
12. De Vries, M.J. *Handbook of Technology Education*; Springer: Berlin/Heidelberg, Germany, 2018.

13. Atmatzidou, S.; Demetriadis, S.; Nika, P. How does the degree of guidance support students' metacognitive and problem solving skills in educational robotics? *J. Sci. Educ. Technol.* **2018**, *27*, 70–85. [CrossRef]
14. Chin, K.Y.; Hong, Z.W.; Chen, Y.L. Impact of using an educational robot-based learning system on students' motivation in elementary education. *IEEE Trans. Learn. Technol.* **2014**, *7*, 333–345. [CrossRef]
15. Tuomi, P.; Multisilta, J.; Saarikoski, P.; Suominen, J. Coding skills as a success factor for a society. *Educ. Inf. Technol.* **2018**, *23*, 419–434. [CrossRef]
16. Yoel, S.R.; Dori, Y.J. FIRST High-School Students and FIRST Graduates: STEM Exposure and Career Choices. *IEEE Trans. Educ.* **2021**, *65*, 167–176. [CrossRef]
17. Caceres, P.C.; Venero, R.P.; Cordova, F.C. Tangible programming mechatronic interface for basic induction in programming. In Proceedings of the IEEE 2018 IEEE Global Engineering Education Conference (EDUCON), Canary Islands, Spain, 18–20 April 2018; pp. 183–190.
18. Sapounidis, T.; Demetriadis, S.; Stamelos, I. Evaluating children performance with graphical and tangible robot programming tools. *Pers. Ubiquitous Comput.* **2015**, *19*, 225–237. [CrossRef]
19. Bers, M.U.; Flannery, L.; Kazakoff, E.R.; Sullivan, A. Computational thinking and tinkering: Exploration of an early childhood robotics curriculum. *Comput. Educ.* **2014**, *72*, 145–157. [CrossRef]
20. McGill, M.M. Learning to program with personal robots: Influences on student motivation. *ACM Trans. Comput. Educ. (TOCE)* **2012**, *12*, 1–32. [CrossRef]
21. Evripidou, S.; Amanatiadis, A.; Christodoulou, K.; Chatzichristofis, S.A. Introducing algorithmic thinking and sequencing using tangible robots. *IEEE Trans. Learn. Technol.* **2021**, *14*, 93–105. [CrossRef]
22. Kaburlasos, V.G.; Dardani, C.; Dimitrova, M.; Amanatiadis, A. Multi-robot engagement in special education: A preliminary study in autism. In Proceedings of the 2018 IEEE International Conference on Consumer Electronics (ICCE), Las Vegas, NV, USA, 12–15 January 2018; pp. 1–2.
23. Amanatiadis, A.; Kaburlasos, V.G.; Dardani, C.; Chatzichristofis, S.A.; Mitropoulos, A. Social robots in special education: Creating dynamic interactions for optimal experience. *IEEE Consum. Electron. Mag.* **2020**, *9*, 39–45. [CrossRef]
24. Amanatiadis, A.; Kaburlasos, V.G.; Dardani, C.; Chatzichristofis, S.A. Interactive social robots in special education. In Proceedings of the 2017 IEEE 7th International Conference on Consumer Electronics-Berlin (ICCE-Berlin), Berlin, Germany, 3–6 September 2017; pp. 126–129.
25. Shim, J.; Kwon, D.; Lee, W. The effects of a robot game environment on computer programming education for elementary school students. *IEEE Trans. Educ.* **2016**, *60*, 164–172. [CrossRef]
26. Garris, R.; Ahlers, R.; Driskell, J.E. Games, motivation, and learning: A research and practice model. In *Simulation in Aviation Training*; Routledge: London, UK, 2017; pp. 475–501.
27. Feurzeig, W.; Lukas, G. LOGO—A programming language for teaching mathematics. *Educ. Technol.* **1972**, *12*, 39–46.
28. Suzuki, H.; Kato, H. AlgoBlock: A tangible programming language, a tool for collaborative learning. In Proceedings of the 4th European Logo Conference, Partenkirchen, Germany, 13–17 September 1993; pp. 297–303.
29. McNerney, T.S. From turtles to Tangible Programming Bricks: Explorations in physical language design. *Pers. Ubiquitous Comput.* **2004**, *8*, 326–337. [CrossRef]
30. Gallardo, D.; Julia, C.F.; Jorda, S. TurTan: A tangible programming language for creative exploration. In Proceedings of the 2008 3rd IEEE International Workshop on Horizontal Interactive Human Computer Systems, Amsterdam, The Netherlands, 2–3 October 2008; pp. 89–92.
31. Wyeth, P.; Wyeth, G.F. Electronic Blocks: Tangible Programming Elements for Preschoolers. In Proceedings of the Human-Computer Interaction INTERACT '01: IFIP TC13 International Conference on Human-Computer Interaction, Tokyo, Japan, 9–13 July 2001; pp. 496–503.
32. Horn, M.S.; Jacob, R.J. Designing tangible programming languages for classroom use. In Proceedings of the 1st International Conference on Tangible and Embedded Interaction, Baton Rouge, LA, USA, 15–17 February 2007; pp. 159–162.
33. Horn, M.S.; Jacob, R.J. Tangible programming in the classroom with tern. In Proceedings of the CHI'07 Extended Abstracts on Human Factors in Computing Systems, San Jose, CA, USA, 7–12 May 2007; pp. 1965–1970.
34. Mondada, F.; Bonani, M.; Riedo, F.; Briod, M.; Pereyre, L.; Rétornaz, P.; Magnenat, S. Bringing robotics to formal education: The thymio open-source hardware robot. *IEEE Robot. Autom. Mag.* **2017**, *24*, 77–85. [CrossRef]
35. De Cristoforis, P.; Pedre, S.; Nitsche, M.; Fischer, T.; Pessacg, F.; Di Pietro, C. A behavior-based approach for educational robotics activities. *IEEE Trans. Educ.* **2012**, *56*, 61–66. [CrossRef]
36. Tsalmpouris, G.; Tsinarakis, G.; Gertsakis, N.; Chatzichristofis, S.A.; Doitsidis, L. HYDRA: Introducing a Low-Cost Framework for STEM Education Using Open Tools. *Electronics* **2021**, *10*, 3056. [CrossRef]
37. Evripidou, S.; Doitsidis, L.; Tsinarakis, G.; Zinonos, Z.; Chatzichristofis, S.A. Selecting a Robotic Platform for Education. In Proceedings of the 2022 IEEE International Conference on Consumer Electronics (ICCE), Las Vegas, NV, USA, 6–8 January 2022; pp. 1–6.

Article

An Omnidirectional Platform for Education and Research in Cooperative Robotics

Majd Kassawat *, Enric Cervera and Angel P. del Pobil

Department of Engineering and Computer Science, Universidad Jaume I, 12071 Castellon de la Plana, Spain; ecervera@uji.es (E.C.); pobil@uji.es (A.P.d.P.)
* Correspondence: majd.kassawat@gmail.com

Abstract: In this paper we present a new, affordable, omnidirectional robot platform which is suitable for research and education in cooperative robotics. We design and implement the platform for the purpose of multi-agent object manipulation and transportation. The design consists of three omnidirectional wheels with two additional traction wheels, making multirobot object manipulation possible. It is validated by performing simple experiments using a setup with one robot and one target object. The execution flow of a simple task (Approach–Press–Lift–Hold–Set) is studied. In addition, we experiment to find the limits of the applied pressure and object orientation under certain conditions. The experiments demonstrate the significance of our inexpensive platform for research and education by proving its feasibility of use in topics such as collaborative robotics, physical interaction, and mobile manipulation.

Keywords: multirobot transportation; mobile robot; omnidirectional

Citation: Kassawat, M.; Cervera, E.; del Pobil, A.P. An Omnidirectional Platform for Education and Research in Cooperative Robotics. *Electronics* **2022**, *11*, 499. https://doi.org/10.3390/electronics11030499

Academic Editor: Jeha Ryu

Received: 22 December 2021
Accepted: 4 February 2022
Published: 8 February 2022

Publisher's Note: MDPI stays neutral with regard to jurisdictional claims in published maps and institutional affiliations.

Copyright: © 2022 by the authors. Licensee MDPI, Basel, Switzerland. This article is an open access article distributed under the terms and conditions of the Creative Commons Attribution (CC BY) license (https:// creativecommons.org/licenses/by/ 4.0/).

1. Introduction

Designing multi-robot systems has captured the attention of many researchers/industries due to its scalability and various applications. As discussed in [1], the majority of the methods used can be categorized into three main strategies: Pushing-only, grasping and caging strategy. Caging strategy was followed in [2] where, using a composition of three behaviors (approach, surround and transport), a group of eight robots were able to displace an L-shaped object to a target location. A pure pushing strategy was discussed in [3] where the swarm takes advantage of the object occluding the visibility of the goal position to decide the direction of pushing. Unlike [4,5], mentioned examples do not realize a solid connection with the object as a preparation step for transporting. The authors in [4] explore a decentralized sliding mode control strategy to move a load along a straight line at a desired velocity. The object is pre-grasped by all robots and the paths of the robots and object are monitored. The authors demonstrate that this strategy does not depend on inter-robot communication, team size, or load related information. Experiments using different object sizes and shapes were performed in [5]. The possibility of having chains of robots or mixed typologies linked to the object was discussed and experimented using an evolutionary algorithm applied to up to 16 robots. These experiments showed that using this method, the swarm can transport heavier objects than using simple one layer caging. While most of the mentioned work concentrates on moving the object from point A to point B, the object is assumed to be pre-grasped or it is pushed on the flat surface of the robots. A mechanical manipulator has been designed to be mounted on mobile robots to be used to collaboratively lift an object to the base of the robots [6,7]. This mechanism relies on friction induced between the set of manipulators and the surface of the object. The solution uses the flexibility of a parallelogram shape with 2 DOF. The structure passively raises once pressure is applied to the end effector. Having two robots applying pressure on opposite sides elevates the object off the ground to be later transported. In [8,9], the problem of object transportation is moved to aerial robots, which have more degrees of freedom and have more possibilities to manipulate the object.

In this article, we will describe a design of a collaborative manipulator which senses the forces induced in the target object by other robots. This technique has been used in leader–follower strategy in [4,10], where force readings are used to analyze the direction of the leader's movements considering that the leader could be a human, a human operated robot, or an autonomous robot. Our concept builds on the approach taken in [6,7], where lift is achieved by friction between the robots and the object, rather than direct grasping as in [4]. Indeed, our design adds the ability to tilt the object while in contact and provides free planar motion to the mobile platform to be used for cooperative transportation compared to a two-motor driven system which is not capable of doing omnidirectional motion. The benefits of omnidirectional motion were shown in [11,12], where a group of two or three omnidirectional robots transport an object to a target destination while avoiding near obstacles. This approach uses an expensive platform equipped with a robotic arm [13] compared to our setup, which simplifies the main components of the agents in order to perform simple, yet effective, lift-transport operation. In [14,15] the authors present interesting low-cost designs for multi-robot manipulators. While those robots are a good fit for research and education, they have drawbacks, such as a two-wheel drive system and having to modify the target object for grasping.

We present a new concept for cooperatively lifting, manipulating, and transporting an object. The concept has already been validated in simulation in [16]. In this paper, we implement an improved version using real hardware and we validate the design in a one-robot scenario with the aim of illustrating the use of the robot platform for research and education in cooperative robotics and manipulation. We believe that it presents a more simplified and affordable approach to multi-robot load sharing and transportation compared to other state-of-the-art approaches. Indeed, it can be applied to lift and manipulate objects that are not prepared for a the usual transporting mechanism—like a forklift—or large objects that could not otherwise be transportable using one agent. Moreover, as it depends on traction, it does not require a special grasping area for each agent or modifying the target object for transportation. Furthermore, having a modular system integrated using ROS and using off-the-shelf components positions it perfectly for use in research and education, since this design allows the addition of new features and modifications without affecting its base platform.

The paper is organized as follows. Section 2 describes the implemented system, Section 3 presents the concept and some additional considerations, and Section 4 reports three experiments with their results in order to validate the system. The paper concludes with a discussion and conclusions, including future work.

2. Description of Implemented System

2.1. Hardware Platform

The design is based on an omnidirectional mobile platform consisting of: three omnidirectional wheels attached to servo motors DYNAMIXEL AX-12A (4), one uEye XS camera (2), two 1KG load cells (5), traction wheels (1) mounted on two servo motors (3), a USB hub (7), and a cable guide (6). Figure 1. Robot chassis and custom links are 3D printed.

The three wheels and motors enable the robot to perform full omnidirectional movements, which simplifies the planning problem for one robot [17–19] and makes a multi-robot object manipulation possible. Load cells (or force sensors) will measure the force exerted from the robot to the object (expected to be less than 1KG for our experiments) [20]. Note that having a higher max value would result in lowering the resolution of measurements. The data collected is passed through a micro-controller to the processing node. Traction motors work as a differential drive to control height and orientation of the target object. The camera is used to know the position and orientation of the target object using a fixed marker. In this model, all sensors and controllers are directly wired to a PC, ensuring cables do not influence the motion of the robot at any time. Power (5v,12v) is provided by an external power supply. This setup allows easy remote access to the experiment.

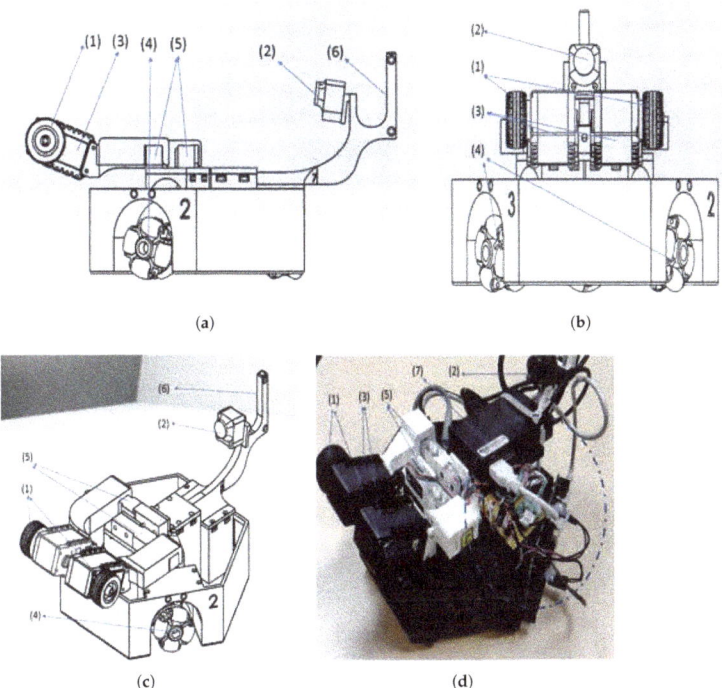

Figure 1. Robot Design: (**a**) side; (**b**) front; (**c**) corner; and (**d**) real.

2.2. Controller Software

2.2.1. Overview

We use ROS nodes as an interface between the low level drivers for the motors and sensors, as well as for implementing the control logic for the robot.

The trajectory file contains a list of trajectory points. Each point is described by a number of constraints (specific required inputs); these inputs could be the position of the robot relative to the marker, force values read using the force sensors, certain torque limit, or simple time conditions. Each condition has its own target, error tolerance, bias, and gain, which should be used in the corresponding error correcting methods in the controller. As usual, K represents the gain in the low-level controller and the bias is a constant value that is summed to the output to the actuators. One point is reached when all the conditions included in that point are reached. Separate points are processed sequentially until the end of the trajectory. Figure 2 shows trajectory points and robot control stages. As mentioned, it is possible to have more than one condition in one point and, our current implementation supports the use of 4 types of control, Figure 3, that we can use to reach said conditions:

- Single: this indicates one correction is going to be processed. This is usually the leaf type for single access corrections;
- Sequential: this indicates that child conditions will be processed sequentially. Once the correction is done, the controller will not check this condition again;
- Parallel: child conditions will be processed at the same time so in each tick all the child corrections are processed and the result output is calculated from the outputs of all child corrections;

- Semi-sequential: in one tick, the controller goes over child corrections sequentially, calculates the first unfinished correction, ignores the rest, and outputs the result. This means that each time, the controller will not proceed to next condition until it has fixed the first ones. The difference with sequential is that this method checks the finished child corrections each tick for any new deviation from target.

It is possible to nest these types as needed. This feature brings certain flexibility to the user to form the trajectory which fits the application the most.

In each tick, the controller checks for all the inputs/references required to process the current point. This check is performed to ensure no null data is introduced to the controller while in action. The frequency used is 40 hz, which is enough, taking into account that camera frame rate is about 20 frame/s.

2.2.2. Available Types of Conditions

- Planar conditions: the conditions are to meet certain position(X,Y)/orientation(Alpha) relative to a reference frame (the marker in our case);
- Boolean: target value is True/False;
- Time (wait): target is reached after certain time;
- Force (single access): target is reached when force sensor reading reach set target.
    1. Total pressure collected from both sensors is within allowed range. This is corrected by moving the robot forward;
    2. Difference between force sensors readings is below a certain tolerance, which is corrected by rotating the robot while applying pressure on target object.

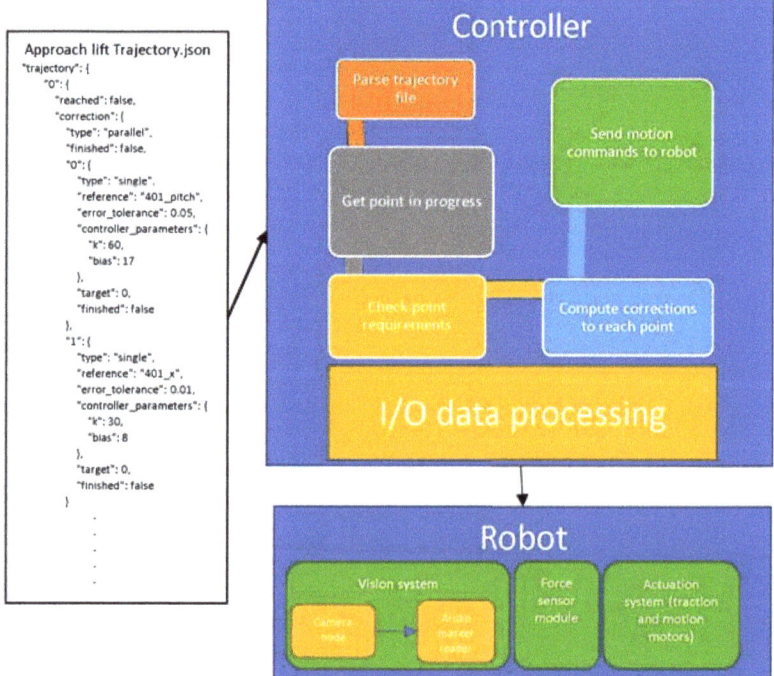

Figure 2. Software components.

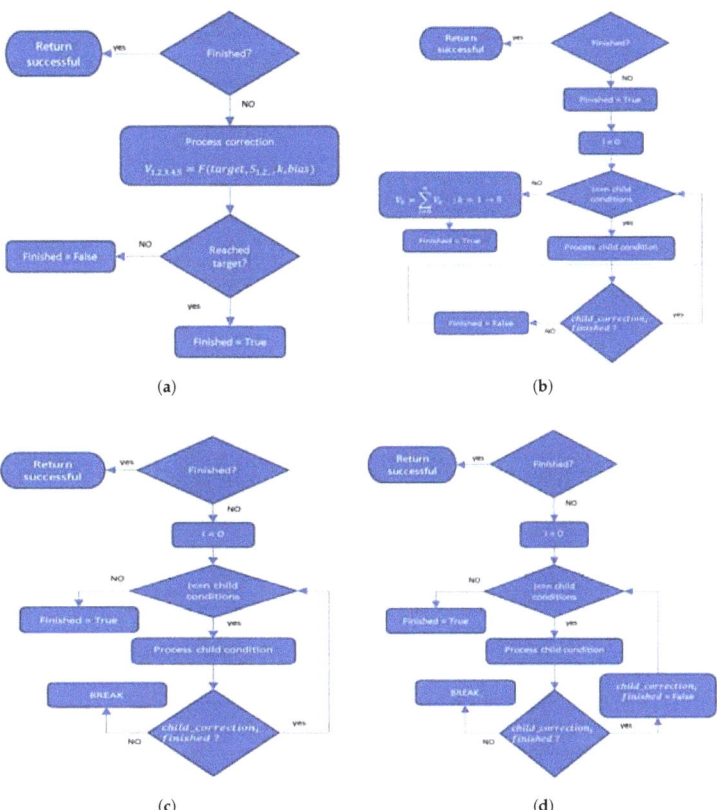

Figure 3. Control Types: (**a**) single correction; (**b**) parallel corrections; (**c**) sequential corrections; and (**d**) semi-sequential corrections.

3. Concept, Approach, and Considerations

The platform described previously is designed for multi-robot object lifting and transportation. This concept has been proven to work in simulation in [16] where we were able to lift a 2 KG object using three robots and displace it about 2 m on a plane surface. Figure 4 shows the forces exerted by each robot on the target object and the total force by which direction the object would move. Having an omnidirectional platform allows each individual robot to move sideways while still maintaining pressure in the contact point. This allows for the possibility to rotate the target object by moving the individual robots at the same local direction.

Using simulation, it is possible to analyze and debug a system of three robots. However, working with hardware adds a certain amount of complexity due to the very dynamic and contact-full nature of the project. Therefore, a minimal scenario is needed (Figure 4). This setup uses one robot which applies force on an object contacting a non-friction surface on the opposite side of the robot. The system still is performing force control and adjusting the altitude of the target object. Using this simplified setup, debugging the system and analyzing force control algorithms becomes more manageable.

Unlike [16], in the following experiments we will not depend on an external observer to guide the robots towards the target object. The object is equipped with a visual marker, which is detected by the camera to guide the robot automatically to the target object.

$$\overrightarrow{F_{total}} = \sum_{i=1}^{i=N*2} \overrightarrow{F_{Pi}}, \&N = \text{number of robots} \qquad (1)$$

The total amount of pressure applied on the object is all the forces applied that didn't participate in total force to move the object, which can be expressed as the following:

$$|F_{pressure}| = \sum_{i=1}^{i=N*2} |F_{Pi}| - |F_{total}| \qquad (2)$$

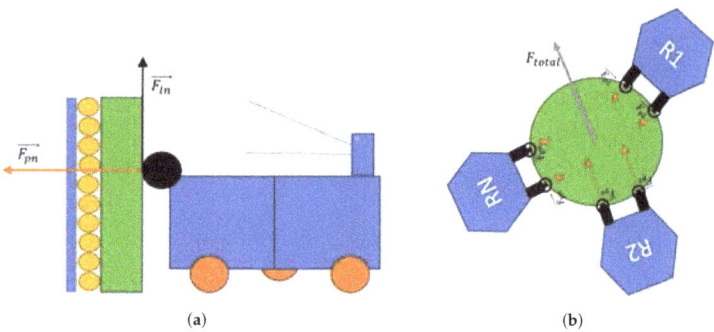

Figure 4. Concept: (**a**) single robot scenario; and (**b**) multi-robot scenario.

4. Experiments and Results

For all our experiments, we will use the setup shown in Figure 5. Our setup is composed of the robot which is wired directly to the controlling PC, the target object in the shape of a rectangular box, and a non-friction surface of free rolling wheels that gives the ability for the box to move freely on the vertical plane. A marker is attached to the target object to easily identify its position and orientation.

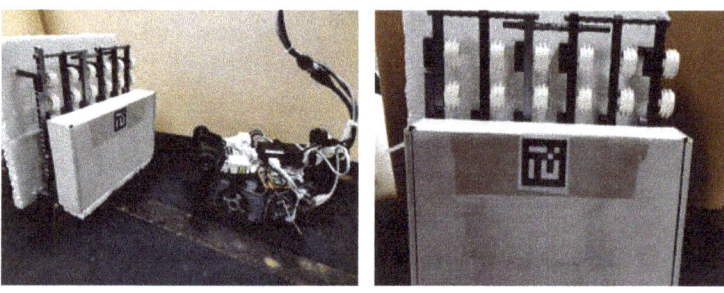

Figure 5. Setup and target object.

4.1. Experiment 1

4.1.1. Description

In this experiment, we set a trajectory of points consisting of force, position, and time conditions. This sequence of points is executed and the corresponding output is shown in Figure 6 where six different phases are identified, Figure 7:

1. Approach: the robot starts in a random location where the target object is visually accessible. The robot detects the target object and performs parallel control to reach a 2 cm distance from the object while keeping the robot parallel and centered relative to the target object.
    *When at the target, the robot calibrates the height of the target object marker and starts next correction;

2. Press: having the robot perfectly parallel to the opposing surface, the system sets the target pressure to 120 g with a total tolerance of 40 g. Once the system reads force values in this range, the target object is "grasped" and ready to be lifted;
3. Lift: the trajectory specifies the system to perform parallel control to lift the object up 4 cm using the traction wheels in front while maintaining the same pressure and keeping the target bottom surface parallel to the ground. Please note that the Z axis value is inverted;
4. Hold: the robot holds the object in the same conditions for 5 s adding a time constraint to the previous parallel control. Note that in this phase, the control is already stable and, since there are not changes on the inputs, the system does not react;
5. Set down: keeping force conditions but changing the target height to original, the robot lowers down the target object;
6. Regress: now the robot can release pressure of the object and leave the area.

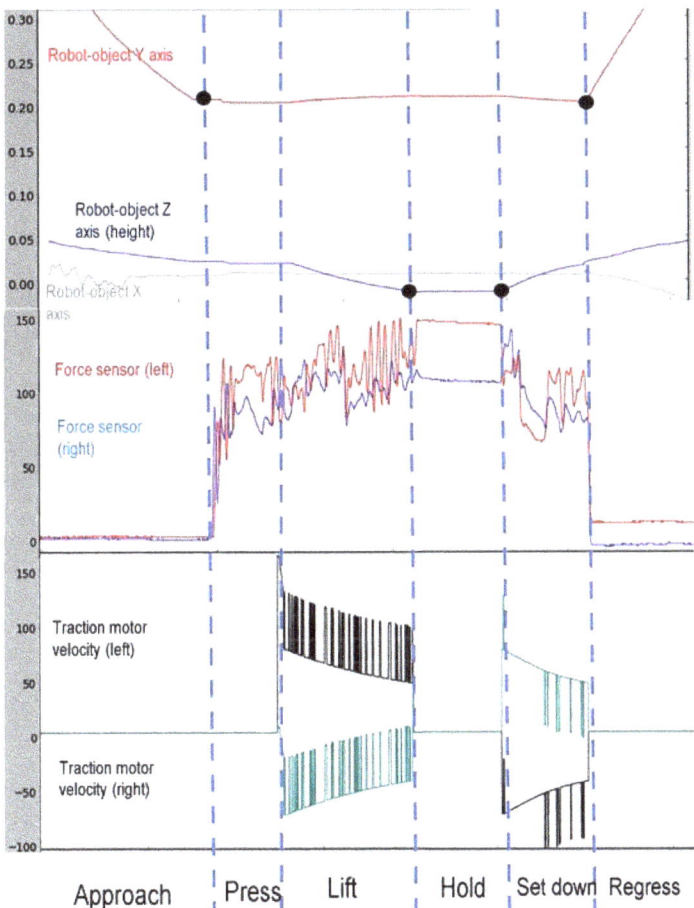

Figure 6. Experiment-1 execution flow.

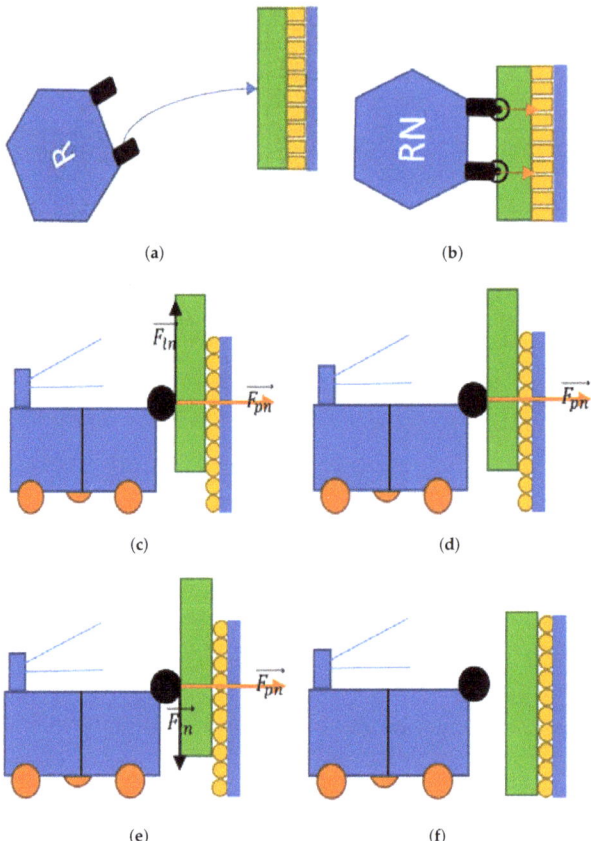

Figure 7. Execution stages: (**a**) approach; (**b**) press; (**c**) lift; (**d**) hold; (**e**) set down; and (**f**) regress.

4.1.2. Results

As seen in Figure 6, the robot was able to complete the entire trajectory as planned. However, in Press and Lift phases, the robot control overshoots the target force threshold and isolates with a maximum variance of 50 g. This problem arises due to the relatively high minimum speed at which the motors can run. Since the motors do not move on very low speeds, the error accumulates until the error is high enough to cause a response from the actuators. Despite this flow, the system didn't lose grip on the object because the target force is at a higher value above the oscillation range.

4.2. Experiment 2

4.2.1. Description

In this experiment, we set the angle of the target object bottom surface with the ground to *alpha* and we measured the average time of 10 iterations of same flow as experiment-1. We then calculated the success rate and defined the most common reason of failure for a certain value of *alpha*.

4.2.2. Results

As demonstrated in Table 1, we can conclude that the possibility of failure increases when *alpha* increases. The performance does not seem to be affected if the angle is below 20 degrees. The reason for this behavior is related to the shape of the target object. In our case, when the angle is higher than 20 degrees, one part of the object would start touching the ground because the object can't be held at a very high altitude. As we see, for 40 degrees, we did not succeed in securely lifting the object; the object would not be in contact with the traction wheels around this angle because the wheels are in a fixed position on the robot, see Figure 8. The average time is higher with lower success rates due to timeouts at 100 s.

Table 1. Results of single robot approach and lift process changing angle *alpha*.

Alpha (Degrees)	Average Time (Seconds)	Reason of Failure	Success Rate
0	35	-	100%
5	33	-	100%
10	41	PRESS	90%
20	53	HOLD	80%
30	64	LIFT	40%
40	110	LIFT	0%

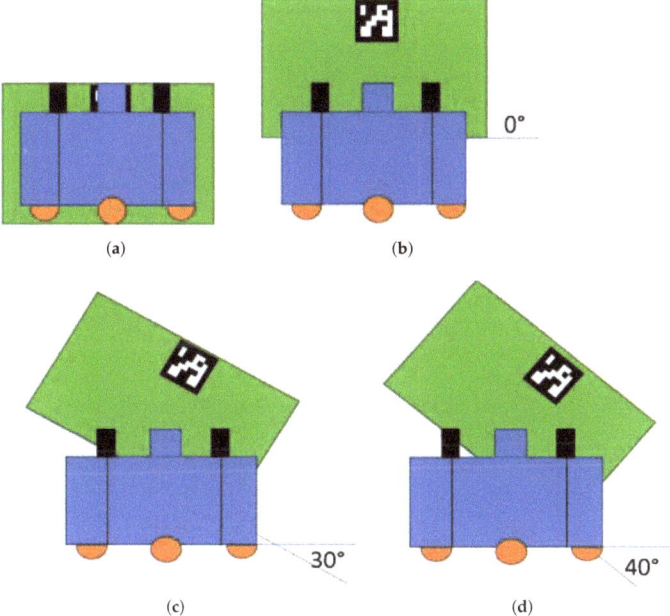

Figure 8. Lifting angle limitation: (**a**) ready to lift; (**b**) lifted (alpha = 0 deg); (**c**) lifted (alpha = 30 deg), and (**d**) failed to lift (alpha = 40 deg).

4.3. Experiment 3

4.3.1. Description

Here, we try to find the limits of pressure that our platform can apply. When the robot is capable of applying more pressure, the target load could have higher weight. In this experiment, we will set the total target pressure to different values to see the optimal pressure for the unloaded robot (900 g) and a very light target object (40 g).

4.3.2. Results

After 10 iterations, we have results in Table 2. It was noted during the executions that on high pressure values (>140), the robot skids on the ground because the platform does not have enough weight to generate more friction between the wheels and the floor. This limitation could be overcome by adding weights to the robot or modifying the flow to start lifting before the pressure threshold is reached to take advantage of the weight of the load and put more pressure on the robots wheels to generate more friction. Low total target pressure results in the robot not having enough pressure to grasp the object and, therefore, the object sometimes falls while being lifted.

Table 2. Results of single robot approach and lift process changing total target pressure.

Total Target Pressure (Grams)	Average Time (Seconds)	Reason of Failure	Success Rate
90	110	PRESS + LIFT	0%
100	45	PRESS	80%
110	33	-	100%
120	35	-	100%
130	52	PRESS	70%
140	90	PRESS	10%

5. Discussion and Conclusions

As observed in the performed experiments, the robot is capable of performing an (approach–press–lift) operation with relatively high repeatability. However, the current implementation of the system has certain performance limitations which can be summarized in 3 issues:

- **Maximum manipulation angle:** as shown in Experiment 2, with more than 20 degree angle the system would have a high failure rate since the object is no longer gaining traction from the wheels' pressure. This issue can be solved by having more traction points with higher altitude so that the lifted object is always in contact with at least two points. Nevertheless, the solution was not implemented because the current limit is more than enough to perform a stable operation at maximum lift height;
- **Pressure overshooting:** in all experiments, it has been noted that our system tends to overshoot the pressure set point. This is due to the relatively high minimum speed of the used servo motors. Although this does not affect the overall results of the system, it has introduced a certain complexity to the process of tuning the low level controller constants to be able to overcome this issue;
- **Maximum pressure limit:** our 3D experiment draws the maximum pressure limit at 120 g. This value correlates with the maximum weight of the object that can be lifted (around 500 g). Counter-intuitively, the problem does not arise from the torque of the wheel motors, but arises from not having enough friction with the ground. The performance could be effortlessly improved by adding passive weight to the robot, increasing its friction force and, therefore, its lifting capacity.

Despite having certain limitations in our current implementation, we believe that it presents a more simplified and affordable approach to multi-robot load sharing and transportation compared to having an entire robotic arm attached to a heavy duty mobile robot. Having a modular system integrated using ROS and using off-the-shelf components positions it perfectly for use in research. The simplified control makes modifying the behavior of the robot straightforward by tuning certain parameters. The process of detecting, analyzing, and fixing a wrong behavior provides an understanding of the physics and control used in this problem. In this paper, we aimed at moving forward with our platform from a simulation environment to a simple hardware environment to validate our method of object lifting and transportation. This is a second step towards having a full multi-robot system. Such a system could be applied to lift and manipulate objects which are not prepared for the usual transporting mechanism, like a forklift or large objects that could not be otherwise transportable using one agent. Since our system depends on traction, it does not require a special grasping area for each agent and, therefore, it provides a solution for such situation where modifying the target object for transportation is a challenge.

Our approach has been to downgrade the problem to one robot for a better understanding of the possible issues in a basic system rather than exploiting the entire problem all at once. Our next step is to increase the complexity of the system by adding more lifting and transporting agents and improving the current design to solve the two pressure problems mentioned.

We validated our platform implementing a simple grasp-release-like experiment and tested the system under various target pressure conditions. The results demonstrate the feasibility of the platform for research and education on cooperative robotics and object manipulation.

Author Contributions: Conceptualization, M.K., E.C., A.P.d.P.; Methodology, M.K., E.C., A.P.d.P.; Validation, M.K., E.C.; Investigation, M.K., E.C.; Experimentation, M.K., E.C.; Writing—Original Draft Preparation, M.K., E.C.; Writing—Review & Editing, M.K., A.P.d.P.; project administration, A.P.d.P.; funding acquisition, A.P.d.P. All authors have read and agreed to the published version of the manuscript.

Funding: This paper describes research conducted at UJI Robotic Intelligence Laboratory. Support for this laboratory is provided in part by Universidad Jaume I (UJI-B2021-42), and by Generalitat Valenciana (PROMETEO/2020/034).

Data Availability Statement: The data that support the findings of this study are available in shared folder at: https://drive.google.com/file/d/1Ue3n79pFKu0FwFRPIOM39qXh5G1KReXq/view?usp=sharing (accessed on 21 December 2021). The repository to the project source code can be found in git hub repository at: https://github.com/majdkassawat/maomt (accessed on 21 December 2021).

Conflicts of Interest: The authors declare no conflict of interest.

References

1. Tuci, E.; Alkilabi, M.H.M.; Akanyeti, O. Cooperative Object Transport in Multi-Robot Systems: A Review of the State-of-the-Art. *Front. Robot. AI* **2018**, *5*, 59. [CrossRef] [PubMed]
2. Fink, J.; Hsieh, M.A.; Kumar, V. Multi-robot manipulation via caging in environments with obstacles. In Proceedings of the 2008 IEEE International Conference on Robotics and Automation, Pasadena, CA, USA, 19–23 May 2008; pp. 1471–1476. [CrossRef]
3. Chen, J.; Gauci, M.; Li, W.; Kolling, A.; Groß, R. Occlusion-Based Cooperative Transport with a Swarm of Miniature Mobile Robots. *IEEE Trans. Robot.* **2015**, *31*, 307–321. [CrossRef]
4. Farivarnejad, H.; Wilson, S.; Berman, S. Decentralized sliding mode control for autonomous collective transport by multi-robot systems. In Proceedings of the 2016 IEEE 55th Conference on Decision and Control (CDC), Las Vegas, NV, USA, 12–14 December 2016; pp. 1826–1833. [CrossRef]
5. Gross, R.; Dorigo, M. Towards group transport by swarms of robots. *Int. J. Bio-Inspired Comput.* **2009**, 1–13. [CrossRef]
6. Hichri, B.; Fauroux, J.-C.; Adouane, L.; Doroftei, I.; Mezouar, Y. Design of cooperative mobile robots for co-manipulation and transportation tasks. *Robot. Comput. Manuf.* **2019**, *57*, 412–421. [CrossRef]
7. Hichri, B.; Adouane, L.; Fauroux, J.-C.; Mezouar, Y.; Doroftei, I. Flexible co-manipulation and transportation with mobile multi-robot system. *Assem. Autom.* **2019**, *39*, 422–431. [CrossRef]
8. Mellinger, D.; Shomin, M.; Michael, N.; Kumar, V. Cooperative Grasping and Transport Using Multiple Quadrotors. In *Distributed Autonomous Robotic Systems*; Springer Tracts in Advanced Robotics; Springer: Berlin/Heidelberg, Germany, 2013; Volume 83. [CrossRef]
9. Kim, S.; Seo, H.; Shin, J.; Kim, H.J. Cooperative Aerial Manipulation Using Multirotors with Multi-DOF Robotic Arms. *IEEE/ASME Trans. Mechatron.* **2018**, *23*, 702–713. [CrossRef]
10. Wang, Z.; Schwager, M. Kinematic multi-robot manipulation with no communication using force feedback. In Proceedings of the 2016 IEEE International Conference on Robotics and Automation (ICRA), Stockholm, Sweden, 16–21 May 2016; pp. 427–432. [CrossRef]
11. Alonso-Mora, J.; Knepper, R.; Siegwart, R.; Rus, D. Local motion planning for collaborative multi-robot manipulation of deformable objects. In Proceedings of the IEEE International Conference on Robotics and Automation, Seattle, WA, USA, 26–30 May 2015; pp. 5495–5502. [CrossRef]
12. Alonso-Mora, J.; Baker, S.; Rus, D. Multi-robot formation control and object transport in dynamic environments via constrained optimization. *Int. J. Robot. Res.* **2017**, *36*, 1000–1021. [CrossRef]
13. Bischoff, R.; Huggenberger, U.; Prassler, E. KUKA youBot-a mobile manipulator for research and education. In Proceedings of the 2011 IEEE International Conference on Robotics and Automation (ICRA), Shanghai, China, 9–13 May 2011. [CrossRef]
14. McLurkin, J.; McMullen, A.; Robbins, N.; Habibi, G.; Becker, A.; Chou, A.; Li, H.; John, M.; Okeke, N.; Rykowski, J. et al. A robot system design for low-cost multi-robot manipulation. In Proceedings of the 2014 IEEE/RSJ International Conference on Intelligent Robots and Systems, Chicago, IL, USA, 14–18 September 2014; pp. 912–918. [CrossRef]

15. Campbell, E.; Kong, Z.C.; Hered, W.; Lynch, A.J.; O'Malley, M.K.; McLurkin, J. Design of a low-cost series elastic actuator for multi-robot manipulation. In Proceedings of the 2011 IEEE International Conference on Robotics and Automation, Shanghai, China, 9–13 May 2011; pp. 5395–5400. [CrossRef]
16. Kassawat, M.; Cervera, E.; del Pobil, A.P. Multi-robot user interface for cooperative transportation tasks. In *From Bioinspired Systems and Biomedical Applications to Machine Learning*; Springer: Berlin/Heidelberg, Germany, 2019; pp. 77–81, ISBN 978-3-030-19650-9. [CrossRef]
17. Doroftei, I.; Grosu, V.; Spinu, V. Omnidirectional Mobile Robot – Design and Implementation. In *Bioinspiration and Robotics: Walking and Climbing Robots*; Habib, M.K., Ed.; I-Tech: Vienna, Austria, September 2007; p. 544, ISBN 978-3-902613-15-8. [CrossRef]
18. Sharbafi, M.A.; Indiveri, G. Swedish Wheeled Omnidirectional Mobile Robots: Kinematics Analysis and Control. *IEEE Trans. Robot.* **2009**, *25*, 164–171.
19. West, M.; Asada, H. Design of Ball Wheel Mechanisms for Omnidirectional Vehicles With Full Mobility and Invariant Kinematics. *J. Mech. Des.* **1997**, *119*, 153–161. [CrossRef]
20. Lebosse, C.; Renaud, P.; Bayle, B.; De Mathelin, M. Modeling and Evaluation of Low-Cost Force Sensors. *IEEE Trans. Robot.* **2011**, *27*, 815–822. [CrossRef]

Article

A Methodological Approach to the Teaching STEM Skills in Latin America through Educational Robotics for School Teachers

Sandra Cano

School of Computer Engineering, Pontificia Universidad Católica de Valparaíso, Valparaíso 2340000, Chile; sandra.cano@pucv.cl

Abstract: The study aims to design a methodological approach that allows educational robotics to develop STEM competences for schoolteachers, but with a gender focus. The phases within consist of designing a set of workshops with a gender approach, making use of Arduino, as it allows for introducing concepts in electronics and programming. For this, a mixed research method was applied, where quantitative and qualitative information was collected. The study was carried out with teachers from Latin American schools, where teachers from Chile and Colombia participated the most, and was conducted in virtual mode through the Zoom platform. As a result, it was found that Arduino and its components can be used to build projects that can be related in a real context, which further motivates students. It was also found that the levels of creativity, attitude, and motivation of the students increased with the workshops that were carried out.

Keywords: educational robotics; computational thinking; STEM

Citation: Cano, S. A Methodological Approach to the Teaching STEM Skills in Latin America through Educational Robotics for School Teachers. *Electronics* **2022**, *11*, 395. https://doi.org/10.3390/electronics11030395

Academic Editors: Savvas A. Chatzichristofis and Zinon Zinonos

Received: 28 October 2021
Accepted: 26 December 2021
Published: 28 January 2022

Publisher's Note: MDPI stays neutral with regard to jurisdictional claims in published maps and institutional affiliations.

Copyright: © 2022 by the author. Licensee MDPI, Basel, Switzerland. This article is an open access article distributed under the terms and conditions of the Creative Commons Attribution (CC BY) license (https://creativecommons.org/licenses/by/4.0/).

1. Introduction

Young girls are generally taught to knit while boys are taught to make wooden boats. Children thus associate various activities with a particular gender. Gender roles, in turn, are culturally stereotyped behaviours. They are thus activities that a person is expected to perform according to his or her gender [1].

Nowadays, gender disparities are especially pronounced in areas such as computer sciences and electronics, female sign-up remains low. Therefore, differential experiences in STEM continue for women and men at the high school level. Some authors indicate inadequate early preparation is problematic for women in computer sciences [2]. Therefore, low participation in STEM courses can limit their ability to access STEM careers later. Margolis et al. [2] found that women lost confidence and interest in computer science because they felt they did not fit with the stereotypical view of a computer scientist. Therefore, women's decisions are very much subject to those barriers arising from basic education, because they do not see themselves identified or feel similar enough to those scientists and computer and/or electronic engineers to enter in these fields [3].

When they do enter the fields in question, they can be penalized socially and professionally for exhibiting leadership skills and qualities [4]. Therefore, some of these barriers contribute to why women choose to enter other fields and lose interest in careers such as electronic and computer science.

In many countries, girls' education is considered an essential element for economic development. Initiatives such as "Roberta initiative" [5] used robot construction kits in combination with gender-balanced didactic material and course concept for girls' interest in technical topics. Another example is WSTEM [6], an Erasmus project to promote STEM careers for women in Latin America. The Girls4STEM project [7] works towards breaking the stereotypes linked to STEM fields, addressing both boys and girls aged from 6 to 18, but especially young girls through interaction with female STEM experts. Therefore, there is great interest in promoting the participation of girls in STEM from an early age, so that women can become more involved in engineering careers and reduce the gender gap, especially in engineering careers such as computer science and electronics.

However, in Latin America. this may not always be the case, and legal, institutional, political, and cultural aspects of their environment mean that many women and girls in the world are excluded from science and technology activities [8,9]. A report presented by UNESCO [10] spoke of the movement taking place in different institutions to promote science, technology, and gender issues. More than 1 billion people live in poverty in Latin America, the majority of whom are women and children; the role of science and technology in society has become vital for improving the quality of life and the socio-economic and environmental situation of any country.

A report published at UNESCO in 2015 [10] mentions that 58% of women in Latin America tend to earn less and are in minority in fields such as sustainable development, information technology, and computer science. In the same document, they also presented a report by country of female researchers in technology, where in 2012 Colombia represented 21.6%, in 2008 Chile had 19%, in 2011 Costa Risa had 30.9%, in 2013 El Salvador had 17.7%, in 2012 Guatemala had 43.5%, and in 2009 Venezuela had 40.4%.

Today, women still suffer from low participation in STEM areas, not only as students, but also as teachers, researchers, and workers [11]. Different factors frame the gender gap. Traditionally, it has been thought that boys have more talent for mathematics and technology and girls have more talent for verbal skills [12]. Studies show that stereotypes associated with technology, physics, and engineering negatively influence girls. However, schools still do not have teachers who are technologically and pedagogically prepared in the areas of STEM, especially in the technology and engineering fields [13]. Therefore, if boys/girls are educated in STEM areas from an early age, one can help gender inclusion from that moment.

Educational robotics is a growing interest in STEM at all levels, especially to promote STEM careers for women. The use of a robot in programming education could help girls understand computer sciences concepts. However, educational robots have a more significant effect on boys than girls [14]. Zhang et al. [14] indicated than there is a "negative stereotype" for girls, which causes them to feel less able to study STEM. Meanwhile, boys are traditionally more familiar with the technology. Educational robotics (ER) is usually seen as an interdisciplinary activity in science, technology, informatics, and mechatronics. Therefore, ER is a powerful, flexible teaching and learning tool to construct robots and control robots using tangible programming languages [15]. Furthermore, ER activities help students become active learners. However, girls appear to need more training time in many situations to reach the same skill level compared to boys [16].

A study conducted by Sullivan and Bers [17] explored the gender differences in student experiences in robotics competitions. Some observations were as follows: "females tend to stand back and let the males take the lead in building even if the males don't know any more about the task", "most of the girls were not as inclined to want to actually build something. They have to be encouraged to use a wrench", "females at my school have had less experience at constructing so they feel insecure or just do not know how to put things together to make what they want". Sullivan and Bers identified that one reason female students may be less confident in their technical and building skills is that female students may simply have less experience with building, tinkering, and constructing prior to joining a robotics competition in middle or high school teams. Research has shown that women have less experience with tinkering during their childhoods compared to men [18], which can be influenced according to the stereotypes they are exposed to and according to interest. In 2018, Sullivan and Bers [19] examined the impact of girls having females as robotics teachers. The study was conducted with female teachers using a prototype of the KIBO robotics kit, which was designed for children aged 4–7 years. The tasks tested were sequencing, a repeat loop, and a conditional statement with two levels, easy and hard, based on how many commands children needed to sequence, with fewer blocks for children to sequence than hard tasks.

In 2020, Román-Graván et al. [20] carried out a study related to perception in the use of educational robotics in training for future teachers. In the study, they performed several robotic kit interventions, such as Colby robot mouse, Ozobot, mBot and the Makey-Makey board. To learn the programming language they used Scratch, where they had to design a video game related to healthy eating using a tangible interface such as the Makey-Makey board. Once they interacted with these kits, the authors applied an instrument that consisted of 42 items that enabled an understanding of the perception of the use of robotics, in which they expressed their motivation to implement it within the subjects. They further indicated that educational robotics in the classroom could promote new teaching–learning methodologies for students and favour the development of self-learning skills.

In order to enhance educational robotics, Peixoto et al. [21] used Raspberry Pi and Arduino as the hardware interface. Cuartielles et al. [22] introduced robotics concepts using an Arduino-like tool. A study conducted by Ntourou et al. [23] used Arduino and Scratch to study their effect on self-efficacy and motivation towards science education and computational thinking in 5th grade students about concepts of electricity. Abidin et al. [24], to promote STEM education learning, designed a process of educational robotics for teachers involved in designing and constructing robots using open source and low-cost technologies such as Arduino. The studies reviewed use robotics in education to promote computational thinking. However, the introduction of concepts of electronic and mechanical parts to build a robot is not considered.

On the other hand, methodologies to teach robotics with robots is not clear. Some studies such as Dimitriou [25] propose a methodology that follows seven steps, such as teaching theory, teaching tools, problem selection, analysis, design, implementation, and evaluation. O. de Azevedo et al. [26] present a methodology composed OF five steps, namely the initial diagnosis, survey of contextualized problems, course planning, classes, and a robotics fair. However, these methodologies do not have a gender approach.

Therefore, the main objective of this study is summarized in the following research questions: What aspects should be considered to propose a methodology with a gender approach to motivate women to choose studies related to engineering, especially computer sciences and electronics?

2. Background
2.1. Educational Robotics

Educational robotics (ER) is a sub-field of robotics that provides students with learning experiences through the creation and implementation of activities, technology, and artifacts related to robots [27]. Educational robotics began with the Logo project developed by Seymour Papert [28], a mobile robot in the shape of a turtle [29] to teach programming to children [30]. The turtle could be programmed to draw pictures on the surface on which it moved using a pen that was in the bottom center of the robot.

Educational robotics has mainly focused on supporting the teaching of subjects that are closely related to the robotics field such as programming, construction, and mechatronics. However, the studies found have used the robot as a passive tool in which students must program the robot. Rush et al. [31] mention that students who are not interested in traditional approaches become motivated when robotics activities are introduced as a way to tell a story or in connection with other disciplines and interest areas. A report from the American Association of University Women [32] argues "girls and other nontraditional users of computer science-who are not enamored of technology for technology's sake-may be far more interested in using technology if they encounter it in the context of a discipline that interest them".

Therefore, robotics construction kits can be used in many different ways, to support many types of activities and different learning styles. Plaza et al. [33] used the Arduino embedded system as an educational tool to introduce robotics, where children built and developed tangible prototypes for problem-solving. PicoCricket [31] is a robotics kit that aims to combine art and technology, enabling young people to create artistic creations. PicoCricket has output devices such as motors, colored lights, and music-making devices and sensors. In 2019, Xenabis et al. [34] made use of recyclable materials and programming with Arduino UNO, where they built the Wall-E robot and programmed the robot through a platform called Ardublock. Another work was carried out by Junior et al. [35] in which they proposed a low-cost educational robotics kit based on the Arduino UNO platform. To design the robotics kit, four requirements were considered: Low-cost, appeal, simplicity, and opensource. For the programing environment, they used block programming called a mini block. For the use of this kit, the following eight learning modules were designed: (1) What are we going to learn? (2) What is robotics? (3) What is Arduino? (4) Learning to program with Minibloq; (5) Electronic components; (6) What are sensors? (7) Robot architecture; and (8) Robot operation. At the end of the course, they asked related questions about whether the kit was a good option for understanding the concepts of electronics and programming.

Educational robotics has in turn been associated with the field of computational thinking [36] and related to STEM learning [37]. Today, educational robotics is being included in the classroom as a form of teaching–learning that can help the development of competencies and promote learning in areas such as engineering, technology, mathematics, and science. Several studies have shown that educational robotics has a positive impact in STEM areas [38–40], as it promotes an understanding of STEM-related concepts. ER can be effective in teaching STEM [41] because it allows one to interact with the real-world concepts of engineering and technology.

Nowadays, ER is being implemented in schools as an alternative to empower students in various related areas in engineering, science, and mathematics [42,43]. Teachers have started to develop activities to incorporate robotics into teaching. However, there are more individual initiatives.

Mataric [30] states that "robotics has the potential to significantly impact the nature of science and engineering education at all levels". In turn, educational robotics began to be used in robotics competitions as a way to encourage their learning. These contests even employ goal-oriented and project-based learning (PBL), and the contests are geared mostly towards the engineering, computer science, and artificial intelligence fields.

On the other hand, Barreto and Vavssori [44] mention that ER is related to thinking skills, the scientific process, problem-solving approaches, and teamwork skills. A study presented by Alves-Oliveira [45] features activities that enhance creativity in children. For this study, they carried out three activities. The first activity was to code the robots. The second activity involved learning to design robots, while in the third activity condition, a control participated in a music class. In the first activity of this study, they learned to use Scratch language.

2.2. Gender in Educational Robotics

Sapounidis et al. [46] found that girls have strong preferences for tangible interfaces, and programming-related tasks can be more difficult for them, due to the manner of teaching. A study conducted by Blue and Gann [47] mentions that girls start kindergarten interested in areas such as math and science but leave high school with that interest far diminished. Therefore, girls lose interest in science and mathematics as they go through school, specifically from fourth grade. Furthermore, girls and women often receive the message that the fields of science, technology, engineering, and mathematics are not for them [48]. Another study [49] examined interactions with a formal educator where they observed that girls are less concerned about being negatively stereotyped when their teacher is female than when their teacher is male. Studies [50] have shown that girls and women are more interested in careers where they can help others.

Sullivan and Bers [43] found differences between girls and boys, where girls tend to back off and let boys take the lead in construction even if boys do not know much about the task. They also found that both boys and girls are good at construction, but boys are more likely to take control or lead. Therefore, girls tend to be more passive when it is a mixed team. At the same time, the girls often do not take control since they are afraid that they will be made fun of by their male companions. However, even the preferences and the correct way to teach girls educational robotics have not been sufficiently researched [51].

2.3. Arduino-Assisted Robotics Coding Applications

Arduino is a microcontroller card created by Massimo Banzi in 2005. This card constitutes easy-to-use hardware and software based on an open-source electronic platform [52]. Arduino allows a wide range of applications, from robotics to automatic control systems. Arduino can be programmed with block-based coding such as the mBlock coding platform, scratch, and TinkerCad. The ability to add advanced technologies to these boards plays an important role in the use and dissemination of Arduino-assisted robotic coding applications in educational environments [53].

Arduino is a card that can handle both analog and digital signals. It integrates a variety of communication protocols such as SPI (Serial Peripheral Interface), I2C (Inter-Integrated Circuit), serial communication, and UART (Universal Asynchronous Reception Transmission). Arduino allows students to control the reactions of a system that they can visibly touch and see and makes it possible for learners to problem solve in situations they encounter in everyday life. This idea is due to the fact that Arduino can be integrated with various sensors such as temperature, humidity, speed, sound, light, gas, color, vibration, and distance, among others. Therefore, with the use of sensors Arduino can sense what is happening around it, which allows a control or monitoring system to be developed. The use of sensors allows a great deal of interaction with science and engineering.

In the literature reviewed, Arduino-assisted robotic coding applications facilitate the teaching of abstract and difficult-to-understand concepts in science subjects, and such applications should be included in the teaching of science subjects such as medical science to monitor or simulate heart rate, detect body temperature, electricity, sound sensors that work with sound waves, etc.

On the other hand, learning Arduino involves many technologies depending on how far you want to go. Therefore, it can help increase the interest, attitudes, and motivation towards technology applications and science teaching.

2.4. Methodologies for Teaching ER

The term educational robotics is used a lot in schools. There is still no clarity on how the teaching of educational robotics ought to be, and especially from a gender perspective. Some methodologies have been proposed for learning, such as the work proposed by Patiño-Escarnina et al. [54], whose main objective is to understand how to introduce the concepts of robotics and related topics into the student curriculum. The authors focus on fields such as mechanics, electronics, control, and computing. The methodology they propose is made up of three phases: (1) Setting up the environment where a problem is defined and topics are selected; (2) definition of the project, where concepts and strategies are developed; and (3) conducting the assessment, where theoretical concepts are applied, and competencies are assessed. For the evaluation of competences, they include four variables: Communication, teamwork, creativity-responsibility, and integration of STEM topics. Based on Vygotsky's socio-cognitive approaches [55], activities involving educational robotics work through collaboration and teamwork.

O. de Azevedo et al. [26] proposed a methodology of contextualized ER, where it is necessary to start working by perfomirng a diagnosis at the school, with the students, and in their community. The methodology is composed of five steps, such as the initial diagnosis, survey of contextualized problems, course planning, classes, and a robotics fair. The methodology was proposed but not evaluated. Another study by Dimitriou [25] proposed a methodology of seven phases. During the first two phases, the teacher follows a predetermined pattern where the main objective is to explain theoretical concepts and train students in software. All other phases require the learning process, so the teacher acts as a coach and cognitive modeler.

Barak and Zadok [56] described three strategies that lead to innovative solutions in robotics tasks—assign a new role (the students find a new use for the robot); remove a component from the system; and examine physical objects available in the environment and apply them to solve a problem. Several studies have demonstrated that educational robotics has a positive impact on the development of skills such as critical thinking [57], problem solving [58], metacognitive skills [59], and creativity [60].

Educational robotics continues to require more research, which would indicate how to work with educational robotics in order to develop skills in students, since these skills have not been evaluated in depth either. Sullivan [61] meanwhile identified that in the various stages in programming a robot, the students (1) write code, (2) test the robot, (3) analyze the problem, (4) propose changes to the model, and (5) test again. The author therefore identifies that the resolution of a problem involves three stages: (1) Identification of the problem, (2) generation of ideas and choice of strategy, and (3) reflection on the process of solving the problem.

Atmatzidou and Demetriadis [62] carried out 11 sessions to train students in robotics for public schools. They proposed a model to develop skills related to computational thinking within educational robotics. The authors focused on five dimensions of the conceptual framework of computational thinking: Abstraction, generalization, algorithm, modularity, and decomposition. They made use of the Lego Mindstorms NXT robot kit as a tool.

The studies reflect that there is no shortage of studies focused on educational robotics. However, the pedagogy of teaching robotics in schools is still in its infancy [63]. More research is therefore required on how to work with educational robotics for teachers in a way that can help students develop specific skills.

A study by [64] proposes a map of terms associated with educational robotics. Within the map of terms, the associated methodologies are project-based learning, problem-based learning, active learning, collaborative learning, experiential learning, and playful learning. All these methodologies are associated with constructivism and constructionism.

Today, many teachers remain unaware of the benefits of educational robotics and are still not prepared enough to be able to teach robotics or concepts involving educational robotics, such as electronics, programming, and technology. As such, there is a lack of specialized training programs for educational institutions focused on teachers since most of the studies found are focused on the student and not on the teacher. Some studies have ICT teachers as participants [65,66], while others feature STEM subject teachers [67]. A study in 2021 by [68] comprised a review of the literature on teacher training in educational robotics. The authors identified that the training programs include participants with different profiles, related to teaching experience, age, familiarity with technology, etc. In addition, many of the ER trainings present training programs without requirements, and those who have studies of programs with requirements have a final project of designing a robot, creating a program, or designing didactic material. However, many of the studies focus on building a robot, despite the fact that the majority of the teachers who enroll are teachers with a background in electronics or programming.

3. Methodology

In this research, a mixed research method was applied including both qualitative and quantitative data collection and analysis processes. The design of the research is given in Figure 1. Therefore, teaching STEM skills with a genre focus follows a set of phases proposed in Figure 1. Following a constructivist approach using a learning model called 5E (Engage, Explore, Explain, Elaborate, and Evaluate) [69], participants can experience meaningful instruction and learning for themselves within a practical, constructive, and active environment.

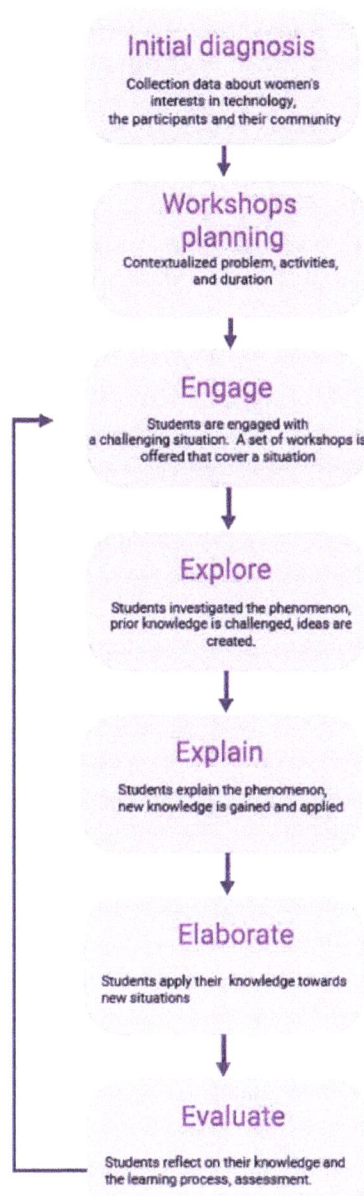

Figure 1. Phases proposed for Teaching STEM Skills in ER.

The first phase called the initial diagnosis collects data about women's interests, the profile of participants, whether they are schoolteachers, level of knowledge in technology, and their background in information technology and robotics. Demographic information is also considered.

The information obtained can help to gain initial insights into the interests and needs of women and the specific robotics/computing topics or curricular content to be further explored.

The second phase is related to initial ideas of possible themes addressing contextual problems. Therefore, the data collected in the first phase are considered. In this phase, it is necessary to propose a set of workshops that relates any topic = to the reality of where the students live, which can be approached with curricular and robotic content. The third phase engages students' prior knowledge about programming, components of electronics, and microcontrollers. The teacher starts the workshops with an interesting question about the subject. Therefore, the teacher shows possible ideas by encouraging students to participate and shows solutions that can be used with the use of technology and engineering. The fourth phase allows students to explore new knowledge through video-clips and lectures and support guides on how to develop the workshop. Moreover, it uses robotics materials such as the Arduino microcontroller, sensors, jumper cables, and other electronic components. The fifth phase involves the teacher creating a discussion environment in the group and in the classroom by asking the participants about the mechanism of how science can be taught with the use of programming and electronics. The sixth phase elaborates, whereby the teacher provides learners with opportunities to apply their acquired knowledge in solving problems. Finally, the seventh phase evaluates, and the students must build assemblies in each workshop, with the objective of understanding theoretical concepts and solving a problem in a specific context.

3.1. Study Group

The study of the research consists of schoolteachers and others interested in educational robotics in Latin America. The reason for the selection of the study participants is that there is still a low participation of women in STEM careers in Latin America. The objective is to promote the participation of girls and women in education robotics.

Two hundred and ninety people from different countries registered: Chile (124), Colombia (98), Ecuador (11), Mexico (26), Costa Rica (3), Peru (23), and Europe (5), where 47.5% of the registered correspond to men and 52.5% to women. Furthermore, 55.2% of those enrolled are college teachers, 23.7% students, 8.7% higher education teachers, and 9% other professions. However, the average number of participants who permanently attended each workshop was between 50 and 60, as they were not required to attend remotely. Workshops were recorded and uploaded to the platform, for those who found it difficult to meet the scheduled timetable.

3.2. Data Collection Tools

Attitudes towards technology is a scale developed by Cross et al. [70], which consists of 24 items and 5-point Likert type. The scale has four sub-dimensions: Learning desire (12 items), self-confidence (5 items), computational thinking (3 items), and teamwork (3 items).

A questionnaire was used to determine information about participants and interest about taking the course. A first part consisted of demographic data, and the second part referred to an open open-ended question about what motivated them to take the course, whether they worked on the robotics activities outside of class, and did they think robotics activities are and will be useful?

In addition, participants were given an opinion questionnaire to fill out individually after the end of the workshops.

3.3. Implement of the Research

Following the proposed steps (Figure 1), the research was first carried out by making an initial diagnosis. Therefore, a literature revision was conducted on the interests of the female gender (see Table 1).

Table 1. Interests of the female gender.

Source	Interests
Michael et al. [71]	The girls showed interest in the use of tangible interfaces.
Su et al. [72]	The women showed interest in artistic areas.
Yamtinah et al. [73] Makarova et al. [74]	Women showed interest in helping people. In STEM areas, women lost interest very quickly in the areas of math and physics.
	Women are more interested in areas of health.
Negrini et al. [75]	Robots tend to be of greater interest to boys, due to their greater interest in technical skills.
Shaqiri et al. [76]	Differences in visual perception, are usually more visual.

According to the identified interests of women, it is proposed to design a set of workshops using Arduino hardware as a platform. Therefore, in the planning workshops, the contents are designed with the aim of combining theory and practice. The theory is developed for 30 min and the rest of the time is practice. Each workshop has a duration of 2 h. The set of workshops has the objective of introducing basic concepts of educational robotics, in the areas of electronics and programming.

Electronics is one of the basic areas for the development of robots. It is the main source of robots to perceive and react according to the environment. Therefore, it includes basic elements to perceive, send, and process signals from/to the different sensors and robotic actuators. The content defined for this discipline is described in Table 2.

Table 2. Thematic fields of the discipline "electronics" associated with learning level.

1. Basic Components	1.1. Definition of Microcontrollers (Arduino)	basic
	1.2. What is a circuit? (Voltage and electricity)	basic
	1.3. Leds	
	1.4. Resistors	basic
	1.5. Jumpler Cables	basic
	1.6. How to make assemblies with a Protoboard?	basic
2. Sensors (inputs)	2.1. definition perception	basic
	2.2. Light based sensors	basic
	2.3. Temperature	basic
	2.4. Humidity	
	2.5. Pressure	basic
3. Responses (outputs, Actuators, electronic components)	3.1. Visual feedback 3.2. Audio feedback	basic

Computing is also one of the most important fields that form the basis of robotics. Therefore, it includes the process of designing computer programs. The contents defined for this discipline are in Table 3.

Table 3. Thematic fields of the discipline "programming" associated with learning level.

5. Programming concepts	5.1. What is programming?	basic
	5.2. Basic Aspects (data types, variables and propositional logic)	basic
6. Control statements	6.1. Conditional sentences	basic
	6.2. Repetitive sentences	basic
	6.3. Variables	basic
	6.4. Operators	basic

Five workshops were proposed (See Table 4): (1) Creating interactive stories with Scratch; (2) medical science and electronics; (3) interactive toys; (4) music and electronics; (5) smart planter. For each workshop, a primer-type digital material was created, which provides information on concepts and can also be used by the teachers themselves to transmit their knowledge to the students. Equally, a low-cost kit was offered, to make it more accessible.

Table 4. Workshops associated with STEM 21st Century Skills.

Workshop	Description	Skills	Tool(s)
Interactive stories	Introduction to programming concepts through storytelling.	Technology use, problem solving	Scratch
Medical sciences and electronics	Introduction to electronics concepts, such as: protoboard, Arduino UNO, Jumper cables, Leds diode and resistors.	Technology use, Problem solving, and creativity	TinkerCad Arduino
Interactive toy	Using basic electronics components to build a face that can simulate reactions or emotions. Visual, tactile, and auditory responses are worked on.	Technology use, Problem solving, and creativity	TinkerCad Arduino
Music and electronics	Introduction to music concepts and piezoelectric sensor.	Technology use, Problem solving, and creativity	TinkerCad Arduino
Smart planter	Using temperature and humidity sensors to build a low-cost smart plant monitor.	Technology use, Problem solving, and creativity	TinkerCad Arduino

To carry out these five workshops, the kit included: Arduino UNO with a USB cable and a 400-point breadboard, (2) red, green, and blue LED diodes, (10) 220 Ohm resistors, (3) 10 Kohm resistors, (1) an LM35 temperature sensor, 1 DHT11 temperature, and humidity sensor module, a hygrometer sensor, a KOhm potentiometer, (2) LDR photoresistors, (5) 27 mm piezoelectric, a buzzer, and a male–female and male–male jumper cable pack. As such, the kit was priced at $30.

Before starting the workshops, instructional material was developed on how to enroll or register on virtual platforms such as Scratch [77] and Tinkercard, since there were schoolteachers who did not have much contact with technology. Moreover, as a way to approach the task, the Flipgrid platform enabled them to make a short video to introduce themselves and their interest in doing the workshops.

Below is a brief description of each workshop:

3.3.1. Workshop 1: Interactive Stories

The aim was to introduce programming concepts using the Scratch platform. Therefore, a digital material was designed (See Figure 2), creating a character called RoboTIC, in which a story could be designed, and the different programming blocks could be taught. It was also explained to them that the creation of stories helps to develop competencies related to creativity [78] and abstraction [79].

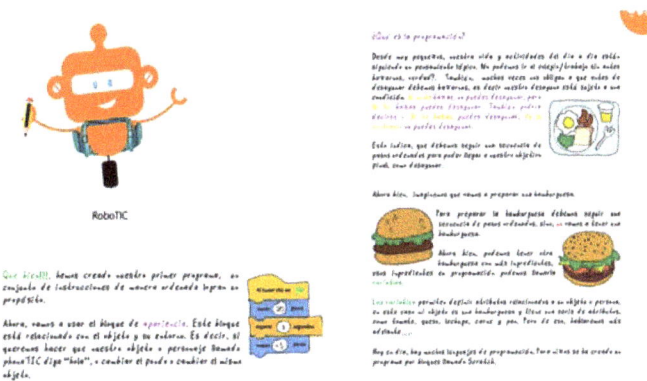

Figure 2. Design of Workshop 1 material (Spanish version).

3.3.2. Workshop 2: Medical Sciences and Electronics

In the second workshop, basic concepts of electronics were introduced. Digital material was designed to teach concepts related to electronics, such as: What is an electrical circuit? What is a diode? What is voltage? How is a breadboard used? What is a resistor? Why should the resistor be used together with the Led diode? Finally, a brief concept was introduced: What is a sensor?

They were also introduced to medical science concepts, for example simulating physiological responses (heart rate) or capturing physiological responses (skin temperature or conductivity).

Before carrying out a physical assembly, the simulation was carried out supported by the Tinkercard platform. Once the assembly and programming were working correctly in the simulation, the code was exported to Arduino. The physical assembly would then be carried out using the basic components: LED diode, resistor, and LM35 (See Figure 3).

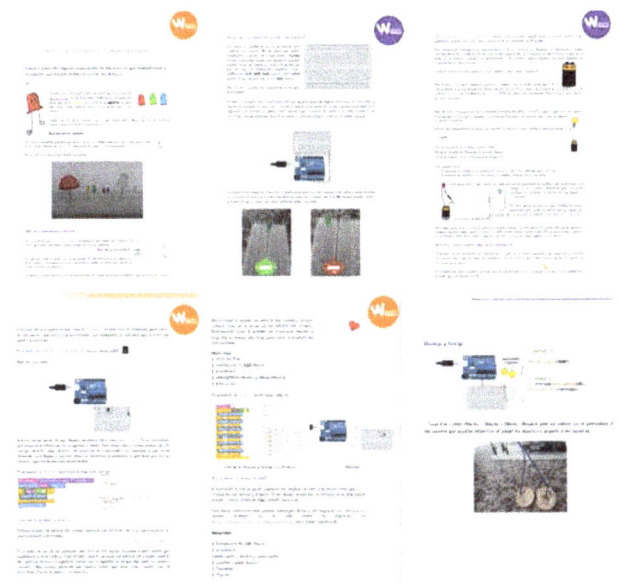

Figure 3. Design of Workshop 2 material (Spanish version).

From this workshop, explanatory videos were made and the whole process was carried out (Figure 4), which consisted of (1) assembly of the circuit using TinkerCard; (2) programming the circuit using Tinkercard; (3) simulation of operation; (4) exporting the code to Arduino; (5) physical assembly; (6) compiling and loading the program in Arduino; and (7) testing the operation in the physical assembly.

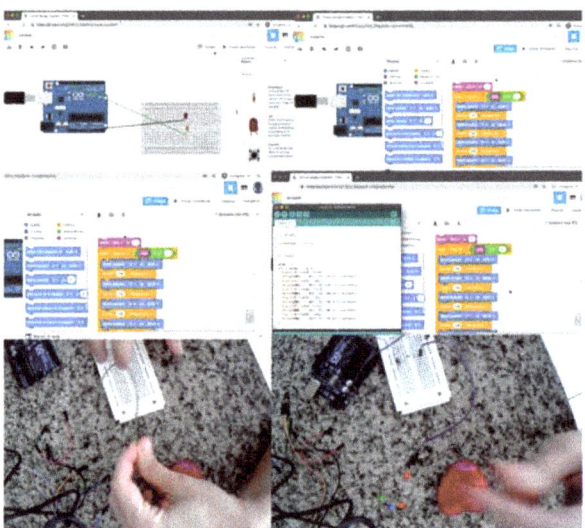

Figure 4. Explanatory video of the "heart rhythm simulation" activity.

3.3.3. Workshop 3: Interactive Toy

In the third workshop, they learn about other electronic components such as variable resistors, the potentiometer, and photo-resistance (See Figure 5). It was also referenced that one can have components that act as outputs or responses to an event, and there are other components that are called sensors that capture physical signals.

Therefore, in this workshop, it was decided to build an interactive face that can react to certain responses. For the construction of the interactive face, facial features and electronic components were selected to capture signals and react to those signals. Therefore, the characteristics that were used were the eyes (LED diodes), the nose (potentiometer), the mouth (buzzer), and the cheeks (Photo-resistances). The interaction was that every time his nose was pinched, he would react to it as if it were painful, so he would have a reaction of blinking his eyes and complaining through the noise that the buzzer produces. In turn, when the cheeks were touched, it would produce another more pleasant reaction using only the eyes but not the mouth.

We performed this workshop so that children, for example with special needs or younger children, could be taught various emotional responses. The activity was therefore called "expressing facial emotions". As a task, they were asked to design a face from recyclable cardboard and place the electronic components where they believed it was more convenient to express one or more emotions.

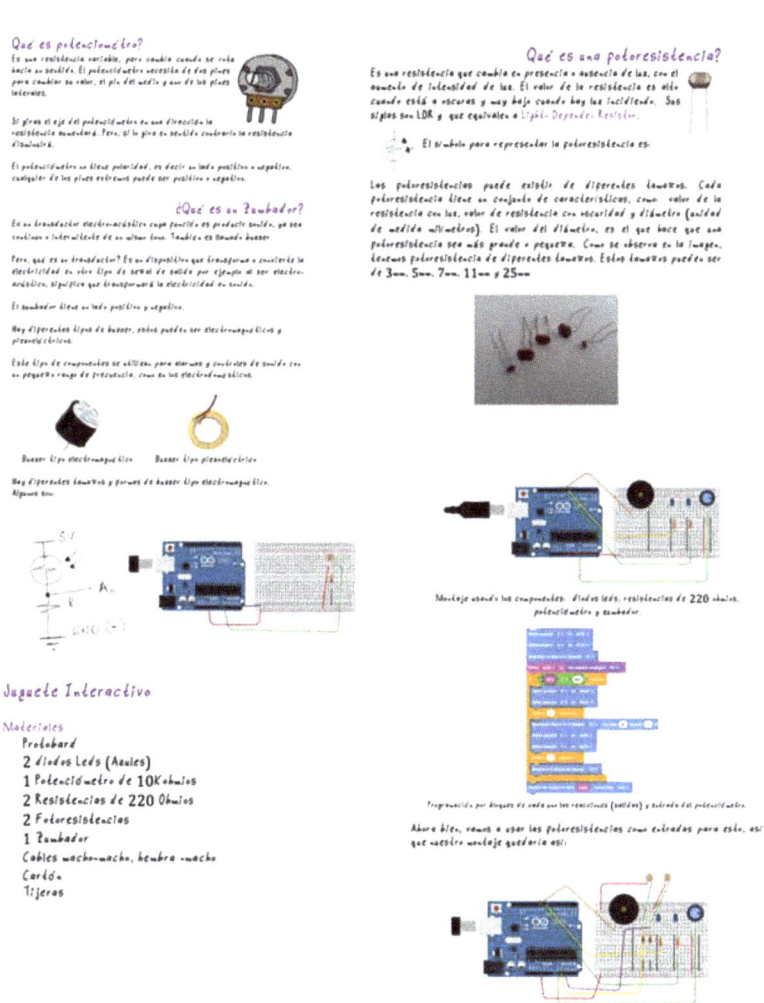

Figure 5. Design of Workshop 3 material (Spanish version).

3.3.4. Workshop 4: Music and Electronics

In the fourth workshop, they learned to use piezoelectric together with the buzzer. Therefore, it was decided to make a musical instrument with recyclable material, where each key is a piezoelectric and the sound is produced through the buzzer (see Figure 6). The idea of this workshop was to introduce them to art through music. Therefore, a brief introduction was given on how music can benefit children.

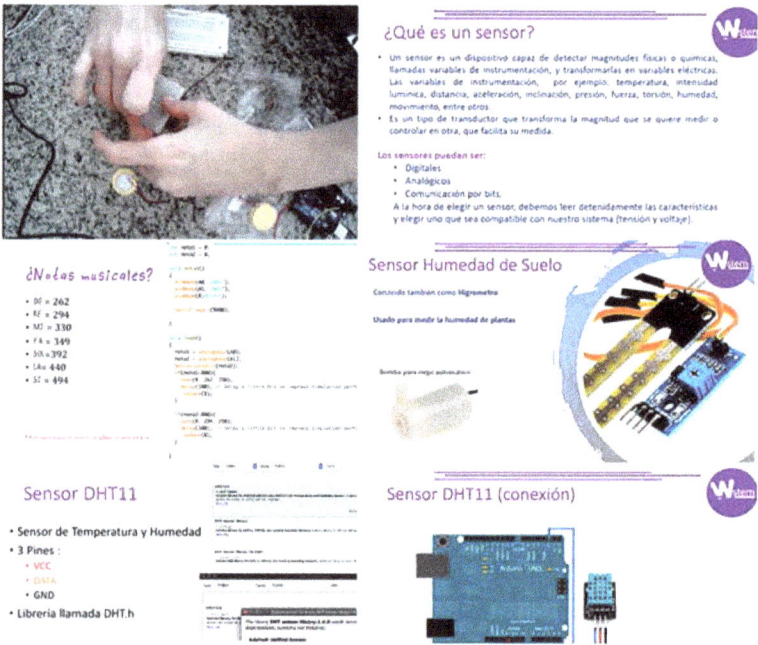

Figure 6. Design of Workshop 4 and 5 materials (Spanish version).

3.3.5. Workshop 5: Smart Planter

This delves deeper into the concepts of sensors (see Figure 6), and how you can build a planter that can emit alerts if a plant needs water, or the temperature is very high, and it needs water. Therefore, LEDs or buzzer diodes were used so that the system was able to react.

From this workshop, explanatory videos were made and the whole process was carried out (Figure 4), which consisted of: (1) Assembly of the circuit using Tinkercard; (2) programming the circuit using Tinkercard; (3) simulation of the operation; (4) exporting the code to Arduino; (5) physical assembly; (6) compiling and loading the program in Arduino; (7) testing the operation in the physical assembly.

The following 5E model was applied for each workshop:

Engagement: Student's prior knowledge about programming concepts, introduction to a microcontroller with Arduino UNO, and electronics components. The teacher starts the workshops with a question to solve a specific problem. The students produce ideas using brainstorming, and these ideas create a discussion environment in class.

Exploration: Each participant is provided with learning material. The teacher introduces these materials to the students and provides information about their use. The students create an algorithm according to the workshop. For example, in Workshop 1, students must create a story using the Scratch platform. The teacher guided the coding on the Scratch coding platform based on this algorithm.

From the second workshop, the teacher guided the coding on TinkerCad and then students made the connection using the breadboard and uploaded the development code to the Arduino card.

Explanation: The teacher creates a classroom discussion environment by asking students about programming and electronics according to the context of the workshop.

Elaboration: Students must carry out the assembly using the Arduino Uno by agreeing on what they have worked on with the TinkerCad platform and the solution to the problem.

Evaluation: The students must carry out the assembly according to the workshop to be solved. Each task consisted of uploading a very short 1 to 2 min video where they shared how it works through Arduino and electronic components (See Figure 7). For example, in Workshop 1, participants were asked to "create your own story" where they were given graphic material so that they could create their interactive story using the Scratch platform.

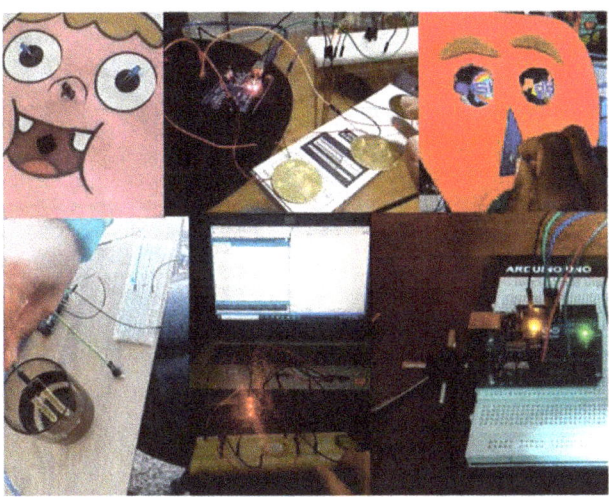

Figure 7. Some activities handed in by the participants.

4. Data Analysis

In the research, quantitative data obtained were demographic data and robotic attitude. The first workshop was held synchronously with 122 participants, and the following 4 workshops had an average of 57 attendees. Attendance was distributed as follows: 50 people attended all 5 sessions, 17 attended 4 of them, 15 attended 3, 12 attended 2, and 200 attended 1 or less. Each week they were assigned a task related to the workshop. A synchronous space was also created to attend to doubts or technical problems.

According to the demographic information of the participants, 52.5% were women and 47.5% were men. Furthermore, 55.2% were schoolteachers, 23.7% were students, 8.7% were higher education teachers, 9% were professionals, and 3.3% were other. Some answers related to motivation and the robotics activities were: "interest in learning about robotics", "teach electronics better to my students", "learn to program with Arduino Uno", "learn more robotics for my classes", "learn more about the scope of the Arduino", "I am a physics teacher and I would love to use Arduino in my classes", "learn robotics to incorporate it into teaching-learning", "learn about new technologies", "develop computational thinking", "learn to program sensors", "improve my robotics skills for my students", and "learn to practice it with preschool children". Therefore, in each of the workshops, there were teachers who knew how to use the technology, as well as others who did not.

Attitudes towards technology were evaluated through aspects such as interest (12 items) and curiosity (8 items) (see Table 5). Moreover, the word "robots" was changed to "electronics and programming". The items were evaluated by a Likert-like scale such as "NO!", "no", "neither yes or no", "yes" and "YES!" [80], which was scored with 1 to 5 scoring where 1 was "NO!" and 5 was "YES!". Items in the interest aspect included computers are interesting to me; I use the internet to find information about computers; I try to do activities related to computers; I like to explore computers; I feel good when I learn about computers, and I have a good feeling about computers. Meanwhile, items evaluated by the curiosity aspect where I am interested in discovering things about computers; I get excited about discussing computers; It is cool to learn new things about robots; I enjoy exploring new ideas about computers; I am often trying to find out more about computers. Participants responded 80% "YES!" and 20% "yes" for both interest and curiosity aspects. Some of the teachers had knowledge of educational robotics, and they had already interacted with Arduino and Scratch, while others did not know either. Moreover, most of them were technology teachers.

Table 5. Attitudes towards technology. Taken from [70].

Sub-Scale	Item
Interest	1. I would like to learn more about robots. 2. Computers are interesting to me. 3. Topics like robots just don't grab my interest. 4. Robots are interesting to me. 5. I use the Internet to find information about computers. 6. I like to watch TV shows and/or read about robots. 7. I try to do activities related to computers. 8. I like to explore computers. 9. I like to do robotics activities. 10. I feel good when I learn about computers. 11. Robots are boring to me. 12. I have a good feeling about computers.
Curiosity	1. I am curious about robots. 2. I am interested in discovering things about computers. 3. I get excited about discussing computers. 4. It is cool to learn new things about robots. 5. I enjoy exploring new ideas about computers. 6. I look for as much information as I can about robots. 7. Everywhere I go, I am out looking for new things about robots. 8. I am often trying to find out more about computers.

At the end of the last workshop, a survey was conducted to receive feedback on the experience of the course. Eighteen participants responded. Some of the questions that were asked were: What was your previous experience in programming and electronics? How do you rate your learning experience of the course? Do you think the proposed activities are attractive for girls and young women? Which workshop was the one that you liked the most? What was the workshop that you liked the least? How do you rate your level of commitment in the course?

Some of the responses obtained were as follows. The workshop that they liked the most was workshop 4 (33.3%). The one they liked the least was their first introductory workshop on programming with Scratch (38.9%). In turn, they would have liked to go deeper into workshop 4. Of the participants, 27.8% had no experience with programming or electronics. Moreover, 55.6% considered that the proposed activities were attractive to girls and young women.

Some of the observations that were obtained were: "the course should have been longer and deepened more in concepts such as scratch", "I thought it was excellent", "I would like the next intermediate level version of the course", "I liked it a lot, I had Zero approach to Arduino. Sometimes I was behind because I had no knowledge and needed support", "the course seemed very didactic to me, an important potential. I would have liked more time for practical activities", and "I really liked it because it can be applied in all professions".

When the participants had interacted with the physical breadboard, we applied a short survey to determine their experience with the use of the breadboard and Arduino. Of the 52 participants who attended remote classes, 2% found the experience "very bad", 4% "bad", 25% "normal", 40% "good", and 29% "very good". Another question asked what they had had the most difficulty with when interacting with Arduino. In total, 23% answered they had understood the concepts, 25% did not have the materials, 8% did not work with Arduino, and 62% did not have much time to do the assigned tasks.

We obtained other open answers to how they would apply the knowledge: "develop play and experimentation activities with high school students", "apply it to students of 1 and 2 means to use different sensors", "the medical science one to explain the behavior of the human body, interactive toy as a toy robot, intelligent planter as a greenhouse, that is, they can be applied at all educational levels"," I am a teacher of preschool education in the classroom. I would apply Scratch as a work tool".

5. Discussion and Conclusions

Learning Arduino involves learning many technologies that allow for developing different projects for different needs. Therefore, the set of workshops introduced hardware elements commonly used in robotics fields, such as actuators, sensors, control boards, and outputs (lights, sound). This type of project allows participants to produce ideas by integrating electronics and programming. These types of ideas can be related to the environment, traffic, energy, recycling, health, and safety; and the ideas produced can be different and design unusual applications.

Therefore, Arduino is an alternative to introduce programming and electronics concepts. It is easy to integrate hardware and mechanical components for application development. However, for younger ages, it requires more attention from the instructor to the students. In addition, it was observed that participants learn to strive to produce ideas to find solutions to the problems they observe by making use of robotics mechanisms. Therefore, it can help improve students' creativity by enabling them to think differently and critically.

The first workshop, "creating storytelling" with Scratch, enables the programmer to become creative. Create a story includes more than one character and scene, which allows one to program dialogs and actions. For example, the user may include audio sounds or time sequences or may construct a message to be passed among different sprites. Digital storytelling is a process of designing and programming digital stories, wherein students can develop computational thinking skills and other skills such as digital literacy and problem-solving skills [81]. There are key elements of the digital story such as the setting of the story, characters, scenes, sequence of events, and narrative [82]. Therefore, making interactive stories with Scratch can help develop a set of skills not only focused on programming.

The application of the methodological approach allowed the design of workshops focused on the needs of a specific user and context. Therefore, the proposal is a process that includes methodological guidelines to apply a robotics curriculum for the implementation of ER through the development of projects with a gender approach.

Zint [83] mentioned that attitudes are learnable and teachable. Therefore, interest and curiosity lead to the development of positive emotions. Therefore, the present research showed greater participation of the female gender and had positive acceptance and impact. The interest of the participants in learning and applying this with their students was thus reflected. Teachers already know the importance of the use of Arduino coding applications integrated into the 5E learning in STEM teaching in improving students' attitudes toward electronic and programming in an interdisciplinary way and from an early age in students. In the workshops, students used engineering concepts to assemble electronic devices and arrive at the solution to the problem. In this way, students are exposed to situations that allow them to generate new ideas and create new algorithms.

However, even schools do not have clear educational policies towards the use of educational robotics to include the topic within the academic curriculum.

6. Limitations

This study has several limitations. The limitations of the present study were (1) there was no control group, so the proposed phases could be validated; (2) there was a wide variety of teachers belonging to private and public schools, so the profile of the participants was not uniform; (3) not all participants performed the assembly with the use of the kit. In addition, it was a zoom course, which did not allow us to see the progress in a certain way.

Lastly, (4) only the Arduino microcontroller card and its basic components are used as it is easy to use and cheap.

Funding: This research received no external funding.

Conflicts of Interest: The authors declare no conflict of interest.

References

1. Cheryan, S.; Master, A.; Meltzoff, A.N. Cultural stereotypes as gatekeepers: Increasing girls' interest in computer science and engineering by diversifying stereotypes. *Front. Psychol.* **2015**, *6*, 49. [CrossRef] [PubMed]
2. Margolis, J.; Fisher, A.; Miller, F. The Anatomy of Interest: Women in Undergraduate Computer Science. *Women's Stud. Q.* **2000**, *28*, 104–127.
3. Dasgupta, N. Ingroup experts and peers as social vaccines who inoculate the self-concept: The stereotype inoculation model. *Psychol. Inq.* **2011**, *22*, 231–246. [CrossRef]
4. Rudman, L.A. Self-promotion as a risk factor for women: The costs and benefits of counter stereotypical impression management. *J. Personal. Soc. Psychol.* **1998**, *74*, 629–645. [CrossRef]
5. Roberta Iniciative. Available online: https://lab.open-roberta.org/ (accessed on 15 December 2021).
6. WSTEM Project. Available online: https://wstemproject.eu/ (accessed on 27 October 2021).
7. Benavent, X.; De Ves, E.; Forte, A.; Botella-Mascarell, C.; López-Iñesta, E.; Rueda, S.; Roger, S.; Perez, J.; Portalés, C.; Dura, E.; et al. Girls4STEM: Gender Diversity in STEM for a Sustainable Future. *Sustainability* **2020**, *12*, 6051. [CrossRef]
8. Herro, D.; Quigley, C.; Jacques, L. Examining technology integration in middle school STEAM units. *Technol. Pedagog. Educ.* **2018**, *7*, 485–498. [CrossRef]
9. Chang, D.F.; Chang Tzeng, H.C. Patterns of gender parity in the humanities and STEM programs: The trajectory under the expanded higher education system. *Stud. High. Educ.* **2018**, *45*, 1108–1120. [CrossRef]
10. UNESCO: Science Report: Towards 2030. Available online: https://en.unesco.org/sites/default/files/usr15_is_the_gender_gap_narrowing_in_science_and_engineering.pdf (accessed on 15 October 2021).
11. García-Holgado, A.; Camacho Díaz, A.; García-Peñalvo, F.J. La brecha de género en el sector STEM en América Latina: Una propuesta europea. In *Actas del V Congreso Internacional sobre Aprendizaje, Innovación y Competitividad*; Sein-Echaluce Lacleta, M.L., Fidalgo-Blanco, Á., García-Peñalvo, F.J., Eds.; Servicio de Publicaciones Universidad de Zaragoza: Zaragoza, Spain, 2019; pp. 704–709.
12. Skaalvik, S.; Skaalvik, E.M. Gender Differences in Math and Verbal Self-Concept, Performance Expectations, and Motivation. *Sex Roles* **2004**, *50*, 241–252. [CrossRef]
13. Margot, K.C.; Kettler, T. Teachers' perception of STEM integration and education: A systematic literature review. *Int. J. STEM Educ.* **2019**, *6*, 2. [CrossRef]
14. Zhang, Y.; Luo, R.; Zhu, Y.; Yin, Y. Educational Robots Improve K-12 Students' Computational Thinking and STEM Attitudes. Systematic Review. *J. Educ. Comput. Res.* **2021**, *59*, 1450–1481. [CrossRef]
15. Mussati, A.; Giang, C.; Piatti, A.; Mondada, F. A Tangible Programming Language for the Educational Robot Thymio. In Proceedings of the 2019 10th International Conference on Information, Intelligence, Systems and Applications (IISA), Patras, Greece, 15–17 July 2019; pp. 1–4. [CrossRef]
16. Chevalier, M.; Giang, C.; Piatti, A.; Mondada, F. Fostering computational thinking through educational robotics: A model for creative computational problem solving. *Int. J. STEM Educ.* **2020**, *7*, 39. [CrossRef]
17. Sullivan, A.; Bers, M. VEX Robotics Competitions: Gender Differences in Student Attitudes and Experiences. *J. Inf. Technol. Educ. Res.* **2019**, *18*, 97–112. [CrossRef]
18. McIlwee, J.S.; Robinson, J.G. *Women in Engineering: Gender, Power, and Workplace Culture*; SUNY Press: New York, NY, USA, 1992.
19. Sullivan, A.; Bers, M.U. The impact of teacher gender on girls' performance on programming tasks in early elementary school. *J. Inf. Technol. Educ. Innov. Pract.* **2018**, *17*, 153–162. [CrossRef]
20. Román-Graván, P.; Hervás-Gómez, C.; Martín-Padilla, A.H.; Fernández-Márquez, E. Perceptions about the Use of Educational Robotics in the Initial Training of Future Teachers: A Study on STEAM Sustainability among Female Teachers. *Sustainability* **2020**, *12*, 4154. [CrossRef]
21. Peixoto, A.; Castro, M.; Blaz, M.; Martin, S.; Sancristobal, E.; Carro, G.; Plaza, P. Robotics tips and tricks for inclusion and integration of students. In Proceedings of the 2018 IEEE Global Engineering Education Conference (EDUCON), Santa Cruz de Tenerife, Spain, 17–20 April 2018; pp. 2037–2041. [CrossRef]
22. Cuartielles, D.; Iriepa, N.; Rodriguez, C.; Lopez, E.; Garcia, J. Educational Robots with Arduino: Annotated Prototypes. In *Educational Robotics in the Context of the Maker Movement*; Moro, M., Alimisis, D., Iocchi, L., Eds.; Edurobotics 2018: Advances in Intelligent Systems and Computing; Springer: Cham, Switzerland, 2020; Volume 946. [CrossRef]
23. Ntourou, V.; Kalogiannakis, M.; Psycharis, S. A Study of the Impact of Arduino and Visual Programming in Self-Efficacy, Motivation, Computational Thinking and 5th Grade Students' Perceptions on Electricity. *Eurasia J. Math. Sci. Technol. Educ.* **2021**, *17*, em1960. [CrossRef]

24. Abidin, Z.; Arifudin, R.; Hardyanto, W.; Akhlis, I.; Umer, R.; Kurniawan, N. Low-cost educational robotics for promoting STEM education. *J. Phys. Conf. Ser.* **2021**, *1918*, 042018. [CrossRef]
25. Dimitriou, K. A more structured way to teach robotics with robotics. In Proceedings of the 3rd International Workshop Teaching Robotics, Teaching with Robotics Integrating Robotics in School Curriculum, Trento, Italy, 20 April 2012; pp. 163–169.
26. de Azevedo, S.O.; Bezerra, J.E.; de Miranda, L.C. A methodology of contextualized educational robotics. In Proceedings of the 2017 IEEE Frontiers in Education Conference (FIE), Indianapolis, IN, USA, 18–21 October 2017; pp. 1–9. [CrossRef]
27. Angel-Fernandez, J.M.; Vincze, M. Towards a Definition of Educational Robotics. In Proceedings of the Processing Austrian Robot Workshop, Innsbruck, Austria, 17–18 May 2018; pp. 37–42. [CrossRef]
28. Papert, S. Teaching Children Thinking. *Program. Learn. Educ. Technol.* **1972**, *9*, 245–255. [CrossRef]
29. Solomon, C.J.; Papert, S. A Case Study of a Young Child Doing Turtle Graphics in Logo. Massachusetts Institute of Technology. Cambridge Artificial Intelligence Lab. National Institute of Education. 1976. Available online: https://files.eric.ed.gov/fulltext/ED207578.pdf (accessed on 16 October 2021).
30. Papert, S. *Mindstorm: Children, Computers, and Powerful Ideas*; Basic Books, Inc.: New York, NY, USA, 1980.
31. Rush, M.N.; Resnick, R.B.; Pezalla-Granlund, M. New pathways into robotics: Strategies for broadening participation. *J. Sci. Educ. Technol.* **2008**, *17*, 59–69.
32. American Association of University Women (AAUW). *Executive Summary: Tech-Savvy: Educating Girls in the New Computer Age [Electronic Version]*; American Association of University Women (AAUW): Washington, DC, USA, 2000.
33. Plaza, P.; Sancristobal, E.; Carro, G.; Blazquez, M.; García-Loro, F.; Martin, S.; Perez, C.; Castro, M. Arduino as an Educational Tool to Introduce Robotics. In Proceedings of the 2018 IEEE International Conference on Teaching, Assessment, and Learning for Engineering (TALE), Wollongong, NSW, Australia, 4–7 December 2018; pp. 1–8. [CrossRef]
34. Xenabis, A.; Brentas, S. STEM activities based on educational robotics, recyclable materials and Arduino Programming. In Proceedings of the Edulearn19 Proceedings 11th International Conference on Education and New Learning Technologies, Palma, Spain, 1–3 July 2019; pp. 1443–1452.
35. Junior, L.A.; Neto, O.T.; Hernandez, M.D.; Martins, P.S.; Roger, L.B.; Guerra, F. A Low-Cost and Simple Arduino-Based Educational Robotics Kit. *Cyber J. Multidiscip. J. Sci. Technol. J. Sel. Areas Robot. Control* **2013**, *3*, 1–7.
36. Charoula, A.; Nicos, V. Developing young children's computational thinking with educational robotics: An interaction effect between gender and scaffolding strategy. *Comput. Hum. Behav.* **2020**, *105*, 105954. [CrossRef]
37. Eguchi, A. RoboCupJunior for promoting STEM education, 21st century skills, and technological advancement through robotics competition. *Robot. Auton. Syst.* **2016**, *75*, 696–699. [CrossRef]
38. Barker, B.; Ansorge, J. Robotics as means to increase achievement scores in an informal learning environment. *J. Res. Technol. Educ.* **2007**, *39*, 229–243. [CrossRef]
39. Hussain, S.; Lindh, J.; Shukur, G. The effect of LEGO training on pupils's school performance in mathematics, problem solving ability and attitude: Swedish data. *Educ. Technol. Soc.* **2006**, *9*, 182–194.
40. Nugent, G.; Barker, B.; Grandgenett, N. The effect of 4-H robotics and geospatial technologies on science, technology, engineering, and mathematics learning and attitudes. In Proceedings of the EdMedia: World Conference on Educational Media and Technology, Vienna, Austria, 30 June 2008; Volume 2008, pp. 447–452.
41. Altin, H.; Pedaste, M. Learning approaches to applying robotics in science education. *J. Balt. Sci. Educ.* **2013**, *12*, 365–377.
42. Jurado, E.; Fonseca, D.; Coderch, J.; Canaleta, X. Social STEAM Learning at an Early Age with Robotic Platforms: A Case Study in Four Schools in Spain. *Sensors* **2020**, *20*, 3698. [CrossRef] [PubMed]
43. Sullivan, A.; Bers, M.U. Girls, boys, and bots: Gender differences in young children's performance on robotics and programming tasks. *J. Inf. Technol. Educ. Innov. Pract.* **2016**, *15*, 145–165. Available online: http://www.informingscience.org/Publications/3547 (accessed on 16 December 2021). [CrossRef]
44. Vavassoru, B.; Barreto, F. Exploring the educational potential of robotics in schools: A systematic review. *Comput. Educ.* **2012**, *58*, 978–988. [CrossRef]
45. Alves-Oliveira, P. Boosting Children's Creativity through Creative Interactions with Social Robots. Ph.D. Thesis, University Institute of Lisbon, Lisbon, Portugal, 2020.
46. Sapounidis, T.; Demetriadis, S.N. Exploring children's preferences regarding tangible and graphical tools for introductory programming: Evaluating the PROTEAS kit. In Proceedings of the 12th IEEE International Conference on Advanced Learning Technologies, Rome, Italy, 4–6 July 2012; pp. 316–320.
47. Jennifer, B.; Debra, G. When Do Girls Lose Interest in Math and Science? Science Sampler. 2008. Available online: https://sc.lib.miamioh.edu/bitstream/handle/2374.MIA/5965/2008%20-%20When%20Do%20Girls%20Lose%20Interest%20in%20Math%20and%20Science%3f.pdf?sequence=1&isAllowed=y (accessed on 16 December 2021).
48. Murphy, M.C.; Steele, C.M.; Gross, J.J. Signaling threat: How situational cues affect women in math, science, and engineering settings. *Psychol. Sci.* **2007**, *18*, 879–885. [CrossRef] [PubMed]
49. Master, A.; Cheryan, S.; Meltzoff, A.N. Reducing adolescent girls' concerns about STEM stereotypes: When do female teachers matter? *Int. Rev. Soc. Psychol.* **2014**, *27*, 79–102.
50. Hughes, R.; Schellinger, J.; Roberts, K. The role of recognition in disciplinary identity for girls. *J. Res. Sci. Teach.* **2021**, *58*, 420–455. [CrossRef]

51. Merdan, M.; Lepuschitz, W.; Koppensteiner, G.; Balogh, R. (Eds.) *Robotics in Education: Research and Practices for Robotics in STEM Education*, 7th ed.; Springer: Vienna, Austria; Cham, Switzerland, 2016; Volume 457.
52. Arduino. Available online: https://www.arduino.cc/ (accessed on 16 December 2021).
53. Dokmetas, G. *Arduino Training Book*; Dikey Eksen Yayincilik: Istanbul, Turkey, 2016.
54. Patiño-Escarcina, R.E.; Barrios-Aranibar, D.; Bernedo-Flores, L.S.; Alsina, P.J.; Gonçalves, L.M. A Methodological Approach to the Learning of Robotics with EDUROSC-Kids. *J. Intell. Robot. Syst.* **2021**, *102*, 34. [CrossRef] [PubMed]
55. Vygotsky, L.S. *Mind and Society: The Development of Higher Mental Processes*; Harvard University Press: Cambridge, UK, 1978.
56. Barak, M.; Zadok, Y. Robotics projects and learning concepts in science, technology and problem solving. *Int. J. Technol. Des. Educ.* **2009**, *19*, 289–307. [CrossRef]
57. Doleck, T.; Bazelais, P.; Lemay, D.J.; Saxena, A.; Basnet, R.B. Algorithmic thinking, cooperativity, creativity, critical thinking, and problem solving: Exploring the relationship between computational thinking skills and academic performance. *J. Comput. Educ.* **2017**, *4*, 355–369. [CrossRef]
58. Kazakoff, E.R.; Sullivan, A.; Bers, M.U. The effect of a classroom-based intensive robotics and programming workshop on sequencing ability in early childhood. *Early Child. Educ. J.* **2013**, *41*, 245–255. [CrossRef]
59. Blanchard, S.; Freiman, V.; Lirrete-Pitre, N. Strategies used by elementary schoolchildren solving robotics-based complex tasks: Innovative potential of technology. *Proc. Soc. Behav. Sci.* **2010**, *2*, 2851–2857. [CrossRef]
60. Miller, D.; Nourbakhsh, I.; Siegwart, R. *Robots for Education in Handbook of Robotics*; Springer: Berlin/Heidelberg, Germany, 2008; pp. 1283–1301. [CrossRef]
61. Sullivan, F.R. Serious and Playful Inquiry: Epistemological Aspects of Collaborative Creativity. *Educ. Technol. Soc.* **2011**, *14*, 55–65.
62. Atmatzidou, S.; Demetriadis, S. Advancing students' computational thinking skills through educational robotics: A study on age and gender relevant differences. *Robot. Auton. Syst.* **2016**, *75*, 661–670. [CrossRef]
63. Alimisis, D. *Teacher Education on Robotics-Enhanced Constructivist Pedagogical Methods*; School of Pedagogical and Technological Education (ASPETE): Athens, Greece, 2009.
64. González-Fernández, M.O.; Flores-González, Y.A.; Muñoz-López, C. Panorama de la robótica educativa a favor del aprendizaje STEAM. *Rev. Eureka Enseñanza Divulg. Cienc.* **2021**, *18*, 2301. [CrossRef]
65. Von Wangenheim, A.; Gresse von Wangenheim, C.; Pacheco, F.S.; Hauck, J.C.R.; Ferreira, M.N.F. Motivating Teachers to Teach Computing in Middle School — A Case Study of a Physical Computing Taster Workshop for K-12 Teachers. *Int. J. Comput. Sci. Educ. Sch.* **2017**, *1*, 35–49. [CrossRef]
66. Major, L.; Kyriacou, T.; Brereton, P. The effectiveness of simulated robots for supporting the learning of introductory programming: A multi-case case study. *Comput. Sci. Educ.* **2014**, *24*, 193–228. [CrossRef]
67. Goodale, T.A. The influence of a ROV themed engineering design workshop on in-service teacher self-efficacy. In Proceedings of the 2013 IEEE Integrated STEM Education Conference (ISEC), Princeton, NJ, USA, 9 March 2013; pp. 1–5. [CrossRef]
68. Schina, D.; Esteve-González, V.; Usart, M. An overview of teacher training programs in educational robotics: Characteristics, best practices and recommendations. *Educ. Inf. Technol.* **2021**, *26*, 2831–2852. [CrossRef]
69. Bybee, R.; Landes, N.M. Science for life and living: An elementary school science program from Biological Sciences Improvement Study (BSCS). *Am. Biol. Teach.* **1990**, *52*, 92–98. [CrossRef]
70. Cross, J.; Hamner, E.; Zito, L.; Nourbakhshh, I.; Bernstein, D. Development of an assessment for measuring middle school student attitudes towards robotics activities. In Proceedings of the IEEE Frontiers in Education Conference (FIE), Erie, PA, USA, 12–15 October 2016; pp. 1–8.
71. Horn, M.S.; Solovey, E.T.; Crouser, R.J.; Jacob, R.J. Comparing the use of tangible and graphical programming languages for informal science education. In Proceedings of the SIGCHI Conference on Human Factors in Computing Systems (CHI '09), Association for Computing Machinery, New York, NY, USA, 4–9 April 2009; pp. 975–984. [CrossRef]
72. Su, R.; Rounds, J.; Armstrong, P.I. Men and things, women and people: A meta-analysis of sex differences in interests. *Psychol. Bull.* **2009**, *135*, 859–884. [CrossRef]
73. Yamtinah, S.; Masykuri, M.; Ashadi Shidiq, A.S. Gender differences in students' attitudes toward science: An analysis of student's science process skill using testlet instrument. *AIP Conf. Proc.* **2017**, *1868*, 030003. [CrossRef]
74. Makarova, E.; Aeschlimann, B.; Herzog, W. The Gender Gap in STEM Fields: The Impact of the Gender Stereotype of Math and Science on Secondary Students' Career Aspirations. *Front. Educ.* **2019**, *4*, 60. [CrossRef]
75. Lucio, N.; Christian, G. How do pupils perceive educational robotics as a tool to improve their 21st century skills? *J. Learn. Knowl. Soc.* **2019**, *15*, 77–87. [CrossRef]
76. Shaqiri, A.; Roinishvili, M.; Grzeczkowski, L.; Chkonia, E.; Pilz, K.; Mohr, C.; Brand, A.; Kunchulia, M.; Herzog, M.H. Sex-related differences in vision are heterogeneous. *Sci. Rep.* **2018**, *8*, 7521. [CrossRef]
77. Balland, C.; Cissé, N.S.; Hergoualch, L.; Kervot, G.; Lidec, J.; Machard, A.; Ribaud-Le Cann, L.; Rio, C.; Sinilo, M.; Dantec, V.; et al. Girls Who Do Scratch a First Round with the Essence Kernel. In Proceedings of the 2017 IEEE 30th Conference on Software Engineering Education and Training (CSEE), Savannah, GA, USA, 7–9 November 2017.
78. Jiang, B.; Li, Z. Effect of Scratch on computational thinking skills of Chinese primary school students. *J. Comput. Educ.* **2021**, *8*, 505–525. [CrossRef]
79. Statter, D.; Armoni, M. Teaching Abstract Thinking in Introduction to Computer Science for 7th Graders. In Proceedings of the 11th Workshop in Primary and Secondary Computing Education, Münster, Germany, 13–15 October 2016; pp. 80–83. [CrossRef]

80. Gibbons, S.J.; Hirsch, L.S.; Kimmel, H.; Rockland, R.; Bloom, J. MIDDLE School Students' Attitudes to and Knowledge about Engineering. In Proceedings of the International Conference on Engineering Education, Gainesville, FL, USA, 16–21 October 2004.
81. Parsazadeh, N.; Cheng, P.-Y.; Wu, T.-T.; Huang, Y.-M. Integrating Computational Thinking Concept into Digital Storytelling to Improve Learners' Motivation and Performance. *J. Educ. Comput. Res.* **2021**, *59*, 470–495. [CrossRef]
82. Hoić-Božić, N.; Dlab, M.H.; Budim, S.U.; Mezak, J. Development of computational thinking skills in primary school through digital storytelling with Scratch. In Proceedings of the 10th International Conference on e-Learning, Belgrade, Serbia, 26–27 September 2019; pp. 114–119.
83. Zint, M. Comparing three attitude-behavior theories for predicting science teachers' intentions. *J. Res. Sci. Teach.* **2002**, *39*, 819–844. [CrossRef]

Article

An Innovative Low Cost Educational Underwater Robotics Platform for Promoting Engineering Interest among Secondary School Students

Andres El-Fakdi *,†,‡ and Xavier Cufí †,‡

VICOROB Institute, University of Girona, 17004 Girona, Spain; xavier.cufi@udg.edu
* Correspondence: aelfakdi@eia.udg.edu
† Current address: Campus Montilivi, Polytechnic School of the University of Girona, Building P4, 17003 Girona, Spain.
‡ These authors contributed equally to this work.

Abstract: The presented article describes the design features of an educational robotics project addressed for secondary school students and carried out at the University of Girona (UdG). The project, called Underwater Robotics Workshop, is about the students building an underwater exploration robotic vehicle using low-cost materials. Its ultimate objective is to promote engineering interest among students and motivate them to direct their future studies towards engineering degrees. The main purpose of this article is to describe this activity and to promote it. Versatility and adaptation are key values as the activity has been designed to be adapted to convenience or replicated. It is a continuation work of a previously published articles, now describing different technological adaptations related to the design of the vehicle's controller, and the gathered experiences from added workshop celebrations in the recent years. The workshop has been defined as a project-based learning approach where the students learn about physics, engineering, electronics, programming, and robotics, as well as to use all kinds of working tools, according to the maker philosophy. To date, the opinions collected from the participants encourage continuation of the activity and, at the same time, ask for the introduction of novelties to keep the workshop updated with the contents of the subjects related to technology and sciences. This project is being held for more than 13 years in the UdG. More than 800 secondary school students have participated in the activity, building about 200 underwater vehicles in more than 50 editions of the workshop.

Keywords: increasing interest for engineering; hands-on experimentation; project-based learning; underwater robots

Citation: El-Fakdi, A.; Cufí, X. An Innovative Low Cost Educational Underwater Robotics Platform for Promoting Engineering Interest Among Secondary School Students. *Electronics* **2022**, *11*, 373. https://doi.org/10.3390/electronics11030373

Academic Editors: Savvas A. Chatzichristofis and Zinon Zinonos

Received: 30 November 2021
Accepted: 21 January 2022
Published: 26 January 2022

Publisher's Note: MDPI stays neutral with regard to jurisdictional claims in published maps and institutional affiliations.

Copyright: © 2022 by the authors. Licensee MDPI, Basel, Switzerland. This article is an open access article distributed under the terms and conditions of the Creative Commons Attribution (CC BY) license (https://creativecommons.org/licenses/by/4.0/).

1. Introduction

The lack of interest of students in Europe and the United States for science, technology, engineering and math (STEM) studies seems not to have changed much in the last ten years. On average, the number of science and engineering students has fallen by about 29% in Europe [1]. The situation is worse in the case of women, with very low representation in engineering studies. This under-representation is also true for minority groups. As early as middle school, these groups start losing interest in STEM fields [2,3]. On the other hand, the labor market demand for engineering related jobs is currently increasing and the ratio of graduated student does not cover that increase. The descending numbers tendency is also confirmed at the local level. Figure 1 shows the engineering students registration numbers recorded at the University of Girona (UdG) over the past years. As can be seen in the graphic, the total number of students registered for engineering studies plots a clearly descending line.

As a general rule, in the initial educational stages of STEM training, each subject is studied separately, as if they were isolated fields and alien to each other, and traditional methodologies based on expository strategies are still the most frequently used activities in learning processes, as opposed to other, more innovative activities. This model does not really fit this teaching, because to be considered as such it is necessary to be accompanied by an integration of these contents, going beyond the concept of subject and proposing an integrative approach, as well as the interactive acquisition of the skills required in that teaching. In addition, the subjects arouse more interest if they present a higher percentage of practical activities, which implies more involvement and a better understanding of these contents. This fact is especially relevant in STEM subjects [4]. The need to adapt compulsory secondary education to the characteristics and demands of a society ruled by the rapid development of technologies, the availability of a vast amount of information and the requirement to increase the population's scientific literacy are generating new training requirements that education systems must meet. Accordingly, the adaptation of teaching practices to learning paradigms that are better suited to the learning of STEM disciplines is one of the most urgent needs, because of the vocational implications for the future generation of scientists, and the danger of them losing interest in these areas during their academic life. It is during Secondary School when students begin to move away from scientific-technical subjects, hence it is necessary to intervene in this educational stage and apply the necessary resources to avoid this distancing. From the age of 12 to 14, most professional vocations are created, orienting the trajectories of the following educational levels accordingly. Students and teachers seem to agree that STEM disciplines are interesting, but do not perceive them as fun but instead as hard and requiring the investment of effort, training methodologies should focus on holding student interest in science and technology by making it accessible and applying it to societal issues. Knowledge related to STEM is crucial to respond to the challenges the society is facing. It is often overlooked that these disciplines have played a key role in addressing some of humanity's greatest challenges in areas such as health, communications, food, and energy.

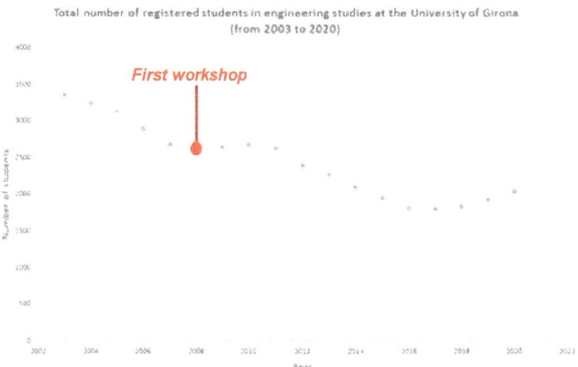

Figure 1. Engineering student annual registration at the University of Girona from 2003 to 2020.

In 2008, the Polytechnic School of the University of Girona considered early interventions to improve interest and encourage pursuit of STEM areas as a priority and greatly needed. As a result, the workshop presented in this article was born. Similar activities with interesting results can be found in [5,6], where the realization of parallel events or activities to teach engineering principles demonstrate the potential for hands-on, biomechanics-based activities to engage students. Also, Ref. [7] shows a designed activity for secondary students focused on engineering and programming which uses app design concepts to build software applications. Deep analysis on the results obtained on those activities demonstrates a general interest increase in engineering, regardless of initial interest, even to the point of positively impacting students' consideration of careers in engineering. The workshop activity described in this article is oriented towards robotics. Real robotics is a highly interdisciplinary field with ties to engineering, programming, and physics. More precisely, in order to take advantage of an expertise contained inside the Computer Vision and Robotics Group (VICOROB) of the UdG, which is focused on underwater robotics. Underwater environments has always been a very important challenge for humanity. Exploring unknown environments using new challenging technological devices has become a compelling necessity, and it is also a very attractive field, especially for young people. The study, development and use of these devices can be a stimulus for their vocation to technological and scientific disciplines. Motivation activities for engaging young students with knowledge and education has always been a major concern for the teaching community. Among state of the art learning possibilities, authors have designed a workshop which explores constructionist learning [8]. Constructionist learning is a student-centered, discovery learning technique based on the creation by learners of mental models to understand the world around them. Students learn through participation in project-based learning where they make connections between different ideas and areas of knowledge facilitated by the teacher through coaching rather than using lectures or direct step-by-step guidance [9]. Constructionist learning holds that learning can happen most effectively when learners are active in making tangible and shareable objects in the real world, which generates an emotional link with them.

There are a lot of mobile robotics activities of many different natures and they use all sorts of terrestrial mobile robots. Most of them are very interesting and are perfectly aligned with the constructionist approaches mentioned above. The peculiarity of our project is to create small-scale, simple, but functional low-cost remote operated underwater prototypes using everyday materials whenever possible. A Remote Operated Vehicle (ROV) is an unmanned submarine vehicle controlled by a command console attached to the vehicle by an umbilical cord. These ROVs are equipped with engines for propulsion, and can be equipped with sensors of different characteristics, underwater cameras and various intervention widgets. Our project is inspired mainly by the Sea Pearch Program of the Massachusetts Institute of Technology (MIT) [10], and the MATE ROV competition from MATE Inspiration for Innovation [11], an annual underwater robotics competition with different amazing challenges that engages a lot of learners and volunteers. Our project seeks to attract and motivate students (and the general public) to technology through the construction and the operation of these underwater vehicles [12–14]. It is also intended to encourage the imagination of students participating in different parts of the design, obviously prioritizing engineering aspects and that the resulting vehicles must respect the underwater environment. These kind of project-based activities are considered highly relevant for exposing students to the fields of Science, Technology, Engineering, and Mathematics (STEM) [15]. The MIT SeaPerch Program was created by the MIT Sea Grant College Program in 2003. Now, SeaPerch program is an initiative from RoboNation [16] that introduces students to basic engineering, design, and science concepts [17], engaging students and fostering skills as for instance, critical thinking, collaboration, and creativity. Also, an interesting approach is presented in the OpenROV open-source hardware project [18] which makes available to the general public a teleoperated submarine robot at a very reasonable cost. In this case the developers provide a list of the submarine parts and instructions on how to assemble them, with the aim to democratize underwater exploration. As far as we know, there are no references to other low-cost underwater robot construction activities such as the one proposed in this article, especially in Europe, and this is something that makes this activity very special and unique.

The presented project is completely in accordance with the maker and do-it-yourself philosophy that is being promoted around the world. The result of the activity is an underwater device made by the participants, using low-cost materials, which reinforces the emotional link of them with the whole activity. The underwater vehicle is very attractive and it navigates underwater graciously and softness, which is very surprising, in the best sense, for all the participants [19]. In some specific cases, when these workshops have been held in the Underwater Robotics Research Center (CIRS) [20] of the UdG, they have been an appropriate way to explain the research in underwater robotics that is carried out there. The close interaction of students with senior researchers at the University can also be a very motivating factor in increasing their interest in science and technology. The activity is a very useful tool to explain and discuss with the participating students about the different research projects and underwater vehicles developed in this research center, where it is shown that these devices are a key to developing underwater technology projects, related to different fields such as marine biology, geology, archaeology projects, which makes the workshop even more transversal. Technology, and especially robotics, is something that is very attractive to young people. Unfortunately, as they grow older, they tend to perceive technology and engineering as difficult and unknown, which causes them to stop considering degrees in technology and engineering. Within the framework of the development of the activity, different types of concepts are considered and worked on, according to the curriculum of technology and science subjects studied in secondary education: Newton's Laws, the Archimedes Principle, control of DC motors, engineering aspects related to the design of the structure and chassis of the vehicle and the location of the engines, the operation of a joystick, the study of different types of sensors, design and construction of different types of actuators with different technologies, use of open-source microcontrolled boards, programming, etc. Not to mention other competences that are very interesting such as teamwork, the correct and safe use of professional tools, the handling of different types of materials, work in a real professional environment, contact with a university research center, compliance with safety regulations, regular use of the English language, etc.

Recently, more advanced concepts have begun to be introduced in the project addressed to students with a higher degree of maturity. These concepts are focused on Autonomous Underwater Vehicles (AUVs) instead of working with ROVs. The students launch a programmable submarine vehicle, which emulates the behavior of the AUVs used in real exploration and research missions. For this purpose, students work with open source electronic platforms based on the use of low-cost and easy-to-use hardware and software, such as Arduino boards [21]. The students program the vehicles in open loop or closed loop (if there is the possibility of incorporating low-cost sensors) and study and program different types of missions to perform trajectories that are tested in the pool. In this case, the students have to adapt the programs they are coding so that the vehicles behave properly as expected. The goal is to discover the difference between the behaviors of real vehicles and those of *ideal* vehicles.

The article is organized as follows. Section 2 gives details about the vehicle and the different teleoperation modes. The workshop carried out by the students is described in Section 3. Finally, the results, conclusions and future sights are discussed in Section 4.

2. The Robot

The main idea is to create prototypes of small-scale ROVs, simple but functional, using everyday materials. By definition, a ROV is an unmanned submarine vehicle, controlled through a command console attached to the vehicle by a tether. A significant example of a vehicle that is built throughout the activity is the one shown in Figure 2.

The control console can be of different types, depending on the technological level of the students who carry out the activity. The console must allow for control of the 3 DC motors that are on board, and it can be made of any material. The basic console holds a frontal panel with a joystick and two buttons to control the 3 motors that propel the vehicle. For students of advanced level, this console can be designed using low cost programmable hardware and DC motor control modules. Also, they can use a mobile device and an app designed by the students themselves as a submarine vehicle control console.

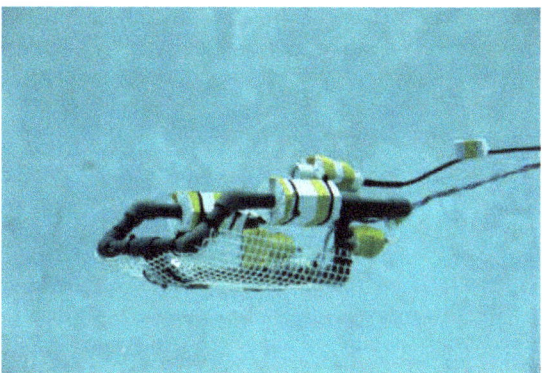

Figure 2. Example of vehicle built at the workshop.

2.1. The Structure of the Vehicle

In Figure 2 details of the low-cost underwater vehicle can be observed. The chassis of the vehicle is very light and robust, built with pipes and joints of PVC of 20 mm in diameter, a material that can be easily manipulated by the students. The structure of the vehicle must be able to accommodate all the components that form part of the vehicle, and which allow it to carry out the mission or missions for which it has been designed (propulsion, buoyancy, sensors, actuators, or cameras). The chassis should house the engines that allow for propulsion and the buoyancy elements. Two horizontal motors and one vertical motor must allow the movement of the vehicle in three dimensions within the underwater environment. The activity allows participating students to propose different chassis models for the submarine vehicle. Students, working in group, make design proposals about possible feature designs. The proposals are made with the missions as the final objective, so students' proposals must be directed to vehicle optimization and mission fulfillment. The final design must be extracted by consensus of the whole group and on the basis of specific advantages for mission success that will be accepted or rejected by workshop supervisors. Figure 3 depicts some suitable design examples for the vehicle chassis.

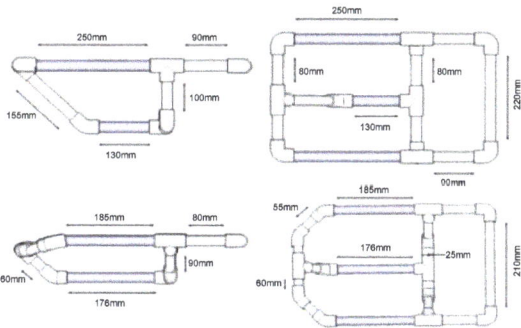

Figure 3. Examples of two possible chassis designs.

The final design must be extracted by consensus of the whole group and on the basis of specific advantages for mission success that will be accepted or rejected by workshop supervisors.

2.2. The Basic Command Console

The most basic control console is a structure built with any type of material, which must be able to house a joystick, two push-buttons and the control circuits of the three

DC motors that equip the underwater robots. Two of these engines are the horizontal motors, which are responsible for the steering movements of the submarine vehicle. These horizontal motors are controlled by the joystick. The third one is the vertical motor, responsible for the ascending and descending movements of the underwater vehicle. This motor is controlled by the two push-buttons provided by the control console.

The push-buttons have a movable mechanical pivot (red in Figure 4) that allows the change in the connections of the terminals: terminals C and NC (Normally Closed) are connected if the pivot is not pressed, and C and NO (Normally Open) are connected if the pivot is pressed. The circuit that controls the movement of each of the DC motors is a standard inverted polarity circuit, governed by two push-buttons, named A and B, as shown in Figure 5. In the case of the two horizontal motors, the two push-buttons on each of the motors are the ones located on the joystick (which has four push-buttons in total). In the case of the vertical motor, the two push-buttons are the ones located on the console near the joystick.

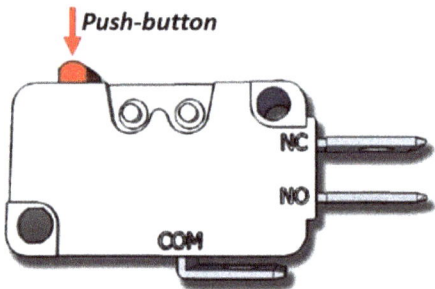

Figure 4. Push-button for DC motor control. Red-dotted line shows the two possible circuit positions depending on the pivot position.

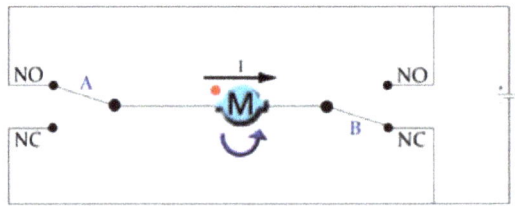

Figure 5. Inverted polarity circuit.

The joystick is basically made up of a handle and four push-buttons placed strategically (see Figure 6). It is crucial that the joystick is placed on the console with a rhomboidal distribution as shown in the figure and not in another distribution, as that fact will be decisive for its correct operation. The joystick should help drive the vehicle in a reasonable and intuitive way. The following Table 1 shows the four possible configurations that this circuit can have:

Table 1. Possible circuit configurations. NO is Connected to +, NC is Connected to −.

Pushbutton A		Pushbutton B		Motor Turning
Pressed	COM A is +	No pressed	COM B is −	Counterclockwise
Pressed	COM A is +	Pressed	COM B is +	No turn
Not pressed	COM A is −	No pressed	COM B is −	No turn
Not pressed	COM A is −	Pressed	COM B is +	Clockwise

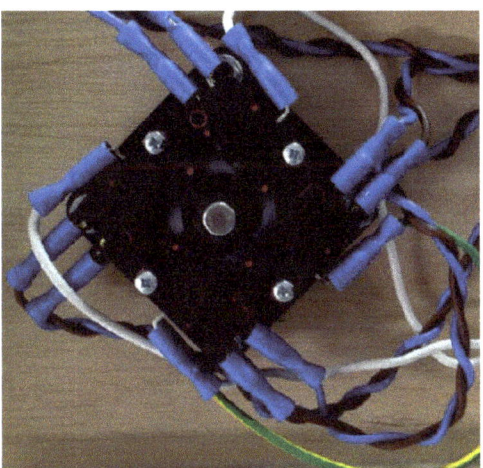

Figure 6. 4 push-buttons of joystick seen from below.

If, for example, we want the vehicle to move forward, the user will push the joystick handle forward, and this gesture should cause the two buttons corresponding to the two horizontal motors to operate simultaneously to move the water both backwards, thus pushing the vehicle forward. This is not possible if the joystick mounting is arranged in a different geometric arrangement.

2.3. The Advanced Programmable Command Console

Considering the educational needs of secondary schools, and with the contents of the curricula of technology subjects in mind, the activity has been adapted from a technological point of view. The new version of the control console incorporates the use of low-cost programmable hardware (mainly based on Arduino UNO boards) and also the possibility to program apps for smart mobile devices. This feature allows for covering a wide range of technology content, and ostensibly increase the overall interest of the activity. Coding is also incorporated into the activity at this level, which gives it a very important added value. It is possible to develop a simple app using programming tools like Appinventor [22], a programming language based on blocks, developed by researchers of MIT, which helps students to build functional apps for Android and IOS smartphones and tablets. Also, Scratch4Arduino-S4A [23], a similar block-based software, can be used if deemed appropriate. Concepts of submarine mission programming, sensor integration, Bluetooth communications, power electronics, and even autonomous behaviors can be also introduced into coding.

Figure 7 shows the complete diagram of the connection of the three DC motors of a submarine vehicle to the power control boards (H-bridges) and to a programmable low-cost hardware. Through the programming cable, the programmable board is connected to a laptop. Some specific keys of the keyboard can be used as buttons to control the movements of the ROV. A mobile device can also be used as a control console using an app developed by the students. From the app, the user can send control commands to the programmable hardware using a Bluetooth link. A specific low-cost Bluetooth module must be connected to the programmable hardware. The development of an app that allows the use of a mobile device as a control console is something that young students value a lot, establishing a powerful link between the student and the project.

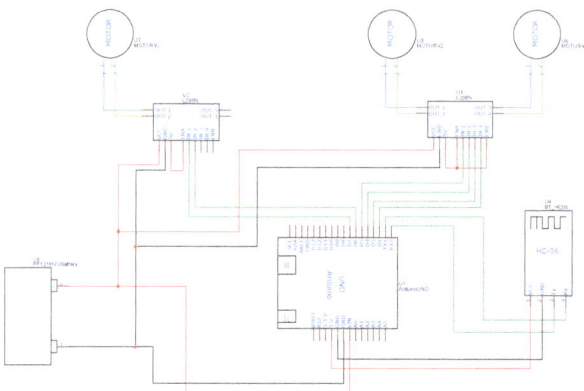

Figure 7. Advanced console connection schematic.

Figure 8 shows an example of the screen of an app that controls the underwater vehicle and a program developed with Appinventor that allows the user to control the underwater vehicle sending control commands to the programmable hardware through a Bluetooth link.

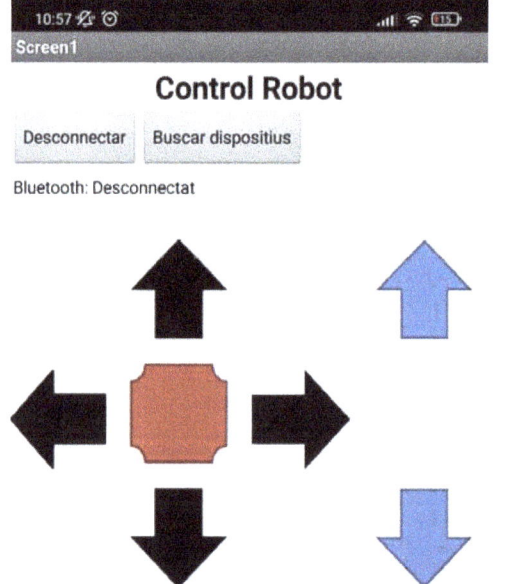

Figure 8. Example of app screen for vehicle control designed with Appinventor.

3. The Workshop Development

The workshop can be carried out in any swimming pool that has minimum dimensions that allow the navigation of the underwater robot. To the date, it has been developed a few times in the CIRS facility at the UdG. This laboratory is one of the most advanced facilities for underwater research built in Spain, it has plenty of space available and all needed machinery and tools for the activity development. In order to fit secondary school requirements, budget and schedules, the workshop has been designed to be developed in two different formats: Standard three-day format and compressed one-day format. The standard three-day format lasts for two and a half days, 20 h approximately. The one-day format divides the workshop in two steps, one at their own school where the students do part of the workshop with their teachers and a second step where they come to the research lab, or a pool for one day. In this compressed format, activities to be done at school or at the lab are studied depending on school equipment. As can be appreciated in Table 2, the standard three-day format is divided into three modules. One module for the teleoperation console and the vehicle chassis, a second module for the motors and console wiring and, finally, a last module for assembling, buoyancy adjustment and mission development.

Table 2. Standard three-day format modules.

Module One	Module Two	Module Three
Presentation	Console wiring	Buoyancy adjustment
Console construction	Motor sealing	Connection check
Chassis construction	Propellers attachment	Final missions
Wires preparation	Umbilical attachment	
Umbilical preparation	Connection check	

The one-day format experience did not exist at the beginning of this project. It was later created as a request from schools demanding for a shorter format, more aligned with their course schedules and economic budgets. Nowadays, the one-day format is the most demanded one among schools. Table 3 shows only the final activities performed during the last part of the workshop, where the pool is needed, while the previous tasks are carried out by the students at their schools and remotely supervised by faculty supervisors. This short format also includes a training session at the school where students' teachers receive all the information and necessary materials to develop the school work. Two weeks before the workshop, school teachers must report supervisors in order to check robot development. School visits by supervisors is an option in case of troubles or delays related with the normal development of the planned activities.

Table 3. One-day format module.

Final Module
Presentation
Buoyancy adjustment
Connection check
Final missions

As can be noted, the tasks contained in the one-day format are almost the same as the ones in the module three of the three-day format. The presentation contains all the information needed by the students about how to operate: mechanical tool usage, safety instructions, and recommendations for quality assurance of the whole experience are given. The last part of the presentation is related with engineering, underwater robotics and research. The numerous industrial applications around underwater technology, such as environmental monitoring, oceanographic research or maintenance/monitoring of underwater structures are presented to the students with the aim of awaking the student's interest in the field. The next sections detail all the tasks listed for every module.

3.1. Module One

The students start the workshop with the design and the construction of its two main elements: the control unit and the vehicle's chassis. As explained in Section 2, the control unit can be implemented using different technology, wired or wireless. Figure 9a shows a finished control unit in the case of a wired selection. In this case, the console is made of wood and the students must combine nails and glue to fix it. The wired control console contains the joystick and the up-down push-buttons for the robot control. Once the glue is dry, students can paint and decorate the console according to their preferences. The vehicle's chassis, shown in (Figure 9b), is made of assembled tubes and joints made of PVC (T, 90° and 45° PVC connectors). Initially, the students propose and discuss several designs on paper. The commencement of the chassis assembly cannot be done without the supervisors approval on the final paper design.

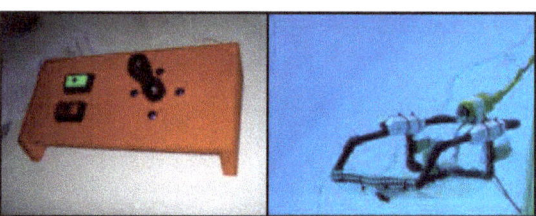

Figure 9. (**Left**) Control unit. (**Right**) Finished chassis.

With the two main frames of the design built, the students must now prepare all the needed wires and connectors that will be used the next day for the console and chassis wiring. A fixed number of cables must be prepared, with a defined color, length and connection type. All wires must be welded with a tin solder in order to facilitate the connection to the console the day after. Also, some extra wires are prepared for motor tests performed during the second module.

3.2. Module Two

As can be seen in Table 2, the second module is related with the assembly of the elements prepared during the first module. Thus, this module is about the console wiring, the motor sealing, and propeller and umbilical assembly. Before the module starts, the students first attend to a lecture session about the electric schematic of the whole design. Here, the student learns the basics about electricity and circuits. The final objective is to apply the acquired knowledge on the proposed schematic. Its is very important to understand the electrical behavior of the design as the success of the final vehicle depends on it. Final assembly of the console wires can be seen in Figure 10.

Figure 10. Assembly of wire connections to the back side of the console.

The chosen vehicle propellers are common 12 V DC motors. They are not specially designed to operate in underwater domains and, therefore, an encapsulation work must be done with them in order to safely use them underwater. To do so, the current design uses a mixture of petroleum jelly and thermal adhesive. The delicate parts of the motors are first covered with electric tape. Also, the motor shaft and the frontal plane of the motor are generously covered with petroleum jelly to prevent water coming inside the motor through the shaft. Then, the motor is introduced into a cylindrical plastic canister. Students have to drill a small hole at the bottom of the case for the motor shaft. Subsequently, the case is filled with thermal adhesive. After a short period of time, when the thermal adhesive hardens, we obtain a solid sealed motor with only a shaft and two wires coming out. The final task of this module is to fix the sealed motors to the chassis of the vehicle and connect them -by means of an Ethernet cable- to the teleoperation console. With respect to the umbilical cable, for this workshop design, an Ethernet cable is used. The advantages of using Ethernet cable are numerous. First of all, the resultant umbilical is thin, flexible and quite light, eliminating drag problems resultant from using heavy and more rigid cabling. An Ethernet cable has four cable pairs, which fit perfectly in our design, which uses three pairs for the motors and leaves an extra unused pair for added gadgets, such as an underwater light, or a grabbing device. The last task of this module is to check all the electrical connections and test the vehicle outside the water to verify its correct behavior.

3.3. Module Three

According to Table 2, the tasks contained in the last module are: buoyancy adjustment, connection check and final mission tests. The one-day format workshop also contains a presentation and a facility visit as, in this format, students do not know the CIRS laboratory and must receive this introductory content as their colleagues from the three-day format did. The last step to be done before performing the real experimental missions in the CIRS pool is to adjust the vehicle's buoyancy. This step is about using a modeled block of foam to be attached to the vehicle in order to compensate for its weight when submerged. The objective of this step is to have a close-to-neutral underwater vehicle in terms of density. Acting this way, the maneuverability and efficiency of the submarine will be close to optimal as its neutral buoyancy helps it to maintain desired depths without spending energy or generating momentum in unnecessarily. Figure 11 illustrates the process.

Figure 11. (**Left**) Buoyancy adjustment step. (**Right**) CIRS experimental pool.

Once the buoyancy has been correctly adjusted and verified, one last electric check is carried out with the objective of validating the prototype for navigation and mission development. The final objectives of the designed missions pursue two main goals: first, to exploit the capabilities of the designed vehicles so the students can appreciate the results of their efforts and, secondly, to show the students what real missions with AUVs look like in the real world. Most of the missions have been designed starting from similar real missions performed by our vehicles at CIRS in open sea conditions and by doing them, the students get the touch of the requirements and performance expected from a real vehicle designed to perform specific tasks.

Figure 12 shows an example vehicle inside the water pool surrounded by a mission set. The designed missions are mostly involved with different recuperation tasks, maneuver the vehicle through complex underwater structures or collaborative tasks where the participation of two or more vehicles is needed to complete the mission. While performing the missions, installed cameras and the installed underwater window allow for recording of the different team's performance in order to evaluate their projects at school.

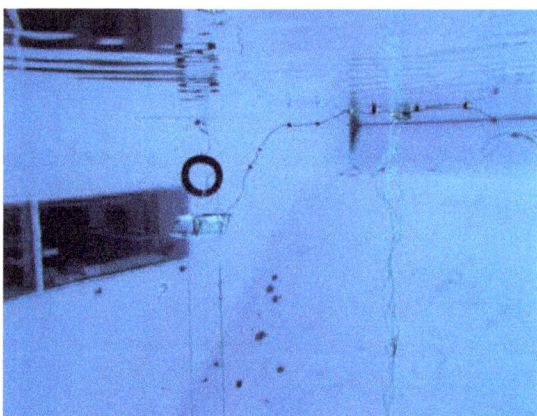

Figure 12. The vehicle and the mission set.

4. Results and Conclusions of the Workshop

Nowadays, there are very few known experiences where secondary students participate in an exciting project-based workshop of building their own underwater vehicle. This fact makes the presented activity very special and characteristic. We have examples of similar activities in the United States, such as the Seaperch project which is a very important national project supported by RoboNation. The activity presented in this article is inspired in the Seaperch project and it has been conveniently adapted to local circumstances. Initiatives like the OpenROV project present a teleoperated submarine robot for a price of approximately $900, nine times the cost of the proposal presented in this article. The activity can be easily adapted to different environments and situations. It can be carried out in a swimming pool, or in other simpler facilities with a minimum amount of water. The workshop has been designed with a series of proposed build materials for its realization but this is just a proposal. Everyone should feel free to try other different approaches that may be as good or even better than the one used here. The use of low cost materials should be a priority and, from this concept in mind, there is always the possibility of incorporating new elements, new aspects, new blocks, and new concepts. For example, it is possible to investigate the incorporation of sensor blocks into the vehicle (sensor blocks that must be isolated from the water) that may be related to parameters of interest that you want to investigate (such as the water quality), or incorporate elements that allow for the cleaning of the water sheet of contaminants (using for example materials based on cellulose nanofibers). The experience gained during all editions of the underwater robotics workshops has determined a number of engineering needs in the design of the chassis of the underwater vehicle:

- The proper location of the two horizontal motors and the vertical motor necessary for the movements of the vehicle. Pieces of vertical PVC pipe are needed to accommodate the two horizontal motors, and a piece of horizontal PVC pipe, at the bottom of the vehicle, to fit the vertical motor.
- The structure of the vehicle chassis must not impede the operation of the propellers when they expel water to provide propulsion.
- The structure of the vehicle chassis must protect the engine-propeller assembly from possible collisions, housing it inside the body of the vehicle.
- The structure of the chassis must allow the buoyancy elements to be located at the top of the vehicle so that it is properly balanced.
- It is necessary to drill the PVC pipes so that the water can flood them, thus preventing possible water bubbles from unbalancing it when it is sailing.

- It is necessary to have a piece of PVC pipe in the back of the vehicle to be able to fix the tether, thus avoiding stresses on the welds of the terminals of the motors, when it is necessary to pick-up it from the water.
- The size of the vehicle should be approximately the size of a shoe box. This is due to the power of the motors used in the activity. With these dimensions, vehicles move underwater with astonishing agility and grace.

The presented activity is completely linked to new ways of learning such as learning based on transversal projects, considering creativity, teamwork, and focusing on different skills, and completely in accordance with the philosophy maker and do it yourself and sometimes related to certain very interesting counterculture movements. The end result of the activity is an artifact made by the students with their own hands, which extraordinarily strengthens the link between them and the theoretical concepts needed to build it. The activity is easily carried out by technology and science teachers in secondary schools. It is considered that after few hours of training and a little practice and audacity, teachers can carry out the activity with complete independence.

Table 4 sums up the total number of editions of the workshop performed to date. As can be appreciated, 53 editions of the workshop have been held, and there are at least three more editions scheduled for 2022. More than 800 students have participated in the activity and more than 200 underwater vehicles have been built. Also, Table 4 describes the format used for the workshops: three-day format or one-day format.

Table 4. Workshops done since November 2008.

Year	Students	ROVs	3-Day Format	1-Day Format
2008	20 (Inaugural Demo Edition)	2	0	0
2009	26	5	1	0
2010	61	11	3	0
2011	85	20	3	2
2012	73	21	2	4
2013	78	19	4	1
2014	78	20	2	2
2015	54	15	3	1
2016	70	20	3	3
2017	80	22	4	1
2018	72	23	4	2
2019	72	21	3	2
2020	All activities cancelled (COV19)	0	0	0
2021	32	8	2	0
2022	3 workshops scheduled	-	-	-
TOTAL	**801**	**207**	**34**	**19**

To the date, the number of experiences that have been carried out is numerous. The last pandemic year asked for a sudden stop in our workshop activities, but we hope to restore pre-pandemic student volumes soon. The participation comes mainly from secondary and high schools inside the Girona area, our territory of influence, and we plan to continue inside this range of reach. Exceptionally, groups of students from other places may be invited to participate in the activity. In all cases, experience feedback from participating students and teachers has been very positive [14,19]. The degree of satisfaction is very high, and the activity covers the learning objectives previously considered. The development of the workshop is associated with a series of strongly related activities that are considered as collateral results of the continued celebration of the event since its beginnings:

- Technology outreach books.
- Scientific publications in national and international journals and conferences.
- Outreach talks addressed to students of different levels and the general public.
- Participation in projects for the dissemination of scientific and technological culture.

- Participation in international cooperation and solidarity projects.
- Participation in national and international science fairs.
- Secondary and high school teacher training activities.
- Distinctions and awards that provide prestige to the project.
- Proposals for research work and practical work in companies for high school students
- Proposals for practical work, final degree and master's thesis in companies for university students.

Authors believe that the presented activity is a successful way to promote research in underwater robotics carried out by VICOROB research group of the University of Girona and, at the same time, encourage engineering studies among secondary school students. Currently, most research projects must be accompanied by appropriate outreach activities, and this activity is a clear example of it. The incidence of this kind of activities in the students decision to carry on with engineering studies has to be deeply analyzed with statistical data. This is one of the most serious aspects we are currently pointing out as our future work, together with improving the design of the workshop, the materials used for construction and the total cost of the activity.

Author Contributions: Conceptualization, A.E.-F. and X.C.; Data curation, A.E.-F. and X.C.; Formal analysis, A.E.-F. and X.C.; Funding acquisition, A.E.-F. and X.C.; Investigation, A.E.-F. and X.C.; Methodology, A.E.-F. and X.C.; Project administration, A.E.-F. and X.C.; Resources, A.E.-F. and X.C.; Software, A.E.-F. and X.C.; Supervision, A.E.-F. and X.C.; Validation, A.E.-F. and X.C.; Visualization, A.E.-F. and X.C.; Writing—original draft, A.E.-F. and X.C.; Writing—review & editing, A.E.-F. and X.C. All authors have read and agreed to the published version of the manuscript.

Funding: This work has been partially funded by the Catalan Government (Generalitat de Catalunya) through ACDC grant number 2012ACDC00129, ACDC grant number 2011ACDC00023, ACDC grant number 2010ACDC00127 and ACDC grant number 2009ACDC00158.

Conflicts of Interest: The authors declare no conflict of interest.

Abbreviations

The following abbreviations are used in this manuscript:

STEM	Science, Technology, Engineering and Math
UdG	University of Girona
VICOROB	Computer Vision and Robotics Group
ROV	Remotely Operated Vehicle
MIT	Massachusetts Institute of Technology
CIRS	Underwater Robotics Research Facility
AUV	Autonomous Underwater Vehicle

References

1. Valero, J.A.; Coca, P. The perception of stem subjects in elementary and secondary students. *Sociol. Techno Sci. Present Future Stem Train. Challenges Defiances* **2021**, *11*, 116–138. Available online: https://revistas.uva.es/index.php/sociotecno/article/view/5144 (accessed on 17 January 2022).
2. National Science Foundation. *Women, Minorities, and Persons with Disabilities in Science and Engineering*; National Science Foundation: Arlington, VA, USA, 2012. Available online: https://ncses.nsf.gov/pubs/nsf21321/downloads (accessed on 17 January 2022).
3. Driver, R.; Guesne, E.; Tiberghien, A. Children's Ideas and the Learning of Science. In *Children's Ideas in Science*; Milton Keynes (Buckinghamshire); Open University Press: Philadelphia, PA, USA, 1985; pp. 1–9. Available online: https://staff.fnwi.uva.nl/e.joling/vakdidactiek/documenten/driver.pdf (accessed on 17 January 2022).
4. Hernandez, M.J.; Muñoz, J.M. Interest in STEM disciplines and teaching methodologies. Perception of secondary school students and preservice teachers. *Educar* **2020**, *56*, 369–386. [CrossRef]
5. Francis, C.; Franz, J.; Leinhart, R.; Kaiser, J.; Towles, J. Work in Progress: Evaluation of Biomechanics Activities at a College-Wide Engineering Outreach Event. In Proceedings of the Annual Conference of the American Society of Engineering Education, New Orleans, LA, USA, 26–29 June 2016. Available online: https://peer.asee.org/work-in-progress-evaluation-of-biomechanics-activities-at-a-college-wide-engineering-outreach-event.pdf (accessed on 18 January 2022).

6. Michaelis, J.; Francis, C.; Acuna, A.; Towles, J. Impact of biomechanics-based activities on individual and situational interests in K-12 students. In Proceedings of the Annual Conference of the American Society for Engineering Education, Columbus, OH, USA, 25–28 June 2017. Available online: https://peer.asee.org/impact-of-biomechanics-based-activities-on-situational-and-individual-interest-among-k-12-students.pdf (accessed on 18 January 2022).
7. Papadakis, S. Evaluating a Teaching Intervention for Teaching STEM and Programming Concepts Through the Creation of a Weather-Forecast App for Smart Mobile Devices. In *Handbook of Research on Tools for Teaching Computational Thinking in P-12 Education*; Kalogiannakis, M., Papadakis, S., Eds.; IGI Global: Hershey, PA, USA, 2020; pp. 31–53. [CrossRef]
8. Cakir, M. Constructivist Approaches to Learning in Science and Their Implications for Science Pedagogy: A Literature Review. *Int. J. Environ. Sci. Educ.* **2002**, *3*, 193–206. Available online: https://files.eric.ed.gov/fulltext/EJ894860.pdf (accessed on 14 January 2022).
9. Alesandrini, K.; Larson, L. Teachers Bridge to Constructivism. *Clear. House J. Educ. Strateg. Issues Ideas* **2002**, *75*, 118–121. [CrossRef]
10. MIT Sea Grant College Program. Available online: https://seagrant.mit.edu/education/ (accessed on 30 November 2021).
11. MATE ROV Competition. Available online: https://materovcompetition.org (accessed on 30 November 2021).
12. Cufi, X.; Villanueva, M.; El-Fakdi, A.; Garcia, R.; Massich, J. Team-based Building of a remotely operated underwater robot as a method to increase interest for engineering among secondary school students. In Proceedings of the 4th International Conference on Education and New Learning Technologies, Barcelona, Spain, 2–4 July 2012; ISBN 978-84-695-3491-5.
13. Villanueva, M.; Cufi, X.; El-Fakdi, A.; Ridao, P.; Garcia, R. Attracting talent to increase interest for engineering among secondary school students. In Proceedings of the IEEE Engineering Education Conference, Learning Environments and Ecosystems in Engineering Education, Amman, Jordan, 4–6 April 2011.
14. El-Fakdi, A.; Cufí, X.; Hurtos, N.; Correa, M. Team-based bulding of a Remotely operated underwater robot, an innovative method of teaching engineering. *J. Intell. Robot. Syst. (Spec. Issue Teach. Robot.)* **2016**, *81*, 51–61. [CrossRef]
15. Stuikys, V.; Burbaite, R. *Smart STEM-Driven Computer Science Education: Theory, Methodology and Robot-Based Practices*; Springer: Berlin/Heidelberg, Germany, 2018.
16. Seaperch. Available online: https://seaperch.org (accessed on 30 November 2021).
17. Bampasidis, G.; Piperidis, D.; Papakonstantinou, V.; Stathopoulos, D.; Troumpetari, C.; Poutos, P. Hydrobots, an Underwater Robotics STEM Project: Introduction of Engineering Design Process in Secondary Education. *Adv. Eng. Educ.* **2021**, *9*, 1–24.
18. OpenROV—The Open Source Underwater Robot. Available online: https://www.kickstarter.com/projects/openrov/openrov-the-open-source-underwater-robot (accessed on 30 November 2021).
19. Cufí, X.; Figueras, A.; Muntaner, E.; Calm, R.; Quevedo, E.; Vega, D.; Loustau, J.; Gil, J.J.; Brito, J.H. EDUROVs: A Low Cost and Sustainable Remotely Operated Vehicles Educational Program. *Sustainability* **2021**, *13*, 8657. [CrossRef]
20. CIRS—Underwater Robotics Research Center. Available online: https://cirs.udg.edu/ (accessed on 30 November 2021).
21. Arduino. Available online: https://www.arduino.cc/ (accessed on 30 November 2021).
22. Appinventor. Available online: https://appinventor.mit.edu/ (accessed on 30 November 2021).
23. Scrath4Arduino. Available online: http://s4a.cat/ (accessed on 30 November 2021).

Article

HYDRA: Introducing a Low-Cost Framework for STEM Education Using Open Tools

Georgios Tsalmpouris [1], George Tsinarakis [2], Nikolaos Gertsakis [3], Savvas A. Chatzichristofis [4] and Lefteris Doitsidis [2,*]

[1] Department of Mechanical Engineering, Hellenic Mediterranean University, 71140 Heraklion, Greece; tsal81@yahoo.com
[2] School of Production Engineering & Management, Technical University of Crete, 73100 Chania, Greece; tsinar@dpem.tuc.gr
[3] Psychology Department, University of Crete, 74150 Rethymno, Greece; gernick2@gmail.com
[4] Intelligent Systems Laboratory, Department of Computer Science, Neapolis University Pafos, Pafos 8042, Cyprus; s.chatzichristofis@nup.ac.cy
* Correspondence: ldoitsidis@dpem.tuc.gr

Abstract: STEM education is of paramount importance, especially in the lower levels of education, and it has been proven beneficial for students in many ways. Although there are various tools available, there are significant drawbacks mainly related to the cost and the ease of use. In this study, we introduce a new low-cost educational framework oriented toward elementary and secondary educational needs. The proposed system exploits open tools and low-cost devices. The system's core is based on the popular Arduino microcontroller, a low-cost device supported by a large community. The overall system was designed and developed, providing an expandable, modular system of low complexity suitable for students with no or low prior knowledge in related subjects, among others, to programming, embedded devices, sensors and actuators, as well as robotics. Our scope was to provide a system with a small learning curve. Practically, this makes it possible in a short amount of time for the students to perform appealing yet straightforward tasks which will boost their self-confidence and creativity, improve their technical skills and simultaneously provide a system with several capabilities usable in different kinds of projects. The introduced system was tested through a preliminary study using flow theory in a team of 68 students of the three last grades in an elementary school in Greece.

Keywords: STEM educational tool; Arduino; Petri Nets

Citation: Tsalmpouris, G.; Tsinarakis, G.; Gertsakis, N.; Chatzichristofis, S.A.; Doitsidis, L. HYDRA: Introducing a Low-Cost Framework for STEM Education Using Open Tools. *Electronics* **2021**, *10*, 3056. https://doi.org/10.3390/electronics10243056

Academic Editor: Carlos J. Bernardos

Received: 25 October 2021
Accepted: 1 December 2021
Published: 8 December 2021

Publisher's Note: MDPI stays neutral with regard to jurisdictional claims in published maps and institutional affiliations.

Copyright: © 2021 by the authors. Licensee MDPI, Basel, Switzerland. This article is an open access article distributed under the terms and conditions of the Creative Commons Attribution (CC BY) license (https://creativecommons.org/licenses/by/4.0/).

1. Introduction

The use of Science, Technology, Engineering and Mathematics (STEM) tools has been proven useful for both teachers and students in many learning contexts. These have been widely used in closely related fields, among others, for programming, automation, and robotics. In [1], the authors introduced conceptual frameworks regarding the practical implementation of STEM education concepts in different countries, while in [2], the authors compared the conceptualization and teaching practices in geographically proximate countries, since no homogeneous standards regarding this issue exist. However, even when students are not interested in STEM-oriented disciplines, they are motivated by them when they are involved as a way of teaching in other fields such as arts and music [3–5]. Reviews of the use of STEM education in early childhood [6] and on the status and trends in STEM education research [7] summarize the majority of the latest publications in this field and discuss a number of issues concerning its increased popularity. Based on the aforementioned publications, STEM tools are considered to be important and innovative and can shape education from kindergarten to university in a variety of fields [8,9].

The core idea behind STEM tools is the constructionism learning theory developed by Papert [10], based on concepts initially introduced in the constructivism theory by Piaget [8,11]. Based on this approach, by manipulating and constructing objects, the students interact with their environment, continually adding new knowledge and building upon existing experiences by adapting previously held ideas to create new information [12].

STEM tools offer hands-on activities that encourage students to become active learners and create an interactive environment where they can investigate and work with complex real-world problems. In this sense, they construct and constantly reconstruct their knowledge and meaning through personal experience as they become active learners [3,8,13,14]. Physical devices can transform the procedure of learning into a fun activity that attracts and keeps students interested in learning, therefore enhancing students' interest and curiosity [9]. Through this procedure, students have the opportunity to improve their critical thinking and problem-solving skills [4,11]. At the same time, many studies report a positive impact on personal development, including collaboration, social and communication skills, cognitive, meta-cognitive, and social responsibilities [4,15]. By developing their self-confidence and self-direction, students increase their creativity, innovation and motivation [4,8,11,16]. Exposure to the use of STEM tools has also been proven useful in assisting students making career choices towards STEM domains and as it was highlighted in [17], a significant, positive, strong correlation between interpersonal skills, STEM exposure, career choice, family and school support, and external motivation exists.

Programming is perceived as an essential skill for everyone to learn with the potential of fostering computational thinking and problem-solving competence. Hence, a variety of different curriculum and different approaches to teaching programming have been proposed [18]. Despite its importance, programming is perceived by students as a difficult task to perform [5,19]. Students in programming courses must familiarize themselves with the fundamental programming concepts while athey must simultaneously learn each programming language's rigid syntax and commands [20]. Learning to program becomes more difficult when learners are not native English speakers, as most programming languages use simple English keywords to represent syntactic and semantic rules. At the same time, students must learn how to solve a problem and transform their solution into a textual representation. Studies also show that the acquisition of programming skills is considered more challenging for female and younger students [14]. In this notion, learners perform a heavy cognitive effort during the programming learning process, leading to decreased motivation and satisfaction. Accordingly, students can adopt a negative attitude towards programming [20].

On these grounds, extensive research has been performed regarding the learning methods and how the educational environment can be transformed when STEM tools, i.e., educational robots, are used as a tool [21,22]. In a programming context, robots as tangible devices can provide a physical environment where students can manipulate physical objects to solve problems through innovative play. With the use of sensors and actuators, robots allow learners to explore and interact with the real world's complex problems while programming. They have the opportunity to constantly design and test their ideas while they receive immediate feedback on their solutions. Through experimentation, students improve their motivation and interest, which leads to easier knowledge acquisition and retention. When they reflect on and correlate problem solving strategies with authentic contexts, students are equipped with the confidence to successfully solve problems in real situations [5,20,21]. Additionally, tangible robots assist the student in solely concentrating on solving a problem and finding the algorithmic solution of a given exercise instead of dealing with each programming language's features. Thus, students perceive programming as a fun and challenging activity instead of a painful procedure [23]. Because of its simplicity, the robot as a means of teaching enables students of different ages, intellectual backgrounds, or with learning disorders to access learning [24–26].

Another aspect of educational robots that can affect the quality and effectiveness of learning is the game factor. Many researchers have noted different game features such as challenge, fantasy, complexity, rules, strategy, and goals can make a game an engaging educational tool [14,21,27]. By using game activities in the learning process, a student's motivation and interest are increased as they are actively involved in an entertaining procedure [21]. At the same time, game activities introduce competition and cooperation, factors that encourage learners to immerse themselves in learning. Given a specific challenge, students tend to discover solutions and new strategies in order to increase their performance and win [14]. Furthermore, games are fun, turning programming tasks perceived by learners into a source of enjoyment. Essentially, users' attention is exclusively devoted to the programming and acquisition or improvement of their algorithmic skills [11,14,20]. However, for a game activity to be effective in education, certain features must be attained. The game cycle is the key component, consisting of the loop triplet judgment–behavior–feedback triggered by specific game features such as the degree of guidance and difficulty. Consequently, integrating the playful aspect of robotics in learning must be done with caution [27].

The application of a tangible user interface has been widely studied with different robotics kits in many different group ages [5]. Several tangible programming projects have a seam to influence the development of tangible programming. AlgoBlockwas one of the first tangible programming tools developed by Suzuki and Kato in which they introduced interlocking blocks representing the commands of a language similar to Logo [18,20].

Tangible programming Brick developed by McNerney added the use of parameters and variables. More precisely, this tangible programming interface used Lego bricks with embedded electronics to program, through the combination of bricks in the correct order, the graphical user interface of Logo Block and Lego Mindstorms [5,20,22].

Lego Mindstorms is a programming and engineering-oriented system consisting of graphical software and handy hardware. The Lego kit includes a control unit in the form of a brick that controls the system, a set of motors, modular sensors (e.g., touch sensors and ultrasonic sensors), and parts from the technic line such as gears and Lego bricks based on the traditional Lego design for the building part. It also includes a graphical programming language where students can manipulate the available picturized commands and connect them just like puzzle pieces to create a program. Learners can build the instructed models included in the kit by following building instructions or experimenting with customizing their robots with different sensors, motor placement, and gearing [13].

More programming concepts were added with systems such as FlowBlock, that enabled students to see the changes in variables based on the movement of lights on a series of arrows-blocks and comprehend the structure of the sequence, repetition, and branch with the use of probes, by counting the times the light passes [14]. Other studies followed, proposing innovating platforms such as TurTan by Gallardo where instructions appear as figures, the Electronic Blocks by Wyeth, which allowed students to build and program robots and mechanisms with blocks and Quetzal–Tern by Horn, which could identify the connected commands with the use of a scanning system [18,20,28,29].

Acknowledging that tangible interfaces enhance learning experiences and increase students' algorithmic/programming thinking skills, a lot of robotics kits were developed to assist students in learning [5]. The most common educational robotic kits used today for teaching programming to younger students are Lego Education (including Mindstorms and Wedo), Engino Robotics, Bee-Bot, and Arduino-based kits. Most of the proposed systems convert written programming to graphical, and others support palpable code over using a computer keyboard, or mouse [30,31]. Even though this is suitable for young novice programmers, students seek more from a tangible programming interface after learning basic programming or reaching a certain age.

Summary of Contribution

Motivated by the wide adoption of STEM approaches in elementary and secondary education and the limited availability of open low-cost tools, we introduce a new educational framework oriented towards the needs mentioned above. The proposed system is based on a two-fold approach. On the one hand, we have the hardware and software based on the popular Arduino microcontroller, a low-cost device supported by a large community, and Ardublockly, a visual programming editor for Arduino. On the other hand, the second part refers to the model of the education procedure using Petri Nets, a typical discrete event-based modeling and simulation method. This enables their use in any STEM-related activity concerning the interacting entities and state-changing events. This, combined with the open nature of hardware and software, can accommodate different kinds of STEM activities. To the best of our knowledge, this is the first formal approach, which combines the tools mentioned above towards developing a working STEM system for elementary and secondary education students.

The overall system is designed and developed to provide an expandable, modular system of low complexity suitable for students with no or low prior knowledge in related subjects, among others, to programming, embedded devices, sensors and actuator, robotics, etc. Furthermore, our scope is to provide a system with a small learning curve. Therefore, the students would be able to perform appealing yet straightforward tasks in a short time period, which will boost their self-confidence and creativity. Simultaneously, it would provide a system with several features that may be adopted in different projects. Furthermore, we decided not to constrain our approach with a robotic device as the majority of the methods in the literature but instead focus on an open architecture that will allow the students to compose their working prototypes/systems.

The rest of the paper is organized as follows. In Section 2, we describe our proposed system in full detail, starting from the overall motivation, the hardware which was developed, and the related software which was adopted and enhanced to accommodate our needs. In Section 3, we present the modeling of the educational process, which was performed using the Petri Nets theory, for the monitoring and observation of the educational procedure. The proposed model ensures the consistency of the followed procedure for all groups of students and that the training process is teacher independent. It also provides a valuable tool to the teacher to detect and solve possible problems during the education process. In Section 4, we describe in detail the procedure followed to preliminary validate our approach using flow theory in an elementary school in Greece. Our main goal was to identify the students' acceptance of the proposed system and how the system managed to put the students in a "flow state". To achieve the goal mentioned above, we accompanied the proposed system with a series of sample courses, with an open-ended structure based on the principles of problem-based learning. Finally, in Section 5, we offer some concluding remarks and some thoughts for future research.

2. The Proposed System

2.1. Motivation

The proposed system was designed, with some key characteristics in mind essential for its proper adaptation from the target group, which consists of 9–15-year-old students. The overall approach is presented in Figure 1. Our design philosophy, was based on an effort to increase access to STEM education, a necessity which was identified in [32], by using low cost, user friendly, modular devices. At the same, the educational goals, align with the approach presented in [33] and the learning outcomes as they were identified in educational robotics, which are applicable to other STEM-related activities [23].

During the design and development phase, it was identified that the user-friendliness of the proposed system was of paramount importance. Creating even simple circuits using the conventional approach requires significant effort and understanding from the students and skills that they may lack, especially during the introductory phase with the equipment at hand. The proposed system minimizes the complexity since the student is required to make simple connections.

Crucial factors for the success of the proposed system were its expandability and modularity since these are the key elements that affect the functionality and adaptability in different educational scenarios. Another key issue was the hardware and software complexity of the proposed system since it has been shown that high levels of complexity create frustration and a lack of focus for the students.

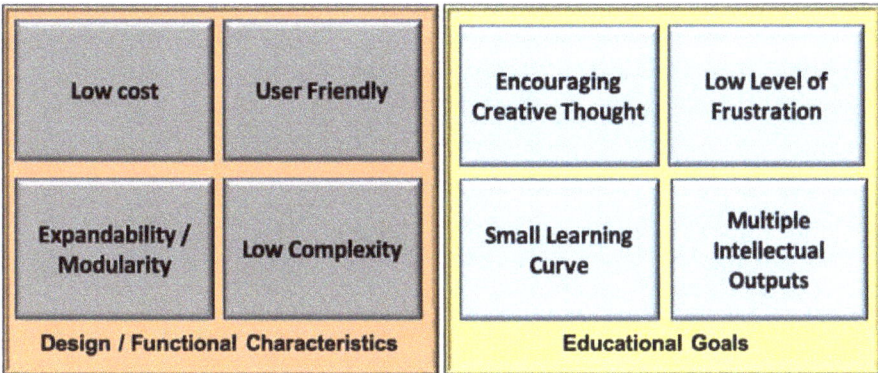

Figure 1. Design philosophy.

The aforementioned design and functional characteristics were considered to meet a diverse set of educational goals. The main one was the encouragement of creative thinking through the simultaneous development of software and the interaction with the environment through different sensors and actuators. In addition, the overall design considered the minimization of the learning curve since the educator has limited time in the classroom to demonstrate the proposed system's functionality and highlight the educational goals of the lecture. By keeping the learning curve small, the student has more time to actually focus on the actual content of the course.

We decided to adopt open tools both for hardware and software during the design process and the maximization of the impact of the proposed system and the minimization of the cost. The core of the hardware system was based on the Arduino family of microcontrollers, which is an extremely popular solution for different kinds of educational projects and the microcontroller of choice is the Arduino Mega 2560. The proposed system's software was based on the popular platform Blockly, which was developed by Google [34], and Ardublockly [35] which is a visual programming editor for Arduino.

2.2. Hardware

Hydra's core module is based on the popular Arduino Mega 2560, which was chosen based on its excellent cost-to-capabilities ratio. It currently consists of eight blocks as presented in Figure 2.

These are divided into four output modules (highlighted with purple): (a) a four LED module; (b) a seven-segment display; (c) a red, green, and blue (RGB) LED; and (d) a DC motor, three input modules (highlighted with cyan): (a) a potentiometer, (b) sonar sensor, and (c) a four-button interaction module and the main control board (highlighted in yellow). All the modules were designed using the Autodesk Eagle PCB.

The Arduino Mega 2560 was adapted to the main control board through proper connectors. All the external modules were connected to the mainboard using RJ45 connectors, which were properly aligned around the mainboard. The usage of the RJ45 connection assures that all the external modules can be connected in a unique way to the mainboard, therefore minimizing the potential errors that the user might make. Overall, the mainboard consists of a USB type-B port (mainly for powering the motors) and nine RJ45 connections grouped in three categories: (a) digital, (b) analog, and (c) PWM, as presented in the schematic in Figure 3.

Figure 2. The complete set of Hydra modules.

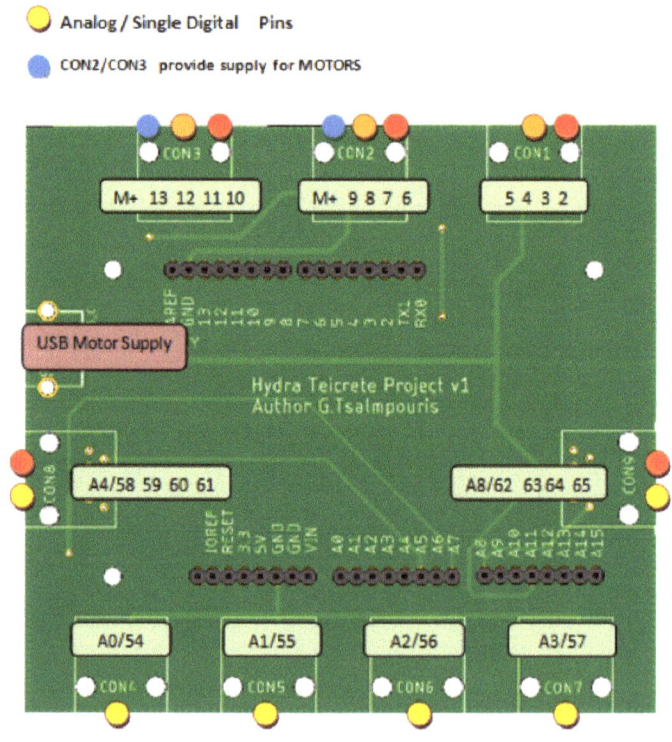

Figure 3. Main board schematic of Hydra.

The digital ports can have two different values: HIGH, which corresponds to 5 V; and LOW, which corresponds to 0 V and can be used as input or output ports, while the analog ports can only be used as input ports for the analog input ranging from 0 to 5 V which corresponds to values ranging from 0 to 1023. Finally, the PWMs can be used as outputs to create rectangular voltage pulses with a variable duty cycle which can control the rotation speed of a motor in the respective module or control the brightness of the LEDs.

The overall approach is modular and allows the students to effortlessly make all the necessary connections without focusing on the time-consuming and sometimes frustrating procedure—especially for non-experienced users—of creating a working circuit. An example of how the proposed system differs from the conventional approach is presented in Figure 4.

(a)   (b)

Figure 4. Comparison between (**a**) the traditional approach and (**b**) the Hydra approach.

As we mentioned earlier, our goal was to provide an affordable platform compared to commercial solutions. In Table 1, the detailed bill of materials used per set is presented, and in this cost, we have to add the cost of printing the PCBs in an external vendor. The overall cost is approximately EUR 35 per set without including an external power supply since most of the commercial USB chargers can be used.

Table 1. Bill of materials (per Hydra set).

Type of Electronic Part	Quantity	Cost (EUR)
Arduino Mega 2560	1	8
PCB RJ45 Connectors	17	4
Male 8pin header 2.54 mm	5	0.5
Red led 5 mm	4	0.1
Tact switch 12 × 12 × 7.3 mm	4	0.2
Linear potentiometer 5–10 kΩ	1	1.5

Table 1. Cont.

Type of Electronic Part	Quantity	Cost (EUR)
7-segment display CK	1	0.5
Sonar sensor HC-SR04	1	2
Motor shield MX1508	1	1
Dual axis Geared DC Motor 5 V	1	1.5
RGB led 10 mm CK	1	0.2
Resistors and transistors	21	0.5
USB type b pcb connector 90 degree	1	0.2
USB cable type b	1	2

2.3. Software

The software of the Hydra platform is an enhanced and modified version of Ardublockly [35], which is a visual programming editor for Arduino based on Google's Blockly, which has been properly modified to generate Arduino code. The main features of Ardublockly, therefore, inherited by Hydra, is that it can generate an Arduino code with visual drag-and-drop blocks, which it can load to an Arduino Board, and it produces useful code block warnings whilst being compatible with a wide range of official Arduino boards. Another key advantage is that the students can access to the Arduino IDE. Therefore, the code as used by the micro-controller is accessible.

Hydra builds upon the original version and provides support for all the hardware modules, which were described in detail in Section 2.2. In order to optimally address the needs of the targeted audience, the main menu of the Ardublockly environment was modified in a minimal manner, and an extra tab for the Hydra modules was added. For every single hardware module, there is a corresponding software module which can access every function. Apart from the single software module for the cases in which there are more than one controllable element in a hardware module, simplified versions that can access single elements were also developed, i.e., the LED case where there is a module responsible for controlling the whole hardware module and a software module responsible for controlling a single LED, as presented in Figure 5.

Figure 5. Ardublockly software modules for 4 LED boards.

A sample Ardublockly program for controlling the rotation direction of a DC motor using two buttons is presented in Figure 6. The Hydra DC motor module and the four-button interaction module were used in the configuration presented in Figure 7.

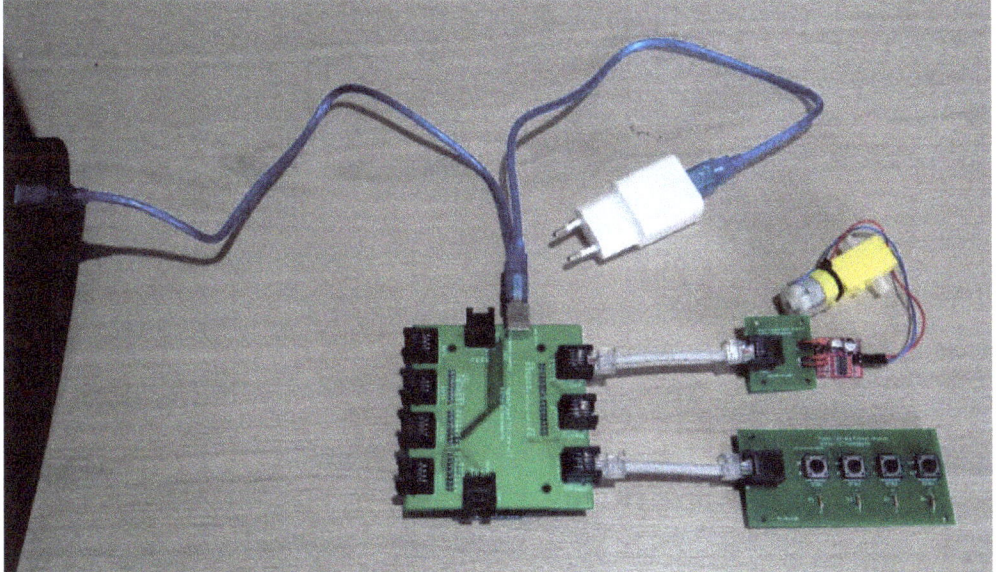

Figure 6. Sample Hydra configuration for DC motor control.

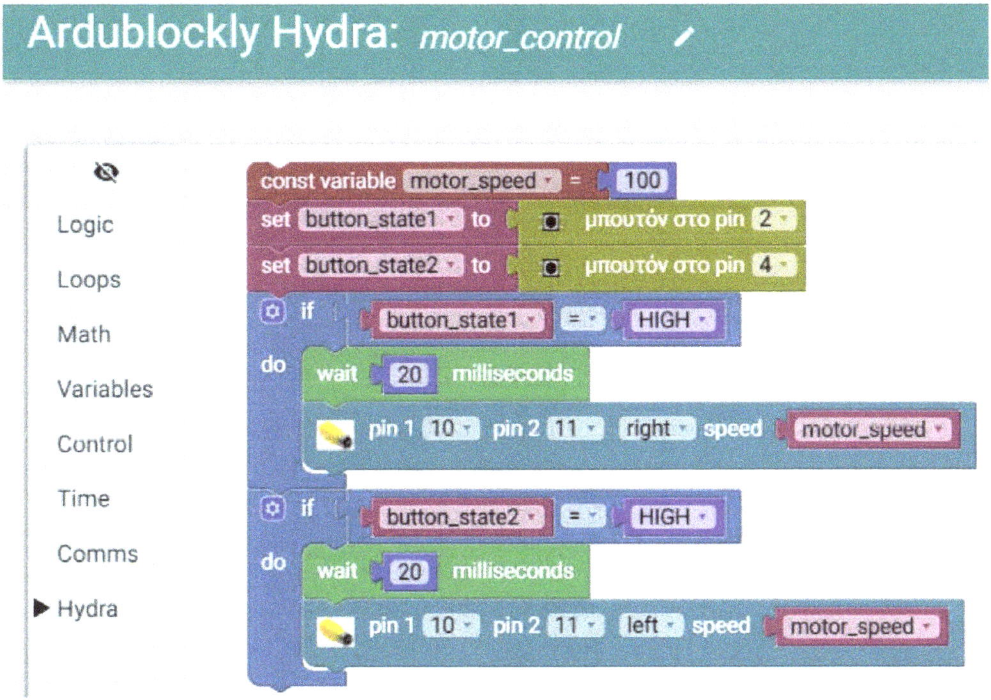

Figure 7. Sample Ardublockly program for controlling Hydra DC motor module.

3. Modeling of the Educational Procedure

Petri Nets (PNs) are a popular mathematical and graphical tool widely used for the modeling, analysis, synthesis, performance evaluation, simulation, and control of processes and systems typically considered as discrete events. They allow the representation and study of the structure as well as of the dynamic behavior of systems and processes and have been proven to be a powerful tool for studying system concurrency, sequential, parallel, asynchronous, distributed deterministic or stochastic behavior, resource allocation, mutual exclusion, and conflicts [36–38]. Popular fields of Petri Nets use include production and manufacturing systems, project management, computer networks, software development and engineering, traffic monitoring and control, power systems, and robotic tasks. However, apart from the typical engineering applications, Petri Nets have been used for studying chemical and biochemical processes, medical and healthcare tasks, and cognitive, educational, and learning procedures.

In [39], the authors used Petri Nets to model the beginning of one lecture and the alternative routes, containing different types of source materials, that a university student could follow to successfully finish the final test of this lecture. In [40], Fuzzy Petri Nets are used to create a concrete model for the adaptation of web-based teaching processes to the individual users of different profiles. In contrast, in [41], the authors introduced a Petri Net-based methodology used to verify the intelligent tutoring system for the English language in Taiwan.

In [42], the authors used Petri Nets to create a model of student behavior in an LMS e-course. In particular, using the available Moodle's log files, the authors were able to see the parts of the course that the students visited, the route that they followed through the different individual parts of the course (Learning part), the parts that were ignored or repeated and the time that they spent in each part. The results from this procedure were used to modify the e-course in order to become more efficient and to compare the actual students' behavior with the respective behavior considered during course design. In [43], the authors introduced a learning evaluation model which applies a high-level fuzzy Petri net (HLFPN) and infers via a fuzzy reasoning method the different answering performances generated by different students' abilities corresponding to the test items with different degrees of difficulty. The results of the test were used to evaluate the overall performance of students not only by considering scores but also by comparing the students' performance. From this study, significant conclusions concerning students' performance as well as indicators for the teachers for the students that need more concern and more efficient guidance were extracted. In [44], the authors introduced a Petri Net-based intelligent tutoring system, used for teaching English courses. The proposed system consists of different parts for teachers and students that can communicate and interact. From all the previous works, it is obvious that Petri nets comprise a valuable tool for a number of applications in education.

In this paper, Petri Nets were used for the monitoring and observation of the educational procedure described. In particular, the implemented model ensures the consistency of the followed procedure for all the groups of students as well as that the training process is teacher independent. Furthermore, monitoring the educational process ensures that the trainer can detect and solve the possible problems such as the timing of the process due to constraints of the overall educational process following the necessary actions.

3.1. Petri Net Fundamentals

Ordinary Petri Nets (OPNs) are bipartite directed graphs formally defined as five-tuple: $PN = \{P, T, I, O, m_0\}$. The respective sets for the two types of nodes are $P = \{p_1, p_2, \ldots, p_{np}\}$ which is a finite set of places and $T = \{t_1, t_2, \ldots, t_{nt}\}$ which is a finite set of transitions. $P \cup T = V$ where V is the set of vertices and $P \cap T = \emptyset$.

In Petri Nets, places describe conditions (e.g., for control purposes) or resource availability. Transitions represent events or actions and arcs (that may have weight equal or greater than one), direct connections, access rights, or logical connections between places and transitions. Thus, places are the passive element of the PN, while transitions are the active one. I represents the input function, the output function by O and m_0 is the PN initial token distribution referred to in the literature as marking. Transitions become enabled when all their input places contain several tokens at least equal to the weight of the arc connecting place to transition and fire by removing tokens equal to these weights from all the input places and adding tokens to all the output to the transition places according to the respective arc weights. PN properties (reachability, coverability, safeness, k-boundedness, conflicts, liveness, reversibility, persistency, deadlock-freeness, P- and T-invariants) capture the precedence relations and structural interactions between system components. More analytically, PN theory was described in [36,45].

The inclusion of time delays (constant, following distribution, or random according to the actions) in the transitions of the initial formalism implements T-timed PNs (TPNs). TPNs are defined as $\{P, T, I, O, m_0, D\}$ with the first five variables responding exactly to the same features as in the case of OPNs and D representing time delay that is a function of the set of non-negative real numbers $\{0, \mathbb{R}+\}$. TPNs have advanced use compared to OPNs as, except for modeling purposes, they can be used for the simulation and calculation of the time duration of sequences of events.

The use of arc extensions increases the modeling power of the initial model as this makes possible the representation of more sophisticated concepts implemented with more compact net structures. Arc extensions were used to activate or deactivate the executions of parts of the PN as long as certain conditions are active. In the literature, three types of arcs are usually used, the standard arcs ($\rightarrow$), inhibitor arcs that are represented by arcs whose end is marked with a small circle (-O), and activator arcs that are drawn as dashed vectors [44].

3.2. Application of Petri Nets for Modeling of the Educational Procedure under Study

The main steps of the followed educational procedure include the introduction of the students to the basic concepts of the Hydra by the teacher, and them interacting with the different hardware modules and the programming environment. The students were then divided into groups, and the teacher assigned different roles, namely "programmer", "electronic", and "manager/secretary". The manager/secretary coordinates the efforts of the team based on the educational material which is available and takes appropriate notes during the experimentation; the electronic interacts with the hardware; and the programmer develops the code modules based on the feedback from the team members and the material that accompanies the different modules. The educational material which is distributed to the students is briefly and concisely written, highlighting the key concepts by simultaneously giving several degrees of freedom to the students to experiment and develop their own working paradigms using the available devices. The goal of each session is that the students will develop small projects of their own using the material at hand. First, the students briefly describe the small projects to the teachers, and afterward, they implement them using the Hydra modules.

Based on the aforementioned concept, we modeled the educational procedure that the student will follow, as presented in Figure 8, using PN models. The overall Petri Net model consists of 15 places and 12 transitions, is conflict-free, and live. Its execution is mainly sequential, with the exception of t_5 that models parallelism and t_6 that models concurrency. The exact meaning of the places in the PN model was presented in Table 2, while the transitions of the model are presented in Table 3.

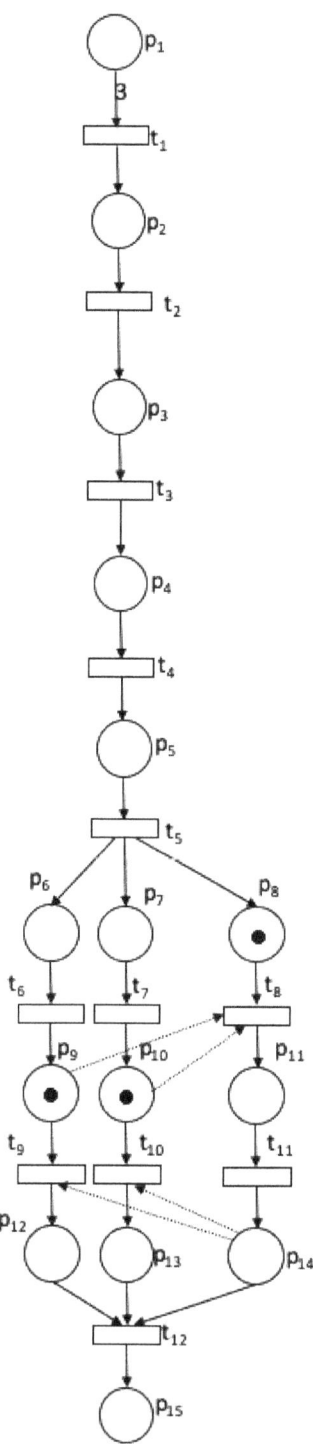

Figure 8. PN model of the educational procedure.

Table 2. Places of the Petri Net model.

Place	Meaning
p_1	Available students
p_2	Team of three students has been created
p_3	Completed predefined laboratory examples
p_4	Team has no more questions
p_5	Open-ended project is defined
p_6	Programmer
p_7	Electronic
p_8	Secretary
p_9	Finished coding
p_{10}	Connections have been implemented
p_{11}	Code and connections are checked
p_{12}	Coding has been approved by secretary
p_{13}	Connections have been approved by secretary
p_{14}	Secretary has finished their tasks
p_{15}	Finished educational procedure

Table 3. Transitions of the Petri Net model.

Transition	Meaning
t_1	Initiation of the educational procedure for the team
t_2	Design of laboratory sheets
t_3	Answer of questions and explanations
t_4	Definition of open ended project
t_5	Role assignment
t_6	Code writing (or coding)
t_7	Implementation of connections
t_8	Secretary checks code and connections
t_9	Coding has been terminated
t_{10}	Connections have been finalized
t_{11}	Approval of code and connections
t_{12}	Measurement recording and operation validation

In the Petri Net model of Figure 8, all the connection arcs have unitary weight apart from the initial ones (from p_1 to t_1). This happens because the educational procedure cannot start if three students are unavailable, as each of these will take a specific role in the following steps. In addition, after the firing of t_5 (role assignment), each of the three students has to do their own tasks which are independent, especially for electronic and programmer, while the secretary interacts with both in a manner. For the electronic and programmer, these tasks are independent in their first stage while the secretary interacts with both in the second stage, giving their final approval. For this reason, in this part of the PN, test arcs were added. In particular, the two test arcs from p_9 and p_{10} to t_8 show that when the programmer and electronic finish their tasks, the secretary will check them and two test arcs from p_{14} to t_9 and

t_{10} to show that when the secretary approves code and connection, the respective tasks can be completed. However, the whole process cannot be terminated unless all three students have finished their tasks. In addition, tokens were added in places p_8, p_9 and p_{10} to show a state of the modeled system. In this state, the programmer finished coding, the electronic finished the connections, and the secretary will start the checking and approval procedure. Since all preconditions are satisfied, t_8 will launch the next step of PN execution.

The presented Petri net model can be used in its present form for the educational process monitoring and observation from the trainer. The simplicity of representation makes it easy to understand even for trainers with reduced technical skills. In addition, it can be used to ensure that different trainers follow exactly the same steps defined during educational process design. Finally, the implemented model can be used for a what-if scenario simulation to distribute the available time between the different stages in the most efficient way with respect to the performance indicators used for assessment.

The advanced capabilities arising from the extensive use of sensors nowadays, as well as the implementation of technologies closely related to the Internet of Things and Industry 4.0, such as digital twins, cyber-physical systems, machine learning, and analytics, increase the significance, the fields of possible application as well as the efficiency of the implemented models. Furthermore, the exploitation of these advances and tools will improve the real-time monitoring, execution, evaluation, design, and update of the educational procedure concerning the feedback received from the students. Thus, the final target is the optimization of the learning procedure and the personal development of the students through an always up-to-date, interactive, and non-static educational procedure.

4. Proof of Concept and Experimental Evaluation

Informatics, robotics, automation, and other STEM-related courses are relatively new in the curriculum of secondary education in Greece and are only integrated at an elementary level in primary education. A detailed study about the courses currently offered and their content can be found in [46]. The tools that are used vary from Lego devices to popular Arduino kits. We decided to perform a preliminary pilot study in primary education to identify the feasibility of our proposed approach. The assessment was based on the basic principles of flow theory that will be described in the following subsection. The main goal was to identify the students' acceptance of the proposed system and how this system managed to put the students in a "flow state". To proceed, we developed a series of sample courses with an open-ended structure based on the principles of problem-based learning [47].

4.1. Flow Theory

Flow experience (flow) is defined as the state in which an individual feels completely absorbed and fully engaged in an activity [48]. Flow is a concept initially introduced by Csikszentmihalyi [49] in their book 'Beyond Boredom and Anxiety'. Flow experience is an extremely rewarding experience, balancing challenge and skill. Flow is often associated with high levels of performance and is a positive psychological experience [50]. It allows the individual to perform at an optimum level. Flow has been used and researched in various fields of everyday life, including but not limited to sports, work-related environments, creative arts, media, and related educational activities where the high state of performance could be beneficial. Flow occurs when one is totally involved in the task at hand. It can occur at different levels of complexity, however, by definition, flow is intrinsically rewarding, regardless of whether it involves a simple game of throw and catch or a complicated and dangerous gymnastics routine [50]. When in flow, one feels strong and positive, not worried about themselves or of failure. To be found in such a psychological state, they must meet two factors which play the most important role: (a) their perception of the difficulty of the challenges they have to face; and (b) their perception of their own skill and ability to deal with this challenge [51].

There are nine key factors that contribute to the appearance of flow which are described in detail in [50,52]. Namely, these nine factors are: (1) challenge–skill balance; (2) action–

awareness merging; (3) clear goals; (4) unambiguous feedback; (5) total concentration on the task at hand; (6) sense of control; (7) loss of self-consciousness; (8) transformation of time; and (9) autotelic experience. All the factors mentioned above contribute to the optimal psychological state of flow.

4.2. Pilot Study

For the pilot study of the proposed approach, we distributed the system to 68 students with their ages ranging from 9 to 12 years old (21 students of the 4th, 26 students of the 5th and 21 students of the 6th grade of the Greek Elementary school). The participants were a mixed group consisting of 35 boys (51.5%) and 33 girls (48.5%). All the students from the three classes participated in the pilot study without considering any prior experience in similar tools or programming. The experiments were conducted inside their school premises, and more specifically, in the school's computer room. Each session with the proposed system lasted approximately 45 min, and at each session, nine students, using one full system per three persons, participated.

The students during their experimentation were monitored by a teacher who was familiar with the system and the related processes. They were initially introduced to the basic concepts of Hydra by the teacher, and afterward, they followed the procedure as described in Section 3.2. The students were only allowed to interact with their team members, while the teacher had minimum intervention, encouraging the students to provide their solutions to any problems that they may have.

Upon the completion of the process, as described in Section 3.2, they answered an anonymous questionnaire consisting of a set of closed-type questions, divided into two main categories. The first category had seven questions concerning the system and its functionality, and the second category had ten questions related to the key factors of flow theory. The structure of the questionnaire and the related questions/statements regarding flow experience were similar to the ones presented in [53]. All the answers were based on a seven values scale where one corresponds to easy/low while seven corresponds to high/hard.

As far as the first category of questions is concerned, the key findings show that 92.6% of students found the overall procedure easy and only 7.4% found it to be of medium difficulty (Figure 9).

None of the students expressed the opinion that the proposed system was difficult to use. The students were self-confident with regard to their skills in the related activity since 89.7% declared that they were highly confident in their skills while only 10.3% perceived that they had medium skills. On the other hand, 69.1% answered that they did not have any previous experience related to programming or automation-related projects, and only 30.9% declared that they had some previous experience with the activities mentioned above. It is worth mentioning that 69.1% stated that they did not have any previous experience with similar systems, highlighting how easy it is to adopt the proposed approach if we consider the answers to the previous question too. Furthermore, the students' opinion was in favor of "Hydra" per se, since they found that: (a) the course demands were medium (79.4%) or low (20.6%); (b) that the software was easy to use (70.6%); and (c) that the hardware was very handy (88.2%).

Flow experience was measured using the flow short scale which measures all components of flow experience with ten items and was used to measure the flow during all activities [53]. The statistical analysis was performed using the SPSS statistical package. The internal consistency for the flow score was $\alpha = 0.92$.

The mean of the answers in the ten questions was combined in a new variable named FLOW. The flow experience reported by the students which participated in the aforementioned study ($t = 19.24$) statistically differed from the average of the scale ($MD = 2.32$, $df = 67$, $p < 0.001$). The high average of the flow experience indicates that the proposed system is appealing in all cases of students independently from factors including sex and age (Figure 10).

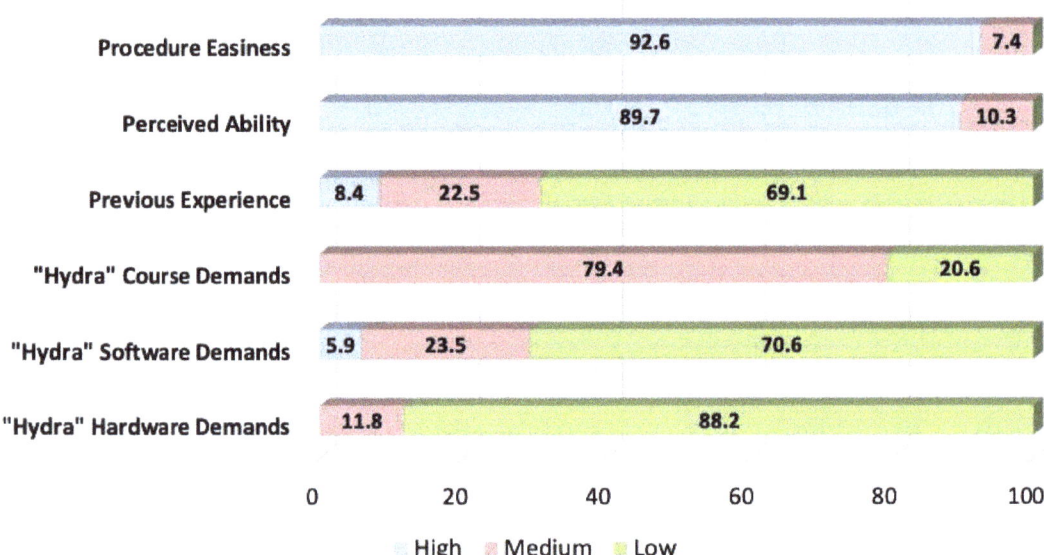

Figure 9. Evaluation findings based on the first set of questions.

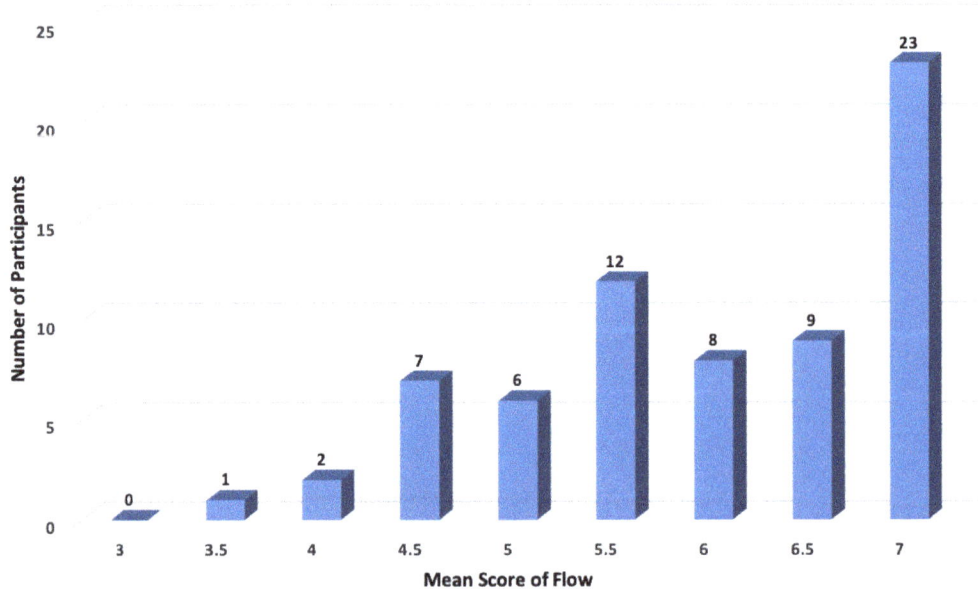

Figure 10. Flow experience distribution.

5. Conclusions

In the proposed manuscript, we present a new low-cost framework for STEM education based on open tools. We present in detail the hardware and software developed in addition to the modeling of the overall educational process using Petri nets. As a proof of concept, we present a preliminary evaluation based on the testing of the proposed system by 68 students of three different grades of a Greek elementary school, using flow theory. The overall adoption rate of the proposed system was high among the participants, highlighting the approach's potential. Although our experiments were conducted using a small sample of students, the reported results are promising. Further research is required to detect the significant effects, confirm our intuitions, and further generalize the findings. In future work, the proposed framework will be tested on a larger sample of participants.

We are currently working on the second prototype of the HYDRA system, which will include a new design aiming to increase the robustness of the system and increase its capabilities by adding new modules. Furthermore, we are developing new structural components which will enclose the electronic components, to allow the users to create complex working prototypes. We also aim to develop an augmented reality application, which will work in tandem with the proposed system. This will significantly enhance the education process by providing an appealing visual tool that will guide the education process using the concept described in detail in Section 3.2. At the same time, it will provide the students with a visual guide that will be accessible using an intuitive interface.

Our vision is to offer the solutions mentioned above through a web-based system, accompanied by the related educational material and detailed electronic and 3D drawings. Thus, the users—both students and teachers—will have the opportunity to interact and simultaneously participate by uploading their material in the aim of a sustainable, low-cost approach to education.

Author Contributions: Conceptualization, G.T. (Georgios Tsalmpouris) and L.D.; investigation, G.T. (Georgios Tsalmpouris), S.A.C. and L.D.; methodology, G.T. (Georgios Tsalmpouris), G.T. (Georgios Tsinarakis), N.G. and L.D.; software, G.T. (Georgios Tsalmpouris); supervision, L.D.; validation, G.T. (Georgios Tsalmpouris) and N.G.; writing—original draft, L.D.; writing—review and editing, G.T. (Georgios Tsinarakis), N.G., S.A.C. and L.D. All authors have read and agreed to the published version of the manuscript.

Funding: This research received no external funding.

Data Availability Statement: Publicly not available nor exploitable by other researchers so as to be shared.

Conflicts of Interest: The authors declare no conflict of interest.

References

1. Hasani, A.L.; Juansah, D.; El Islami, R. Conceptual Frameworks on How to Teach STEM Concepts in Bahasa Indonesia Subject as Integrated Learning in Grades 1–3 at Elementary School in the Curriculum 2013 to Contribute to Sustainability Education. *Sustainability* **2021**, *13*, 173. [CrossRef]
2. Tawbush, R.L.; Stanley, S.D.; Campbell, T.G.; Webb, M.A. International comparison of K-12 STEM teaching practices. *Int. J. STEM Educ.* **2020**, *13*, 115–128. [CrossRef]
3. Benitti, F.B.V. Exploring the educational potential of robotics in schools: A systematic review. *Comput. Educ.* **2012**, *58*, 978–988. [CrossRef]
4. De Vries, M.J. *Handbook of Technology Education*; Springer: Berlin/Heidelberg, Germany, 2018.
5. Kwon, D.Y.; Kim, H.S.; Shim, J.K.; Lee, W.G. Algorithmic bricks: A tangible robot programming tool for elementary school students. *IEEE Trans. Educ.* **2012**, *55*, 474–479. [CrossRef]
6. Han, Z.H.; Jiang, Y.; Zhan, Y. STEM Education in Early Childhood: A Review of Empirical Studies. *Int. J. STEM Educ.* **2020**, *32*, 940–962.
7. Li, Y.; Wang, K.; Xiao, Y.; Froyd, E.J. Research and trends in STEM education: A systematic review of journal publications. *Int. J. STEM Educ.* **2020**, *7*. [CrossRef]
8. Alimisis, D. Educational robotics: Open questions and new challenges. *Themes Sci. Technol. Educ.* **2013**, *6*, 63–71.
9. Eguchi, A.; Shen, J. Student learning experience through CoSpace educational robotics. In *Society for Information Technology & Teacher Education International Conference*; Association for the Advancement of Computing in Education (AACE): Waynesville, NC, USA, 2012; pp. 19–24.
10. Papert, S.; Harel, I. *Constructionism*; Ablex Publishing Corporation: New York, NY, USA, 1991.
11. Atmatzidou, S.; Demetriadis, S.; Nika, P. How Does the Degree of Guidance Support Students' Metacognitive and Problem Solving Skills in Educational Robotics? *J. Sci. Educ. Technol.* **2018**, *27*, 70–85. [CrossRef]
12. Papert, S. *Mindstorms: Children, Computers, and Powerful Ideas*; Basic Books, Inc.: New York, NY, USA, 1980.

13. Miglino, O.; Lund, H.H.; Cardaci, M. Robotics as an educational tool. *J. Interact. Learn. Res.* **1999**, *10*, 25–47.
14. Shim, J.; Kwon, D.; Lee, W. The effects of a robot game environment on computer programming education for elementary school students. *IEEE Trans. Educ.* **2016**, *60*, 164–172. [CrossRef]
15. Chin, K.Y.; Hong, Z.W.; Chen, Y.L. Impact of using an educational robot-based learning system on students' motivation in elementary education. *IEEE Trans. Learn. Technol.* **2014**, *7*, 333–345. [CrossRef]
16. Tuomi, P.; Multisilta, J.; Saarikoski, P.; Suominen, J. Coding skills as a success factor for a society. *Educ. Inf. Technol.* **2018**, *23*, 419–434. [CrossRef]
17. Yoel, S.R.; Dori, Y.J. FIRST High-School Students and FIRST Graduates: STEM Exposure and Career Choices. *IEEE Trans. Educ.* **2021**, 1–10. [CrossRef]
18. Caceres, P.C.; Venero, R.P.; Cordova, F.C. Tangible programming mechatronic interface for basic induction in programming. In Proceedings of the 2018 IEEE Global Engineering Education Conference (EDUCON), Santa Cruz de Tenerife, Spain, 17–20 April 2018; pp. 183–190.
19. Ali, A.; Mensch, S. Issues and challenges for selecting a programming language in a technology update course. In Proceedings of the Information Systems Education Conference, Phoenix, AZ, USA, 2008. Available online: https://www.researchgate.net/publication/228651088_Issues_and_challenges_for_selecting_a_programming_language_in_a_technology_update_course (accessed on 25 September 2021).
20. Sapounidis, T.; Demetriadis, S.; Stamelos, I. Evaluating children performance with graphical and tangible robot programming tools. *Pers. Ubiquitous Comput.* **2015**, *19*, 225–237. [CrossRef]
21. Bers, M.U.; Flannery, L.; Kazakoff, E.R.; Sullivan, A. Computational thinking and tinkering: Exploration of an early childhood robotics curriculum. *Comput. Educ.* **2014**, *72*, 145–157. [CrossRef]
22. McGill, M.M. Learning to program with personal robots: Influences on student motivation. *ACM Trans. Comput. Educ. (TOCE)* **2012**, *12*, 4. [CrossRef]
23. Evripidou, S.; Georgiou, K.; Doitsidis, L.; Amanatiadis, A.A.; Zinonos, Z.; Chatzichristofis, S.A. Educational Robotics: Platforms, Competitions and Expected Learning Outcomes. *IEEE Access* **2020**, *8*, 219534–219562. [CrossRef]
24. Kaburlasos, V.G.; Dardani, C.; Dimitrova, M.; Amanatiadis, A. Multi-robot engagement in special education: A preliminary study in autism. In Proceedings of the 2018 IEEE International Conference on Consumer Electronics (ICCE), Las Vegas, NV, USA, 12–14 January 2018; pp. 1–2.
25. Amanatiadis, A.; Kaburlasos, V.G.; Dardani, C.; Chatzichristofis, S.A. Interactive social robots in special education. In Proceedings of the 2017 IEEE 7th International Conference on Consumer Electronics-Berlin (ICCE-Berlin), Berlin, Germany, 3–6 September 2017; pp. 126–129.
26. Amanatiadis, A.; Kaburlasos, V.G.; Dardani, C.; Chatzichristofis, S.A.; Mitropoulos, A.C. Social Robots in Special Education: Creating Dynamic Interactions for Optimal Experience. *IEEE Consum. Electron. Mag.* **2020**, *9*, 39–45. [CrossRef]
27. Garris, R.; Ahlers, R.; Driskell, J.E. Games, motivation, and learning: A research and practice model. *Simul. Gaming* **2002**, *33*, 441–467. [CrossRef]
28. Gallardo, D.; Julia, C.F.; Jorda, S. TurTan: A tangible programming language for creative exploration. In Proceedings of the 2008 3rd IEEE International Workshop on Horizontal Interactive Human Computer Systems, Amsterdam, The Netherlands, 1–3 October 2008; pp. 89–92.
29. Horn, M.S.; Jacob, R.J. Tangible programming in the classroom with tern. In *CHI'07 Extended Abstracts on Human Factors in Computing Systems*; ACM: New York, NY, USA, 2007; pp. 1965–1970.
30. Mondada, F.; Bonani, M.; Riedo, F.; Briod, M.; Pereyre, L.; Rétornaz, P.; Magnenat, S. Bringing robotics to formal education: The thymio open-source hardware robot. *IEEE Robot. Autom. Mag.* **2017**, *24*, 77–85. [CrossRef]
31. De Cristoforis, P.; Pedre, S.; Nitsche, M.; Fischer, T.; Pessacg, F.; Di Pietro, C. A behavior-based approach for educational robotics activities. *IEEE Trans. Educ.* **2012**, *56*, 61–66. [CrossRef]
32. English, L.D. Advancing Elementary and Middle School STEM Education. *Int. J. Sci. Math. Educ.* **2017**, *15*, 5–24. [CrossRef]
33. Fallon, G.; Hatzigianni, M.; Bower, M.; Forbes, A.; Stevenson, M. Understanding K-12 STEM Education: A Framework for Developing STEM Literacy. *J. Sci. Educ. Technol.* **2020**, *29*, 369–385. [CrossRef]
34. Fraser, N. Ten things we have learned from Blockly. In Proceedings of the 2015 IEEE Blocks and Beyond Workshop (Blocks and Beyond), Atlanta, GA, USA, 22 October 2015; pp. 49–50. [CrossRef]
35. Ardublockly's Web Page. Available online: https://ardublockly.embeddedlog.com (accessed on 29 January 2019).
36. Murata, T. Petri nets: Properties, analysis and applications. *Proc. IEEE* **2014**, *77*, 541–580. [CrossRef]
37. Desrochers, A.; Al-Jaar, R. *Applications of Petri Nets in Manufacturing Systems-Modeling, Control and Performance Analysis*; IEEE Press: New York, NY, USA, 1995.
38. Proth, J.; Sauer, N. Scheduling of piecewise constant product flows: A Petri net approach. *Eur. J. Oper. Res.* **1998**, *106*, 45–56. [CrossRef]
39. Kuchárik, M.; Balogh, Z. Student Learning Simulation Process with Petri Nets. In *Recent Developments in Intelligent Computing, Communication and Devices*; Patnaik, S., Jain, V., Eds.; Advances in Intelligent Systems and Computing; Springer: Singapore, 2018; Volume 752, pp. 1115–1124.
40. Balogh, Z.; Turøáni, M. Possibilities of Modelling Web-Based Education Using IF-THEN Rules and Fuzzy Petri Nets in LMS. In *Informatics Engineering and Information Science: International Conference*; Springer: Berlin/Heidelberg, Germany, 2011; pp. 93–106.

41. Wang, Y.Y.; Lai, A.F.; Shen, R.K.; Yang, V.; Chu, Y.H. Modeling and verification of an intelligent tutoring system based on Petri net theory. *Math. Biosci. Eng.* **2019**, *16*, 4947–4975. [CrossRef] [PubMed]
42. Balogh, Z.; Drozda, M.; Kuchárik, M. Petri net model of student choices in a LMS moddle e-course. In Proceedings of the 12th International Scientific Conference on Distance Learning in Applied Informatics, Sturovo, Slovakia, March 2019. Available online: https://www.researchgate.net/publication/331546741_PETRI_NET_MODEL_OF_STUDENT_CHOICES_IN_A_LMS_MOODLE_E-COURSE (accessed on 25 September 2021).
43. Shen, V.R.L.; Yang, C.Y.; Wang, Y.Y.; Lin, Y.H. Application of high-level fuzzy Petri nets to educational grading system. *Expert Syst. Appl.* **2012**, *39*, 12935–12946. [CrossRef]
44. Wang, J. *Timed Petri Nets: Theory and Application*; Kluwer: New York, NY, USA, 1998.
45. Zurawski, R.; Zhou, M.C. Petri nets and Industrial Applications: A Tutorial. *IEEE Trans. Ind. Electron.* **1994**, *41*, 567–583. [CrossRef]
46. Tsalmpouris, G. Design and Development of a STEM Platform for the Needs of Secondary Education. Master's Thesis, Hellenic Mediterenean Univeristy, Heraklion, Greeece, 2019.
47. Hmelo-Silver, C.E. Problem-Based Learning: What and How Do Students Learn? *Educ. Psychol. Rev.* **2004**, *16*, 235–266. [CrossRef]
48. Vasiliou, C.; Ioannou, A.; Zaphiris, P. Measuring Students' Flow Experience in a Multimodal Learning Environment: A Case Study. In *Lecture Notes in Computer Science*; Zaphiris, P., Ioannou, A., Eds.; Springer International Publishing: Cham, Switzerland, 2014; Volume 8523.
49. Csikszentmihalyi, M. *Beyond Boredom and Anxiety: Experiencing Flow in Work and Play*; Jossey-Bass: San Francisco, CA, USA, 1975.
50. Jackson, S.A.; Eklund, R.C. *The Flow Scales Manual*; Fitness Information Technology: Morgantown, WV, USA, 2004.
51. Giasiranis, S.; Sofos, L. Flow Experience and Educational Effectiveness of Teaching Informatics using AR. *J. Educ. Technol. Soc.* **2017**, *24*, 78–88.
52. Jackson, S.A.; Csikszentmihalyi, M. *Flow in Sports*; Human Kinetics: Champaign, IL, USA, 1999.
53. Engeser, S.; Rheinberg, E. Flow, performance and moderators of challenge-skill balance. *Motiv. Emot.* **2008**, *32*, 158–172. [CrossRef]

Article

Utilizing Educational Robotics for Environmental Empathy Cultivation in Primary Schools

Dimitris Ziouzios [1,*], Dimitrios Rammos [2], Tharrenos Bratitsis [2] and Minas Dasygenis [1]

1. Department of Electrical & Computer Engineering, Faculty of Engineering, University of Western Macedonia, 50100 Kozani, Greece; mdasygenis@uowm.gr
2. Department of Early Childhood Education, School of Humanities and Social Sciences, University of Western Macedonia, 53100 Florina, Greece; drammos@uowm.gr (D.R.); bratitsis@uowm.gr (T.B.)
* Correspondence: dziouzios@uowm.gr; Tel.: +30-698-760-4110

Abstract: The fostering of empathy among primary school students is an important goal because it enhances the improvement of behavior and the development of positive social contacts. Empathy can contribute to understanding and supporting others' needs. In most cases, empathy in young children is developed through listening to sad stories, experienced first-hand by others. In the educational scenario presented in this article, the dramatic effects of climate change were conveyed to the pupils through a message said to originate from the future, delivered by an educational robot. The message was expressed by a peer living in Iran in 2050. In addition to delivering the message, the robot called on children to prevent climate change from rapidly worsening by changing their own way of thinking and attitudes. Thus, students called upon a formulated educational problem to understand and handle through their own emotional and cognitive performance through the robot's storytelling. This performance was intensely affected by empathy towards the Iranian peer's difficult personal living conditions. The research focused on measuring the evidence of empathy development. Additionally, the design and implementation aspects of the robot are presented, utilizing the implemented teaching intervention as means of demonstrating the innovative nature of the robot.

Keywords: empathy; climate change; educational robot; sustainability; teaching scenario; primary education

Citation: Ziouzios, D.; Rammos, D.; Bratitsis, T.; Dasygenis, M. Utilizing Educational Robotics for Environmental Empathy Cultivation in Primary Schools. *Electronics* **2021**, *10*, 2389. https://doi.org/10.3390/electronics10192389

Academic Editor: Ngai-Man (Man) Cheung

Received: 9 September 2021
Accepted: 27 September 2021
Published: 30 September 2021

Publisher's Note: MDPI stays neutral with regard to jurisdictional claims in published maps and institutional affiliations.

Copyright: © 2021 by the authors. Licensee MDPI, Basel, Switzerland. This article is an open access article distributed under the terms and conditions of the Creative Commons Attribution (CC BY) license (https://creativecommons.org/licenses/by/4.0/).

1. Introduction

Educational robotics is increasingly being exploited by primary school teachers, especially in projects aimed at developing 21st century skills [1,2]. Empathy is one such kind of skill which is deemed to crucially beneficial for students since it helps students better understand people's social behavior and shape their own attitudes towards different social issues [3,4]. Many studies highlight the contribution of empathy to the cognitive and behavioral development of young students within school and family environments [5,6].

Various factors related to other people's behavior or changes in the social environment may cause empathy development in children. In most cases, the degree of development is greater when descriptions of unpleasant incidents or difficulties faced by someone are processed [7,8]. Thus, addressing a difficulty experienced by one or more people raises the reflection and expression of emotions in a safe and secure personal context. In an educational context, these kinds of descriptions and stories from others could be presented as part of teaching scenarios to develop empathy for major problems worldwide. This article presents an educational scenario aimed at developing empathy for the current problem of climate change and global warming. Climate action is one of the 17 UNESCOs Sustainable Development Goals, promoted in young people's education in accordance with European Union directives [9,10].

Novel tools to develop empathy in pupils are always welcomed by the educational community, especially if they utilize modern technologies and capture everyone's attention.

Here, we present our contribution to this field. Concerning the most appropriate way to measure empathy in children, there are ongoing discussions from various esteemed researchers [11–13]. Specifically, the accuracy of research measuring tools is limited in children, especially younger ones, due to the influence from their environment and their cautious attitude towards scientific measurement procedures in general [11]. For this reason, systematic observation of student's performance during project activities is the strategy proposed in this article for assessing the development of empathy. This observation was followed by filling in an evaluation rubric, developed by the members of the research team.

The paper is structured as follows: initially, the notion of empathy and its significance within education and social interaction is discussed; then, the utilization of robots in education is examined, leading to the proposed implementation of the EI-EDUROBOT; after that, a case study in which the robot was utilized for the facilitation of environmental and social empathy is presented, showcasing the unique functionalities of the robot's design, before the concluding discussion.

2. Empathy: A Very Important and Useful Aspect of Social Life

Empathy is a set of processes which affect and shape the way people comprehend other people's behavior. Fostering empathy between members of a society could be directly reflected in every aspect of social life. According to Hoffman [14], empathy is " ... the spark of human concern for others, the glue that makes social life possible" (p. 3). Research findings consistently demonstrate that empathy contributes to developing positive and supportive relationships and to understanding and supporting others' needs [15]. Empathy is valuable for all age groups and all types of societies. Consequently, the development of empathy among young people can enhance the well-being of the whole society [13].

Although there is no unanimity among researchers as to the definition and the elements that constitute empathy, there are three distinct strands which emerge in most empirical studies [13,16,17]. These are empathic resonance, empathic reasoning and empathic response.

- Empathic resonance, which comprises the emotional aspect of empathy, is the impulsive mirroring of another's emotional experiences, such as sorrow or joy;
- Empathic reasoning, which comprises the cognitive element of empathy, is a conscious perception whereby an individual imagines themself 'in the other's shoes' while taking several environment considerations into account;
- Empathic response, which comprises the behavioral aspect of empathy, is an internal cognitive and inspirational process that motivates an individual to act on behalf of the other's needs.

The empathic process begins with an emotional resonance between two individuals, followed by the empathizer taking perspective on the other's situation, and conclude on a supportive behavior [18]. Empathy, as a whole, is considered one of the most seminal social–emotional competencies [19].

3. Empathy in Children

Empathy in childhood is particularly important and has therefore piqued the interest of researchers. A typical example was the research of the Department of Psychology of the University of Chicago in September 2013, published in the journal *Frontiers in Human Neuroscience*, according to which children aged from six to twelve years old had the ability to feel compassion for people who felt pain [20]. More specifically, it appeared that additional aspects of the brain were activated when they were confronted with a person who was deliberately harmed by another. These aspects significantly included the area concerning moral reasoning of the brain. Moral reasoning, however, is also influenced by the way parents behave towards their children, because children learn and enhance their emotional world through interactions within their family environment [20,21].

On the other hand, school has always been a crucial formative factor of a child's emotional world. Therefore, empathy should be part of the pedagogical process because cultivating the psychoemotional culture of the individual is an important objective of education [22].

The learning process is particularly influenced by the emotions experienced by the child. Educators must be able to attract and understand their pupils in order to be able to serve their mental and learning needs. In each school class, there are pupils with different cognitive and emotional backgrounds, which makes the role of the teacher complex but crucial.

Goleman [23] argued that teachers are able to develop the emotional intelligence of students. They should therefore plan appropriate activities as part of a broader strategy. In this case, the teacher's initiative can cover the absence of emotional intelligence programs in the curriculum. According to the majority of relevant surveys, the development of emotional skills such as empathy is more easily achieved in the early years of a child's life, specifically at the age of 6–8 years [13,17]. Of course, the formation of empathy is evolutionary and continues in older ages. Primary school age, however, is when children's emotions are considered to be the most malleable and decisive.

Some other studies highlight the importance of having teachers with a high empathy level [24,25]. This leads to appropriate learning environments where teachers seek to cooperate and cultivate a friendly learning climate. When this is achieved, it is very likely that the needs of pupils are understood and properly taken into account. This, in turn, can lead to conflict resolution and the formation of a collaborative climate. The latter guarantees the creative and efficient work of children in all kinds of teaching activities. This develops a high degree of empathy among children, which enhances the implementation of demanding educational scenarios.

In conclusion, as Goleman [23] says, students who have experienced emotional education appear to perform better and not adopt delinquent behavior. In addition, they acquire skills that will help them in their later school years and adulthood. Empathy helps to understand the world and to take initiatives to improve the lives of all people. In this study, students were guided to understand the issue of climate change by listening to the personal problems experienced by a peer in 2050.

4. Utilizing Robots in Education

The use of robots in education is not a new idea. Starting from the 1980s, mainly though the Logo programming language, it has been based on constructivism and constructionism theories [26]. Educational robotics (ERs), in general, is the teaching method where robots are used by students usually under the guidance of a teacher [27]. Today, the use of robots in classrooms starts from the early ages. Jung and Won [28] systematically studied the literature and recorded the trends in educational robotics used as tools for STEAM education and other disciplinary areas, involving children aged 4 to 13 years old. Toh et al. [29] studied the literature and focused on the impact of robots on young children and education.

Nowadays, there are many robots utilized in educational contexts, starting from the age of 4. Most of them focus on disciplines which fall under the sciences area, when examined in the typical education context. The robot presented in this paper, named Emotional Intelligence Educational Robot (EI-EDUROBOT), can be utilized by students from the age of 4 and over without limits.

4.1. The Design Principles and Idea of the EI-EDUROBOT

The research team decided to design a new robotic system for the needs identified for empathy training in school settings. Prior to that, an extensive literature review was carried out, leading to the accumulation of 57 papers which were related to empathy, educational robotics and young age groups (4–9 years old). Regarding the content of the studies is out of the scope of this paper, although it is important to mention that no approach such as the one presented in this paper exists in the literature (focusing on environmental and social empathy in an interconnected manner).

For the needs of this paper, the type of robotic constructs was examined. Overall, there are three main categories of such constructs: floor roamers, humanoid or animal-like robots, and complex constructs. The first category refers to simple programmable robotic devices which are designed for moving on a simple surface (e.g., the floor or a table). The programming of such devices merely includes direction commands (e.g., forward, backward, left, right) with a predefined or varying step. A representative example of this category is BeeBot, a bee-like robot which can only receive directional commands (up to 44) and incorporates movements of 15 cm lengths or 90° turns. The concept of utilizing this robot involves printed floor mats. Depending on the pictures on the mats, various teaching activities can be designed and contextualized. Other examples of robots in this category are BlueBot, Gigo first coding, Edison and Bottley. All of them are more appropriate for younger ages. Some of them (e.g., ProBot, which is a car-like robot) also incorporate touch sensors so that they can identify obstacles when moving.

The second category is that of humanoid robots, or ones which have the appearance of some life form. One example is the PLEO robot, a dinosaur-like robot which has been widely used for training social skills, because it can interact with a child in a social manner. It replicates behaviors based on fundamental feelings (e.g., fear, affection). Another example is Alpha 1S Pro, a humanoid robot which incorporated several servomotors and can execute various movements with very high precision and balance. It can also transmit pre-recorded audio files which are synchronized with the movements of the robot. Interaction with this robot is rather minimal and it can be utilized as a programmable device for solving realistic spatial problems. More sophisticated and much more expensive examples in this category are the NAO and the Pepper robots. Both are humanoid and they incorporate a large set of sensors which allows more realistic interaction with a person. NAO is a "close-to-real" humanoid robot which replicates physical movement and can also interact with a person with sound triggers (incorporating sound recognition). Pepper incorporates a screen on its chest for displaying multimedia content and can also interact via audio. Both are very expensive solutions and have been mainly used in controlled laboratory environments (NAO) or for other social activities (e.g., Pepper has been used as a guide in exhibitions or as a welcoming agent in airports).

The third category refers to robotic solutions which require some sort of construction that integrates sensors and/or motors. Probably the most known devices of this category are Lego sets (WeDo, EV3 and Spike). The kits provide structural elements such as building blocks, sensors (color, distance, infrared, tilt, etc.) and motors in order to create interactive constructs which can also be programmed to react to the inputs of the sensors. Depending on the complexity of the kits, they can be used by children of various age groups (e.g., from 7 to 18 years old). Usually, these robots do not have the ability to incorporate multimedia material in a native manner.

Considering all the aforementioned options, the research groups reached the conclusion that none of them would meet the needs of the designed studies. They all appeared to have several advantages and disadvantages. For example, the roamers are easy to program but do not actually interact with the children. The humanoid robots are more capable of interaction, but they are either too expensive (e.g., NAO) or they have limited interaction capabilities (Alpha 1S Pro). Other robots such as PLEO are designed for very specific tasks and have limited or no programming potential; thus, they are unfit for other types of educational activities. The last category requires building and programming block-based constructs which involve more complex skills (e.g., fine-motor skills), are more time consuming (due to the need to design and implement the construction), and have limited interactivity.

Thus, a strategic decision was made to design a new robot based on the review of the state of the art. Considering the target group (young students), the robot was designed in a humanoid form, incorporating a head, hands and movement capabilities. Taking into account safety issues, the robot incorporated wheels instead of legs, so as to be more sturdy and secure for both the children and itself. Various sensors were incorporated for that matter (see Section 4.2). The research team focused mainly on the interactivity of the robot with children. Consequently, several sensors were attached to the robot's body, which allowed interaction via touching. The face of the robot was selected to be a touch screen, allowing the robot to present multimedia material of any kind but also provide an additional interaction method (via the touch screen). Additionally, a camera, a microphone and speakers were incorporated to the robot which, with its various connectivity capabilities (Wi-Fi and Bluetooth), would allow free-form interaction with another human peer (e.g., a teacher or a researcher) via the robot in a realistic and free manner. For example, an adult with a plain headset would be able to carry out free-form and real-time verbal interaction with a child by listening through its microphone and talking through its speakers. This would be totally transparent for the child, because they would perceive that the interaction occurs with the robot only. These interactivity capabilities combined in a single device are not met in any of the existing solutions in the market.

All these elements were considered for designing the robot. Additionally, an attempt was made to keep the cost as low as possible while incorporating functionalities which can be seen in more sophisticated robots in the market (e.g., NAO, which costs over 10 times more than the EI-EDUROBOT). Lastly, the design of the EI-EDUROBOT had to allow expandability in both programming and mechanical aspects, enabling it to be very versatile and adaptable to any possible teaching interventions. The next section briefly presents the electromechanical design of the robot.

4.2. Technical Aspects of EI-EDUROBOT

EI-EDUROBOT was developed in the base of Open-Source Software and Open Hardware, where the research community and anyone with basic programming knowledge will be able to develop it further. With this philosophy, the robot was designed in-house in a 3D CAD software and manufactured with our 3D printer, utilizing the fused deposition modeling (FDM) technique. As for the electronic and mechanical systems, we followed the COTS (components off the shelf) principle for fast prototyping, and easily obtaining them from the market. As with any cyberphysical system such as our robot, it is a codesign process of hardware and software, which includes the robot's code, the online handling platform, and a mobile app.

All parts of the robot were constructed using polylactic acid (PLA) or polylactide, obtained from renewable and natural raw materials such as corn, because they are biodegradable and bioactive [30]. The frame of the robot was designed (Figure 1) with the aim of stability, endurance and protection, both for the robot itself and for the children, as the highest priorities, in order to achieve optimal distribution of its weight, resulting in stable and smooth movement. The interior of the robot is allocated to the electronic components. The robotic system had two arms with double hinges and were designed in such a way as to allow the user to add various components to the robot's hands, which were also designed and printed in FDM. The head could move on two axes: the horizontal axis (right–left) and the vertical axis (up–down). This design option allowed the robot to express the desired emotions (agreement, denial, irritability, etc.) with high precision due to the seven-inch touchscreen.

The 'brain' of the robot was based on a Raspberry Pi 4 model B with a high-performance 64-bit quad-core processor, with up to 4 GB of RAM, which supports dual-band 2.4/5.0 GHz wireless LAN and Bluetooth 5.0 and has dual-display support at resolutions up to 4K via a pair of micro-HDMI ports. These specifications met the project's requirements, and due to the low cost and low energy usage, made it cost-effective. The use of Raspberry Pi gives huge possibilities to both manufacturers and users to customize various accessories.

Figure 1. The EI-EDUROBOT.

The robot integrated a variety of sensors that can be divided into two major categories: (i) security-related, and (ii) operationally related. As for the first category, the robot incorporated ultrasonic sensors in the front and rear, which were activated when the robot moved. If an obstacle was detected, the robot stopped moving. Additionally, at the bottom (in front and behind the wheels), there were infrared (IR) sensors, so if the robot was placed at an elevated point, it stopped moving when it reached its edge (by detecting the corresponding gap). The second sensor category concerned the functions of the robot, where the educator could optionally make use of it, if they wished. Specifically, it had two pressure sensors in the hands (right–left), and a button on the chest, for which the usage was dependent on the loaded scenario, so the robot executed different commands. On the head, a thin membrane potentiometer was placed. Its resistance changed linearly from 100 to 10,000 Ohms by simply pressing down on various places of the sensor strip, making it possible to calculate the pressure position on the strip with precision. This was critical for the proposed implementation because the robot could detect a touch on the head and react in response to the pressure. Each sensor could perform different tasks which depended on the script developer. Figure 2 presents a diagram of the sensors.

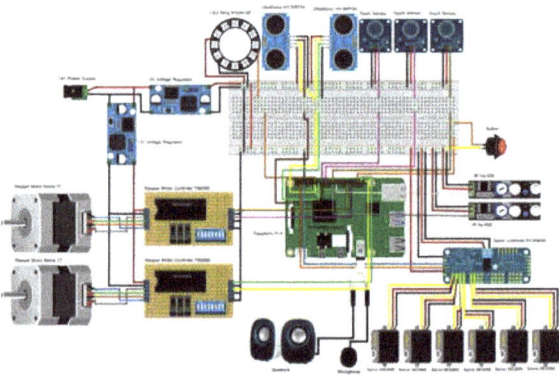

Figure 2. Diagram of the sensors.

For easier connection of the robot's sensors and motors, a printed circuit board (PCB) was developed as illustrated in Figure 3. Two TB6560 chips controlled the motors, while a PCA9685 16-Channel controlled the servos. The system's smooth operation was ensured by the employment of two voltage reducers, one at 12 volts and the other at 5 volts.

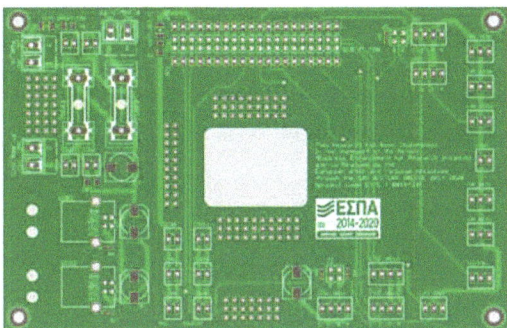

Figure 3. Printed circuit board of our robot.

Moreover, in terms of software, three basic tools have been developed for using the robot: (i) the robot user platform, (ii) the robot code, and (iii) the application for smartphones with the Android operating system. Through these tools, the trainer could utilize all the functions of the robot and even develop them further. Raspberry Pi controlled the Raspbian operating system (OS), a free OS based on Debian that is customized for the Raspberry Pi hardware. Python, a sophisticated and quick programming language, was utilized to control the robot and use all of its capabilities. Python is a user-friendly programming language in which anyone with basic knowledge of programming can develop a scenario. The robot's graphical user interface (GUI) was created using the PyQt toolkit, which is a Python add-on. The Python programming language was used to create various educational scenarios. Users with the required programming skills can use the Python programming language to create programs that control robot sensors and motors. The research team aspired for this platform to become a useful tool at the disposal of teachers who know basic programming concepts so that they can develop their own scenarios, depending on the needs they recognize.

An information system was designed to coordinate the transmission of information from the user's device to the robot in order to achieve communication between the user and the robot. The web application and the Rest API made up this information system. The MEAN architecture, which consisted of MongoDB, Express framework, Angular framework and NodeJS, was used to develop all aspects of the system. The advantages of the MEAN architecture include the fact that it is an open-source framework that can be used as a standalone solution in a complete application and that it includes extra frameworks, libraries, and reusable modules to speed up development. The system is highly scalable and maintenance-friendly thanks to these technologies. It is also feasible to create new applications that can support the system's capabilities by using JSON files for data transmission between the user, the API, and the robot.

The humanoid robot was controlled via an Android app by its operators. The app used the Rest API (application programming interface) to communicate directly with the robot and the (IS) information system and provide critical information about the robot's smooth movement and operation. Particularly, the Android application allowed the user to control the robot's legs, hands, and head directly, as well as execute a pre-configured script including a sequence of movement commands. This allows users to choose and execute an installed scenario of the robot. The Microsoft Xamarin framework was used to create the Android application, which was written in C# and XAML. The robot communicated with the information system via the Wi-Fi protocol at predetermined intervals (polling). All data (including scenarios and movement-related information) were compressed and encrypted before the transmission process began. Lossless compression formats, such as PNG and WebP, were utilized for photos and movies. The robot used the asymmetric encryption algorithm RSA for encryption, which meant that even if the robot was stolen or communication was intercepted, malicious users would not be able to decrypt the data because they will not have access to the secret RSA key. The Android App was could very easily be used by teachers and students from the age of 4 years old.

5. Education on Climate Change and Empathy

Action on climate change is one of the timeliest goals for improving people's lives. According to scientists' data, climate change is expected to cause intolerable living conditions in the future [31]. In addition, problems in daily life of societies are expected to occur. The actions of people today directly affect climate change. Raising awareness and taking immediate action at all levels are, therefore, very crucial factors in preventing the phenomenon [32].

Even more important is the awareness of young people and children from their early school years. Therefore, raising awareness of climate change in students should be part of the broader goal of active citizenship and participation in social dialogue and decision-making.

The modern reality about the climate and predictions for its future development are complex issues with scientific implications. Thus, it is quite difficult for children to accurately understand how it affects their lives. In addition, the issue of climate change has political and economic implications that confuse and disorient the mind from the daily and immediate dimensions of the problem [31,32].

Perhaps the most effective method for children to process the issue in a meaningful and practical way is to develop empathy about the problems that climate change has created or is expected to create in people's lives in the future: to put themselves in their place, in other words, so that they understand their phobias and feelings [31].

In terms of teaching methodology, the implementation of an educational scenario aimed at developing empathy for climate change depends on many factors such as the age of children and their cognitive background. In addition, it depends on elements that will give originality and attractiveness, such as the possibility of using new technologies. The model of such an educational scenario is presented in this article.

6. The Implemented Educational Scenario

The specific educational scenario of utilizing the educational robot was designed to be carried out with elementary school students. The robot's programming presented an educational problem to the students through the projection of multimedia material on the screen located on its head. Solving the educational problem required interaction of the robot with the children. Therefore, the whole didactic approach was performed through the robot; the researchers were responsible for its programming. At the same time, the research team was able to determine and differentiate the flow of the scenario through a corresponding application for smart devices. At the research level, the members of the research team acted as observers, filling in observation rubrics on the topic of developing empathy in the students.

The learning strategy of the educational scenario combined the problem-solving method through STEAM activities. Problem-based learning (PBL) is a learning strategy in which complex problems from real life are utilized to promote student learning and to develop learning skills as opposed to the direct presentation of facts. Complementary to course content, PBL can promote the development of empathy. It can also provide opportunities for evaluating research materials, and for developing active citizenship [33]. PBL can be incorporated into any learning situation. The core thread is a real-world problem, which ensures relativity and increases children's interest.

Moreover, the problem should motivate students to seek out a deeper understanding of concepts. Additionally, they should be required to make reasoned decisions and to defend them, as well as express their feelings and relate them to these decisions.

On the other hand, STEAM teaching methodology reinforced the interdisciplinary approach of the educational problem, combining robotics with the scientific fields of meteorology, environment, mathematics and geography. For the needs of the scenario, the

EI-EDUROBOT presented itself to the students as ENVIE S-50, a robot from the future. ENVIE S-50 had returned to 2021 from the distant 2050 in order to inform children about the climate conditions and to convey a message to them from a 12-year-old child, Reza, who lived in Iran in 2050.

The theoretical framework of the educational scenario concerned the causes of climate change and the greenhouse effect. Most of it was incorporated into the video messages presented to children through the robot's screen/face. This practically means that new knowledge was mainly delivered by the educational robot. The videos were divided into two categories: those addressed to the children by the robot itself, where information was presented and missions were assigned; and those in which Reza told his digital story to the children in the form of an animated hero, as shown in Figures 4 and 5.

Figure 4. The image of Reza, as shown on the robot screen.

Figure 5. The scenario of Reza in a classroom.

Reza's message was far from pleasant, describing in detail the extremely difficult living conditions of Iran's inhabitants in 2050 due to overheating. These descriptions concerned his daily and school life as well as the government's actions to tackle the problem. In turn, the robot asked children to reflect on people's responsibilities in previous decades in terms of not caring and acting enough to prevent these negative developments. In addition, the children had to think and record the initiatives they intended to undertake themselves in their daily lives to prevent catastrophic climate change. This treaty actually created an «educational problem» which student were asked to solve by identifying changes in their personal perceptions and attitudes towards climate change (UNESCO/UNEP, 2011).

After the completion of the process and the proposed solutions on the educational problem, the robot reviewed the children's proposals through a new journey to 2050. This journey aimed the check whether the new way of thinking and attitudes of the children had had a prompt impact on future climate change. After that, the robot returned to 2021 to announce the findings of his observations to the children. In fact, the robot's ability to travel to and from the future was a unique opportunity for children to understand the power and impact of their decisions on the evolution of individual and social life.

Cumulatively, the educational scenario was implemented in five stages. In the first stage, the teacher referred to the concepts of sustainable development and climate change by highlighting the great importance given worldwide to the subject/problem through the projection of audiovisual material. Children's previous knowledge and thoughts on the subject were then illustrated in digital conceptual maps.

The second stage concerned the theoretical framework of the phenomenon of climate change which extends, cross-thematically, to the cognitive regions of natural sciences, mathematics, geography, language, and social and political education. The teacher presented scientific data and information on the causes of climate change and its present and future impacts on people's lives on a global scale. The whole teaching approach was theoretically integrated under the study of the United Nations' 17 Sustainable Development Goals. The term 'sustainability' was, initially, clarified through empirical examples and applications of everyday life. It was then connected with the 13th SDG goal, namely, the cognitive area of climate study and action.

The third stage of the scenario was related to the exploitation of the educational robot in the teaching process. Following relevant preparation, the teacher introduced ENVIE S50 to children. The movement and playback of audiovisual material by the robot was handled by a corresponding application on the teacher's smart device. According to the educational script, ENVIE S50 chose the particular classroom so as to deliver a crucial message about the evolution of climate change in Iran in 2050. As for the teaching strategy, the main purpose of this stage was to develop the "educational problem" which children would be asked to solve with their stories. The problem was expressed throughout the digital stories of both the robot and Reza. It was about detecting people's responsibilities for worsening climate change and also about taking action through the change of thinking and lifestyle. Reza's descriptions of his country's extremely difficult living conditions were especially aimed at developing empathy in children living in 2021, following the relevant literature review. These are the two indicative texts that were included in the digital stories displayed in the robot's screen, located in its head. The first one was delivered by the robot, and the second one by Reza:

> "Good morning guys, my name is ENVIE–S50 and I am a new generation technological robot. I was created in 2048 in a modern digital sustainable development laboratory. My mission is to check up on the achievement of the United Nations' sustainable development goals. I am sure you are aware of these objectives. I know how you understand the importance to have those objectives accomplished for the future of all mankind. I have been programmed in such a way to be able to travel back in time in order to communicate and deliver important data and information to selected people. For this reason, I arrived today in Greece after a back in time journey. This journey lasted exactly 86,400 s. It started in 2050. I'm currying a really crucial message related, in particular, to global warming and climate change . . . "

> "Hello, mates. I'm Reza and I live in Tehran, Iran. This the year 2050 and I am 12 years old. Envi–S50 informed me about his mission to travel to 2021 to deliver important information about the climate condition of my country and the whole world. I would definitely wish to travel along to get to know each other and learn about the climate of your country, my country and the whole world in 2021. In return, I am recording this message for you. After a brief research on the climate records of your time, I realized that global climate condition was in a logical and tolerable level despite people's concern about their gradual rise. Additionally, looking at photos and videos from my city in early twenties caused me a great surprise. This is because I realized that people were freely walking the streets throughout the whole year, without restrictions and bans on account of burn risk. I can tell you, my friends, that this seems ideal and magical to me. As I speak to you, it's May fifteen, five in the afternoon and the temperature in Tehran is close to 55 Celsius degrees. People can't go out without special uniform nor walk around outside without permission. School was closed due to high temperature and lessons were remotely carried out through computers. We are actually informed whether schools will be open or closed from special weather forecasts . . . "

The fourth stage of the scenario mainly concerned students' storytelling. More specifically, they were asked by the educational robot to think and write down their own stories using the information about the planet's future climate situation. These stories actually highlighted the potential change of their attitude towards climate change global problem. They also reflected the impact of the negative image of the future global climate on their emotional word and their feelings. It was a kind of a solution to the "educational problem" expressed by Reza, their Iranian peer from 2050. The stories were recorded in the robot's memory. According to the scenario, the robot would travel back to the future so as to check whether children's attitude changes could potentially reverse the negative developments of climate change. Thus, a general teaching objective was fulfilled, where people could form their future through active citizenship.

In the final stage, children were asked to complete a worksheet based on the knowledge they came across through the scenario activities. It had, mainly, to do with the understanding of the terms *sustainability* and *climate change*, together with their effects on people's lives. In terms of empathy development, they were also asked to draw something for Reza together with a small written message for him. Additionally, the completion of an evaluative rubric regarding the degree of involvement and the level of children's empathy was completed by teachers at this stage. The rubric mainly concerned stages C, D and E. It was developed by the research team using a Likert scale model (Figure 6). The rubric was chosen because it is a useful grading tool which adds reliability and validity to the observation results. It is often used to increase transparency in school projects and to decrease subjectivity [34]. A well-designed rubric is one that helps educators to judge students' work effectively, and to also keep records on attitude change incidents throughout teaching activities.

Child's name:					
Stage C					
	Strong Obvious	Obvious	Neutral	Poor	Strong Poor
Use of emotional words and phrases					
Change in emotional state					
Self-awareness of empathy development					
Stage D					
Use of emotional words and phrases					
Use of emotional words and phrases in written stories					
Change in emotional state					
Self-awareness of empathy development					
Stage E					
Use of emotional words and phrases					

Figure 6. The evaluative rubric regarding the development of children's empathy.

7. Research Methodology

This pilot research project was conducted in a primary school in Athens, Greece. In particular, two sixth grade classes took part, with a sum of 50 students. Children of both classes attended the elementary curriculum, and no serious learning difficulties were recorded. All children were excellent native speakers. The project was piloted with groups of 10 students. Each group volunteered for 3 h in total, and the whole project lasted three days. Naturalistic observation was the method adapted by the research group. This type of observation was appropriate because participants' behaviors were studied in natural surroundings. Additionally, there were no predetermined behavioral codes established either by researchers or teachers. Instead, rigorous notes on children's performance during project activities were taken and all data were coded later. In such qualitative studies, researchers actively participate or observe the teaching intervention and complete an observation journal during or right after the process (in order to not forget details which may be significant). Then, the notes are coded and interpreted in order to extract conclusions. This was the case in this study.

Institutional approval was obtained for this study. All project stages were recorded so as to make the validity of the observation findings more accurate and valid. Teachers of two classes participated in the study, helping in the collection of the data. They were also interviewed at the beginning in terms of shaping the empathy level of each student. Thus, data to evaluate the potential of the teaching strategy related to empathy development were obtained from student self-assessments of empathy and reflective writings throughout the school year. Taking children's age into account, equally important were the teachers' evaluation of the empathy level of each child, along with their yearly development. Finally, teachers were responsible for keeping records on the evaluative rubric during the whole procedure. Such rubrics which rely on observations represent an objective, although justified, constituent, which is very common in qualitative research.

Children's written stories from the project activities were read and coded independently by two members of the research group with no affiliation to the previous level of empathy of participants. Coders were also blind to any information about students because any identifying and other kind of information was deleted from the reflections. Coding occurred after the end of all group work. Apart from the written stories, coders determined how many times students experienced a change in their level of empathy across the recordings. These changes were noted either through relevant emotional phrases, expressed written or orally by students, or when the coders noted a change in their emotional state through their comments and attitude throughout the activities. They also noted phrases and dialogues which indicated that students became more aware of their own empathetic development.

8. Results and Discussion

The rubrics and recordings debriefing highlighted the high degree of empathy development in children, especially with regard to Reza's personal history. The expression of emotions both in the stories about their attitude change and the messages to him was remarkable (Figure 7). More specifically the highest percentages occurred in stages D and E, where the "obvious" indicator reached a total average of 60% and "obvious strong" in 20%.

	S.O.	Ob.	N.	Po.	S. Po.
Stage C					
Use of emotional words and phrases	4%	16%	52%	20%	8%
Change in emotional state	12%	32%	46%	8%	2%
Self-awareness of empathy development	4%	4%	4%	76%	12%
Stage D					
Use of emotional words and phrases	12%	64%	16%	6%	2%
Use of emotional words and phrases in written stories	42%	38%	10%	6%	4%
Change in emotional state	10%	62%	4%	2%	2%
Self-awareness of empathy development	20%	30%	40%	5%	5%
Stage E					
Use of emotional words and phrases	18%	68%	6%	6%	6%
Use of emotional words and phrases in written messages	14%	64%	14%	6%	2%
Expression of emotions in drawing	6%	30%	38%	20%	6%
Self-awareness of empathy development	12%	48%	24%	10%	6%

Figure 7. The percentages resulting from debriefing the rubric.

At stage C, the students did not express their feelings through corresponding words and phrases to a large extent. Similarly, their emotional state remained stable, according to the researchers' observation. For this reason, the 'neutral' category had the highest proportion, i.e., 52% and 46%, respectively. This is a reasonable and expected research finding, because students at this age need time to emotionally process the information received and express themselves in response.

It is still considered particularly important to note that at this stage, students did not seem to understand the change in their emotional state while the educational robot and Reza presented the negative scientific data and the difficult daily living of people in 2050. Most students (88%) reacted cautiously to listening to digital stories, taking a rational stance. This percentage was considered unexpectedly high in view of the large difference with the percentages in stages D and E. It therefore confirmed the tendency of children not to change their feelings easily and quickly, but to process them internally and to externalize them on some occasions, such as through the work assigned to them by the research team.

In stage D, the percentages clearly indicated both the change in emotional state and the understanding of this change by students themselves. A total of 76% of them used spoken words and expressions that manifested feelings. At the same time, 80% incorporated these expressions into written stories. Obvious or very obvious changes in emotional state were recorded in a staggering 92% of participants, although only 50% of children themselves seemed to perceive that they had been emotionally affected. Consequently, emotional involvement in the stage is significant, creating a noticeable change from the previous stage.

Similar results occurred at stage E, as far as the use of oral emotional expressions was concerned. In the written stories, i.e., the personal messages to Reza, the use of emotional expressions was less evident than in the written stories in stage D, but overall, students continued to show empathy for his difficult living conditions. Less obvious was the expression of emotions in the drawings. This came as a small surprise in relation to the research forecasts. On the one hand, it could be interpreted as due to the age of the students; on the other hand, by the "emotional fatigue" caused by the written stories.

Finally, after the teaching activities of the project, it was attempted to capture the development of empathy for each student individually in comparison with the degree of empathy in previous school activities, without the use of the educational robot or another form of educational technology. A five-point scale was used. Children's teachers were asked to set the grade for each student before they were even informed about the project with the educational robot. They were also asked to describe the criteria by which they decided on this scoring. After the implementation of the project, they were asked to re-rate the students on the same criteria, evaluating empathetic development. Once again, the results for the 50 students, shown in Figure 8, demonstrate the significant impact of this project on the development of empathy. Most students exhibited an increase of one to two points, whereas there were very few who increased by less than one unit or remained stagnant. Although this measurement is empirical and therefore less valid, it is of great interest because it reflects the opinion of teachers who are better aware of the characteristics of students and their previous levels of empathy.

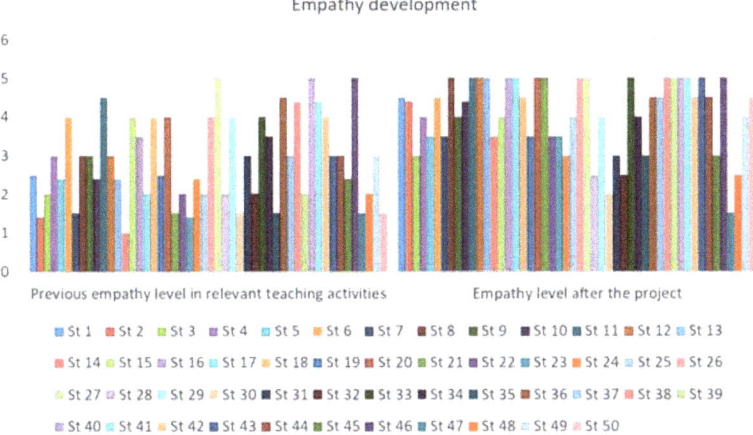

Figure 8. Comparative representation of 50 students' empathy levels.

Moreover, the fact that this project's activities were mainly presented and carried out by the educational robot and Reza contributed to the development of an immediate and comfortable climate in relation to traditional teaching practice where this role belongs to the teacher. This leads to the conclusion that the development of empathy in school teaching is stronger in a differentiated context than standard, usual practice.

9. Conclusions

Measuring children's levels of empathy and the factors that influence them is a particularly difficult issue. Naturalistic observation by members of the research team and by teachers at the school was chosen as the research method because children functioned independently, without coming into contact with any rubrics or other measurement tool. The research results of the observation and rubrics completed by the researchers were varied enough and gave the opportunity to compare and synthesize in order to draw as many objective conclusions as possible.

The alternation of emotions of the children was intense and evident, and all researchers observed responses of the children as an evolution of the educational scenario. The robot's programming contributed to this by clearly highlighting the educational information. This programming was performed through a relevant application on smart devices developed by the research team. Implementation has made a key contribution to the flexibility of this scenario. Specifically, it gave researchers the ability to adjust the view of the videos on the robot's screen in real time depending on the interaction of the students. Additionally, the robot's programmed movements gave it anthropomorphic characteristics and contributed to the immediacy of the messages of Envi-S50 and Reza.

The researchers' conclusions about the development of children's empathy and the effectiveness of programming on the robot were complemented and enriched with the pre-existing knowledge of teachers. Teachers' comments were certainly more complete but more subjective. The teachers' opinions on the presence of the robot were universally positive, because everyone recognized the successful completion of the scenario at a technical and educational level. In addition, the comparative juxtaposition of the pre-existing image of the level of empathy of children with this project highlighted the development of empathy in the majority of children.

At the same time, the presence of the robot increased the interest and participation of children and also facilitated the research process. Its technical characteristics, in particular, have been instrumental in the rapid and effective implementation of the activities. The ability to project multimedia material on the robot's screen and the children's interaction with it offered immediacy and flexibility. The presentation of information and the formulation of the educational problem were carried out by the robot itself, which significantly differentiated it from traditional school practice, creating a greater teaching interest in children.

Author Contributions: Methodology, D.Z., D.R., T.B. and M.D.; software, D.Z. and M.D.; validation, D.R. and T.B.; data curation, D.R.; writing—original draft preparation, D.Z., D.R., T.B. and M.D.; writing—review and editing, D.Z., D.R., T.B. and M.D.; supervision, T.B. and M.D.; funding acquisition, D.Z. All authors have read and agreed to the published version of the manuscript.

Funding: This research has been implemented in the framework of the Action "Business Enhancement for Research projects" and co-financed by the European Union and national resources through the B.P. WESTERN GREECE 2014–2020 (project code: DEP5-0019433).

Institutional Review Board Statement: Real teaching settings within the school's official curriculum by the teaches of the specific school, one of which is a member of the authoring/research team. This study falls under the category in which teachers reported upon their in-class intervention and thus no humans are identifiable or directly involved by providing personal information of any kind or being affected by the study in any way, so as to require such approval according to the directives of the UOWM Ethical committee.

Informed Consent Statement: Informed consent was obtained from all subjects involved in the study.

Data Availability Statement: Publicly not available nor exploitable by other researchers so as to be shared.

Conflicts of Interest: The authors declare no conflict of interest.

References

1. Yang, Y.; Long, Y.; Sun, D.; Van Aalst, J.; Cheng, S. Fostering students' creativity via educational robotics: An investigation of teachers' pedagogical practices based on teacher interviews. *Br. J. Educ. Technol.* **2020**, *51*, 1826–1842. [CrossRef]
2. Massaty, M.H.; Budiyanto, C.W.; Tamrin, A. Revisiting the roles of educational robotics in improving learners' computational thinking skills and their positive behaviour. *J. Phys. Conf. Ser.* **2020**, *1511*, 012088. [CrossRef]
3. Ewin, N.; Chugh, R.; Muurlink, O.; Jarvis, J.; Luck, J. Empathy of Project Management Students and Why It Matters. *Procedia Comput. Sci.* **2021**, *181*, 503–510. [CrossRef]
4. Berliner, R.; Tracy, L.M. Review of research: Promoting empathy development in the early childhood and elementary classroom: April Bedford and Renée Casbergue, editors. *Child. Educ.* **2015**, *91*, 57–64. [CrossRef]
5. Wang, M.; Wang, J.; Deng, X.; Chen, W. Why are empathic children more liked by peers? The mediating roles of prosocial and aggressive behaviors. *Pers. Individ. Differ.* **2019**, *144*, 19–23. [CrossRef]
6. O'Conner, R.; De Feyter, J.; Carr, A.; Luo, J.L.; Romm, H. A Review of the Literature on Social and Emotional Learning for Students Ages 3–8: Teacher and Classroom Strategies That Contribute to Social and Emotional Learning (Part 3 of 4). REL 2017-247. *Reg. Educ. Lab. Mid-Atl.* **2017**. Available online: https://files.eric.ed.gov/fulltext/ED572721.pdf (accessed on 9 September 2021).
7. Ratka, A. Empathy and the development of affective skills. *Am. J. Pharm. Educ.* **2018**, *82*, 7192. [CrossRef]
8. Lee, J.; Lee, Y.; Kim, M.H. Effects of Empathy-based Learning in Elementary Social Studies. *Asia-Pac. Educ. Res.* **2018**, *27*, 509–521. [CrossRef]
9. UNESCO/UNEP. Climate change starter's guidebook. In *An Issues Guide for Education Planners and Practitioners*; United Nations Educational: Paris, France, 2011.
10. European Commission. Climate Change Consequences. Available online: https://ec.europa.eu/clima/change/consequences_en (accessed on 20 May 2021).
11. Akos, P. Building empathic skills in elementary school children through group work. *J. Spec. Group Work* **2000**, *25*, 214–223. [CrossRef]
12. Coll, M.-P.; Viding, E.; Rütgen, M.; Silani, G.; Lamm, C.; Catmur, C.; Bird, G. Are we really measuring empathy? Proposal for a new measurement framework. *Neurosci. Biobehav. Rev.* **2017**, *83*, 132–139. [CrossRef]
13. Feshbach, N.D. Empathy in Children: Some Theoretical and Empirical Considerations. *Couns. Psychol.* **1975**, *5*, 25–30. [CrossRef]
14. Hoffman, M.L. *Toward a Comprehensive Empathy-Based Theory of Prosocial Moral Development*; American Psychological Association: Washington, DC, USA, 2001.
15. Jennings, P.A.; Mark, T.G. The prosocial classroom: Teacher social and emotional competence in relation to student and classroom outcomes. *Rev. Educ. Res.* **2009**, *79*, 491–525. [CrossRef]
16. Koopman, E.M.E.; Frank, H. Effects of literature on empathy and self-reflection: A theoretical-empirical framework. *J. Lit. Theory* **2015**, *9*, 79–111. [CrossRef]
17. Brooks, S. Historical empathy in the social studies classroom: A review of the literature. *J. Soc. Stud. Res.* **2009**, *33*, 213–234.
18. De Waal, F. *The Age of Empathy: Nature's Lessons for a Kinder Society*; Broadway Books: New York, NY, USA, 2010.
19. Bar-On, R.; Richard, H.; Suzanne, F. The Impact of Emotional Intelligence on Performance. *Linking Emotional Intelligence and Performance at Work: Current Research Evidence with Individuals and Groups*, Psicothema, Spain 2006, pp. 3–19. Available online: https://books.google.co.jp/books?hl=zh-CN&lr=&id=a_OryLZ2W2cC&oi=fnd&pg=PA3&dq=The+impact+of+emotional+intelligence+on+performance&ots=vtw5OxYER5&sig=gg8WN4lhh8EQtkc40NwAXsJ-VXU#v=onepage&q&f=false (accessed on 9 September 2021).
20. Malikiosi-Loizou, M. A critical look at empathy. *Psychol. J. Hell. Psychol. Soc.* **2003**, *10*, 295–309. (In Greek)
21. Ozbaci, N. Emotional intelligence and family environment. *Sos. Bilim. Derg.* **2006**, *16*, 169–175.
22. Orpinas, P.; Arthur, M.H. Creating a positive school climate and developing social competence. In *Handbook of Bullying in Schools*; Routledge: Washington, DC, USA, 2009; pp. 59–70.
23. Goleman, D. *Leadership: The Power of Emotional Intelligence*; More Than Sound LLC: Florence, MA, USA, 2021.
24. Stojiljković, S.; Gordana, D.; Blagica, Z. Empathy and teachers' roles. *Procedia-Soc. Behav. Sci.* **2012**, *69*, 960–966. [CrossRef]
25. Goroshit, M.; Meriav, H. Teachers' empathy: Can it be predicted by self-efficacy? *Teach. Teach.* **2016**, *22*, 805–818. [CrossRef]
26. Ackermann, E. Piaget's Constructivism, Papert's Constructionism: What's the Difference? 2001. Available online: https://learning.media.mit.edu/content/publications/EA.Piaget/_/Papert (accessed on 10 January 2020).
27. Misirli, A.; Komis, V. Robotics and programming concepts in early childhood education: A conceptual framework for designing educational. In *Research on e-Learning and ICT in Education*; Karagiannidis, C., Politis, P., Karasavvidis, I., Eds.; Springer: New York, NY, USA, 2014; pp. 99–118.

28. Jung, S.E.; Won, E. Systematic Review of Research Trends in Robotics Education for Young Children. *Sustainability* **2018**, *10*, 905. [CrossRef]
29. Toh, L.P.E.; Causo, A.; Tzuo, P.W.; Chen, I.M.; Yeo, S.H. A Review on the Use of Robots in Education and Young Children. *Educ. Technol. Soc.* **2016**, *19*, 148–163.
30. Pang, X.; Zhuang, X.; Tang, Z.; Chen, X. Polylactic acid (PLA): Research, development and industrialization. *Biotechnol. J.* **2010**, *5*, 1125–1136. [CrossRef] [PubMed]
31. Vidal, G.; Eyraud, C.-H.; Larose, C.; Lejan, É. Teaching Scientific Evidences of Climate Change to K12: A Key to Reach Social Acceptance of Mitigation and Adaptation Strategies. *EGU General Assembly Conference Abstracts*; Göttingen, Germany, 2021. Available online: https://meetingorganizer.copernicus.org/EGU21/EGU21-8097.html?pdf (accessed on 9 September 2021).
32. Rousell, D.; Amy, C.-M.-K. A systematic review of climate change education: Giving children and young people a 'voice' and a 'hand' in redressing climate change. *Child. Geogr.* **2020**, *18*, 191–208. [CrossRef]
33. Duch, B.J.; Susan, E.G.; Deborah, E.A. *The Power of Problem-Based Learning: A Practical How to for Teaching Undergraduate Courses in any Discipline*; Stylus Publishing, LLC: Sterling, VA, USA, 2001.
34. Silvestri, L.; Jeffrey, O. Using Rubrics to Increase the Reliability of Assessment in Health Classes. *Int. Electron. J. Health Educ.* **2006**, *9*, 25–30.

Article

A Framework for Using Humanoid Robots in the School Learning Environment

Deepti Mishra [1,*], Karen Parish [2], Ricardo Gregorio Lugo [3] and Hao Wang [1]

[1] Department of Computer Science (IDI), NTNU—Norwegian University of Science and Technology, 2815 Gjøvik, Norway; hawa@ntnu.no
[2] Faculty of Education, Inland Norway University of Applied Sciences, 2624 Lillehammer, Norway; Karen.Parish@inn.no
[3] Department of Information Security and Communication Technology (IIK), NTNU—Norwegian University of Science and Technology, 2815 Gjøvik, Norway; ricardo.g.lugo@ntnu.no
* Correspondence: deepti.mishra@ntnu.no

Abstract: With predictions of robotics and efficient machine learning being the building blocks of the Fourth Industrial Revolution, countries need to adopt a long-term strategy to deal with potential challenges of automation and education must be at the center of this long-term strategy. Education must provide students with a grounding in certain skills, such as computational thinking and an understanding of robotics, which are likely to be required in many future roles. Targeting an acknowledged gap in existing humanoid robot research in the school learning environment, we present a multidisciplinary framework that integrates the following four perspectives: technological, pedagogical, efficacy of humanoid robots and a consideration of the ethical implications of using humanoid robots. Further, this paper presents a proposed application, evaluation and a case study of how the framework can be used.

Keywords: school learning environment; human–robot interaction; pedagogy; education; efficacy; ethics

Citation: Mishra, D.; Parish, K.; Lugo, R.G.; Wang, H. A Framework for Using Humanoid Robots in the School Learning Environment. *Electronics* **2021**, *10*, 756. https://doi.org/10.3390/electronics10060756

Academic Editors: Savvas A. Chatzichristofis, Zinon Zinonos, Ying Tan and Jungong Han

Received: 29 January 2021
Accepted: 18 March 2021
Published: 23 March 2021

Publisher's Note: MDPI stays neutral with regard to jurisdictional claims in published maps and institutional affiliations.

Copyright: © 2021 by the authors. Licensee MDPI, Basel, Switzerland. This article is an open access article distributed under the terms and conditions of the Creative Commons Attribution (CC BY) license (https://creativecommons.org/licenses/by/4.0/).

1. Introduction

According to Oxford University researchers, many white and blue-collar jobs are at risk of the Fourth Industrial Revolution [1,2] with its increasing supply and demand of industrial robots globally [3]. According to the Economist Intelligence Unit's recently released Automation Readiness Index, not a single nation included in the study was fully prepared to address the challenge [4]. Robotics and efficient machine intelligence are the building blocks for the coming revolution [5,6]. Countries need a long-term strategy to deal with the challenges of automation and education must be at the center of it. Countries must provide students with a grounding in certain technical skills, such as computational thinking, which are likely to be required in many future roles [4]. Many such roles will also require an understanding of robotics [4].

Humanoid robots have already been used with children to examine various phenomena [7–9]. However, the use of humanoid robots in classrooms is a recent development [10]. The understanding of how children use and learn with these robots is beginning to display signs of future potential [10]. Much of the research to date has focused on the technological capabilities of robots to act as educational tools, focusing for example on language acquisition, Science, Technology, Engineering and Mathematics (STEM) and the basic principles of programming [11,12].

Educational robotics (ER) offer the possibility both of the facilitation and the evaluation of learning as "pedagogical agents" [13]. Through human–robotic interactions and targeted feedback, ER can be programmed to help with learning and develop technical skills through individual and collaborative learning [14]. In particular, ER can be used to target specific learning outcomes of subject knowledge (i.e., math), skills (i.e., programming and critical thinking) [15]. A recent meta-analysis [16] has shown that ER has been shown to improve knowledge and skills, help with transferring skills to other domains, increase creativity and motivation, increase the inclusion of broad and diverse populations and have an added benefit of increasing teacher development. ER has also shown benefits in STEM subjects [17], but in general, there are mixed findings on the effectiveness of ER [18]. This may be due to methodological shortcomings in design and evaluation [19].

In the context of educational robotics, there have been many efforts made to improve the teaching work in STEM programs to aid both teachers and learners; however, there is a lack of clear-cut guidelines or standards [20]. While ER is a growing field, the benefits to learning outcomes and the evaluations of these interventions need standardized and validated frameworks to assess the efficacy of ER in schools.

Robots have also been used as educational agents with a focus on developing social psychological skills. For example, the iCat robot has been used to teach children to play chess [21] and the Keepon robot for robot-assisted therapy with children on the autistic spectrum [22,23]. Research with the NAO, RoboVie and Tiro humanoid robots have provided insights into the psychological dynamics characterizing social human-robot interaction (HRI) in educational settings [24]. However, multiple studies [25,26] have acknowledged a lack of understanding of the efficacy of humanoid robots in school learning environments (SLEs).

In recent reviews, it has been found that humanoid robots largely act as novices, tutors or peers in educational settings to support learning and that the majority of these applications are driven by technological feasibility and not grounded in didactical theory [12,26]. When theory has provided some didactical frame-working for working with robots in educational contexts, the following approaches have been used: project-based learning, experiential learning and constructionist learning [27].

From the technological perspective, the social element of the interaction between robot and human is difficult to automate and fully autonomous social tutoring behavior in unconstrained environments remains elusive [28]. The robots are limited by the degree to which they can accurately interpret the learner's social behavior [28]. Building artificial "social interaction requires a seamless functioning of a wide range of cognitive mechanisms and their interfaces" ([28] p. 7). This social element of the interaction is especially difficult to automate [12] and needs further research.

In Reference [27], the benefits of incorporating robotics as an educational tool in different areas of knowledge are explored. Another study [29] investigated how robots in the classroom reshape education and foster learning. A recent study has reported that students are generally motivated and have a very positive reaction to the introduction of educational robotics in the academic curriculum [30]. Although humanoid robots have the potential to bring benefits, the incorporation of such technology into SLEs brings its own set of challenges for teachers. These are due to the robot's presence in the social and physical environment and the expectations that the robot creates in the user [28]. In Reference [31], the influence of robots on children's behavior and development and their reaction to the robot's appearance and visual characteristics were examined. There is a call for research into people's interactions with and social reactions towards humanoid robots as a way to shape ethical, social and legal perspectives on these issues as a prerequisite to the successful introduction of robots into our societies [32].

There is a lack of empirical research involving the use of robots in SLEs; therefore, there is a need for more effective analysis of the potential of robotics as a teaching tool for schools [27]. A recent review of the literature [16] observed that the majority of the existing studies lacked an experimental or quasi-experimental design. Another study [33] proposed having more intervention studies with focused research design in K–12 spaces. Recently emphasis has been put on the importance of conducting these interventions with effective robotic pedagogies and underlying theoretical foundations that are required for educational modules in STEM education to make robot-based pedagogies more efficient [16].

Further to this, it has been argued that educational robotics allows for an integrated, multidisciplinary approach and it is essential to provide a more holistic portrayal of the research on educational robots [16]. In response, this article contributes to the field by presenting a multidisciplinary framework. The multidisciplinary nature of the framework acknowledges that the use of humanoid robots in SLEs must be holistic, rather than focusing on just the technical, or the pedagogical for example. As a position paper, our intention is to present the framework with a proposed application, evaluation and case study by way of an illustration. In particular, we propose that the introduction and evaluation of technology in the classroom should be explored from the following four perspectives: pedagogical, technological/human robot interaction, psycho-social development and a consideration of the ethical implications of using humanoid robots.

Firstly, from an educational perspective and in light of the United Nations Sustainable Development Goal 4 which seeks to "Ensure inclusive and equitable quality education and promote lifelong learning opportunities for all." [34], can humanoid robots contribute anything to the promotion of quality education? Can a humanoid robot offer a learning experience tailored to the learner, supporting and challenging students in ways unavailable in current resource-limited classrooms? Can humanoid robots contribute to adapted or differentiated education? Can robots be used and thereby "... free up precious time for human teachers, allowing the teacher to focus on what people still do best: providing a comprehensive, empathic, and rewarding educational experience" [12]? What are the pedagogical and didactical foundations or frameworks for the use of humanoid robots in educational settings?

Secondly, how can Artificial Intelligence (AI) and robotic technology be integrated to develop humanoid robots to teach children in SLEs?

Thirdly, how do the human factors interaction with humanoid robotics influence psycho-social development in children (i.e., motivation, self-efficacy, resilience)?

Finally, as AI technology develops and the social interactions between robots and students become more complex, what are the ethical implications of using humanoid robots in educational settings and how do we address these?

This article firstly in Section 2 presents the multidisciplinary framework for using humanoid robots in SLEs. Section 3 includes concrete suggestions on how the proposed framework could be applied and evaluated by researchers and practitioners in different contexts and settings. Section 4 describes a case study related to the application of this framework in a real setting followed by a conclusion and future work.

2. A Multidisciplinary Framework for Humanoid Robots in School Learning Environments

In this section, we present the presuppositions upon which the framework is built. We then present an outline of the framework, including a brief description of each of the four aspects.

2.1. Presupposition

The framework is grounded in the values of inclusive education and the right to education for all. The foundations of inclusive education are built upon the principles of universal human rights and supported by international organizations, such as UNICEF, UNESCO, the Council of Europe, the United Nations and the European Union [35]. The Salamanca Declaration includes all groups of students in danger of marginalization highlighting the right to participate in common learning activities within the ordinary school system, regardless of special needs, gender, ethnicity, culture, social background, etc. [36]. If inclusive education is to become a reality, we must develop learning environments to embrace diversity. For example, some students understand quickly through images, others may prefer texts and readings. Some may deal well with theories, others may learn through experiments and examples and some may have specific learning difficulties [37]. Some learn through engaging in discussion with others, whilst some learn through having the opportunity to work alone. What are the potential ways in which humanoid robots can contribute to the development of SLEs that embrace diversity and help to promote inclusive education?

With the focus on the learning of each individual, the student is placed at the center of our proposed framework as shown in Figure 1.

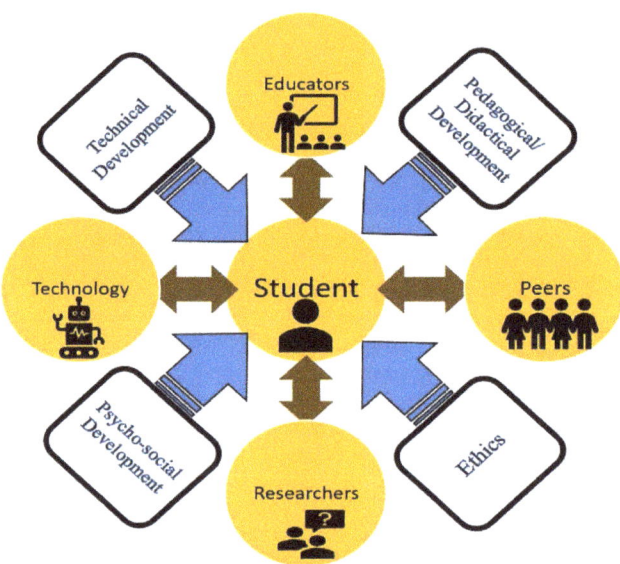

Figure 1. A framework for introducing humanoid robots in school learning environments.

In a two-way collaboration with the student, educators (teachers and assistants), technology (humanoid robots), peers and researchers contribute to the SLE. Through the development of this collaborative learning environment, we seek to explore the following areas.

2.2. Pedagogical/Didactical Development

It is proposed that the pedagogical/didactical aspect of the framework should be grounded in experiential learning theory (ELT) which defines learning as "the process whereby knowledge is created through the transformation of experience. Knowledge results from the combination of grasping and transforming experience" [38] (p. 41). With the focus on learning as a "process", the ELT model proposes two dialectically related modes of grasping experience—Concrete Experience (CE) and Abstract Conceptualization (AC) [39]. In addition, the ELT model proposes two dialectically related modes of transforming experience—Reflective Observation (RO) and Active Experimentation (AE). The ELT model allows for a diversity of learning styles in students and acknowledges that for some, concrete experience helps them to grasp, perceive and gain new knowledge. However, for others, grasping or taking hold of new information happens through symbolic representation or abstract conceptualization. In the same way, some of us transform or process experiences by watching others and reflecting on the observation of others who are involved in the experience, whereas others actively experiment, jumping right in and doing things [39].

We propose that the ELT model be used as the theoretical foundation for the didactical approach. Further, the didactical approach must be developed as part of an iterative process in collaboration with those working in the specific SLE context.

2.3. Technological Development for Human–Robot Interaction

In order to realize a successful human–robot interaction, a key element—a spoken dialog system—needs to be implemented. A spoken dialog system consists of multiple components: speech recognition, natural language understanding, dialog management, natural language generation and speech synthesis [40]. On the other hand, social signal processing [41], social expression generation, turn-taking [42] and physical action generation including pose, hand, arm, head movements [43] are also important elements of a spoken dialog system, especially in multiparty dialogs. In order to maintain a multi-turn dialog, the robot has to maintain and understand the conversational history and context [44].

2.4. Psycho-Social Development

We propose that the individual and social behaviors, capabilities, constraints and limitations should be explored as the humanoid robot is incorporated into the SLE. The development of behavioral prediction models for user-behavior and performance outcomes can then be used to develop the framework further for human cognition in socio-technical systems. We propose the modeling of user–task interaction at the individual and group level of the SLE through systematic experimentation and naturalistic testing. The research findings then have the potential to be used in the development of evidence-based training modules that cover both the needs of the students and teachers.

2.5. Ethical Development

We recognize the need for applied ethical engagement when it comes to the use of humanoid robots in social settings such as learning environments. In particular, we wish to see research with humanoid robots that moves beyond the question of "what can we do technically?" to "what should we do, ethically?"

This framework requires a theoretical contribution by developing a didactical approach that can be used and evaluated through working with humanoid robots in SLEs. The proposed framework allows for the expansion of the boundaries of artificial intelligence by implementing various components of spoken dialog systems for humanoid robots. Further, we propose that the key performance indicators, to assess different aspects of HRI in SLEs, are identified to determine the efficacy of existing HRI metrics and propose new HRI metrics if required. Finally, we propose the development and evaluation of the humanoid robot's efficacy to help pupils to learn. The framework enables the promotion of students and teachers learning about how robots work, but it also uses robots to help them to learn competencies needed for a future with robots. In particular, the framework incorporates applied ethical engagement as an important aspect of the competencies needed for a future with robots.

3. Proposed Application and Evaluation of the Framework

In this section, we first present our methodological standpoint for the framework followed by an outline of how the framework can be applied, evaluated and executed.

3.1. Methodology

The proposed framework requires a multidisciplinary and multiple-methods approach that will include applied, qualitative and quantitative aspects. Whilst respecting the integrity of the different paradigms, we propose the utilization of different ways of knowing to expand our understanding of the potential ways in which humanoid robots can be used in SLEs to promote student learning. With such a research design, we can expand the scope of our understanding as different methods will be used to assess different aspects of the phenomenon [45]. By combining qualitative and quantitative aspects in our evaluation of humanoid robots in the SLE, we incorporate both subjective experiences and objective observations [46,47].

3.2. Methodological Implications

Research into understanding and learning the effects of human–robotic interactions in schools is still in the early stages. The applied nature and real-world complexity of this field mean this research is multidisciplinary. The use of a mixed-methods research design that includes qualitative, quantitative and theory can lead to insights and discoveries in this novel domain. There are few existing theoretical frameworks in the literature encompassing these research questions and validated approaches. This requires using validated approaches from different disciplines, that is, psychology, human factors and educational research.

This framework also promotes using naturalistic settings over laboratory settings due to the nature of the domain studied. Socio-technical domains incorporate human-technology interactions while in social settings (i.e., classroom) but research frameworks need to be validated across domains. Experimental laboratory settings are applicable to identify the impact of variable manipulation on outcome variables and may give high internal validity, but it is limited in generalizations. Naturalistic design allows the observation of participants in their natural settings and observes for outcomes. While this approach may have low internal validity, it is high in ecological validity, therefore the findings can be generalized to other populations.

Both quantitative and qualitative approaches need to include their respective approaches to validity (See for qualitative approaches [48]). By using a mixed-methods design and triangulation methods, new insights on ELT approaches can be validated and form the foundations for future work that are applicable to all four domains (technological, psychological, educational and ethical). This approach will allow for the reflective observation and active experimentation of the ELT framework.

3.3. Preparation

We propose that the framework must be situated within the specific context and take into account the needs of the teachers and SLE. In particular, the needs of the SLE must be established regarding the identification and definition of scenarios related to existing educational contents suitable for the use of humanoid robotics, for example, grade/age, types of school, state/private, types of learning formats, group/individual/whole class. In order to complete this task, the researcher will need to engage in a period of consultation and information gathering with school teachers. This activity may take multiple sessions as the researchers learn about existing educational content to be able to develop a set of scenarios involving humanoid robots depending upon the learner profile(s) to deliver context-appropriate and tailored educational content.

This preparation stage also involves organizing information sessions for teachers and parents along with obtaining necessary permissions from relevant ethical boards and parents since these activities involve children.

In addition, in this preparation stage, the researchers must identify and design appropriate data collection tools that measure learning outcomes, performance, user interface experience and psychosocial skill development.

3.4. In-Context Development of Various Aspects and Evaluation Instruments

3.4.1. Pedagogical

As stated in Section 2.2, we propose the development of a didactical approach to working with humanoid robots in SLEs based on ELT [38]. The didactical approach should, however, be developed in collaboration with the teachers and based on the needs of the specific SLE context. We propose that this should be an iterative process to allow for the investigation of both how the development of a didactical approach can contribute to more effective working with humanoid robots in specific SLEs, and in what ways educational activities with humanoid robots can promote learning.

We propose that to evaluate the effectiveness of the pedagogical aspect of the framework the main approach should be qualitative and exploratory. Since programming robots for social interaction and for teaching is highly creative, it requires co-design and development with stakeholders, and an iterative development methodology will be highly beneficial. Semi-structured interviews could be used to evaluate humanoid robots in

SLEs with respect to HRI, robot behavior, natural language understanding and social signal processing.

In addition, a qualitative approach could be used to focus on both student and teacher experiences of introducing and working with humanoid robots in the classroom. The advantage of adopting a qualitative approach is that it allows us to explore how the students and teachers interact with the humanoid robots, including feelings, strengths/challenges and ethical considerations of working with humanoid robots.

3.4.2. Technical

The main approach for technical development can be iterative, requiring continuous qualitative and quantitative evaluation. We propose to implement a spoken dialog system consisting of various components (as shown in Figure 2) to create engaging educational activities with humanoid robots.

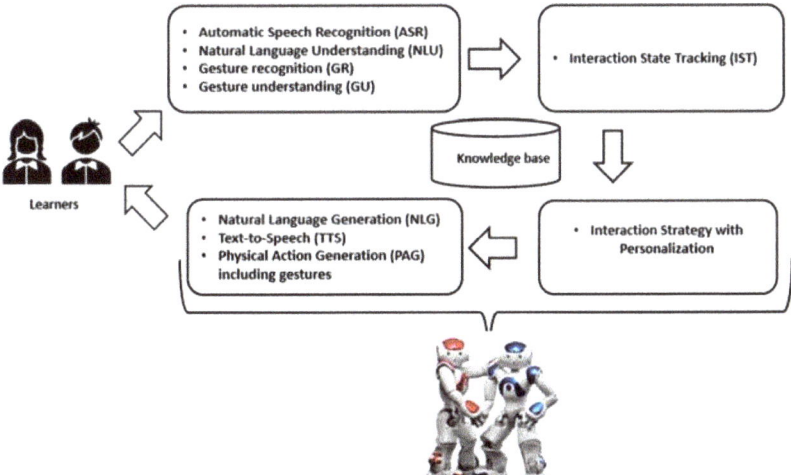

Figure 2. Proposed implementation of spoken dialog system (SDS) in SLEs.

(a) Automatic speech recognition, natural language understanding, gesture recognition and understanding so that the robot can perceive the learning environment and human participants;
(b) Interaction state tracking so that the robot can determine the current state comprising of the dialog act and/or gesture by maintaining a "memory" to store interaction history and contextual information;
(c) The robot will then form an interaction strategy plan consisting of various actions with personalization;
(d) Natural language generation, text to speech and physical action generation including gestures with personalization for adaptive learning customized according to the level and learning speed of the user.

The above-mentioned activities can be designed for two settings, individual educational activities and multi-party educational activities with group interactions and teamwork between peers.

Existing tools and libraries provided with commercially available humanoid robots can be explored for components such as automatic speech recognition and generation, natural language understanding and generation, text to speech synthesis and the main focus can be on components such as creating a knowledge base for efficient dialog management to be used with the humanoid robot in SLEs. Other available techniques and methods such as for natural language understanding, deep learning methods involving Convolutional Neural

Networks [49] or Recurrent Neural Networks [50] and for leveraging external knowledge for natural language understanding [51] and natural language generation [52], knowledge graphs can also be explored.

Various metrics (e.g., cognitive interaction, degree of monotonicity, human awareness—human recognition, characterization and adaptation, robots' self-awareness, safety) have been discussed to evaluate and assure functionality of humanoid robots [53]. However, a key factor that limits the success of human–robot teams is the lack of consistent test methods and metrics for assessing the effectiveness of HRI [54] since existing metrics are not sufficient to capture all aspects of HRI [53] in every setting [55]. Therefore, HRI metrics in conjunction with observations, quantitative (e.g., questionnaire) and qualitative methods (e.g., semi-structured interviews) can be used to evaluate humanoid robots in SLEs.

3.4.3. Psycho-Social

We propose the development of behavioral prediction models for user-behavior and performance outcomes that are situated in the specific context of the SLE. This can be achieved through the modeling of user-task interaction at the individual and group level of the SLE through systematic experimentation and naturalistic testing.

We propose that by using validated approaches from human factors and cognitive engineering, we can evaluate the efficacy of humanoid robots on the psycho-social development of learners (i.e., motivation, self-efficacy, resilience). This can be achieved by developing and validating applied interventions based on human factors and cognitive engineering aspects where the interaction of individual aspects of human behavior (microcognition; i.e., self-efficacy, resilience, metacognition) and naturalistic environments (macrocognition; i.e., shared situational awareness, communication) are considered in both human–robot interaction and human–human interactions. These measures will be analyzed using social science paradigms (i.e., statistical analysis, cognitive task analysis, qualitative interviews).

3.4.4. Ethics

Careful consideration must be given to ethics and it is proposed that these considerations are situated in the specific context in which the research is taking place. Some considerations to be taken are, first, what are the implications for the students and teachers/assistants in introducing humanoid robots into the SLE? As researchers, we have an ethical responsibility to "do no harm" to those who participate in such studies. Secondly, as the technological advancement of artificial intelligence continues and humanoid robots become more autonomous, what ethical applications apply to the robots? Thirdly, and related to the above two, how do we prepare students and teachers/assistants for a future with robots which are founded upon ethical considerations?

4. Case Study

This section presents an example of how the framework can be implemented.

Aim: To explore how humanoid robots can assist teachers to promote Mathematics and programming skills.

Sample: Grade 6 students ($n = 20$) and teachers ($n = 2$)

Preparation: Researchers have two meetings with the grade 6 teachers to prepare the content of the three-day workshop, including discussion surrounding the learning needs of the students. Ethical consent is gained from the relevant body to conduct the research. An information meeting is held for teachers and parents/guardians of participants under the age of 16. Informed consent is gained from participants and the parents/guardians of participants under the age of 16. The discussion related to the selection of evaluation methods (e.g., observations, quantitative and qualitative) and instruments is also initiated at this stage.

Didactical approach: Execution of a three-day workshop which involves the following activities for the participants:

Activity 1—Introduction to robots—including a presentation and class discussion led by the researchers. Informed consent is explained to the participants.

Activity 2—Participants complete a pre-test structured questionnaire of their metacognitive judgment on how they expect to do working with the robot, math and programming.

Activity 3—Participants are separated into groups of four or five by the regular class teachers. Each group participates in a one-hour practical session led by the researchers. The session includes basic programming and math tasks using the robot.

Activity 4—Participants complete a post-test structured questionnaire of their metacognitive judgment about how well they think they did working with the robot, math and programming.

Activity 5—The researchers conduct semi-structured group interviews with each of the four groups of grade 6 students to gather in-depth data about the experiences of working with the robot.

Activity 6—Plenary—including a presentation and class discussion surrounding the experiences of working with robots, what a future with robots looks like and the ethical considerations to working with robots, led by the researchers.

Activity 7—The researchers conduct semi-structured group interviews with the grade 6 teachers to gather in-depth data about the experiences of working with the robot.

Technical development: The robots are programmed for activities related to mathematics and programming tasks. This is done in multiple iterations so that other researchers and teachers can provide feedback in order to improve these activities before the workshop with the participants. Questionnaire and semi-structured interviews are used to evaluate human–robot interaction along with participants' views on the current technical capabilities, limitations and potential improvements in robot activities for future workshops.

Psycho-social development: This is explored during the three-day workshop and in particular through the collecting of pre- and post-test data that explores the participants' self-efficacy and meta-cognition.

Ethical development: This occurs primarily through the discussions during Activity 6 and in the semi-structured interviews. This is also covered through following ethical guidelines such as informed consent.

Evaluation: Both qualitative and quantitative analysis of the interviews and pre- and post-test data can be analyzed using validated methodologies. Inferential statistics can be used for quantitative data, while qualitative approaches such as Interpretive Phenomenological Analysis or Thematic Analysis can be used to analyze interview data. These approaches have been validated across social and technical domains to measure experiences, interactions and outcomes.

5. Conclusions and Future Work

This position paper has proposed a framework that addresses an under-researched and not well-understood aspect of humanoid robots in SLEs. Rapid technological progress in SLEs needs to be balanced with a holistic approach to research that attempts to support human adaptation in rapidly changing socio-technical system dynamics. With such a multidisciplinary framework, we offer the possibility to move beyond extending the technical possibilities to evaluating how technological advancements can be used in an ethical way to benefit individuals and society through education. In particular, the multidisciplinary framework presented here integrates the technological, pedagogical, psycho-social and ethical aspects of HRI. Further, this paper has presented a possible way to apply and evaluate the framework, methodologically, along with an example of a case study. It is hoped that readers will be inspired to adopt this interdisciplinary framework as their starting point for research into how humanoid robots can be used effectively in SLEs and contribute to the development of the research base within this field.

Although this study includes concrete suggestions regarding the application and evaluation of the proposed interdisciplinary framework along with a case study describing its application in a real setting with a focus on learning mathematical and programming concepts, it is beyond the scope of this paper to include empirical data. Further research is needed to empirically evaluate the framework in order to derive more grounded conclusions. Therefore, future work will report on the comparative analysis, both by longitudinal research and by comparison with the results of experiments designed within different courses and also at other schools.

If humanoid robots can contribute positively towards the SLE and increased learning opportunities (motivation, self-efficacy, resilience) then this will benefit both students in the short and long-term, and in turn society. This framework has the potential to impact the teaching and training of future generations of students that can be reached and benefit from the implementation of the proposed framework. The addition of humanoid robotics in the classroom may facilitate the learning process in students who struggle and may decrease apprehensive behaviors in students, allowing for cognitive processes to open up for more efficient learning and the promotion of inclusive education for all.

Author Contributions: Conceptualization, D.M., K.P. and R.G.L.; Investigation, D.M., K.P., R.G.L. and H.W.; Methodology, D.M., K.P., R.G.L. and H.W.; Visualization, D.M. and K.P.; Writing—original draft, D.M. and K.P.; Writing—review and editing, D.M., K.P., R.G.L. and H.W. All authors have read and agreed to the published version of the manuscript.

Funding: This research received no external funding. The APC cost is covered by NTNU—Norwegian University of Science and Technology.

Institutional Review Board Statement: The study was conducted according to the guidelines of the Declaration of Helsinki, and approved by the NSD—Norwegian Centre for Research Data (reference number: 238991 and date of approval: 28 September 2020).

Informed Consent Statement: Informed consent was obtained from all subjects involved in the study.

Data Availability Statement: No new data were created or analyzed in this study. Data sharing is not applicable to this article.

Conflicts of Interest: The authors declare no conflict of interest.

References

1. BBC. Written Evidence to UK Parliment Artificial Intelligence Select Committee's Publications. Available online: https://publications.parliament.uk/pa/ld201719/ldselect/ldai/100/10001.htm (accessed on 23 March 2021).
2. Frey, C.B.; Osborne, M.A. The future of employment: How susceptible are jobs to computerisation? *Technol. Forecast. Soc. Chang.* **2017**, *114*, 254–280. [CrossRef]
3. Robots double worldwide by 2020. In Proceedings of the International Federation of Robotics Press Conference, Tokyo, Japan, 18 October 2018.
4. Economist Intelligence Unit. *The Automation Readiness Index: Who Is Ready for the Coming Wave of Automation?* Economist Intelligence Unit: London, UK, 2018.
5. Accenture UK Limited. Written Evidence to UK Parliment Artificial Intelligence Select Committee's Publications. Available online: https://www.gov.uk/government/publications/government-response-to-the-house-of-lords-select-committee-on-artificial-intelligence (accessed on 23 March 2021).
6. Kim, J.-H.; Myung, H.; Lee, S.-M. Robot. Intelligence technology and applications. In Proceedings of the 6th International RiTA Conference 2018, Kuala Lumpur, Malaysia, 16–18 December 2018; Springer: Berlin/Heidelberg, Germany, 2019; Volume 1015.
7. Tanaka, F.; Cicourel, A.; Movellan, J.R. Socialization between toddlers and robots at an early childhood education center. *Proc. Natl. Acad. Sci. USA* **2007**, *104*, 17954–17958. [CrossRef]
8. Mazzoni, E.; Benvenuti, M. A robot-partner for preschool children learning English using socio-cognitive conflict. *J. Educ. Technol. Soc.* **2015**, *18*, 474–485.
9. Ioannou, A.; Andreou, E.; Christofi, M. Pre-schoolers' interest and caring behaviour around a humanoid robot. *TechTrends* **2015**, *59*, 23–26. [CrossRef]
10. Crompton, H.; Gregory, K.; Burke, D. Humanoid robots supporting children's learning in an early childhood setting. *Br. J. Educ. Technol.* **2018**, *49*, 911–927. [CrossRef]
11. Balogh, R. Educational robotic platform based on arduino. In Proceedings of the 1st International Conference on Robotics in Education RiE 2010, Bratislava, Slovakia, 16–17 September 2010; pp. 119–122.
12. Powers, K.; Gross, P.; Cooper, S.; McNally, M.; Goldman, K.J.; Proulx, V.; Carlisle, M. Tools for teaching introductory programming: What works? In Proceedings of the 37th SIGCSE Technical Symposium on Computer Science Education, New York, NY, USA, 3–5 March 2006; pp. 560–561.

13. Tang, A.L.; Tung, V.W.S.; Cheng, T.O. Dual roles of educational robotics in management education: Pedagogical means and learning outcomes. *Educ. Inf. Technol.* **2020**, *25*, 1271–1283. [CrossRef]
14. Scaradozzi, D.; Screpanti, L.; Cesaretti, L. Towards a definition of educational robotics: A classification of tools, experiences and assessments. In *Smart Learning with Educational Robotics*; Springer: Berlin/Heidelberg, Germany, 2019; pp. 63–92.
15. Ronsivalle, G.B.; Boldi, A.; Gusella, V.; Inama, C.; Carta, S. How to implement educational robotics' programs in Italian schools: A brief guideline according to an instructional design point of view. *Technol. Knowl. Learn.* **2019**, *24*, 227–245. [CrossRef]
16. Anwar, S.; Bascou, N.A.; Menekse, M.; Kardgar, A. A systematic review of studies on educational robotics. *J. Pre-Coll. Eng. Educ. Res.* **2019**, *9*, 2. [CrossRef]
17. Arís, N.; Orcos, L. Educational robotics in the stage of secondary education: Empirical study on motivation and STEM skills. *Educ. Sci.* **2019**, *9*, 73. [CrossRef]
18. Zhong, B.; Xia, L. A systematic review on exploring the potential of educational robotics in mathematics education. *Int. J. Sci. Math. Educ.* **2020**, *18*, 79–101. [CrossRef]
19. Hoorn, J.F.; Huang, I.S.; Konijn, E.A.; van Buuren, L. Robot tutoring of multiplication: Over one-third learning gain for most, learning loss for some. *Robotics* **2021**, *10*, 16. [CrossRef]
20. Phan, M.-H.; Ngo, H.Q.T. A multidisciplinary mechatronics program: From project-based learning to a community-based approach on an open platform. *Electronics* **2020**, *9*, 954. [CrossRef]
21. Leite, I.; Castellano, G.; Pereira, A.; Martinho, C.; Paiva, A. Modelling empathic behaviour in a robotic game companion for children: An ethnographic study in real-world settings. In Proceedings of the Seventh Annual ACM/IEEE International Conference on Human-Robot Interaction, Boston, MA, USA, 5–8 March 2012; pp. 367–374.
22. Feil-Seifer, D.; Mataric, M. Robot-assisted therapy for children with autism spectrum disorders. In Proceedings of the 7th International Conference on Interaction Design and Children, Chicago, IL, USA, 11–13 June 2008; pp. 49–52.
23. Kozima, H.; Michalowski, M.P.; Nakagawa, C. Keepon. *Int. J. Soc. Robot.* **2009**, *1*, 3–18. [CrossRef]
24. Lehmann, H.; Rossi, P.G. Social robots in educational contexts: Developing an application in enactive didactics. *J. eLearn. Knowl. Soc.* **2019**, *15*, 27–41.
25. Kazakoff, E.R.; Sullivan, A.; Bers, M.U. The effect of a classroom-based intensive robotics and programming workshop on sequencing ability in early childhood. *Early Child. Educ. J.* **2013**, *41*, 245–255. [CrossRef]
26. Ros, R.; Baroni, I.; Demiris, Y. Adaptive human-robot interaction in sensorimotor task instruction: From human to robot dance tutors. *Robot. Auton. Syst.* **2014**, *62*, 707–720. [CrossRef]
27. Benitti, F.B.V. Exploring the educational potential of robotics in schools: A systematic review. *Comput. Educ.* **2012**, *58*, 978–988. [CrossRef]
28. Belpaeme, T.; Kennedy, J.; Ramachandran, A.; Scassellati, B.; Tanaka, F. Social robots for education: A review. *Sci. Robot.* **2018**, *3*, eaat5954. [CrossRef] [PubMed]
29. Karim, M.E.; Lemaignan, S.; Mondada, F. A review: Can robots reshape K-12 STEM education? In Proceedings of the 2015 IEEE International Workshop on Advanced Robotics and Its Social Impacts (ARSO), Lyon, France, 1–3 July 2015; pp. 1–8.
30. Román-Graván, P.; Hervás-Gómez, C.; Martín-Padilla, A.H.; Fernández-Márquez, E. Perceptions about the use of educational robotics in the initial training of future teachers: A study on steam sustainability among female teachers. *Sustainability* **2020**, *12*, 4154. [CrossRef]
31. Toh, L.P.E.; Causo, A.; Tzuo, P.-W.; Chen, I.-M.; Yeo, S.H. A review on the use of robots in education and young children. *J. Educ. Technol. Soc.* **2016**, *19*, 148–163.
32. De Graaf, M.M. An ethical evaluation of human-robot relationships. *Int. J. Soc. Robot.* **2016**, *8*, 589–598. [CrossRef]
33. Xia, L.; Zhong, B. A systematic review on teaching and learning robotics content knowledge in K-12. *Comput. Educ.* **2018**, *127*, 267–282. [CrossRef]
34. United Nations. *The Sustainable Development Goals Report 2019*; United Nations: New York, NY, USA, 2019.
35. Haug, P. Understanding inclusive education: Ideals and reality. *Scand. J. Disabil. Res.* **2017**, *19*, 206–217. [CrossRef]
36. Unesco. The Salamanca Statement and Framework for action on special needs education. In Proceedings of the World Conference on Special Needs Education—Access and Quality, Salamanca, Spain, 7–10 June 1994; Unesco: Salamanca, Spain, 1994.
37. Truong, H.M. Integrating learning styles and adaptive e-learning system: Current developments, problems and opportunities. *Comput. Hum. Behav.* **2016**, *55*, 1185–1193. [CrossRef]
38. Kolb, D.A. *Experiential Learning: Experience as the Source of Learning and Development*; Prentice-Hall International: Upper Saddle River, NJ, USA, 1984.
39. Kolb, D.A.; Boyatzis, R.E.; Mainemelis, C. Experiential learning theory: Previous research and new directions. *Perspect. Think. Learn. Cogn. Styles* **2001**, *1*, 227–247.
40. Lison, P.; Meena, R. Spoken dialogue systems: The new frontier in human-computer interaction. *XRDS Crossroads ACM Mag. Stud.* **2014**, *21*, 46–51. [CrossRef]
41. Funakoshi, K. A multimodal multiparty human-robot dialogue corpus for real world interaction. In Proceedings of the Eleventh International Conference on Language Resources and Evaluation (LREC 2018), Miyazaki, Japan, 7–12 May 2018; pp. 35–39.
42. Baxter, P.; Kennedy, J.; Belpaeme, T.; Wood, R.; Baroni, I.; Nalin, M. Emergence of turn-taking in unstructured child-robot social interactions. In Proceedings of the 2013 8th ACM/IEEE International Conference on Human-Robot Interaction (HRI), Tokyo, Japan, 4–6 March 2013; pp. 77–78.

43. Jokinen, K.; Wilcock, G. Multimodal open-domain conversations with robotic platforms. In *Multimodal Behavior Analysis in the Wild*; Elsevier: Amsterdam, The Netherlands, 2019; pp. 9–26.
44. Yang, L.; Qiu, M.; Qu, C.; Chen, C.; Guo, J.; Zhang, Y.; Croft, W.B.; Chen, H. IART: Intent-aware response ranking with transformers in information-seeking conversation systems. In Proceedings of the Web Conference 2020, Online, 20–24 April 2020; pp. 2592–2598.
45. Greene, J.C. *Mixed Methods in Social Inquiry*; John Wiley & Sons: Hoboken, NJ, USA, 2007; Volume 9.
46. Almalki, S. Integrating quantitative and qualitative data in mixed methods research—Challenges and benefits. *J. Educ. Learn.* **2016**, *5*, 288–296. [CrossRef]
47. Golafshani, N. Understanding reliability and validity in qualitative research. *Qual. Rep.* **2003**, *8*, 597–607.
48. Flick, U. *An Introduction to Qualitative Research*; SAGE Publications: Thousand Oaks, CA, USA, 2018.
49. Kim, S.; Banchs, R.E.; Li, H. Exploring convolutional and recurrent neural networks in sequential labelling for dialogue topic tracking. In Proceedings of the 54th Annual Meeting of the Association for Computational Linguistics, Berlin, Germany, 7–12 August 2016; Volume 1, pp. 963–973.
50. Yao, K.; Peng, B.; Zhang, Y.; Yu, D.; Zweig, G.; Shi, Y. Spoken language understanding using long short-term memory neural networks. In Proceedings of the 2014 IEEE Spoken Language Technology Workshop (SLT), South Lake Tahoe, NV, USA, 7–10 December 2014; pp. 189–194.
51. Heck, L.; Hakkani-Tür, D.; Tur, G. Leveraging knowledge graphs for web-scale unsupervised semantic parsing. In Proceedings of the 14th Annual Conference of the International Speech Communication Association, Lyon, France, 25–29 August 2013; pp. 1594–1598.
52. Li, W.; Peng, R.; Wang, Y.; Yan, Z. Knowledge graph based natural language generation with adapted pointer-generator networks. *Neurocomputing* **2020**, *382*, 174–187. [CrossRef]
53. Murphy, R.R.; Schreckenghost, D. Survey of metrics for human-robot interaction. In Proceedings of the 2013 8th ACM/IEEE International Conference on Human-Robot Interaction (HRI), Tokyo, Japan, 4–6 March 2013; pp. 197–198.
54. Marvel, J.A.; Bagchi, S.; Zimmerman, M.; Aksu, M.; Antonishek, B.; Wang, Y.; Mead, R.; Fong, T.; Amor, H.B. Test methods and metrics for effective HRI in collaborative human-robot teams. In Proceedings of the 2019 14th ACM/IEEE International Conference on Human-Robot Interaction (HRI), Daegu, Korea, 11–14 March 2019; pp. 696–697.
55. Begum, M.; Serna, R.W.; Kontak, D.; Allspaw, J.; Kuczynski, J.; Yanco, H.A.; Suarez, J. Measuring the efficacy of robots in autism therapy: How informative are standard hri metrics. In Proceedings of the Tenth Annual ACM/IEEE International Conference on Human-Robot Interaction, Portland, OR, USA, 1–4 March 2015; pp. 335–342.

Review

A Systematic Review on Oral Interactions in Robot-Assisted Language Learning

Vivien Lin [1], Hui-Chin Yeh [2] and Nian-Shing Chen [3,*]

[1] Graduate Institute of Children's English, National Changhua University of Education, Changhua City 50007, Taiwan; vivienster@gmail.com
[2] Department of Applied Foreign Languages, National Yunlin University of Science and Technology, Douliou City 64002, Taiwan; hyeh@gemail.yuntech.edu.tw
[3] Program of Learning Sciences, Institute for Research Excellence in Learning Sciences, National Taiwan Normal University, Taipei City 10610, Taiwan
* Correspondence: nianshing@gmail.com

Abstract: Although educational robots are known for their capability to support language learning, how actual interaction processes lead to positive learning outcomes has not been sufficiently examined. To explore the instructional design and the interaction effects of robot-assisted language learning (RALL) on learner performance, this study systematically reviewed twenty-two empirical studies published between 2010 and 2020. Through an inclusion/exclusion procedure, general research characteristics such as the context, target language, and research design were identified. Further analysis on oral interaction design, including language teaching methods, interactive learning tasks, interaction processes, interactive agents, and interaction effects showed that the communicative or storytelling approach served as the dominant methods complemented by total physical response and audiolingual methods in RALL oral interactions. The review provides insights on how educational robots can facilitate oral interactions in language classrooms, as well as how such learning tasks can be designed to effectively utilize robotic affordances to fulfill functions that used to be provided by human teachers alone. Future research directions point to a focus on meaning-based communication and intelligibility in oral production among language learners in RALL.

Keywords: educational robots; oral interactions; communicative language teaching; instructional design; robot-assisted language learning

Citation: Lin, V.; Yeh, H.-C.; Chen, N.-S. A Systematic Review on Oral Interactions in Robot-Assisted Language Learning. *Electronics* **2022**, *11*, 290. https://doi.org/10.3390/electronics11020290

Academic Editors: Savvas A. Chatzichristofis and Zinon Zinonos

Received: 30 November 2021
Accepted: 11 January 2022
Published: 17 January 2022

Publisher's Note: MDPI stays neutral with regard to jurisdictional claims in published maps and institutional affiliations.

Copyright: © 2022 by the authors. Licensee MDPI, Basel, Switzerland. This article is an open access article distributed under the terms and conditions of the Creative Commons Attribution (CC BY) license (https://creativecommons.org/licenses/by/4.0/).

1. Introduction

Educational robots are known as capable interactive pedagogical agents in language learning situations. Previous research has reported on educational robots' affordances for training skills in one's first, second, or foreign language [1–3]. Despite claims about the potential of educational robots for helping learners improve language skills [4], no previous review has focused on instructional design that leads to positive learning outcomes in robot-assisted oral interactions. This review study, therefore, aims to fill this gap by analyzing 22 empirical studies in terms of the interactive design of oral tasks by highlighting the teaching methods used, the oral task types, the role served by the robot and the instructor/facilitator, as well as their effectiveness in improving oral competence.

1.1. Scope and Definitions

Educational robots can be divided into hands-on robots and service robots [5]. While hands-on robots are programmable robots for engineering-related practice (e.g., LEGO Mindstorm), service robots are intelligent robots that can be used by teachers as complementary tools for incorporating specific learning content and activities suitable in their teaching contexts [5,6]. This study focuses on educational robots used in language education. In language learning, the use of educational service robots can effectively facilitate the presentation of digital content, task repeatability, interactivity, flexibility for incorporating different learning theories, and embodied interactions conducive to learning [7,8]. In particular, interactions that enable oral communication between learners and robots serve as the core of robot-assisted language learning (RALL).

Defined as interactive language learning through systems that involve the physical presence of a robot, RALL provides learners face-to-face communication opportunities that resemble real conversation situations [9]. In RALL, verbal (e.g., question-and-answer) and non-verbal modalities (e.g., gesturing, nodding, face tracking) can be used to facilitate language practice, leading to increased learning motivation, interest, engagement, as well as cognitive gains [9]. Furthermore, based on principles of instructional design for technology-enhanced language learning, appropriate use of language teaching methods for designing learning activities [10], as well as the roles played by various interactive agents in RALL, need to be examined closely in order to yield insights on effective pedagogy [11]. This systematic review thus provides details about actions taken by various interacting agents (e.g., learner, robot, instructor/facilitator) in RALL and their effects on learning outcomes to help language practitioners develop interactive course design using robots in their classrooms.

1.2. The Review Study

This study aimed to conduct a systematic review, which is a type of review under the Search, Appraisal, Synthesis, and Analysis (SALSA) framework [12,13]. A systematic review adheres to a set of guidelines to address research questions by identifying reliable and quality data on a topic. Researchers who conduct this type of review (a) undertake exhaustive, comprehensive searching, (b) apply inclusion/exclusion to appraise the data, (c) synthesize the data through a narrative accompanied by tabular results, and (d) analyze what is known to provide recommendations for practice, or analyze what is unknown and state uncertainty around findings with recommended directions for future research [12].

Previous research has investigated the affordances of educational robots, and analyzed the learning goals of their use of robots for different age groups [7]. However, one research topic that remains unexplored in RALL is the cooperation between the teacher and robot and the resulting language teaching and learning model in this cooperation mode [5]. It is therefore necessary to delve into the implementation of RALL in the classroom by focusing on the interactions, including the activity design, the interactive agents involved, and interaction processes. It is also important to identify how these interaction elements affect the learning outcomes and shape learners' experiences in RALL. Four research questions were therefore formulated as follows:

RQ1: What language teaching methods are incorporated in the design of oral interactions in RALL?
RQ2: Which types of oral interaction task design are employed in RALL?
RQ3: What roles do robots and instructors fulfill when facilitating oral interactions in RALL?
RQ4: What are the learning outcomes of RALL oral interactions in terms of learners' cognition, language skills, and affect?

2. Literature Review

2.1. Oral Interactions in Language Classrooms

Traditionally, interaction is the process "face-to-face" action channeled either verbally through written or spoken words, or non-verbally through physical means such as eye-contact, facial expressions, gesturing [14]. In second or foreign language development, comprehensible input plays an important role [15]. That is, language learners must be able to understand the linguistic input provided to them in order to communicate authentically through spoken or written forms. In particular, classroom oral interaction involves listening to authentic linguistic output from others and responding appropriately to continue in a communicative event such as role play, dialogue, or problem-solving [16,17]. Classroom oral exchanges involve two interlocutors speaking and listening to each other in order to predict the upcoming content of the communicative event and prepare for a response [18]. As a consequence, providing the context for negotiation of meaning becomes a crucial part of facilitating classroom oral exchanges that range from formal drilling to authentic, meaning-focused communication such as information exchange [19,20]. Aside from establishing the context for oral interactions, creating intended communication behaviors among learners is another goal for language instructors. According to Robinson [14], two types of interaction can be found in a classroom—verbal and non-verbal interaction. Verbal oral interactions refer to communicative events such as speaking to others in class, answering and asking questions, making comments, and taking part in discussions. Non-verbal interaction, on the other hand, refers to interacting through behaviors such as head nodding, hand raising, body gestures, and eye contact [17]. As educational robots assume humanoid forms, they can help achieve various types of classroom oral interactions in RALL.

2.2. Affordances of Educational Robots for Language Learning

As [21] reported, educational robots began to emerge in North America, South Korea, Taiwan, and Japan in the mid-2000s. These robots took anthropomorphic forms and assumed the role of peer tutors, care receivers, or learning companions. They have an outer appearance of anthropomorphized robots with faces, arms, mobile devices, and tablet interfaces attached to their chests [21]. With different functions such as voice/sound, facial, gestural, and position recognition, RALL is perceived to be more fun, credible, enjoyable, and interactive than computer-assisted language learning, which relies on mobile devices (e.g., smartphones or tablets) only. Different stimuli can be provided as robots assume roles such as human or animal characters that speak, move, or make gestures [21] to tell stories. The various multimodal sources of input and interactions make RALL a promising field with numerous possibilities in interactive design for language learning. In addition, as the robot-assisted learning mode is still at its infant stage, there remains a great potential for researchers and educators to postulate language learning models for best practices.

2.3. Human-Robot Interaction in RALL

Prior research has shown that human–robot interaction (HRI) can lead to language development. In a review study [22], comprehensive insights were provided about the effects of HRI on language improvement, including robots' positive impact on learner motivation and emotions due to novelty effects, and the multifaceted robotic behaviors that provide social and pedagogical support to learners. Through immersing in real-life physical environments and manipulating real-life objects, learners can also experience embodied learning to improve their vocabulary, speaking, grammar, and reading. Whole body movements and gestures have been found conducive to vocabulary learning, for example.

Robots are capable of complementing humans in language learning scenarios that focus on specific language skills such as speaking, grammar, or reading. Studies have concluded that robots can help children gain vocabulary equally well as human teachers. Furthermore, the use of robots in language learning has a great impact on learners' affective state, including learning-related emotions. In the presence of a robot, instead of a human teacher, learners' anxiety is reduced, and they are less afraid of making mistakes in front of a humanoid robot. Higher confidence has also been reported among teenage students when they practiced speaking skills in robot-assisted situations [22].

2.4. Applying Language Teaching Methods in Interactive Design in RALL

Cheng et al. [7] claimed that language education is ranked at the top as a learning domain with the application of educational robots. The reported types of language learning varied from general, foreign, to second or additional language skills; and the popular age levels for applying RALL were between ages of three and five (preschool), and prior to puberty (primary school), as these are two critical periods for language learning. Further connection needs to be made between language teaching methods and RALL instructional design. In this regard, the notion of *didaktik* can be applied [23]. *Didaktik* is a German term comparable to the North American concept of instructional design that considers learner needs, task design, and learning materials. Jahnke and Liebscher [23] argued that an emphasis should be put on the role of the teacher and how his/her course design translates or connects to student learning and performance. The *Didaktik* system has three components—the instructor, the learner, and the course content or design. The design of second and/or foreign language learning activities involves the incorporation of teaching methods as a basis for the intended learning experience.

As outlined by [24], twentieth-century language instruction mainly employed a number of language teaching methodologies in second or foreign language learning settings. According to [24], language practitioners continuously swing between methodologies that are strictly managed and those that are more laissez faire in terms of content and amounts. On one side of the pendulum swing stand the traditional methods developed in early twentieth century, these include grammar translation, direct method, and the reading method. By the mid-twentieth century, the audiolingual method (ALM) emerged mainly for teaching oral skills. Highlighting drill-based practice, ALM presents specific language structures (e.g., sentence patterns) to learners in a systematic and organized manner and helps them replace native language habits with target language habits. The method also includes pronunciation and grammar correction through drills.

Following ALM was the emergence of total physical response (TPR) and teaching proficiency through reading and storytelling (TPRS). As a method, TPR [25] directs learners to listen to commands in the target language and immediately respond with a commanded physical action. TPRS also extended from TPR and aimed to develop oral and reading fluency in the target language. By having learners tell interesting and comprehensible stories in the classroom, TPRS has been perceived as a useful technique for fostering 21st century speaking skills, connecting closely with the concept of comprehensible input and the natural approach [26].

As ALM gradually faded in the 1980s, communicative approaches such as communicative language teaching (CLT) became the dominant foreign and second language teaching paradigm, and has continued to gain popularity worldwide in the 21st century [27]. In a way, CLT makes up for shortcomings of ALM by focusing on the functional aspect of language rather than the formal aspect. Therefore, CLT mainly trains learners' communicative competence through authentic interactions (e.g., role-play scenarios) instead of ensuring pronunciation or grammatical accuracy [28]. CLT activities usually incorporate meaningful tasks such as interviews, role-play, and opinion giving [29].

3. Methods
3.1. Search Strategy

The authors employed a search strategy to retrieve articles published between 2010 and 2020 [30,31] in order to survey the development of RALL in the past decade. The databases included Web of Science, ERIC, and Ebsco, while journal sources included ten journals, most of which were from the Social Sciences Citation Index, in the field of educational technology and computer-assisted language instruction (e.g., Computers & Education, British Journal of Educational Technology, Computer-Assisted Language Learning, Educational Technology Research & Development, Interactive Learning Environments, System). The researchers conducted six searches using the following key terms—"Interactive robots AND language learning," "L1 learning AND robots," "L2 learning AND robots," "Educational robots," "Robot," and "Humanoid," which led to the retrieval of 1897 articles.

3.2. Study Selection

After the initial article retrieval, the researchers underwent a study selection process. The researchers first eliminated inaccessible, duplicate, and non-English articles, which reduced the number of articles to 1887. After these articles were removed, the remaining studies were screened by title, abstract, and type of study. Specifically, titles and abstracts that indicated the use of robots for language learning were selected. Also, only empirical studies were selected. Therefore, other article types such as review studies, book reviews, proceedings, and editorials were eliminated, leading to 1202 studies remaining for further screening based on the Method, Results, and Discussion sections. In particular, the researchers evaluated the rigor of the Method section, evidence of learning outcome in the Results, and pedagogical implications in the Discussion. This led to 49 eligible studies for inclusion/exclusion.

3.3. Eligibility: Inclusion/Exclusion Criteria

With a total of 49 studies eligible for assessment, rigorous inclusion/exclusion criteria were applied to obtain valid data on interactions in RALL. The criteria were as follows:

- The study must present physical use of robots;
- The study must focus on language learning;
- The study must employ rigorous methodology with sufficient details;
- The study must report about robot-learner interactions in detail, including the specific language input and output during the interactions.

As shown in Figure 1, articles that failed to meet the inclusion criteria were removed. For example, studies that used virtual robots or studies with a focus on subjects other than language learning were removed. Similarly, studies that did not provide thorough accounts of the instructional design for oral interactions (including the language input and output in RALL) were eliminated. The final number of selected articles was twenty-two with the publication period spanning from 2010 to 2020.

3.4. Data Extraction

The data extraction process involved close reading of the 22 selected studies. First, the general research profile (See Table A1) with characteristics (e.g., country, target language, implementation duration, research design, technological components) were coded. Second, based on the *Didaktik* instructional design model, which includes three components—the instructor, the learner, and the course design, the researchers coded content on the learning activity, role of the robot as a pedagogical agent, interactive task design, language input and output, and learning outcome in terms of cognition, affect, and skill (see Tables A2 and A3). Table 1 provides the coding scheme for the interactive oral task design (See Table A3).

3.5. Tabulations

A series of tabulations were conducted by one of the co-authors and one experienced research assistant. First, general characteristics were identified. For example, the target language for each study was categorized as (a) a first language, (b) a foreign language, and (c) a second language (See Table A1). Another general characteristic identified was the major theoretical foundations in RALL and their benefits and drawbacks across the 22 studies. The last general characteristic concerned the technological affordances in RALL, including the type of robot and the sensors used (See Table A1).

Second, the distribution of major language teaching methods (e.g., audiolingual method, communicative language teaching) applied in the 22 reviewed studies was tabulated (See Table A2). Many studies employed more than one language teaching method in their activities. Third, oral interaction tasks that were considered effective in the selected studies were categorized into (a) storytelling, (b) role-play, (c) action command, (d) question-and-answer, (e) drills (e.g., repeating/reciting), and (f) dialogue (See Table A3). Fourth, the roles played by the robot and the support provided by the instructor/facilitator were coded (See Table A2). The robot's main roles included (a) role-play character, (b) action commander, (c) dialogue interlocutor, (d) learning companion, and (e) teacher assistant; while the support by human instructors/facilitators included (a) procedural support, (b) learning support, and (c) technical support. Fifth, the language input and output were coded (See Table A3). Specifically, the language input mode was categorized into (a) linguistic, (b) visual, (c) aural, (d) audiovisual, and (e) gestural/physical modes; and the language output was categorized into four levels based on linguistic complexity, including (a) phonemic level (referring to the smallest sound unit in speech, e.g., the phonetic entities /b/, /æ/, and /t/, respectively in the word bat), (b) lexical level, (c) phrasal level, and (d) sentential level. During the entire inter-coding process, one of the researchers served as the first coder and created a coding scheme to train the second coder. Then, after initial coding trials on three studies, the two coders met and discussed the resulting discrepancies to engage in another trial. After all the studies were coded, the inter-coder reliability in terms of percent agreement was calculated to be 87%.

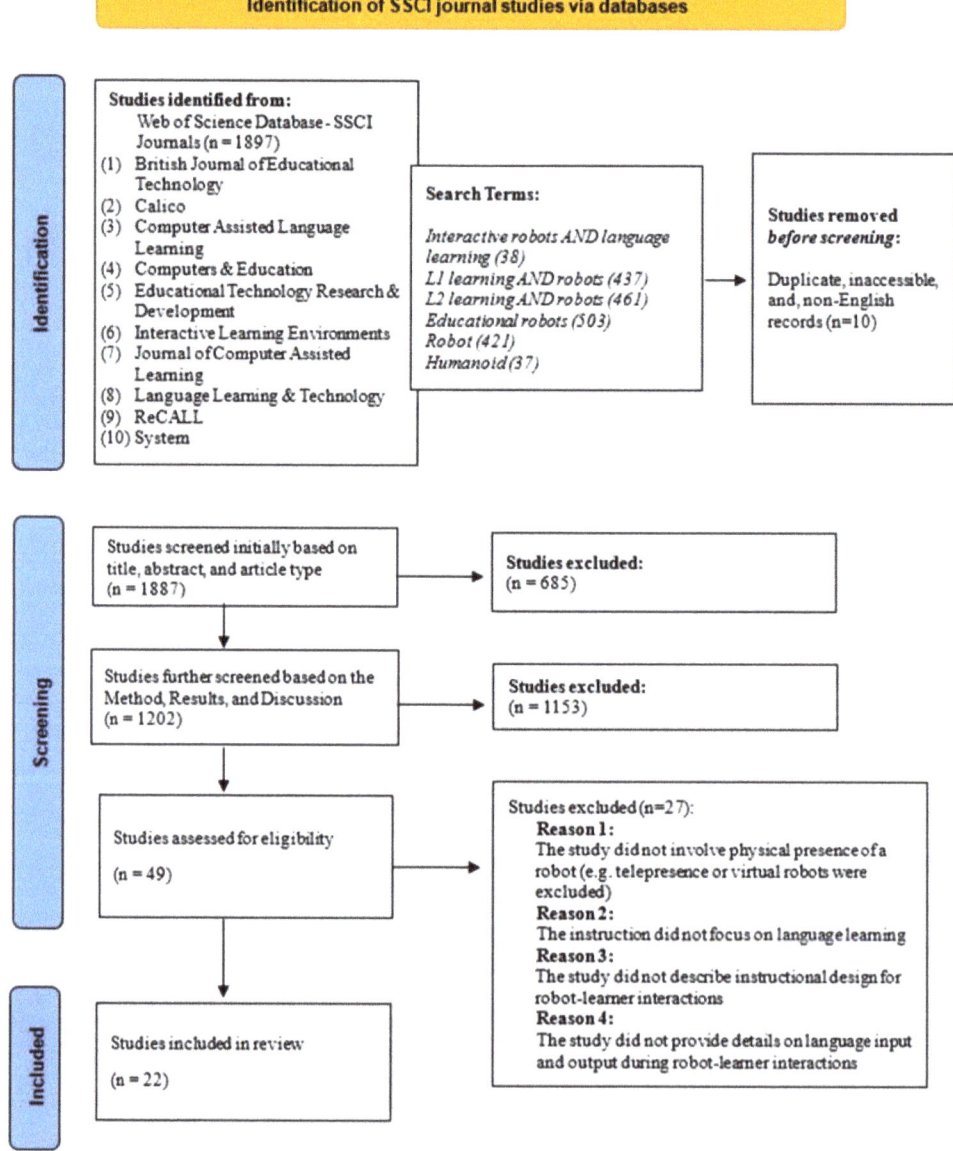

Figure 1. PRISMA flow chart showing the selection process (available online: http://www.prisma-statement.org/ (accessed on 7 March 2021).

Table 1. Coding Scheme for Task Design for Oral Interactions in RALL.

Code	Descriptor	Example Coded Item	Reference
Interactive Task Design	The type of task designed to engage learners in oral interactions (e.g., drill, question-and-answer, dialogue, role-play, action commands, acting out a story)	Drill: Recite - Robot questioning - Total physical response storytelling	[32]
Interaction Mode	The number of learners in the two-way robot-learner interaction (e.g., one-to-one or one-to-many)	Robot-Learner Interaction: - One-to-many	[33]
Instructional Focus	Specific goal for learning the target language items—focus on form (e.g., accuracy) or focus on meaning (e.g., communicative competence) Opened = With open-ended answers Closed = With fixed answers	Form-Focused: Closed - Identifying the 26 alphabets Meaning-Focused: Closed - Making self-introductions	[34]
Teacher Talk by Robot	The type of teacher talk fulfilled by the robot, (e.g., knowledge teaching, skill training, procedural prompts, motivational elements, and affective feedback)	Knowledge Teaching: - 26 English alphabets Skill Training: - Naming body parts - Conversation - Storytelling Motivational Elements: - Song and dance motions	[34]
Input Mode	The type of multimodal input provided in the robot-assisted learning environment to facilitate the learners to acquire the target language (e.g., linguistic, visual, aural, audiovisual, and gestural/physical).	Visual: - Animation on robot screen - Robotic facial expressions and gestures Aural: - Robotic talk - Robotic sounds (e.g., music) Audiovisual: - Video	[35]
Oral Output	The complexity level of linguistic output produced by the learner during RALL oral interactions (e.g., phonemic, lexical, phrasal, or sentential level) with the possibility of closed or open answers	Phonemic level: Closed Lexical level: Closed Sentential level: Closed	[34]

3.6. Synthesis

Synthesis on the detailed instructional design for oral interactions in RALL was based on the type of task design and the actions performed by the robot, learners, and human facilitators/instructors. The researchers synthesized the coded data to connect the nature of each task type to the actual interactions induced by the task. For example, through storytelling, a robot could read a story aloud for the learner to listen and receive the linguistic input. The learners could then be asked to recite, repeat, or act out the story in a role play task to produce language output following the robot's content delivery or action commands. Furthermore, the language input and output, as well as the type of teacher talk afforded by the robot in each oral interactive task among the 22 studies were analyzed to help the researchers understand the mechanisms that enriched the oral interactions. The researchers sought evidence of stimulating and engaging elements in the designed oral tasks and were able to see that the oral interactive tasks were conducive to heightening the level of motivation, interest, and cognitive engagement, which in turned fostered the development of oral skills in language education.

4. Results
4.1. General Characteristics

Several characteristics in the general profile of the 22 studies were worth noting—the geographic research settings, education levels, the target language for acquisition with the robot-assisted activities, the research design, theoretical bases, and technological affordances in RALL. The countries that implemented robot-assisted oral interactions for language learning included Taiwan ($n = 6$), Japan ($n = 3$), Sweden ($n = 3$), Iran ($n = 3$), South Korea ($n = 2$), United States ($n = 2$), Turkey ($n = 2$), and Italy ($n = 1$). In terms of the distribution of RALL by learners' education levels, the results showed that primary schools engaged their learners in RALL most frequently ($n = 11$), followed by preschools ($n = 4$), higher education ($n = 4$), and secondary schools ($n = 3$). This finding indicates that robots best serve children in formal, primary schooling years, as children between the ages of 7 and 12 (the primary schooling age in most countries) still find robots fun and appealing as opposed to older teenagers who might find them somehow childish or less intellectually engaging. The second age group that benefited most from RALL was preschoolers. Similarly, toddlers and young children still enjoy interacting with humanoid robots. Coincidentally, primary school children and preschoolers belong to the two critical periods for language development. It is possible that since learners from these two developmental stages benefit most from enriched language learning activities, language educators devote more efforts by incorporating robot-assisted oral interactive learning activities to engage learners from these two age cohorts.

Target languages in the 22 RALL studies focused primarily on foreign language learning, especially learning English as a foreign language ($n = 14$) occurred most frequently, followed by Russian ($n = 1$) and Dutch ($n = 1$), while first and second language learning occurred less frequently, with three studies for both categories. As for the research design, the majority of the studies employed either single-group ($n = 7$) or between-group ($n = 6$) experiments; some of these experiments adopt pre-/post-test instruments ($n = 6$), while others adopt survey evaluation design ($n = 2$). Other research designs include quasi-experiments ($n = 4$), ethnographic study design ($n = 1$), and system design and implementation evaluation ($n = 1$). Overall, the research instruments revealed a trend of using quantitative, summative assessment in RALL. Specifically, over 70% of the studies employed tests such as listening, speaking, word-picture association, vocabulary, reading, and writing tests to measure learners' performance of target skills. Only less than 15% used qualitative, formative assessment on skills such as storytelling and drawing artifacts. Although 29% of the studies did use video recording to collect data on learning performance, the assessment methods remained test-oriented in RALL.

Two major theoretical bases were identified among the RALL studies—technologies for creating human–robot relationships and embodied cognition through robot-based content design. The first theoretical basis was developing robots for forming human–robot relationships through HRI interactions. Attempts to enable humanoid robots to autonomously interact with children using visual, auditory, and tactile sensors were realized [36]. Also, RFID tags enabled mechanisms such as identifying individual learners and adapting to their interactive behaviors to successfully engage learners in actual language use. Such findings support theoretical perspectives from social psychology by highlighting similarity and common ground in learning. Applying this perspective to RALL, it was imperative that robots bear similar attributes and knowledge as target users [36]. Doing so led to benefits such as engaged language use, improved oral skills, and higher motivation and interest in learning. However, novelty effects were reported [37]. Also, highly structured activities for autonomous robot responses led to little variation among learner responses. Recommendations were thus made about adapting robot behaviors to learners' responses.

The second theoretical basis was applying embodied cognition through robot-based content design. Robot-based content design, as opposed to computer-based content design, which consists of static user model and two-dimensional, visual and audio content displayed on screen consists of dynamic user models with visual, audio, and tangible, human-like humanoids with an appearance and body parts that perform face-to-face interactions [37]. In addition to tangible, interactive design, RALL design provided bidirectional interactive content through installing e-book materials, reaping combined benefits of e-learning tools and embodied language learning to improve learners' reading literacy, motivation, and habit [38].

As for technological affordances in RALL, the general functionalities included identifying multiple learners, recalling interaction history, speech recognition and synthesis, body movements, oral interactions, teaching, explaining, song playing, dancing, face recognition, language understanding and generation, dialogue interactions, motions on wheels, and interaction event tracking. Sensors such as wireless ID tags, eye/stomach/arm LEDs, RFID readers/sensors, infrared sensors, tactile sensors, sonars were used to support the various affordances.

4.2. Language Methods Used in RALL Oral Interactions (RQ1)

The language teaching methods that were used to create RALL oral interactions were based on language instruction theories that emerged during the 20th and 21st centuries. Moreover, some studies employed more than one language teaching method in their RALL oral interaction activity design. Figure 2 shows that the most popular method adopted was CLT ($n = 13$), followed by TPRS ($n = 7$), TPR ($n = 6$). Other methods such as multimedia-enhanced instruction, learning by teaching, socio-cognitive conflict ($n = 6$), ALM ($n = 4$), and multimodal stimuli ($n = 2$). In addition, studies that adopted multiple language teaching methods employed combinations such as CLT plus TPR plus TPRS ($n = 4$), CLT plus TPR ($n = 2$), CLT plus TPR plus ALM ($n = 1$), ALM plus TPRS plus TPR ($n = 1$), and CLT plus TPRS ($n = 1$).

4.3. Task Design for Oral Interactions in RALL (RQ2)

The task design for oral interactions was analyzed through a learner-centered perspective. The instructional design elements included (a) the task itself, (b) the language input provided by the robot and received by the learner, as well as (c) the oral language output produced by the learner. In terms of the interactive task design, the task design that led to oral interactions included dialogue ($n = 11$), storytelling/story acting ($n = 8$), question-and-answer ($n = 7$), Role Play ($n = 5$), drill ($n = 4$), and action commands ($n = 3$). The instruction embedded in the task design was more form-focused ($n = 12$) than meaning-focused ($n = 8$), with only a few studies that included both in the design ($n = 2$). Figure 3 presents the results on the interactive task design.

The mode of language input provided by the robot served as input from the learner's perspective, and mainly consisted of *aural* input ($n = 18$), followed by *visual* ($n = 11$), *linguistic* ($n = 4$), and *gestural/physical* input ($n = 3$), as shown in Figure 4.

Language output produced by the learners mostly consisted of sentential, closed answers ($n = 11$), followed by lexical, closed answers ($n = 13$), and others (See Figure 5).

4.4. Role of Robots and Instructors (RQ3)

From a design-based perspective, there were five possible roles the robots played in RALL oral interactions (Figure 6). The most common role was a dialogue interlocutor ($n = 12$). This referred to pre-determined dialogues where the robot conversed with the learners using fixed phrases or sentences. The second most frequent role fulfilled by the robot was a role-play character, where the robot acted out a story as one of the characters in the story ($n = 9$), followed by a companion that sings, dances, played with the learner, or showed pictures on its screen ($n = 5$), a teaching assistant that helped the teacher with any part of the instructional procedure (4), and action commander that acts out certain movements commanded by the learner during an activity (*n* = 1).

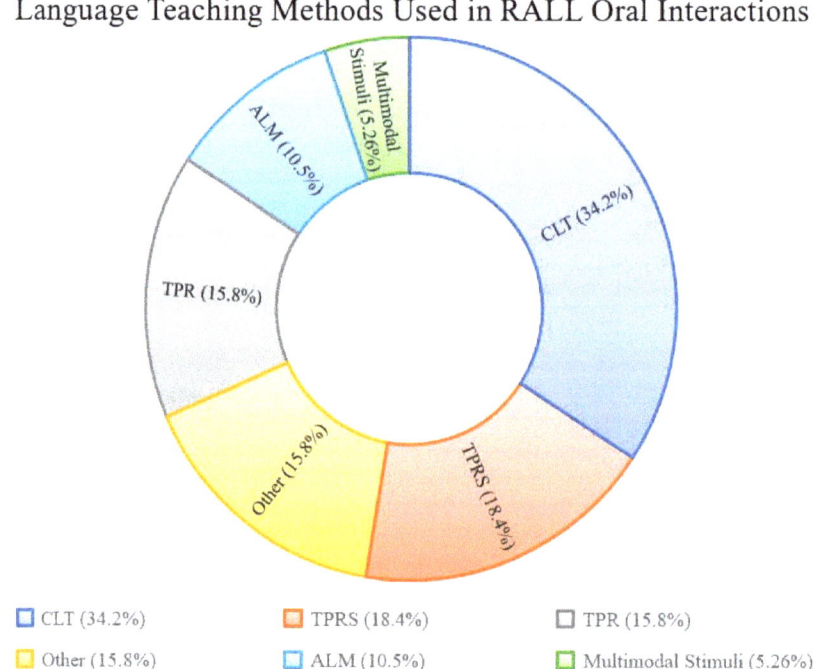

Figure 2. Language teaching methods in RALL oral interactions. NOTE: CLT = Communicative Language Teaching. TPRS = Teaching Proficiency through Reading and Storytelling. TPR = Total Physical Response. ALM = Audiolingual Method.

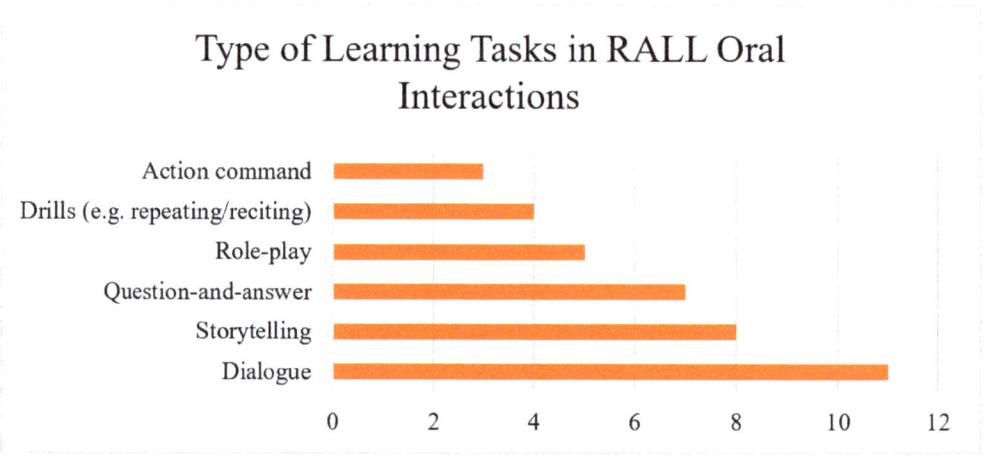

Figure 3. Type of task design for RALL oral interactions.

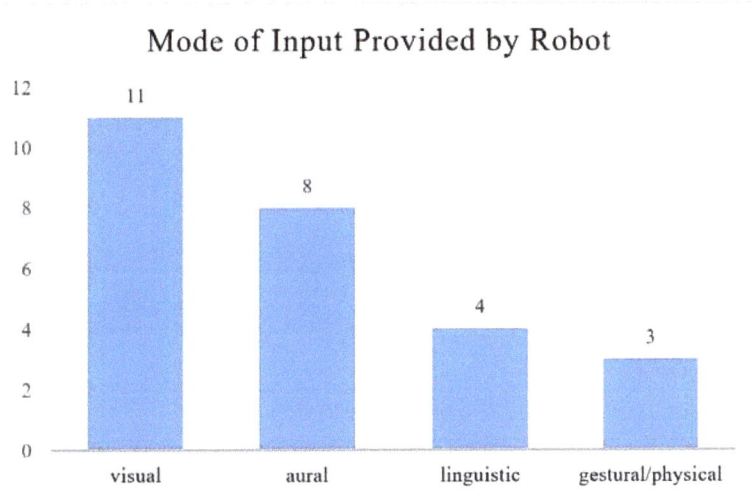

Figure 4. The mode of input the robot provides to the learner.

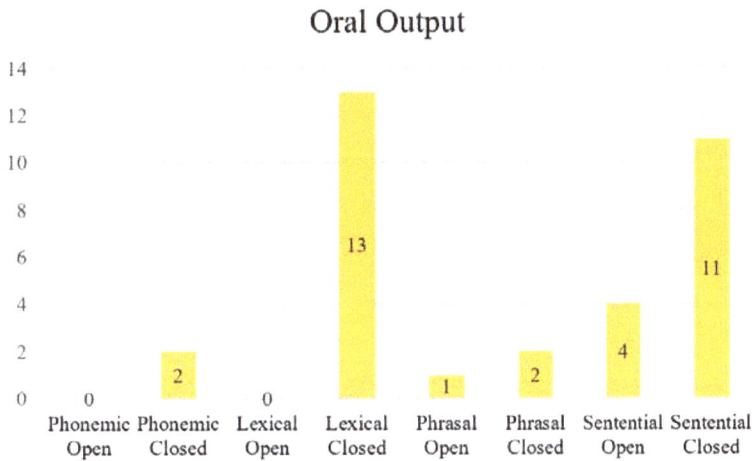

Figure 5. Type of oral output produced by learners.

In addition, the robot served a major function of providing teacher talk. Five kinds of teacher talk were provided, including skill training ($n = 12$), affective feedback ($n = 11$), knowledge teaching ($n = 7$), motivational elements ($n = 3$), and procedural prompts ($n = 2$). Finally, the instructor or facilitator would, in some studies, serve to provide additional support in RALL. The types of support included procedural support ($n = 9$), learning support ($n = 7$), and technical support ($n = 1$) for those studies that mentioned them.

The interactive oral task design allowed the robot, human facilitators, and learners to engage in a well-orchestrated speaking practice in a contextualized and meaningful way. Some example actions performed by the interacting agents are summarized in Table 2. It is evident that RALL oral interactive mechanisms can be multifarious, each specific to the oral communicative goal and context. In most cases, the interactions were based on robotic functions such as (a) speaking [32], (b) making gestures and movements [39],

(c) singing [34], (d) object detections [40,41], (e) voice recognition functions [42], and (f) display of digital content on the accompanying tablets [43]. While robots were used to facilitate bi-directional communication by initiating or engaging in verbal, gestural, and physical interactive processes to allow learners to practice receptive (e.g., listening and reading) and productive (e.g., speaking and writing) language use, human facilitators constantly provided procedural, learning, and technical support [34,38] to learners during the interactive tasks.

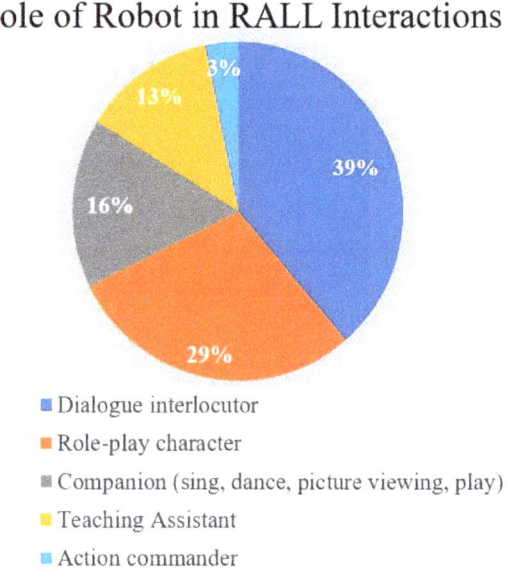

Figure 6. Roles played by robots in oral interactions.

Learners engaged mostly in productive language practice such as asking questions [33], repeating or creating words or sentences orally [34,39], creating stories orally [44] or in writing [33], performing movements [39], and acting in role plays [45]. They also relied on the guidance of human facilitators with various task needs such as game introduction [46] and provision of feedback [39].

4.5. Learning Outcomes of RALL Oral Interactions (RQ4)

The cognitive learning outcome of engaging learners in RALL oral interactions was reflected by effective academic achievement [35], increased concentration [35], understanding of new words through pictures, animation, and visual aid [44], and significant improvement in word–picture association abilities [46]. Children also gained the ability in picture naming [41]. In terms of the acquisition of language skills, there was significant improvement in learners' speaking skills [45]. Specifically, student-talk rate and response ratio increased [39], and the RALL system helped to significantly improve speech complexity, grammatical and lexical accuracy, number of words spoken per minute, and response time [43]. Pronunciation also became more native-like [43]. Efficient vocabulary gains [37,40,42] and retention [42] also occurred.

Table 2. Synthesis of Actions Performed by Interacting Agents in RALL.

Robot	Instructors/Facilitators	Learners
Uni-Directional Output • Recite words/sentences • Sing • Tell stories Bi-Directional Interaction • Answer questions with corpus database • Ask learners questions • Display learning content on screen or tablet • Encourage learners to read • Give commands for learners to act out • Perform movements upon detection of specific objects or learner commands/triggers • Play a role and react to learners' talk • Provide feedback • Reward correct answers with a dance	Directing the Robot • Allow the robot to interact with learners • Initiate teacher–robot dialogues • Show cards to the robot to make it perform movements Guiding the Learners • Ask questions • Ensure safety of learners • Explain the story • Give corrective feedback • Give instructional cues and praise • Introduce game goal • Introduce game narrative • Initiate the learning • Lead learners to practice • Model the play activity • Provide live-coaching • Respond to learners' questions/comments • Respond to participants' questions and comments Technical Facilitation • Fix technical problems • Help operate the robot and tablet PC • Use remote control to direct the robot in responses	Receptive Language Use • Listen to the robot read aloud a story • Place pictures in right position on robot's touch screen • Select the correct picture as an answer Productive Language Use • Answer questions posed by the robot (sometimes with actions or poses) • Command the robot to perform actions • Create a story using RFID tags for interacting with the robot • Create long sentences • Create storybooks about the robot • Imitate robot's recitations • Interact with the robot with different physical movements, greetings, or self-introductions • Perform movements commanded by the robot • Play a role in dialogue-based scenarios • Read aloud a story by following robotic guidance • Repeat after robot

In terms of language skills, there was significant improvement in listening and reading skills [39]. The slightly structured repetitive interaction pattern was perceived as beneficial for adult Swedish learners with low proficiency levels [47]. Evidence of the development of other skills such as physical motor skills due to the use of the robot [33] and children's ability in teaching [40] was also reported. As for affective learning outcomes, increased satisfaction, interest, confidence, motivation, and attitudes [34,45,47–49] were found toward the use of RALL and toward learning English [48,50]. In RALL, students became more active in a native-like setting [49]. Also, the robots reduce learner anxiety about making mistakes in front of native speakers [51]. Class atmosphere improved effectively due to RALL.

Moreover, positive emotional responses were identified from various studies. Of the coded emotional responses, over 91% were positive. Only several negative responses were identified, which showed learners' dissatisfaction with the robot's synthesized voice, facial expressions, and feelings of anxiety and fear of making mistakes in RALL. The positive responses are summarized as bolded keywords, which reflect the affective states of learners during RALL (See Table 3). The positive affect included emotional states such as eagerness, enthusiasm, satisfaction, appreciation, motivation, and enjoyment.

Table 3. Positive Cognitive, Skill, and Affective Learning Outcome.

Type of Cognition	Contributing Factor to Learners' Cognitive Development
Retention	Dialogue interactions with the robot supported by multimodal stimuli on target vocaublary items
Identification	Using a robot to guide learners through a picture naming task improved the ability to detect the right word
Understanding	Effective robot e-learning contents lead to better concentration
	Using an integrated robot learning system with pictures and animation visual aid helped learners understand new words
Association	Working with a humanoid robot using the socio-cognitive conflict paradigm to induce the knowledge acquisition process leads to significant improvement in word–picture association abilities
Social-cognition	Humanoid robots have the advantage of creating scenarios similar to child–child social-cognitive conflict situations
Analysis	Students were intellectually curious when learning with the robot (e.g., generate questions about mathematics and science reasoning)
Application	Asking a robot to take action using action commands (e.g., drink, sweep, play, brush)
Language skill	Contributing factor to learners' language development
Conversation	Repeated practice in comprehension and oral skills that resembled natural conversation
Vocabulary usage	Efficient learning of vocabulary (verbs) through teaching a robot to take actions or actual vocabulary use
Speaking, listening, and reading	Role-play and dialogue supported by principles of communicative language teaching, storytelling, total physical response, and audiolingual methods
Grammar accuracy	Focus on lexical items and sentence patterns in dialogues
Reading fluency	Focus on lexical items and sentence patterns in dialogues
Pronunciation	Focus on lexical items and sentence patterns in dialogues
Affective state	Keyword reflecting affective outcome through learners' feedback
Eagerness	Eager to find out what the robot would say or do
Enthusiasm	Enthusiastic to participate in answering or interacting with the robot
Laughs	Laughing at silly robotic actions
Enjoyment	Enjoyed conversing with robot and that the robot understood what the learner said
Appreciation	Appreciative of learning a word and its pronunciation without having to look it up
Confidence	Confident to speak English
Satisfaction	Satisfied with the robot's social interaction capabilities
Interest	Interested in learning English using robots
Likes	Liked playing with robots/Liked reading a book with robots/Liked one-on-one communication with robots
Encouragement	Encouraged by the happy atmosphere
Fun	The learning is a fun and interesting experience
Motivation	Highly motivated to study English using a robot

5. Discussion

The review identified recent efforts in the field of RALL that applied various types of robotic sensing technologies (e.g., personal identification mechanisms with RFID tags) to enrich robot–human interactive design. By integrating other tools such as e-books into robots, the field of RALL was advanced with more diverse instructional design. Detailed findings concerning each question are described below and summarized in Table 4.

With regards to the first research question, findings about the language teaching methods incorporated in RALL oral interactions revealed a heavy emphasis on communicative skill training with the use of Communicative Language Teaching and Teaching Proficiency through Reading and Storytelling. On the other hand, many studies also applied Total Physical Response and Audiolingual Method to train bottom-up language skills such as word recognition. Through RALL interactions, learners were able to experience receptive language learning [52] of vocabulary and sentences by mimicking authentic scenarios, reading the storylines, or seeing pictures in word-association tasks. Moreover, they engaged in productive language use by giving robot commands or creating stories. Such interaction opportunities in RALL can effectively enhance both productive communication (e.g., oral skills) and creative skills, which are important for 21st century learners [53].

Table 4. Alignment of research questions to review findings on RALL.

RQ #	Corresponding Findings
1	Communicative language teaching and teaching proficiency through reading and storytelling are often complemented by total physical response and audiolingual method, which train bottom-up oral interaction skills.
2	Applying communicative, meaning-based language learning principles, interactive oral tasks (e.g., dialogue, storytelling, role play) with robots were used to provide speaking practice with a focus on communicative competence instead of grammatical accuracy.
3	Robots' roles included a dialogue interlocutor, role-play character, learning companion, teaching assistant; instructors' roles included providing additional support such as procedural support, learning support, and technical support
4	Learning outcomes in RALL consisted of cognitive gains in target subject domains, skill-based improvements in various aspects of speaking, and a more exciting, enjoyable, fun, and encouraging affective learning experience

Although the dominant language teaching methods were communicative and storytelling approaches, existing affordances of educational robots such as giving commands and voice recognition have allowed traditional methods such as audiolingual and total physical response methods to complement the top-down, communicative approach in many of the studies reviewed. To a certain extent, the audiolingual and total physical response methods reflect a bottom-up approach that drills learners with simple instructional design (e.g., dialogues or question-and-answer). This implies that activity design using CLT, TPRS, ALM, and TPR may be easy for RALL practitioners to implement and is especially applicable to the majority of RALL research settings in East Asian contexts. Many traditional English classrooms rely on grammar translation and audiolingual methods for English learning, therefore, the drill-based practices that combine ALM or TPR with communicative approaches appears to be a feasible design combination.

To address the second research question on the types of oral interaction task design in RALL, the designed tasks were aligned to language teaching methods such as teaching proficiency through reading and storytelling to fulfill such goals as (a) learning the meaning of a set of vocabulary confined to the content of a story, (b) forming personalized questions through a spoken class story, (c) reading specific language structures in a story, and (d) acting out parts of a story by repeating certain language structures in the actors' lines [54]. The results showed that through communicative, meaning-based language teaching methods, RALL practitioners could create interactive language learning tasks such as storytelling and role play with robots acting as human- or animal-like characters. However, it is worthy to note that the oral output produced by learners tended to be closed answers at lexical and sentential levels, which points to future efforts to develop tasks that highlight intelligibility to fulfill meaning-focused instruction.

The pedagogical implication for RALL instructional design therefore highlights oral and reading fluency as well as communicative competence instead of grammatical accuracy. Language teachers that integrate RALL can adopt a wide array of methods along the skill-training spectrum. On one end, the tasks can focus on communicating in situated dialogues, and on the other end, the tasks can aim to improve accuracy in pronunciation or word-picture association. The instructional design consisting of these methods allows educational robots to engage learners in a context-specific manner to appeal to learners in various educational levels. This further confirms previous researchers' arguments that RALL is a feasible and valuable language learning mode for oral language development [55]. Furthermore, robots no longer are perceived as merely machines that automatically carry out a sequence of programmed actions, but as interactive pedagogical agents with multisensory affordances conducive to language learners' oral communication development [56].

In response to the third research question concerning the roles played by the robots and instructors, the findings showed that the robot usually played the most essential role during oral interactions in RALL, with timely support by a human instructor or facilitator. The findings are in line with previous claims that compared to books, audios, and web-based instruction, humanoid robots can best engage learners in language learning through human-like interactions [21]. The input–output process of comprehensible linguistic content that is vital in language learning [15] can be effectively fulfilled by oral interactions provided by robots.

As for the fourth research question, various learning outcomes in terms of cognition, language skills, and affect were identified. For cognitive learning outcomes, RALL effectively facilitated learners' understanding of vocabulary across all age levels. This echoed the findings by [57] that robot-assisted learning can effectively lead to cognitive gains in target subject domains (e.g., mathematics and science) with robots' complex, multi-sensorial content, and interactions. In this study, the subject domain is language, therefore, the cognitive learning gain is mostly focused on vocabulary comprehension (e.g., closed answers at the lexical level), which was reported as a major focus in the RALL oral instructional design. For the skill-based learning outcomes, significant improvement in terms of speaking abilities, including the complexity, accuracy, and pronunciation was evident in numerous studies. This suggests that oral interactions facilitated by robots are promising for improving oral proficiency among language learners. As put forth by Mubin et al. [58], robots have efficient information and processing affordances, which can reduce learners' cognitive workload and anxiety compared to traditional instructional modes. The review findings support the view that robots can foster speaking abilities without incurring anxiety or extra cognitive demands on the learners.

In terms of the affective learning outcome, which is an important aspect of language acquisition, the presence and affordances of educational robots made the learning experience more exciting, enjoyable, fun, and encouraging. The learners became more eager, enthusiastic, and confident in class under RALL conditions. These positive emotional states serve as advantages of incorporating educational robots in language education. In this respect, previous research has included emotional design as one of the instructional conditions in multimedia learning that enhanced learning [59] with increased motivation and better performance. It has been proven that positive emotional states during learning can activate retention and comprehension during learning according to [59]. The review thus confirms the positive impact of robot-assisted interactions in language learning scenarios.

This review study had three limitations. The first limitation concerns the small sample size of the articles reviewed (n = 22). This limitation is mainly due to the current limited number of studies on RALL oral interactions in existing databases, as RALL is a new research niche with gradual, growing efforts focusing on the analysis on instructional design involving various interacting agents. However, with a narrow research focus and strict inclusion/exclusion procedures, the review did reach data saturation since the studies provided rather rich data for answering the research questions. Other systematic reviews with relatively small sample sizes have also proven to be valuable with rigorous systematic review procedures [60]. Secondly, the studies varied in terms of educational levels, which in part was also due to the constraint of a small sample size. Despite the limitation, the authors were able to obtain the expected patterns as the focus was on analyzing instructional design for interactions in language learning with the use of educational robots. The third limitation was the duration of the 22 studies, most of them were not longitudinal, therefore, the researchers cannot make claims about valid learning outcomes in the long run.

6. Conclusions

This systematic review reported on general research trends for RALL and analyzed interactions among various agents, the robot, the learners, and the human facilitator across educational levels. Specifically, the research questions focused on (a) the language teaching methods, (b) instructional design, (c) roles of robot and instructors/facilitators, and (d) cognitive, skill-based, and affective learning outcomes. The review findings suggested that RALL instructional design employ communicative language teaching and storytelling as the most dominant language learning methods, and these two methods are often complemented by audiolingual and total physical response methods. The learning tasks are based on the principles of the identified language learning teaching methods, and the resulting interaction processes and effects proved to be conducive to language acquisition. Interaction effects from the learning tasks led to positive cognitive, skilled-based, and affective outcomes in language learning.

By examining the benefits and drawbacks of RALL theoretical perspectives and design practices, the review contributes to the research field of robot-assisted language teaching and learning with in-depth exploration and discovery about effective instructional design elements and their effects on interaction processes and language learning. The detailed analysis helps to add new insights and provide specific design elements to guide RALL practitioners including teachers, instructional designers, and researchers.

Future research should aim to develop more sophisticated functions to improve the accuracy and adaptivity for mechanisms such as speech recognition, feedback giving, and personal identification, and engage multiple learners in RALL interactions via collaborative oral tasks. In addition, as storytelling appears as a recent trend of activity design in RALL, forming detailed and applicable storytelling rubrics that emphasize intelligibility in oral production via functions such as automatic speech recognition will help ensure the meaning-focused nature of interactive RALL. Finally, it will be worthwhile to investigate innovative ways to design and assess interactions for learners at different educational levels using innovative teaching methods. Efforts should also aim to combine RALL with other emerging technologies such as the use of tangible objects and internet-of-things technology [61] to better facilitate authentic and embodied language learning for young learners. Finally, specific emotional design in RALL leading to socio-emotional development among young learners holds promises in the RALL research area.

Author Contributions: Conceptualization, V.L. and N.-S.C.; methodology, V.L. and N.-S.C.; validation, V.L. and H.-C.Y.; investigation, V.L.; writing—original draft preparation, V.L.; writing—review and editing, H.-C.Y.; supervision, N.-S.C.; funding acquisition, N.-S.C. All authors have read and agreed to the published version of the manuscript.

Funding: This research was partly funded by the Ministry of Science and Technology, Taiwan under grant numbers MOST-109-2511-H-003-053-MY3, MOST-108-2511-H-003-061-MY3, MOST-107-2511-H-003-054-MY3, and MOST 108-2511-H-224 -009. This work was also financially supported by the "Institute for Research Excellence in Learning Sciences" of National Taiwan Normal University (NTNU) from The Featured Areas Research Center Program within the framework of the Higher Education Sprout Project by the Ministry of Education (MOE) in Taiwan".

Conflicts of Interest: The authors declare no conflict of interest.

Appendix A

Table A1. General Profile of the Reviewed Studies on RALL.

No.	Authors and Year	Country/Language TL = Target Language	Participant Profile	Implementation Duration	Research Purpose	Robot Type and Affordances	Sensors and Accompanying Tools	Research Design	Instruments
1	Kanda, Hirano, Eaton, and Ishiguro, 2004 [36]	Japan L1: Japanese TL: English	119 first-grade students and 109 sixth-grade students	2 weeks	Analyze the effect of the robots on social interaction over time and learning	Humanoid robot/Robovie - Identify multiple learners simultaneously - Recall interaction history	- Wireless ID tags - Camera - Microphone	Single-group experiment with pretest-posttest design	**Quantitative:** - Tests (the order of sentences) - Video recording - Questionnaires **Quantitative:** - Listening test
2	Han, Jo, Jones, and Jo, 2008 [35]	Korea L1: Korean TL: English	90 fifth to sixth graders	Forty minutes	Investigate if the effect of the use of home robots in children's learning is more effective for their concentration, learning interest, and academic achievement than the other two types of instructional media	Humanoid robot/IROBI - Voice recognition and synthesis - 3D simulation - Head action - Wheel action	- Eye LED - Heart LED - Mouth LED Software: - eR-Author - eR-Player - Window XP	Between-group experiment	**Quantitative:** - Observation - Questionnaires - Interviews - A test
3	Chang, Lee, Chao, Wang, and Chen, 2010 [32]	Taiwan L1: Mandarin TL: An unspecified second language	100 fifth graders	5 weeks	Explore the possibility of using robots to teach a second language	Humanoid Robot - Body movement - Oral interactions - Teaching	Unknown	Quasi-experimental intervention	**Qualitative:** - Video recording
4	Chen, Quadir, and Teng, 2011 [44]	Taiwan L1: Mandarin TL: English	5 EFL fifth graders	80 min	Investigate the effect of the integration of book, digital content, and robots on elementary school students' English learning	Humanoid robot (pedagogical social agent) - Robot's song playing and dancing as learners touched pictorial icons	- RFID reader - Computer - English book	Test-driven experiment/System design and implementation	**Qualitative:** - Interviews - Video recording

Table A1. Cont.

No.	Authors and Year	Country/Language TL = Target Language	Participant Profile	Implementation Duration	Research Purpose	Robot Type and Affordances	Sensors and Accompanying Tools	Research Design	Instruments
5	Lee, Noh, Lee, Lee, Sagong, and Kim, 2011 [43]	South Korea L1: Korean TL: English	21 EFL third to fifth graders	Eight weeks	Investigate the effect of RALL on elementary school students	Animal-like robots (Mero and Engkey) - Face recognition - Speech functions - Speech recognition and synthesis - Language Understanding - Dialog Management - Language generation	-RFID sensors	Single-group experiment with pretest–posttest design	**Quantitative:** - Listening test - Speaking test
6	Hsiao, Chang, Lin, and Hsu, 2015 [38]	Taiwan L1: Mandarin TL: Mandarin	57 pre-kindergarteners	11 months	Explore the influence of of educational robots on fostering kindergarteners' reading motivation literacy, and behavior	Humanoid robot/iRobiQ - Broadcasting sound - Express human-like emotion	-Infrared sensors	Between-group experiment	**Quantitative:** - Reading comprehension test - Word Recognition **Qualitative:** - Storytelling
7	Tanaka and Matsuzoe, 2012 [40]	Japan L1: Japanese TL: English	18 preschool students	Phase 1: Six days Phase 2: one month	Investigate the effect of care-receiving robots on preschool students' vocabulary learning	Humanoid robot/NAO (care-receiving robot) - Perform locomotion and gestures - Classroom dialogs	- Graphic cards - Monitoring camera - Microphone	Single-group experiment with pretest–posttest design	**Quantitative:** - Word-picture association test
8	Wang, Young, and Jang, 2013 [36]	Taiwan L1: Mandarin TL: English	65 fifth graders	Not vailable	Investigate the effectiveness of tangible learning companions on students' English conversation	Animal-like robot - Speech recognition - Bi-directional language learning	Unknown	Quasi-experiment	**Quantitative:** - Cloze test - Pair test - Speaking test

Table A1. Cont.

No.	Authors and Year	Country/Language TL = Target Language	Participant Profile	Implementation Duration	Research Purpose	Robot Type and Affordances	Sensors and Accompanying Tools	Research Design	Instruments
9	Alemi, Meghadari, and Ghazisaedy, 2014 [42]	Iran L1: Iranian TL: English	46 seventh graders	Five weeks	Investigate the effect of RALL on students' vocabulary learning and retention	Humanoid robot/ NAO - *Motion* - *Vision* - *Audio* - Human detection, tracking, and recognition - Noisy object detection, tracking, and recognition - Speech recognition - Speaker recognition - Remote monitoring - Entertainment applications	- Tactile sensors - Infrared emitter/receiver - Eye LEDs - Ear LEDs - Prehensile hands - Joints - Sensor pressure - Chest buttons - Sonars - English textbook	Quasi-experiment	**Quantitative:** - Vocabulary test
10	Alemi, Meghdari, and Ghazisaedy, 2015 [45]	Iran L1: Iranian TL: English	Seventy female students between 12 and 13 years of age in junior high	5 weeks	Examine the effect of robot-assisted language learning (RALL) on anxiety level and attitude in English vocabulary acquisition	Humanoid robot/ NAO - Exercising - Singing - Shaking hands - Playing rock-scissors-paper - Brief conversations	- Tablet for display - Choreograph Software: - visual graphical programming language - Urbi and Python languages: - C++ modules	Between-group experiment	**Quantitative:** - Questionnaires - A placement test
11	Mazzoni and Benvenuti, 2015 [46]	Italy L1: Italian TL: English	10 preschool students	Three days	Investigate whether humanoid robots can assist students in learning English as effective as a human counterpart in terms of social-cognitive conflict paradigm	Humanoid robot/MecWilly - Replication and recognition of human emotions - Perform movements - Recognizing human language, objects, and environmental changes	Sensors for recognizing human language	Between-group experiment	**Quantitative:** - Word-picture association test

Table A1. Cont.

No.	Authors and Year	Country/Language TL = Target Language	Participant Profile	Implementation Duration	Research Purpose	Robot Type and Affordances	Sensors and Accompanying Tools	Research Design	Instruments
12	Wu, Wang, and Chen, 2015 [34]	Taiwan L1: Mandarin TL: English	64 EFL third graders	200 min	Investigate the effect of in-house built teaching assistant robots on EFL elementary school students' English learning	Humanoid robot/ PET - Teaching - Facial expression - Gestures - Motions on wheels	LEDs(head, face, ears, arms)	Between-group experiment	Quantitative: - Test on learning content (multiple choice and filling the blanks) - Survey Qualitative: - Interviews - Observations - Video Recording
13	Hong, Huang, Hsu, and Shen, 2016 [39]	Taiwan L1: Mandarin TL: English	52 fifth graders	Not available	Investigate the effects of design robot-assisted instructional materials on elementary school students' learning performance	Humanoid robot/Bioloid - Motions - Graphic content display (pictures, videos, audios)	- Sensors - Instructional material editing tool - Material displaying system	Between-group experiment	Quantitative: - Listening Test - Reading Test - Speaking Test - Writing Test
14	Lopes, Engwell, and Skantze, 2017 [17]	Sweden L1: 14 different mother tongues TL: Swedish	22 L2 Swedish learners (average age 29.1)	Two 15 min interactions	Explore using a social robot in a conversational setting to practice a second language	Humanoid Robot/ Furhat - Gestures - Text-to-speech synthesis - Facial animation - Automatic speech recognition - Interaction event tracking - Conversations	- Java-based framework for robot control - Rotating head - Video camera - Head-mounted microphone - Gopro camera		Quantitative: - Observation - Questionnaires
15	Westlund, Dickens, Jeong, Harris, DeSteno, and Breazeal, 2017 [44]	USA L1: English TL: English	36 preschool students	Not available	Investigate the effects of non-verbal cues on children's vocabulary learning	Animal-like robot/ DragonBot - Conversations	- Robot control software - A tablet - A mobile phone	Single-subject experiment	Quantitative: - Recall Test - Questionnaire Qualitative: - Video Recording

159

Table A1. *Cont.*

No.	Authors and Year	Country/Language TL = Target Language	Participant Profile	Implementation Duration	Research Purpose	Robot Type and Affordances	Sensors and Accompanying Tools	Research Design	Instruments
16	Crompton, Gregory, and Burke, 2018 [33]	USA L1: English TL: English	Three teaching assistants and 50 preschool students	Not available	Investigate how the use of humanoid robots can support preschool students' learning	Humanoid robot/ NAO - Interactions with children	Unknown	Ethnographic study design	Qualitative: - Semi-structured interviews with teachers - Student artifacts (drawings and storytelling)
17	Sisman, Gunay, and Kucuk, 2018 [62]	Turkey L1: Turkish TL: English	232 secondary school students broken into small sessions of 20 students each	Four months	Investigate an educational robot attitude scale (ERAS) for secondary school students	Humanoid robot/ NAO - Responding to utterances - Acting on one's commands - Shaking hands and dancing	Unknown Mobile phone	Experiment with evaluation survey design	Quantitative: - Questionnaire
18	Lio, Maede, Ogawa, Yoshikawa, Ishiguro, Suzuki, Aoki, Maesaki, and Hama, 2019 [43]	Japan L1: Japanese TL: English	Nine university students	Seven days	Investigate the effect of RALL system on college students' English-speaking development	Humanoid robot/ CommU - Explain rules of noun judgement	Unknown Tablet for display	Single-group experiment with pretest-posttest design	Quantitative: - Speaking test
19	Wedenborn, Wik, Engwall, and Beskow, 2019 [63]	Sweden L1: Unknown TL: Russian	Fifteen university students	15 min per participant	Investigate the effect of a physical robot on vocabulary learning	Humanoid Robot/ Furhat - Dialogues - Animated face - Modules for using speech synthesizers - Rotating head	Java-based framework for constructing multi-modal dialogue systems	Quasi-experiment	Quantitative: - Observation - A Friedman test - A post-trial Questionnaire
20	Alemi and Haeri, 2020 [49]	Iran L1: Iranian TL: English	38 kindergarteners	Two months	Investigate the impact of applying the robot-assisted language leaning (RALL) method to teach request and thanking speech acts to young children.	Humanoid robot/ NAO - Text-to-speech - Playing games - Singing songs - Dancing - Talking - Interacting	Unknown Robot Control Software Choregraphe program - Flash cards - Real classroom objects - CD player	Single-group experiment with pretest-posttest design	Quantitative: - Pictorial test - t-test

Table A1. Cont.

No.	Authors and Year	Country/Language TL = Target Language	Participant Profile	Implementation Duration	Research Purpose	Robot Type and Affordances	Sensors and Accompanying Tools	Research Design	Instruments
21	Engwell, Lopes, and Ålund, 2020 [51]	Sweden L1: Varied TL: Swedish	Robot-led Conversations:6 adults beyond teriary education level;Survey:32 participants	Three days	Investigate how the post-session ratings of the robot's behavior along different dimensions are influenced by the robot's interaction style and participant variables	Humanoid Robot/ Furhat - Dialogue interactions	- Rotating head Cameras - Head-mounted micro phones	Experiment with evaluation survey design	Quantitative: - Survey - Observation
22	Leeuwestein, Barking, Sodacı, oudgenoeg, Verhagen Vogt, Aarts, Spit, Haas, Wit, and Leseman, 2020 [37]	Turkey L1: Turkish TL: Dutch	67 kindergarteners	2.4 days with 40 min sessions	Investigate the effects of providing translations in L1 on the learning of L2 in a vocabulary learning experiment using social robots	Humanoid robot/ NAO - Text-to-speech - Speech recognition	Unknown - Tablet - Plush toys - Videotape	Single-group experiment with pretest-posttest design	Quantitative: - Words tests

Appendix B

Table A2. Instructional Design and Learning Outcome of RALL.

Communicative Skill	Learning Activity	Language Teaching Method	Role of Robot	Role of Instructor or Facilitator	Learning Outcomes
1 Vocabulary	Engaging students in learning a vocabulary of about 300 words for speaking and 50 words for recognition with 18 day trial.	- Communicative language teaching - Total physical response	Dialogue interlocutor Play Mate	Teacher/facilitator is absent/not mentioned	Skill: - Improvement in English
2 Speaking	Engaging the students in speaking and dialogue with NCB, WBI, or HRL for about 40 min	- Communicative language teaching; role play/scenario-based language learning	Role-play character	Teacher/facilitator is absent/not mentioned	Cognition: - Effective academic achievement - Increased concentration Affect: - Increased learning interest

Table A2. Cont.

	Communicative Skill	Learning Activity	Language Teaching Method	Role of Robot	Role of Instructor or Facilitator	Learning Outcomes
3	Listening Speaking	Five weekly practice scenarios each with a different interaction mode	- Audiolingual method - Storytelling - Total physical response	Role-play character Action commander	Learning support: - Give cues - Initiate robot–learner interaction - Teach - Check learning progress	Affect: - Active responses and heightened interactions Skill: - Repeated practice in comprehension and oral skills that resembled natural conversation
4	Vocabulary	A system contains five RALL activities; students took turns to have a test drive on the system in a total amount of 40 min	Multimedia-enhanced instruction	Role-play character Dance- and sing-along partner	Teacher/facilitator is absent/not mentioned	Cognition: - The integrated system helped the learners understand new words through pictures and animation visual aid.
5	Listening Speaking: - pronunciation - vocabulary - grammar - communicative ability	Engaging students in learning 68 English lessons in four different RALL classrooms	- Dialogue-context model of language understanding - Communicative language teaching; role-play	Role-Play Character (Sales clerk)	Technical support	Skills: - Significant improvement in speaking skills Affect: - Positive affective effects in satisfaction, interest, confidence, and motivation
6	Reading Vocabulary Grammar	Experimental group: read e-book with the aid of iRobiQ Control group: read e-book with the aid of tablet-PC	- Bidirectional interaction in storytelling for reading literacy development	Content display on robot partner screen	Procedural support: - Ensuring operation smoothness	Affect: - iRobiQ is an effective learning companion as compared to tablet-PCs Skills - Bidirectional interactions with iRobiQ leads to better peer collaboration and competition for preschoolers

Table A2. Cont.

	Communicative Skill	Learning Activity	Language Teaching Method	Role of Robot	Role of Instructor or Facilitator	Learning Outcomes
7	Vocabulary	Engaging students in four verb-learning games with the aid of care-receiving robot for 30 min per section	Learning by teaching: - Direct teaching - Gesturing - Verbal teaching	Respondant to learners' action commands	Procedural support: - Modeling play activity procedure	Skill: - Efficient learning of vocabulary (verbs) through care-receiving robot - Children's ability gains in teaching
8	Speaking	Experimental group: engaging 32 students in practicing English conversation with tangible learning robot Control group: engaging 31 students in practicing English conversation with classmates	- Audiolingual method - Co-discovery	Dialogue interlocutor Dance- and sing-along partner	Procedural support: - Modelling a dialogue with robot	Skill: - Significant improvement in speaking Affect: - Class atmosphere improved effectively - More positive attitude toward learning English
9	Vocabulary	Experimental group: learn English vocabulary from humanoid robot Control group: learn English vocabulary from human teachers	- Vocabulary learning through multimodal stimuli/input	Dialogue interlocutor Teacher assistant	Procedural support: - Initiate robot–learner Interaction - Ensure operation smoothness Learning support: - Provide instant feedback through robot control - Give praise	Skill: - Significant vocabulary gains - Significant vocabulary retention
10	Vocabulary	Experimental group: learn English vocabulary through the RALL system Control group: learning English vocabulary based on the Communicative Approach	- Communicative language teaching - Total physical response - Teaching proficiency through reading and storytelling	Dialogue interlocutor Teacher assistant (show vocabulary-related motions)	Procedural support: - Demonstrate human-robot interaction	Affect: - A very positive attitude toward the use of RALL

Table A2. Cont.

	Communicative Skill	Learning Activity	Language Teaching Method	Role of Robot	Role of Instructor or Facilitator	Learning Outcomes
11	Vocabulary	Experimental group: learn English vocabulary in children-SCC condition Control group: learning English vocabulary in robot-SCC condition	- Socio-cognitive conflict	Dialogue interlocutor (remotely controlled)	Procedural support: - Introduce the game narrative, goal, and activity to learners	Cognition: - Significant improvement in word-picture association abilities - Humanoid robots have the advantage of creating scenarios similar to child-child social-cognitive conflict situations
12	English Alphabets Listening Speaking	Experimental group: learn English with PET Control group: learn English with human teacher	- Communicative language teaching - Total physical response - Storytelling	Teacher assistantDialogue interlocutorRole-play character	Learning support: - Provide instant feedback through robot control	Skill: - Significant improvement in learning the content presented - Enhanced English learning experiences Affect: - Increased learning motivation - Increase learning interest
13	Listening Speaking Reading Writing	Experimental group: have English class by humanoid robot Control group: have English class by human teacher	- Audiolingual method - Storytelling - Total physical response - Communicative language teaching	Role-play characterDialogue interlocutor	Learning support: - Explain the story - Provide direct evaluative feedback without robot control - Encourage participation	Skill: - Significant improvement in listening and reading skills - Student-talk rate and response ratio increased Affect: - Increased learning motivation
14	Speaking	Experimental group: have conversational setting to practice with two second language learners, one native moderator and a human Control group: Have conversational setting to practice with two second language learners, one native moderator and a robot n	- Communicative language teaching: scenario-based	Dialogue interlocutor	Procedural support: - Lead robot–learner conversation Learning support: - Help learners overcome language difficulties	Skill: - The slightly structured repetitive interaction pattern was perceived as beneficial for adult Swedish learners with elementary proficiency levels.

Table A2. Cont.

	Communicative Skill	Learning Activity	Language Teaching Method	Role of Robot	Role of Instructor or Facilitator	Learning Outcomes
15	Vocabulary	Engaging students in vocabulary learning with the aid of robot and human teacher	Learning by following non-verbal cues	Picture viewing partner	Teacher/facilitator is absent/not mentioned	Cognition: - The children gained the ability to detect which picture in the pair was being referred to by the robot in the picture naming task
16	Listening Speaking	Phase 1: planning RALL lessons Phase 2: RALL lessons implementation Phase 3: reflect on the process of designing and implementing RALL lessons	- Communicative language teaching - Storytelling	Dialogue interlocutor	Procedural support: - Tell participants to ask robot questions	Cognition: - The use of the robot provided cognitive development in mathematics - Promotion of language and communication, physical, cognitive, and social-emotional learning experiences Skill: - Development of physical motor skills by the use of the robot
17	Listening Speaking	Engaging students in four robot-assisted English tasks for 40 min per class	- Communicative language teaching; role play/scenario-based language learning	Role-play character (remotely controlled)	Procedural support: - Facilitate learners with task fulfillment	Affect: - RALL can be validly measured by the Educational Robot Attitude Scale (ERAS) based on four constructs: engagement, intention, enjoyment, and anxiety. - The most effective aspect of the RALL experience was engagement.

165

Table A2. Cont.

	Communicative Skill	Learning Activity	Language Teaching Method	Role of Robot	Role of Instructor or Facilitator	Learning Outcomes

18	Speaking	Engaging the students in speaking practices with the aid of RALL system for a total of 30 min per day for seven days	- Communicative language teaching; role play/scenario-based language learning	Dialogue interlocutor	Teacher/facilitator is absent/not mentioned	Skill:
						 - The RALL system helped to improve significantly in the following aspects:
						  - speech complexity
						  - grammatical and lexical accuracy
						  - number of words spoken per minute
						  - response time
						 - Pronunciation became more native-like

19	Vocabulary	Learn vocabulary exercises in three different conditions: First condition: disembodied voice Second condition: screen Third condition: robot	- Vocabulary learning through multimodal stimuli/input - Audiolingual method	Teacher assistant	Learning support: - Provide instant feedback through robot control	Cognition: - Significant effects on learning when the virtual tutor takes the step from screen into the physical world Affect: - Robot face increases the task motivation and extrinsic motivation due to a more human like connection
20	Speaking Vocabulary	Experimental group: learn English with a humanoid robot and the teacher Control group: learn English with the teacher	- Total physical response - Storytelling - Communicative language teaching; scenario-based	Dialogue interlocutor Teacher assistant	Learning support: - Provide content instruction - Procedural support - Facilitate learners with task fulfillment	Affect: - Increase interest and motivation - Help students be more active in a native-like setting
21	Speaking	Engaging the students in four stereotypic interaction styles with social robot Furhat for three days	- Communicative language teaching; role play	Role-play character Dialogue interlocutor	Teacher/facilitator is absent/not mentioned	Affect: - Robots reduce learner anxiety about making mistakes in front of native speaker

Table A2. Cont.

	Communicative Skill	Learning Activity	Language Teaching Method	Role of Robot	Role of Instructor or Facilitator	Learning Outcomes
22	Vocabulary	Engaging students in vocabulary learning with the monolingual or the bilingual robot for 40 min	- Communicative language teaching: scenario-based	Role-play character	Teacher/facilitator is absent/not mentioned	Skill: - Using social robots enhanced L2 word learning among Turkish-Dutch kindergarteners.

Appendix C

Table A3. Interactive Oral Task Design in RALL.

No.	Interactive Task Design	Interaction Mode	Instructional Focus	Teacher Talk by Robot	Input Mode	Oral Output
1	- Action commands	Robot–learner - One-to-one	Form-focused	Skill training: - Sentence recognition Affective feedback: - Physical, verbal, gestural responses showing care from robot (e.g., hugs)	Aural: Robotic talk Robotic sensory output	- Sentential level (closed)
2	- Drill - Role play	Robot–learner - One-to-one	Form-focused	Skill training: - Sentence recitations Affective feedback: - Facial expressions and gestures showing various emotions	Visual: Animation on robot screen Robotic facial expressions and gestures Aural: Robotic talk Robotic sensory output Audiovisual: Video	- Sentential level (closed)

Table A3. Cont.

No.	Interactive Task Design	Interaction Mode	Instructional Focus	Teacher Talk by Robot	Input Mode	Oral Output
3	- Drill: recite - Robot questioning - Total physical response - storytelling	Robot–learner - One-to-many	Form-focused:Meaning-focused	Knowledge teaching: - Word meanings Skill training: - Recitations Procedural prompts: - Storytelling instructions Motivational elements: - Cheerleading	Aural Robotic talk	- Lexical level (closed) - Sentential level (closed)
4	- Dialogue - Role play	Robot–learner - One-to-many	Form-focused	Knowledge teaching: - Word meanings	Linguistic: Text Aural: Robotic talk Songs	- Lexical level (closed) - Sentential level (closed)
5	- Role play	Robot–learner - One-to-one	Meaning-focused	Motivational elements: - Situational talk between customers and store clerks Affective feedback: - Facial expression of various emotions	Aural: Robotic talk	- Phrasal level (open) - Sentential level (open)
6	- Robot questioning - Storytelling	Robot–learner - One-to-one	Form-focused	Skill training: - Pronunciation of words	Visual: Pictures	- Lexical level (closed) - Phrasal level (closed) - Sentential level (closed)

Table A3. Cont.

No.	Interactive Task Design	Interaction Mode	Instructional Focus	Teacher Talk by Robot	Input Mode	Oral Output
7	- Learning by teaching	Robot–learner - One-to-one	Meaning-focused	Procedural prompts	Linguistic: Flashcard Visual: Flashcard	- Lexical level (closed) - Sentential level (closed)
8	- Dialogue	Robot–learner - One-to-many	Meaning-focused	Skill training: - Conversation in English	Aural: Robotic talk (short conversation patterns)	
9	- Robot questioning - Dialogue	Robot–learner - One-to-many	Meaning-focused	Knowledge teaching: - Word meanings Affective feedback: - Verbal comments such as "well done" and "good job" - Physical feedback such as movements that signal praise	Visual: Pictures Aural: Robotic vocabulary read-aloud Robotic feedback Gestural: Pantomime actions	- Lexical level (closed) - Sentential level (closed)
10	- Role play - Action commands	Robot–learner - One-to-many	Form-focused	Knowledge teaching: - Word meanings Affective feedback: - Physical and gestural responses (e.g., cheering and clapping)	Aural: Robotic talk	- Lexical level (closed) - Phrasal level (closed)
11	- Robot questioning	Robot–learner - One-to-one	Form-focused	Motivational elements: - Inducing socio-cognitive progress with questions that show doubt	Visual: Pictures Aural: Robotic feedback	- Lexical level (closed)

Table A3. *Cont.*

No.	Interactive Task Design	Interaction Mode	Instructional Focus	Teacher Talk by Robot	Input Mode	Oral Output
12	- Robot questioning - Dialogue - Storytelling - Drills	Robot–learner - One-to-many	Form-focused and meaning-focused	Knowledge teaching: - 26 English alphabets Skill training: - Naming body parts - Conversation - Storytelling - Self-introductions Motivational elements: - Songs and Dance Motions Affective feedback: - Thumbs-up gesture signaling 'good job'	Visual: Pictures Aural: Robotic talk songs	- Phonemic level (closed) - Lexical level (closed) - Phrasal level (closed) - Sentential level (closed)
13	- Robot questioning - Dialogue - Storytelling	Robot–learner - One-to-many	Form-focused	Skill training: - Pronunciation - Grammar Procedural prompts: - Giving action commands Affective feedback: - Clapping as signal of praise	Aural: Robotic talk Gestural: Robotic actions	- Phonemic level (closed) - Lexical level (closed) - Sentential level (closed)
14	- Dialogue	Robot–learner - One-to-two	Meaning-focused	Skill training: - Café language Affective feedback: - Facial expressions of various emotions	Aural: Robotic talk	- Sentential level (open)

Table A3. Cont.

No.	Interactive Task Design	Interaction Mode	Instructional Focus	Teacher Talk by Robot	Input Mode	Oral Output
15	- Robot questioning supported by non-verbal cues through gazing	Robot–learner (remote human control of robot) - One-to-one	Form-focused	Knowledge teaching: - Word meanings Affective feedback: - Facial expressions showing various emotions	Visual: Pictures Robotic gaze Aural: Robotic talk	- Lexical level (closed)
16	- Action commands - Storytelling	Robot–learner - One-to-many	Form-focused	Skill training: - Language on counting numbers - Understand action commands	Aural: Robotic talk Gestural: Robotic actions	- Lexical level (closed)
17	- Dialogue	Robot–learner (remote human control of robot) - One-to-many	Meaning-focused	Skill training: - Self-introduction - Asking questions	Aural: Robotic talk	- Sentential level (open)
18	- Drill - Role play	Robot–learner - One-to-one	Form-focused	Skill training: - Sentence practice - Conversation	Linguistic: Sentence-picture flashcards Visual: Sentence-picture flashcards Aural: Robotic talk	- Sentential level (closed)

Table A3. Cont.

No.	Interactive Task Design	Interaction Mode	Instructional Focus	Teacher Talk by Robot	Input Mode	Oral Output
19	- Dialogue	Robot–learner - One-to-one (remote human control of robot)	Form-focused	Skill training: - Pronunciation	Linguistic: Text Visual: Pictures Visible speech through facial features during word pronunciation Aural: Robotic talk	- Lexical level (closed)
20	- Dialogue - Storytelling	Robot–learner - One-to-one	Meaning-focused	Skill training: - Speech acts Affective feedback: - Applause Motivational elements: - Short songs	Visual: Pictures Aural: Robotic talk Gestural: Robotic gestures	- Sentential level (closed)
21	- Dialogue	Robot–learner - One-to-one - One-to-two Learner–learner - One-to-one	Meaning-focused	Skill training: - Conversation Affective feedback: - Facial expressions showing various emotions	Visual: Facial expressions Aural: Robotic talk	- Sentential level (open)
22	- Dialogue	Robot–learner - One-to-one	Form-focused	Knowledge teaching: - Word meanings	Visual: Pictures Aural: Robotic talk	- Lexical level (closed)

References

1. Kory-Westlund, J.M.; Breazeal, C. A long-term study of young children's rapport, social emulation, and language learning with a peer-like robot playmate in preschool. *Front. Robot. AI* **2019**, *6*, 1–17. [CrossRef]
2. Liao, J.; Lu, X.; Masters, K.A.; Dudek, J.; Zhou, Z. Telepresence-place-based foreign language learning and its design principles. *Comput. Assist. Lang. Learn.* **2019**. [CrossRef]
3. So, W.C.; Cheng, C.H.; Lam, W.Y.; Wong, T.; Law, W.W.; Huang, Y.; Ng, K.C.; Tung, H.C.; Wong, W. Robot-based play-drama intervention may improve the narrative abilities of Chinese-speaking preschoolers with autism spectrum disorder. *Res. Dev. Disabil.* **2019**, *95*, 103515. [CrossRef]
4. Alemi, M.; Bahramipour, S. An innovative approach of incorporating a humanoid robot into teaching EFL learners with intellectual disabilities. *Asian-Pac. J. Second Foreign Lang. Educ.* **2019**, *4*, 10. [CrossRef]
5. Han, J. Robot-Aided Learning and r-Learning Services. In *Human-Robot Interaction*; Chugo, D., Ed.; IntechOpen: London, UK, 2010. Available online: https://www.intechopen.com/chapters/8632 (accessed on 5 July 2021).
6. Spolaor, N.; Benitti, F.B.V. Robotics applications grounded in learning theories on tertiary education: A systematic review. *Comput. Educ.* **2017**, *112*, 97–107. [CrossRef]
7. Cheng, Y.W.; Sun, P.C.; Chen, N.S. The essential applications of educational robot: Requirement analysis from the perspectives of experts, researchers and instructors. *Comput. Educ.* **2018**, *126*, 399–416. [CrossRef]
8. Merkouris, A.; Chorianopoulos, K. Programming embodied interactions with a remotely controlled educational robot. *ACM Trans. Comput. Educ.* **2019**, *19*, 1–19. [CrossRef]
9. Kahlifa, A.; Kato, T.; Yamamoto, S. Learning effect of implicit learning in joining-in-type robot-assisted language learning system. *Int. J. Emerg. Technol.* **2019**, *14*, 105–123. [CrossRef]
10. Warschauer, M.; Meskill, C. Technology and second language learning. In *Handbook of Undergraduate Second Language Education*; Rosenthal, J., Ed.; Lawrence Erlbaum: Mahwah, NJ, USA, 2000; pp. 303–318.
11. Woo, D.J.; Law, N. Information and communication technology coordinators: Their intended roles and architectures for learning. *J. Comput. Assist. Learn.* **2020**, *36*, 423–438. [CrossRef]
12. Grant, M.J.; Booth, A. A typology of reviews: An analysis of 14 review types and associated methodologies. *Health Inf. Libr. J.* **2009**, *26*, 91–108. [CrossRef]
13. Samnani, S.S.S.; Vaska, M.; Ahmed, S.; Turin, T.C. Review Typology: The Basic Types of Reviews for Synthesizing Evidence for the Purpose of Knowledge Translation. *J. Coll. Physicians Surg. Pak.* **2017**, *27*, 635–641.
14. Robinson, H.A. *The Ethnography of Empowerment—The Transformative Power of Classroom Interaction*, 2nd ed.; The Falmer Press; Taylor & Francis Inc.: Bristol, PA, USA, 1994.
15. Pica, T. From input, output and comprehension to negotiation, evidence, and attention: An overview of theory and research on learner interaction and SLA. In *Contemporary Approaches to Second Language Acquisition*; Mayo, M.D.P.G., Mangado, M.J.G., Martínez-Adrián, M., Eds.; John Benjamins Publishing Company: Philadelphia, PA, USA, 2013; pp. 49–70.
16. Rivers, W.M. *Interactive Language Teaching*; Cambridge University Press: New York, NY, USA, 1987.
17. Tuan, L.T.; Nhu, N.T.K. Theoretical review on oral interaction in EFL classrooms. *Stud. Lit. Lang.* **2010**, *1*, 29–48.
18. Council of Europe. *The Common European Framework of Reference for Languages: Learning, Teaching, Assessment*; Council of Europe: Strasbourg Cedex, France, 2004. Available online: http://www.coe.int/T/DG4/Linguistic/Source/Framework_EN.pdf (accessed on 6 July 2021).
19. Brown, H.D. *Teaching by Principles: Interactive Language Teaching Methodology*; Prentice Hall Regents: New York, NY, USA, 1994.
20. Ellis, R. *Instructed Second Language Acquisition: Learning in the Classroom*; Basil Blackwell. Ltd.: Oxford, UK, 1990.
21. Han, J. Emerging technologies: Robot assisted language learning. *Lang. Learn. Technol.* **2012**, *16*, 1–9.
22. Van den Berghe, R.; Verhagen, J.; Oudgenoeg-Paz, O.; van der Ven, S.; Leseman, P. Social Robots for Language Learning: A Review. *Rev. Educ. Res.* **2019**, *89*, 259–295. [CrossRef]
23. Jahnke, I.; Liebscher, J. Three types of integrated course designs for using mobile technologies to support creativity in higher education. *Comput. Educ.* **2020**, *146*, 103782. [CrossRef]
24. Mitchell, C.B.; Vidal, K.E. Weighing the ways of the flow: Twentieth century language instruction. *Mod. Lang. J.* **2001**, *85*, 26–38. [CrossRef]
25. Asher, J. The Total Physical Response Approach to Second Language Learning. *Mod. Lang. J.* **1969**, *53*, 3–17. [CrossRef]
26. Muzammill, L.; Andy, A. Teaching proficiency through reading and storytelling (TPRS) as a technique to foster students' speaking skill. *J. Engl. Educ. Linguist. Stud.* **2017**, *4*, 19–36. [CrossRef]
27. Chen, Y.M. How a teacher education program through action research can support English as a foreign language teachers in implementing communicative approaches: A case from Taiwan. *Sage Open* **2020**, *10*, 2158244019900167. [CrossRef]
28. Savignon, S.J. Communicative competence. *TESOL Encycl. Engl. Lang. Teach.* **2018**, *1*, 1–7.
29. Bagheri, M.; Hadian, B.; Vaez-Dalili, M. Effects of the Vaughan Method in Comparison with the Audiolingual Method and the Communicative Language Teaching on Iranian Advanced EFL Learners' Speaking Skill. *Int. J. Instr.* **2019**, *12*, 81–98. [CrossRef]
30. Lin, V.; Liu, G.Z.; Hwang, G.J.; Chen, N.S.; Yin, C. Outcomes-based appropriation of context-aware ubiquitous technology across educational levels. *Interact. Learn. Environ.* **2019**. [CrossRef]
31. Petticrew, M.; Roberts, H. *Systematic Reviews in the Social Sciences: A Practical Guide*; Blackwell: Oxford, UK, 2006.

32. Chang, C.W.; Lee, J.H.; Chao, P.Y.; Wang, C.Y.; Chen, G.D. Exploring the Possibility of Using Humanoid Robots as Instructional Tools for Teaching a Second Language in Primary School. *Educ. Technol. Soc.* **2010**, *13*, 13–24.
33. Crompton, H.; Gregory, K.; Burke, D. Humanoid robots supporting children's learning in early childhood setting. *Br. J. Educ. Technol.* **2018**, *49*, 911–927. [CrossRef]
34. Wu, W.C.V.; Wang, R.J.; Chen, N.S. Instructional design using an in-house built teaching assistant robot to enhance elementary school English-as-a-foreign-language learning. *Interact. Learn. Environ.* **2015**, *23*, 696–714. [CrossRef]
35. Han, J.; Jo, M.; Jones, V.; Jo, J.H. Comparative Study on the Educational Use of Home Robots for Children. *J. Inf. Processing Syst.* **2008**, *4*, 159–168. [CrossRef]
36. Kanda, T.; Hirano, T.; Eaton, D.; Ishiguro, H. Interactive robots as social partners and peer tutors for children: A field trial. *Hum.-Comput. Interact.* **2004**, *19*, 61–84.
37. Leeuwestein, H.; Barking, M.; Sodacı, H.; Oudgenoeg-Paz, O.; Verhagen, J.; Vogt, P.; Aarts, R.; Spit, S.; Haas, M.D.; Wit, J.D.; et al. Teaching Turkish-Dutch kindergartners Dutch vocabulary with a social robot: Does the robot's use of Turkish translations benefit children's Dutch vocabulary learning? *J. Comput. Assist. Learn.* **2020**, *37*, 603–620. [CrossRef]
38. Hsiao, H.S.; Chang, C.S.; Lin, C.Y.; Hsu, H.L. "iRobiQ": The influence of bidirectional interaction on kindergarteners' reading motivation, literacy, and behavior. *Interact. Learn. Environ.* **2015**, *23*, 269–292. [CrossRef]
39. Hong, Z.W.; Huang, Y.M.; Hsu, M.; Shen, W.W. Authoring robot-assisted instructional materials for improving learning performance and motivation in EFL classrooms. *Educ. Technol. Soc.* **2016**, *19*, 337–349.
40. Tanaka, F.; Matsuzoe, S. Children teach a care-receiving robot to promote their learning: Field experiments in a classroom for vocabulary learning. *J. Hum.-Robot. Interact.* **2012**, *1*, 78–95. [CrossRef]
41. Westlund, J.M.K.; Dickens, L.; Jeong, S.; Harris, P.L.; DeSteno, D.; Breaseal, C.L. Children use non-verbal cues to learn new words from robots as well as people. *Int. J. Child-Comput. Interact.* **2017**, *13*, 1–9. [CrossRef]
42. Alemi, M.; Meghdari, A.; Ghazisaedy, M. Employing humanoid robots for teaching English language in Iranian junior high-schools. *Int. J. Hum. Robot.* **2014**, *11*, 1450022. [CrossRef]
43. Lio, T.; Maede, R.; Ogawa, K.; Yoshikawa, Y.; Ishiguro, H.; Suzuki, K.; Aoki, T.; Maesaki, M.; Hama, M. Improvement of Japanese adults' English speaking skills via experiences speaking to a robot. *J. Comput. Assist. Learn.* **2019**, *35*, 228–245. [CrossRef]
44. Chen, N.S.; Quadir, B.; Teng, D.C. Integrating book, digital content and robot for, enhancing elementary school students' learning of English. *Aust. J. Educ. Technol.* **2011**, *27*, 546–561. [CrossRef]
45. Lee, S.; Noh, H.; Lee, J.; Lee, K.; Lee, G.G.; Sagong, S.; Kim, M. On the effectiveness of robot-assisted language learning. *ReCALL* **2011**, *23*, 25–58. [CrossRef]
46. Mazzoni, E.; Benvenuti, M. A robot-partner for preschool children learning English using socio-cognitive conflict. *Educ. Technol. Soc.* **2015**, *18*, 474–485.
47. Lopes, J.; Engwell, O.; Skantze, G. A first visit to the robot language café. In Proceedings of the 7th ISCA Workshop on Speech and Language Technology in Education, Stockholm, Sweden, 25–26 August 2017; pp. 25–26.
48. Alemi, M.; Meghdari, A.; Ghaziseady, M. The impact of social robotics on L2 learners' anxiety and attitude in English vocabulary acquisition. *Int. J. Soc. Robot.* **2015**, *7*, 523–535. [CrossRef]
49. Alemi, M.; Haeri, N.S. Robot-assisted instruction of L2 pragmatics: Effects on young EFL learners' speech act performance. *Lang. Learn. Technol.* **2020**, *24*, 86–103.
50. Wang, Y.H.; Young, S.S.C.; Jang, J.S.R. Using tangible companions for enhancing learning English conversation. *Educ. Technol. Soc.* **2013**, *16*, 296–309.
51. Engwell, O.; Lopes, J.; Ålund, A. Robot interaction styles for conversation practice in second language learning. *Int. J. Soc. Robot.* **2020**, *13*, 251–276. [CrossRef]
52. Uriarte, A.B. Vocabulary teaching: Focused tasks for enhancing acquisition in EFL contexts. *MEXTESOL J.* **2013**, *37*, 1–12.
53. Rios, J.A.; Ling, G.; Pugh, R.; Becker, D.; Bacall, A. Identifying critical 21st-century skills for workplace success: A content analysis of job advertisements. *Educ. Res.* **2020**, *49*, 80–89. [CrossRef]
54. Lichtman, K. *Teaching Proficiency through Reading and Storytelling (TPRS): An Input-Based Approach to Second Language Instruction*; Routledge: New York, NY, USA, 2018.
55. Neumann, M.M. Social robots and young children's early language and literacy learning. *Early Child. Educ. J.* **2019**, *48*, 157–170. [CrossRef]
56. Toh, L.P.E.; Causo, A.; Tzuo, P.W.; Chen, I.M.; Yeo, S.H. A Review on the Use of Robots in Education and Young Children. *Educ. Technol. Soc.* **2016**, *19*, 148–163.
57. Papadopoulos, I.; Lazzarino, R.; Miah, S.; Weaver, T.B.; Koulouglioti, C.T. A systematic review of the literature regarding socially assistive robots in pre-tertiary education. *Comput. Educ.* **2020**, *155*, 103924. [CrossRef]
58. Mubin, O.; Stevens, C.; Shahid, S.; Mahmud, A.; Dong, J.-J. A review of the applicability of robots in education. *Technol. Educ. Learn.* **2013**, *1*, 13. [CrossRef]
59. Heidig, S.; Muller, J.; Reichelt, M. Emotional design in multimedia learning: Differentiation on relevant design features and their effects on emotions and learning. *Comput. Hum. Behav.* **2015**, *44*, 81–95. [CrossRef]
60. Barrett, N.; Liu, G.Z. Global trends and research aims for English Academic Oral Presentations: Changes, challenges, and opportunities for learning technology. *Rev. Educ. Res.* **2016**, *86*, 1227–1271. [CrossRef]

61. Lin, V.; Yeh, H.C.; Huang, H.H.; Chen, N.S. Enhancing EFL vocabulary learning with multimodal cues supported by an educational robot and an IoT-Based 3D book. *System* **2021**, *104*, 102691. [CrossRef]
62. Sisman, B.; Gunay, D.; Kucuk, S. Development and validation of an educational robot attitude scale (ERAS) for secondary school students. *Interact. Learn. Environ.* **2018**, *27*, 377–388. [CrossRef]
63. Wedenborn, A.; Wik, P.; Engwall, O.; Beskow, J. The effect of a physical robot on vocabulary Learning. *arXiv* **2019**, arXiv:1901.10461.

 electronics

Review

Social Robots in Special Education: A Systematic Review

George A. Papakostas [1,*], George K. Sidiropoulos [1], Cristina I. Papadopoulou [1], Eleni Vrochidou [1], Vassilis G. Kaburlasos [1], Maria T. Papadopoulou [2], Vasiliki Holeva [3], Vasiliki-Aliki Nikopoulou [3] and Nikolaos Dalivigkas [4]

[1] HUMAIN-Lab, Department of Computer Science, International Hellenic University, 65404 Kavala, Greece; georsidi@cs.ihu.gr (G.K.S.); mysapad@cs.ihu.gr (C.I.P.); evrochid@cs.ihu.gr (E.V.); vgkabs@cs.ihu.gr (V.G.K.)

[2] 4th Department of Pediatrics, Papageorgiou General Hospital, Aristotle University of Thessaloniki, 56403 Thessaloniki, Greece; mtpapado@gmail.com

[3] 1st Psychiatric Clinic, Papageorgiou General Hospital, Aristotle University of Thessaloniki, 56403 Thessaloniki, Greece; vholeva@yahoo.gr (V.H.); v.a.nikopoulou@gmail.com (V.-A.N.)

[4] Euroaction, 54655 Thessaloniki, Greece; dalivigkas@gmail.com

* Correspondence: gpapak@cs.ihu.gr; Tel.: +30-2510-462-321

Citation: Papakostas, G.A.; Sidiropoulos, G.K.; Papadopoulou, C.I.; Vrochidou, E.; Kaburlasos, V.G.; Papadopoulou, M.T.; Holeva, V.; Nikopoulou, V.-A.; Dalivigkas, N. Social Robots in Special Education: A Systematic Review. *Electronics* **2021**, *10*, 1398. https://doi.org/10.3390/electronics10121398

Academic Editor: Dah-Jye Lee

Received: 4 May 2021
Accepted: 7 June 2021
Published: 10 June 2021

Publisher's Note: MDPI stays neutral with regard to jurisdictional claims in published maps and institutional affiliations.

Copyright: © 2021 by the authors. Licensee MDPI, Basel, Switzerland. This article is an open access article distributed under the terms and conditions of the Creative Commons Attribution (CC BY) license (https://creativecommons.org/licenses/by/4.0/).

Abstract: In recent years, social robots have become part of a variety of human activities, especially in applications involving children, e.g., entertainment, education, companionship. The interest of this work lies in the interaction of social robots with children in the field of special education. This paper seeks to present a systematic review of the use of robots in special education, with the ultimate goal of highlighting the degree of integration of robots in this field worldwide. This work aims to explore the technologies of robots that are applied according to the impairment type of children. The study showed a large number of attempts to apply social robots to the special education of children with various impairments, especially in recent years, as well as a wide variety of social robots from the market involved in such activities. The main conclusion of this work is the finding that the specific field of application of social robots is at the first development step; however, it is expected to be of great concern to the research community in the coming years.

Keywords: social robots; child–robot interaction; special education; robot-assisted learning; systematic review

1. Introduction

There is no doubt that in recent years we have witnessed the Fourth Industrial Revolution, the so-called *Industry 4.0* [1] in Europe and *Society 5.0* [2] in Japan. Among the main features of this technological advancement is the use of artificial intelligence algorithms in processing the available large volume of data and making decisions from it. The role of robotic systems appears to be enhanced in the field of executing specific actions based on the derived decisions.

In this context, there is a growing trend in the application of robots outside of industrial workplaces, in people's daily lives, through the development of the so-called *cyber-physical* systems. As a direct consequence of this high integration of robots into society, the term *social robots* has been adopted [3] to include the new generation of robotic systems that interact with humans in daily activities such as entertainment [4–6], healthcare [7,8], and education. An outstanding work about the social acceptance of robots in different application fields is presented systematically in [9].

The field of application of social robots in the education of children is of paramount interest for the following important reasons: (1) the education of the young people in each country is a critical factor for maintaining and promoting the culture and traditions of each nation and (2) the provision of specialized education services to children with various impairments contributes to their integration into the society with equal opportunities and rights by fighting the social exclusions. Additionally, in the particular conditions that humanity is experiencing, such as the current pandemic of COVID-19, the need for distance education of special categories of children can be met to a satisfactory degree with the use of social robots [10].

In recent years, several approaches have been proposed for the use of social robots in the education of adults, with the robot participating in the educational process with multiple roles, as a presenter, teaching assistant, teacher, peer, or tutor [11]. Recent studies have highlighted the great acceptance of social robots by children and their parents [12,13]. Children are very willing to interact with social robots for the following reasons: (1) children treat robots not just as simple machines but as cute toys; (2) robots gain children's attention because of their childlike appearance, while they have many interactive abilities (movements, sounds, colored lights, etc.); (3) social robots have the patience to teach children through many repetitions without getting tired; and (4) social robots are emotionally and behaviorally stable during their interaction with children.

The aforementioned advantages of using social robots in the educational process are much more valuable when the children interacting with the robots have some impairment. In these cases, the educational process is adapted to the special requirements of the children, with social robots being the center of attention for children. For example, in the case of children with autism, a critical factor in the effectiveness of an educational process is the children's engagement in the lesson, as they present several difficulties in concentrating their attention. In this regard, several attempts to study the degree of children's engagement during the lesson, as well as to develop ways to attract children's attention in social robots, have been presented [14,15]. To this end, several multimodal behavioral analysis methods have been proposed [16,17]. Summarizing, the study of the methodologies applying social robots in special education is of particular interest, as it includes several scientific and technological challenges for various scientific disciplines, e.g., child psychology, developmental psychology, cognitive science, neuroscience, computer science.

1.1. Related Work

In order to better identify the contribution of this work to the research field of social robots for educational purposes, it will be constructive to present and comment on similar works that have been proposed so far.

The first systematic review of the application of social robots in education was presented in 2013 by Mubin et al. [18]. This review presented the published approaches based on the following four criteria: (1) the field of educational activity, (2) the role of the robot in the educational process, (3) the type of robot, and (4) the way the robot behaves. Following this categorization of publications and without mentioning any specific methodology for mining the included studies, about 60 papers published from 1996 to the beginning of 2013 were examined.

The second systematic literature review was presented in 2018 by Belpaeme et al. [11]. This study focused on identifying the technological challenges that exist in the development of robots for education, as well as the role of the appearance and behavior of robots in the outcomes of the educational procedure. For the analysis of the literature, three main criteria were adopted: (1) the effectiveness of the application of social robots in education, (2) the impact of integrating social robots into education and (3) the different roles that a social robot can play in the educational process. In light of the above criteria, about 80 papers published by 2018 were studied.

The third bibliographic study that investigates in a systematic way the application of social robots in education was presented in 2019 by Ismail et al. [19]. In this publication, for the first time in the literature, a thorough analysis and review of the application of social robots in the education of children with autism were presented. The study identified significant gaps in the international literature on the application of social robots to the education of children with autism. The identified gaps were (1) the lack of high diversity in the objectives of the researches, (2) the bias of the researches concerning the environment and the applied methodology in relation to the expected behaviors of children with autism and (3) the long-term effectiveness of interventions. The study analyzed about 130 papers published by 2018 and constitutes by far the most complete analysis of the use of social robots in educating children with autism.

1.2. Contribution of This Study

From the analysis of the previous section, it is concluded that most review publications regarding the application of social robots in education are limited to researches on typical education and only one review is dedicated to the case of children with ASD. The research field of integrating social robots into typical education is characterized by many scientific and technological challenges. However, the use of social robots in special education involves additional challenges, as the behavior and skills of children who may have one or multiple impairments vary.

The research community has identified and raised significant awareness of these challenges in special education, with the result that a significant number of efforts have been made in recent years. Although few [20], with limited scope, and non-systematic works have been published that review the application of social robots in special education, the gap for a systematic bibliographic review of this field still exists from the literature. This work seeks to fill this gap by identifying, organizing, processing, and creatively presenting research proposals for the use of social robots in special education in a holistic way.

The high importance of the application of robots in special education, both for children and for society, along with the lack of a systematic study in this field were the main pillars of inspiration for the present work. In addition to the systematic presentation of the research in this field, this paper seeks to contribute in the direction of answering specific questions formulated as follows:

A. **Question 1—What is the degree of integration of social robots in special education?**

This question is answered through a quantitative and statistical analysis of the research attempts published in recent years. For this purpose, Section 2 presents in detail the research activity by presenting specific quantitative measures.

B. **Question 2—In which impairments have the social robots been used, under what conditions and experimental settings and with what results?**

This question is answered in Section 3 through a structured presentation of the qualitative and quantitative characteristics of the research protocols that have been carried out, with a simultaneous reference to their technical settings.

C. **Question 3—What types of social robots are appropriate for each impairment and what is their performance?**

In Section 4, a detailed analysis of the used robots and their performance for each impairment is presented as an attempt to answer this question. Conclusions about the appropriateness of the used social robots are drawn, towards defining a user guide for future research.

D. **Question 4—What are the challenges that need to be addressed by the researchers in this field, in order to achieve the successful integration of social robots in special education?**

The information presented in the first four sections stimulates a constructive discussion in Section 5, in the direction of defining the main challenges provided by the researchers or concluded by this study.

Finally, Section 6 concludes this study by summarizing the answers to the above questions and puts forward the next actions that need to be planned for promoting social robots in special education to the next readiness level.

2. Materials and Methods

The methodology followed in this systematic review is based on the principles proposed by Kitchenham [21]. The proposed method consists of three main phases: *planning*, *conducting*, and *reporting* the review. Khalid [22] suggested preparing a checklist for conducting a systematic review, which was followed in the present systematic review. Some of the items in the checklist that are also used herein are: (1) the sources that were searched and the search terms used, (2) the inclusion/exclusion criteria and (3) the data extraction procedure.

2.1. Sources and Search Terms

The search was conducted in the *Scopus* [23] abstract and citation database, which provides a large amount of peer-reviewed literature from different fields. The search rules incorporating specific terms that were used in this study were the following:

(1) "(human–robot interaction) AND ((special education) OR (special needs education) OR disorder)" and
(2) "human–robot interaction" AND "autism".

It should be noted that in both cases the search rules were applied to the *article title*, *abstract* and *keywords*. Both search rules overlap each other to a certain degree. The first case, though, searches for cases where a human–robot interaction was applied in any of the cases of special education or special needs education or generally a disorder. The second case searches for cases where a human–robot interaction was applied only on cases with autism.

2.2. Inclusion and Exclusion Criteria

The studies that were found needed to include at least two of the search terms that were used during the search. This means that one such study should certainly include the use of a robot and the target group should have at least one kind of impairment so that the group is considered to have special needs. Moreover, an additional constraint was applied; the studies should have been conducted between 2008 and 2020, meaning that the survey focused on the studies conducted in the last 13 years. This constraint is applied in order to analyze the recent status and trends. A diagram showing the exclusion procedure is shown in Figure 1, according to which 99 papers were further processed after removing duplicates and less relevant records by checking their titles and abstracts.

Figure 1. Source selection procedure.

2.3. Data Extraction

The data that were extracted from each study were the following:
- The impairment type of the target group.
- The age range of the target group.

- The role of the robot in the interaction (if the interaction occurred only with the robot or with the cooperation of other persons, namely an instructor, other children, or a family member).
- The type of interaction between the target group and the robot (game, interaction, lessons, or other).
- The name of the robot that was used.
- The type of robot (humanoid, non-humanoid).
- The challenges faced during the study from the aspect of the functionality of the robot.

The above data were extracted from each study and organized into an Excel file.

2.4. Statistical Results

With the application of the aforementioned methodology, a sufficient set of published research papers were collected in the context of this work. The statistical analysis of all published publications is presented in this section.

2.4.1. Demographics

Figure 2 shows that most of the studies are conducted in Europe (47%, N = 46), followed by Asia (29%, N = 29) and North America (16%, N = 16). The rest (8%, N = 8) of the studies were conducted in South America, Oceania, while some studies included children from multiple continents.

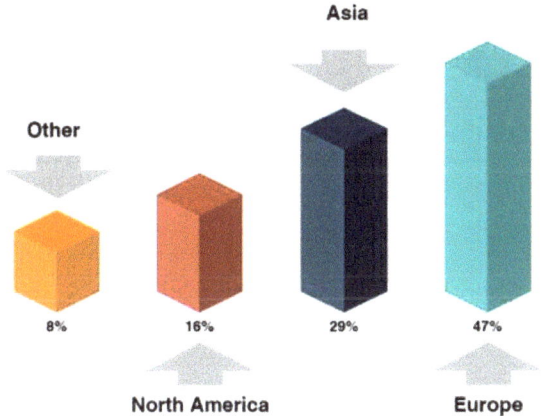

Figure 2. Percentage of studies per continent.

The detailed country map of the conducted studies is illustrated in Figure 3. Most studies were conducted in the U.S.A. (14%, N = 14), followed by the UK (12%, N = 12), Italy (8%, N = 8), Malaysia (6%, N = 6), Iran (5%, N = 5) and Romania (5%, N = 5). The countries in which the studies were conducted are very sparse, with 50% (N = 49) of all corresponding to the following 28 countries: China (4), Portugal (4), France (4), Japan (4), Korea (3), Saudi Arabia (1), Qatar (2), Pakistan (2), New Zealand (2), the Netherlands (2), Australia (2), Greece (2), Belgium (2), the International Consortium (2), Kazakhstan (1), Azerbaijan (1), Turkey (1), Skopje (1), Singapore (1), Brazil (1), Quebec (1), Canada (1), Colombia (1), Ecuador (1), Finland (1), Ukraine (1), and Luxemburg (1).

2.4.2. Timeline

Figure 4 shows the number of publications per year. It seems that 2018 and 2019 were the years with the most publications (N = 16), followed by 2016 with 14 publications. It is worth mentioning that the last year (2020) of this study reveals a very low research activity, mainly due to the pandemic conditions caused by COVID-19.

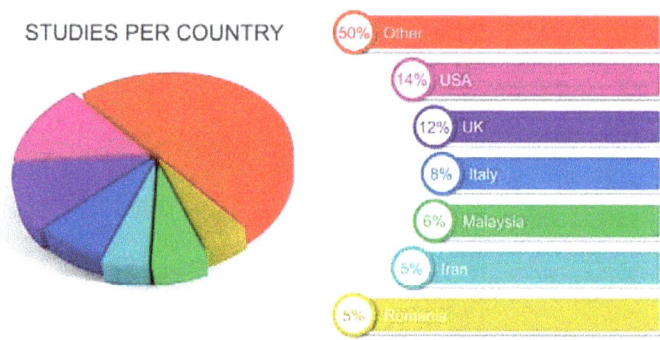

Figure 3. Percentage of studies per country.

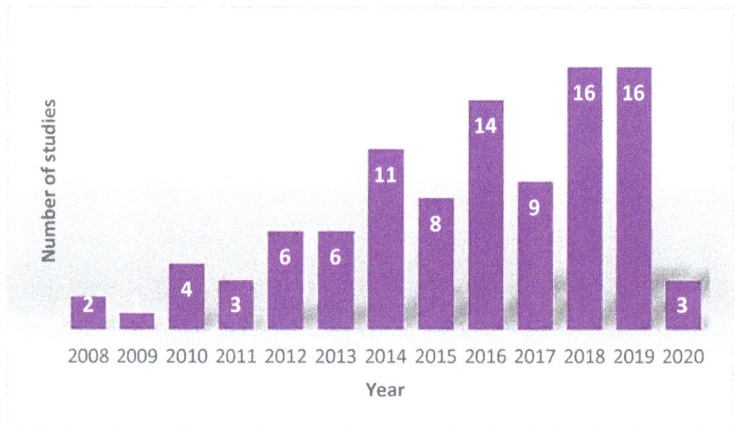

Figure 4. Publications per year.

The above publications are divided into publications for conferences, journals and books, as shown in Figure 5. Furthermore, there is an additional category showing that a study was conducted in the context of a dissertation.

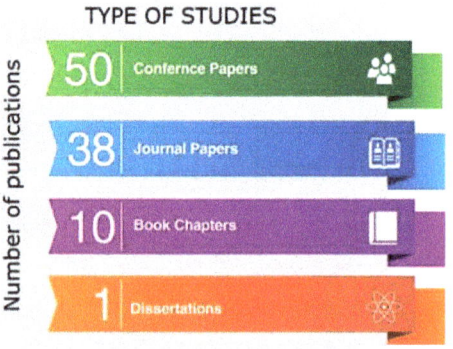

Figure 5. Number of publications per publication type.

2.4.3. Impairments

The variety of impairments for which the social robots have been applied is very large. Figure 6 illustrates that most of the studies were conducted with children with autism spectrum disorder (ASD), as, according to CDC's Autism and Developmental Disabilities Monitoring Network [24], it is a very common disorder among children in the past years (1 in 59 children).

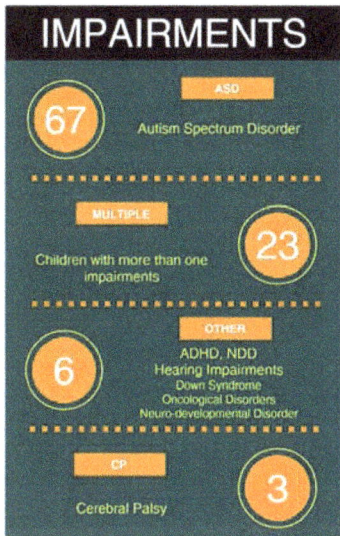

Figure 6. Number of applications of robots on different kind of impairments.

Following this impairment, most cases included children with cerebral palsy—CP (3). The applications of social robots in cases of cerebral palsy are training-oriented interactions. These interactions focus on training the child's movements through training and other activities. Some of those cases also use a ball kicking interaction as a training method.

It should be noted here that the cases named "multiple" are cases where the participating children in the studies had multiple impairments. In addition to that, there were studies where the target group had a variety of disabilities, for example, two children with ASD and two children with Down Syndrome.

It seems that the different impairments on which social robots were applied are quite sparse: intellectual disabilities, down syndrome, developmental disorder, attention deficit hyperactive disorder (ADHD), psychosis, Prader–Willi syndrome, oncological disorders, learning disabilities, joint attention impairments, physical disabilities, spinal muscular atrophy, Asperger, amentia, hearing impairments, neuro-developmental disorder (NDD), etc.

3. Impairments Taxonomy

In this section, an attempt to constructively discuss the findings of the literature analysis of the published studies, based on the type of impairments of the children participating in the research, is presented. Moreover, Tables 1–4 summarize the main quantitative characteristics of the examined studies of each impairment category.

3.1. Autism Spectrum Disorder (ASD)

Children with autism spectrum disorder impairment constitute the bigger target group for delivering social robot-aided special education. According to the literature analysis presented in the previous section, 66 studies focused on children with ASD, aiming to improve the social skills, attention, etc. of the children. The high percentage of the studies belonging to this category shows that ASD seems to be a priority in these types of studies. In 2019, Ismail et al. [19] presented a thorough study in deploying social robots for educating children with ASD. For this reason, it was decided to discuss herein only the approaches proposed in 2019 and 2020, since the works published before 2019 have been analyzed in-depth in the outstanding review of Ismail et al. [19].

Taheri et al. [25] aimed to improve the children's social skills by teaching them music with the NAO robot. In the context of music-based scenarios, four children, at the age of six years old, interacted with the robot and learned to play drum and xylophone. The study showed several different results derived from questionnaires answered by both parents and therapists, having significant improvements on the children, such as: positively affecting their walking, speaking and handwriting, autism severity and parental stress decreased, social skills increased and improvement of the stereotyped behaviors. Those results though are limited due to the small number of participants and having no control group and the results can be highly affected by classes taken by children outside the study.

A study that was part of the EC-FP7 funded DREAM project [26] developed a system to make the NAO robot autonomous in therapy, in order to improve the children's joint attention, imitation and turn-taking skills. They divided the experiments into two phases, one with a teleoperated robot (11 children, three to five years old) and one with the autonomous system (27 children), conducting experiments with a single-case alternative treatment design. The children took part in six to eight game sessions, with both groups showing signs of improvement within a significant time effect.

Study [27] also followed a simple approach, by teleoperating the CommU robot to provide daily-life guidance to the individuals and aimed to explore if caregivers can better address concerns of adolescents via the robot. The two participating girls (15 and 18 years old) were simply communicating with the robot, in the presence of the therapist, disclosing problems with human relationships or the identity of an individual they disliked, behaviors that had not previously occurred in direct conversations with teachers in their daily lives.

Attention is another highly affected aspect by ASD, which many studies have tried to improve through robotic interventions. Joint activities are a common interaction setup in this case, as they are a common interaction to elicit the children's attention through various ways, through specific tasks therapies. Quite a few studies have used the NAO robot in these types of interactions; for example, the study in [28] incorporated two NAO robots to introduce the concept of multi-person communication to the children, testing cases with inter-robot communication and without. They validated the effectiveness of the intervention by analyzing the children's cognitive state of the brain before and after the interventions. Twelve children (11 males and one female) participated in the study between the ages of 3.7 to 10.4 years old, which managed to improve their multi-communication skills. Specifically, the Childhood Autism Rating Scale showed the effectiveness of the therapy, with statistical results for joint attention and EEG module with F value = 20.36, p-value = 1.74×10^{-6} and F critical value = 3.28; joint attention and imitation were F value = 23.93, p-value = 3.79×10^{-7} and F critical value = 3.28 and the eye contact duration of each participant improved over the experiments. Another study that carried out a joint attention therapy was presented in [29], which aimed to find the effect of different visual stimuli in order to improve the children's joint attention, by measuring the total eye contact time and number of times for each visual cue. The study included 12 children (11 males and one female), aged between 3.5 and 7.2 years old. Two attention cues were examined, with one them being more effective (blinking or rasta), with the blinking having 32.4 s and 65.1% accuracy eye contact and rasta having 38.8 s with 80.3%. The results showed that the prominence of the cue is important in establishing eye contact, showing effectiveness in the improvement of joint attention.

The INSIDE system, which allows for complex, semi-unstructured interactions and assessed the autonomy of the proposed system in the context of therapy sessions with children, was proposed by Melo et al. [30]. They used the non-humanoid social robot ASTRO, in therapy sessions with the children. The study was executed with three different groups of children (five boys 3.9 to 5.9 years old, six children and 18 children) targeting different scientific goals. The study with the last group of children included four weeks of interventions and 121 total sessions. All participants managed to complete more than 50% of the tasks during the intervention, with times being lower when the completion rate was higher. The eye gaze percentages showed that high percentages did not necessarily correspond to desirable behaviors and, lastly, most of their speech was directed to the robot, showing high engagement with the robot.

Ishak et al. [31] developed a new framework for robot and human interaction. They selected the humanoid social robot Rero, due to its reconfigurable capability, its ability to be developed in many forms, mobility, speech, its ability to be controlled and programmed and its attractiveness. The nine boys that participated, aged five to six years old, participated in introductory, listening and following instructions, looking and naming objects, focusing and learning colors and focusing and matching colors interaction modules. From the questionnaires that were answered, three out of five modules obtained high scores, with module 4 having the highest score.

Wood et al. [32] were developed some interaction games, to be played with the robot Kaspar to improve the children's Visual Perspective Taking and Theory of Mind. The study was divided into an initial proof of concept that included three children, ages from three to five years old, and then a pilot study with 12 children (five female and seven males), aged from 11 to 14 years old. The sessions included the Smarties test, Sally–Anne test and the Charlie test, showing no significant differences between the pre- and post-test assessments. They utilized the McNemar test to analyze the results, with the Smarties test having $p > 0.05$, Sally–Anne $p > 0.05$ and the Wilcoxon signed ranks for the Charlie test ($z = -1.41$, $p > 0.05$). Despite those results, 7 out of 12 children achieved a higher success level in at least one post-test, with seven children showing an increased number of successful tasks in the post-test.

Sign language teaching has also been studied in [33], by designing a humanoid social robot InMoov by taking into account the characteristics of children with ASD (impaired language, communication, social behavior and narrow flexibility in daily activities). The robot taught nine assistive signs to 10 children, who managed to imitate the robot and keep their focus on it, reporting positive experiences, with a one-sample Wilcoxon signed rank test revealing that the median number of total successful repetitions was significantly greater than zero ($p = 0.011$).

The impact of a robot through storytelling, games, exercises and singing interactions with the children was tested and analyzed by Qidwai et al. [34]. The NAO robot that was used in the study, with the teacher being present, showing improved performance with the children. Fifteen children participated in the study, aged from 7 to 11 years old. The improvement was quantified in terms of the robot activity as an independent variable, following dependent behavioral variables from the responses of the children, specifically: the number of trials, activity response time, response type and behavior retention. Applying the null hypothesis, showing that it was too significant and could be disqualified through the experiments, meant that the use of NAO showed significant improvement in several aspects and confirmed the confidence level for the techniques used.

Study [35] was part of an ongoing project and included the NAO robot and a pet-like robot MiRo, in interaction with play activities within a simulated clinical procedure. Five five-year-old children took part in the study, with which parents and carers were present during the interactions to ensure that they were comfortable. From the video analysis they conducted, along with the parents' feedback, they confirmed that there were possible benefits to reducing the children's anxiety and increased their compliance with instructions. Specifically, four out of five children enjoyed the interaction with both robots, executing on average 82% of the robot's instructions, while one engaged with only 17% of those. The same four children completed the procedures and were happy to stay longer.

Zhang et al. [36] investigated the ability of children with ASD to develop social skills through playing distrust and deception games with the NAO social robot. Two equally sized groups of children participated in this study: twenty children (two females, 18 males) with ASD and ages between five and eight years old and twenty (three females, 17 males) typical developing children. All the children participated in three main tasks, namely the "warm-up session", "distrust and deception, and "interview" about their anthropomorphic thinking of the robot. An important outcome of this study was the observation that children with ASD seemed to more readily consider the robot anthropomorphic than the children with TD. Moreover, children with ASD liked to interact with a robot more than with a human in distrust tasks.

Some useful quantitative information of the studies discussed in this section is summarized in Table 1. It is noted that the symbol "-" implies that this information is not provided in the corresponding reference.

Table 1. Quantitative information of the examined ASD studies.

Ref.	Objectives	Interaction	Age Range (Years)	Participants Total (Female, Male)	Robot Name	Robot Type	Robot Role
[25]	Teach fundamentals of music, improve social/cognitive skills	Music-based scenario	6	4 (0, 4)	NAO	Humanoid	Main interaction
[26]	Improve joint attention, imitation and turn-taking skills	Games	3–5 (Phase 1) - (Phase 2)	11 (-, -) (Phase 1) 27 (-, -) (Phase 2)	NAO	Humanoid	Main interaction. Therapist present
[27]	If caregivers can better address concerns of adolescents with ASD via a desktop humanoid robot	Conversations	15, 18	2 (0, 2)	CommU	Humanoid	Main interaction, tele-operated by caregiver, cases of caregiver being in the same room and in a different room
[28]	Find parameters that can improve the multi-communication skills	Intervention adaptive therapy games (joint attention and imitation)	3.7–10.4	12 (1, 11)	2 NAO	Humanoid	Main interaction
[29]	Find effect of different visual stimuli in order to improve the joint attention	Joint attention therapy	3.5–7.2	12 (1, 11)	NAO	Humanoid	Main interaction
[30]	Assess autonomy of robot	Therapy sessions	3.9–5.9 - -	5 (0, 5) 6 (-, -) 18 (-, -)	ASTRO	Non-Humanoid	Main interaction
[31]	Measure effectiveness of interaction module	Interaction modules	5–6	9 (0, 9)	Rero	Humanoid	Main interaction, therapist present, experimenter hidden
[32]	See whether the games played with the robot improve the children's visual perspective taking (VPT) and theory of mind (TOM)	Games	3–5 (initial proof of concept), 11–14 (pilot study)	3 (-, -) 12 (5, 7)	Kaspar	Humanoid	Main interaction, therapist present
[33]	Examine whether children successfully imitate the robot and if they focus attention on the robot	Sign language teaching	-	10 (-, -)	InMoov	Humanoid	Main interaction, therapist and companions present
[34]	Test and analyze impact of robot	Storytelling, games, exercises, song	7–11	15 (-, -)	NAO	Humanoid	Main interaction, teacher present
[35]	Evaluate benefits in anxiety reduction and instruction compliance	Mixed play activities	5	5 (-, -)	NAO, MiRo	Humanoid, Non-Humanoid	Main interaction, therapist and parents present
[36]	Develop social skills	Distrust and deception games	5–8	20 (2, 18)	NAO	Humanoid	Main interaction

3.2. Multiple Impairments

Table 2 shows the information for each study that included children with multiple impairments (children that had more than one impairment). These studies seem to have several differences in the kind of interactions, the target of improvement and the type of robot that was used. This is reasonable, as these cases seem to be more complex as the impairment is not strictly defined, meaning that each child has more than one impairment and the "group" of impairments being different from child to child and from study to study.

In detail, some of the disabilities that the children had in these studies include ASD, motor and language impairments, tuberous sclerosis, Down syndrome, ADHD, cognitive impairments, cerebral palsy, epilepsy and intellectual disabilities.

That being said, the aims of those studies can be grouped as follows: investigation of the effects of the robot, improvement of cognitive skills and mobility, improvement of mobility, improvement of communication and interaction skills, improvement of communication and learning a specific skill. One can see that some of those aims have similarities; for example, one study may aim to improve just the cognitive skills of the robot while another will aim to improve the children's cognitive skills along with its mobility. The aims of those studies were achieved with a different kind of interaction. Those interactions were exercises for the specific aim (speech exercises for speech therapy, movement exercises for mobility therapy, etc.), games and play sessions with the robot, free interactions and communication and interaction with the robot. It is obvious that the studies that aim to improve specific skills do so using the same kind of interaction.

Following that, the different robots that were used in those studies are NAO, Iromec, Kaspar, SPELTRA, Paro, and in two cases, a Lego robot (WeDo and Lego Mindstorms). Most of those robots are humanoid (NAO, Kaspar, SPELTRA and Lego Mindstorms) and it seems that they are closely related to the improvement of the social skills and mobility of the children. This is because those robots can carry out movements that children can imitate and, as a result, improve their mobility. In the case of non-humanoid robots (Iromec, Paro and WeDo), they are connected with the improvements of the children's cognitive skills as in those cases the interaction is a game/play session or a free interaction.

More specifically, Lindsay and Hounsell [37] helped to address the educational, cognitive, physical and social needs of the children, engaging youth with disabilities in a robotics program; as a result, the children enjoyed and learned about computer programming and building robots, while also considering working in this area in the future. Children with spinal muscular atrophy, cerebral palsy, developmental disorder, and intellectual disabilities participated in this study. They aimed to engage the children in STEM by performing workshops with other engineers and teachers in which the children had to program the robot to solve problems.

In this kind of study, the type of the robot does not seem to be an important factor as the children's main aim was to program the robots so that they can solve problems. This is because the children did not have direct interaction with the robot (for example, playing a game or social interaction) and so the robot did not need to have human-like characteristics. The robots that were used in the study were WeDo [38] and Lego Mindstorms [38], which, although one is humanoid, have quite a few differences in appearance compared to other social robots.

During the study, the children had to build the robots in addition to programming them, with the help of teachers and other staff members of the hospital in which the study was conducted. The 18 children that participated in the workshops were between the ages of six and 13 years old, four of which were female and 14 male. Concerning the weaknesses of the study, the first one is that it was a pilot study and was conducted at only one site. Secondly, girls were under-represented in the program, and therefore, they recommended that future studies make concerted efforts to include more girls. Thirdly, they recognized that STEM learning for children with various disabilities may have different meanings and is an area worthy of further exploration.

In [39], the results obtained in the experimental plan shown that children with cerebral palsy and communication disorders can adapt quickly to the robot, and in the case of the phonemic area, an immediate improvement in the results has been demonstrated. In [40], it was stated that the children with global cognitive retardation, developmental disorder, epilepsy, and language retardation were interested in the robot and in the play activity, regardless of their different disabilities, and they were engaged in the activity from the very beginning of the session. The robot's appearance and behavior did not seem to evoke an agent with its inner states intentionality and this radically reduces the potential of the robot as a mediator of social exchanges. The main issues are mainly related to the functional aspect of the visual interface that does not adequately support a life-like metaphor and meaning attribution processes. Another problem was related to the design of the physical appearance of the robot: children perceived the two screen displays (one used for the face and the other one located on top of the main body) as separate components that do not constitute a whole. Most of the child's attention was focused on the body screen where the commands of the game are entered. The face disappears in the background as well as most of the robot expressiveness. This negatively impacted the interpretation process, thus forbidding the emergence of the role of social mediator.

Three studies focusing on attention, imitation, joint attention and turn-taking were presented in [41]. One subject's "no response" count decreased and flattened out with a noticeable improvement in a future session. Likewise, the "correct response" count consistently increased with a noticeable improvement at a later session. These counts are consistent with the increase of total directives over time. For another subject, the results were inconclusive, although they performed well during the first session (total directives = 16, no response = 1, and correct response = 15), were despondent during the second session and were turn-taking during the third session, and thus were removed from the therapy in both cases. Another subject made considerable progress according to the speech and language pathologist (SLP) and the special education teacher.

A study to identify the utility of interacting with the NAO robot was presented in [42], including six children with several impairments, e.g., ASD, global developmental delay, cerebral palsy, epilepsy. The Wilcoxon signed-rank test showed that for the group as a whole, ratings were significantly ($z = 2.023$, $p = 0.043$) higher when working with the robot examining the individual results indicates that for three of the pupils (S.H., S.T. and T.H.) the engagement increased over time.

Marti and Iacono [43] investigated the utility of the Iromec robot to support the educational activities of four children by playing, concerning the following areas of development: sensory development (S), motor development (M), social and emotional development (SE), cognitive development (C) and communication and interaction (CI). They did not record any positive changes for the sensory developmental area, even if these data were not confirmed from the qualitative analysis and the comments of the special education teachers. The motor developmental area was the only one that did not report any negative changes. Overall, the unchanged items for all the children were 334, the decremented items were 128 and the incremented items were 120, with 144 items being recorded for two of the children and 147 for the other two.

The study in [44] included 11 children aged between 6 and 10 years old with different and multiple neuro-developmental disorders (ASD, Down syndrome, intellectual disabilities, Prader–Willi syndrome and psychosis). It aimed to investigate the potential of the robot as a tool to help children with NDD learn through free play. As some of the children had severe cognitive deficits and others had socialization problems, they were split into two groups in which the first group played alone with the robot and the second played with a peer. They used the non-humanoid robot Teo, which was co-designed by a team of designers, engineers and NDD therapists in the context of the study. This means that the choice of the robot may be critical in cases of children with different NDD disorders. In this case, Teo should be able to have multimodal interactions, offer different types of stimuli, provide clear feedback and have consistent behavior.

During unforeseen situations, the trainer (therapist) had to assist the robot with problems it could not solve for the children by itself. In scenarios where the robot was teaching a child different skills or behaviors, they needed to reduce unforeseen situations to a minimum. The robot's speech, however, provoked multiple reactions. The children reacted verbally to the rate of the robot's speech and some inaccuracies in pronunciation were obviously noticed by the children, prompting critical remarks from the children.

The variables that were analyzed during this study were: communication with Teo, manipulation of Teo, externalization of need, positive emotions, negative emotions, creativity, body stereotypes and social play (for the case of children that were paired with the robot and a second peer). Overall, two children had the highest increase on the variable "communication with Teo" during the second session, while others had a high decrease. In addition, for four children, there was an increase in some variables from the first session to the second, while there was a strong decrease in two children. The variable "manipulation of Teo" had a decrease for all children except for two of them. Additionally, the variables "externalization of needs", "positive emotions" and "negative emotions" showed a positive trend in the second session in both groups of children. Lastly, the study mentions that in empirical researches involving subjects with severe and multiple disabilities, causality relationships are hard to measure and it is almost impossible to isolate all potentially confounding variables that may influence the improvement.

In [45], the two participating adolescents with ASD and mental impairment had resistances and challenges during the interaction with the robot initially, for example, not being able to distinguish the colored cards or not being able to activate the robot's motions. However, they had improvements in the interaction and understanding of the interaction and its tools, managing to activate its movements with cards or not, without problems. Additionally, the behaviors "ignores robot" and "stares at the robot" that were measured decreased throughout the sessions and the children became more engaged with the robot.

Children with physical disabilities (cerebral palsy or brain injury), and cognitive impairments, some of them unable to walk, participated in a study in [46]. For this reason, the interaction between the robot and the children was based on body exercises that focused on improving their movements and their cognitive skills, as most of them also had cognitive impairments. The humanoid robot used in this study was ZORA (NAO) due to its simplified software, which is focused on the application in the rehabilitation and care sector and due to its attractive appearance, variation of interaction and communication skills. This study included 17 participants, of which seven were female and 10 male, between the ages of 2.6 to 18 years old. The quantitative results of the study showed a positive contribution of the robot towards achieving therapeutic and educational goals as measured with the IPPA (individually prioritized problem assessment). Specifically, the mean score of IPPA before the sessions was 11.8, with a minimum of 6 and a maximum of 15 (SD: 3.0), and the mean score after the sessions was 8.8, with a minimum of 3 and a maximum of 15.3 (SD: 3.5).

Iacono et al. [47] compared the Iromec and Kaspar social robots in interacting with 10 children with ASD and cognitive impairments. This study has shown positive results in the developmental target areas. Additionally, and according to the teachers' statements, the interaction with the robots seemed to have had a positive influence on individual development.

In another study [48], three students with ASD and intellectual disabilities became more confident and willing to engage in conversation after interacting with the NAO robot over a period of time. All of the students enrolled in the disability unit (DU) took the opportunity to interact with the robot. For some students, progress was more marked than for others, and the acquired skills were relative to the cognitive ability of the student. In the fourth study, the children were interested in the robot and in the play activity regardless of their different disabilities. Children were engaged in the activity from the very beginning of the session.

Nakadoi [49] investigated the effectiveness of the Paro robot in the therapy of nine children with ASD, developmental disorders, mood disorder, anxiety disorder, etc. aged between 8 and 19 years old. The first patient seemed to treat Paro like a living animal. They saw a pleased expression on her face when some patients were interested in Paro and gathered around her and Paro. Two weeks later, though her autistic trait remained completely unchanged, she gradually started to talk in a relaxed way. For the second patient, they gave him Paro instead of an antipsychotic drug when he had the impulse to go back home. He liked Paro and held it with pleasure in the day room of the ward almost every day, though they could not find deep interaction between him and other patients. He often said hello to Paro. He seemed to treat Paro like a living animal. He sometimes went to sleep with Paro, which was an exceptional allowance for him. Two weeks later, they saw a calm expression on his face.

In [50], the 30 participating children with cognitive disabilities were interacting with the NAO robot towards improving their cleaning skills. They answer a pre-test and post-test questionnaire with six verb and picture questions to assess their improvement after the tests. All groups improved their knowledge and skills between the pre-test (M = 5.43, SD = 1.85) and the post-test (M = 7.05, SD = 1.60). The students' IQ levels showed an improvement in functional knowledge and skills at the end of this study. Although all groups' scores increased, students with moderate cognitive disabilities and severe cognitive disabilities achieved significantly better improvements than those with mild cognitive disabilities.

The authors in [51] focused on the impact of children with ASD and intellectual disabilities (ID) interacting with social robots. They applied the robot as an assisting tool for the Verbal Behavior Milestones Assessment and Placement Program (VB MAPP). The humanoid robot NAO was used due to its 25 degrees of freedom, face detection capabilities, its ability to mimic eye contact by moving its head accordingly, simulate emotions by changing its eye colors and because it can capture a lot of information about the environment. Only six males participated with a mean age of 8.7 years old.

The children with mild, moderate, and severe ID were successful at the end of the therapy; in fact, they were able to adequately perform the VB-MAPP tasks. On the other side, two children with profound ID did not benefit from the robot-assisted therapy, as they were not able to perform any task. The video analysis shows that all children increased the time spent imitating the robot. More significant is the progress of those that learned how to perform the task, while the increase of the two children that were not successful, at around 5%, was negligible.

The results suggest that there is a need to find more advanced solutions and approaches for persons with profound ID. This is the case that requires more care and, thus, the robot-assisted therapy may be very welcome by the therapeutic team, who can reduce their workload by allowing parts of the treatment to be taken over by a robot. Due to the relatively low number of participants and the absence of a control group, the results of this study only indicate the underlying potential of research in this field.

Wan et al. [52] conducted a medium-scale study for investigating the preferences of 74 children with ASD and developmental delay (DD), for the appearances and functionalities of the robots interacting with them. The authors applied a visual attention analysis methodology, as well as a statistical analysis of questionnaires, in order to derive conclusions regarding the physical robot design and the ability of three different robots (Dabao, XiaoE, and Mika) to attract the attention of the children. Dabao robot was the most popular for the children and their parents, while the proposed attention analysis method was able to provide quantitative information w.r.t. the engagement level of the participating children.

In [53], the authors aimed to study the effect of the Cozmo robot on the behavior of six adults with ASD, intellectual disabilities and Down syndrome when they play with it in groups. This interaction with the robot had a positive effect on the development of collaborative and competitive attitudes between the participants.

Zhanatkyzy et al. [54] analyzed the video recordings of several sessions in which 21 children (three female, 18 male) with ASD, ADHD and delayed speech development (DSD) interacted with a NAO robot during play. This study aimed to discover behavioral patterns of the children as well as to measure their engagement in the play. Due to the interaction with the robot, children showed an increasing engagement and eye contact with the robot session by session. The same authors in another study [55] proposed a novel robot behavior targeting children with ASD and ADHD, aiming to increase the engagement level of the 15 boys who participated in a series of sessions. The experimental results showed an increase in the level of engagement and therefore the improvement of the acceptance by the children of the educational process.

Table 2. Quantitative information of the examined studies with multiple impairments.

Ref.	Impairments	Objectives	Interaction	Age Range (Years)	Participants Total (Female, Male)	Robot Name	Robot Type	Robot Role
[37]	Spinal muscular atrophy, cerebral palsy, developmental disorder, intellectual disabilities	Engage children in STEM	Workshops	6–13	18 (4, 14)	WeDo, Lego Mindstorms/EV3	Non-Humanoid, Humanoid	Main interaction
[39]	Cerebral palsy, communication disorders	Speech therapy	Exercises	-	14 (-, -)	SPELTRA	Humanoid	Main interaction, therapist present
[40]	Global cognitive retardation, developmental disorder, epilepsy, language retardation	Investigation of effects of robot	Game	6–11	5 (3, 2)	Iromec	Non-Humanoid	Main interaction, single and two child tests, one teacher involved in activity, another observing
[41]	ASD, speech–language impairment,	Improve social and attentions skills	Social interaction and exercises	6–9	3 (1, 2)	NAO	Humanoid	Main interaction, parent and researcher present, robot operated
[42]	ASD, Global developmental delay, cerebral palsy, epilepsy	Improve mobility	Sessions	9–17	6 (2, 4)	NAO	Humanoid	Main interaction
[43]	Global cognitive disability, tuberous sclerosis, ADHD, motor impairments	Improve mobility and cognitive skills	Play sessions	6–11	4 (3, 1)	Iromec	Non-Humanoid	Main interaction, individual or group sessions, teacher and facilitator present
[44]	Prader–Willi disorder, psychosis, Down syndrome, intellectual disabilities	Learn through play with the robot Investigation of effects of robot	Free play	6–10	11 (-, -)	Teo	Non-Humanoid	Main interaction, therapist present
[45]	ASD, mental impairment	Improve mobility	Play sessions	adolescents	2 (-, -)	Lego Mindstorms NTX	Humanoid	Main interaction, researcher present
[46]	Physical disabilities, cognitive impairments	Improvement of movements and cognitive skills	Body exercises	2.6–18	17 (7, 10)	ZORA (NAO)	Humanoid	Main interaction, Wizard of Oz
[47]	ASD, cognitive impairments	Improve social and cognitive skills	Play scenarios	8.3 avg.	10 (1, 9)	Iromec, Kaspar	Non-Humanoid, Humanoid	Main interaction, experimenter present
[48]	ASD, intellectual disabilities	Improve communication skills	Communication and interaction.	8–13	3 (0, 3)	NAO	Humanoid	Main interaction

Table 2. Cont.

Ref.	Impairments	Objectives	Interaction	Age Range (Years)	Participants Total (Female, Male)	Robot Name	Robot Type	Robot Role
[49]	ASD, developmental disorders, mood disorder, anxiety disorder	Investigation of effects of robot	Free interaction	8–19	9 (5, 4)	Paro	Non-Humanoid	Main interaction
[50]	Different levels of cognitive disabilities	Learn cleaning skills	Training session	10–18	30 (-, -)	NAO	Humanoid	Main interaction, controlled by experimenter
[51]	ASD, intellectual disability	Rehabilitation	Imitation tasks	8.7 avg.	6 (0, 6)	NAO	Humanoid	Main interaction, teacher present
[52]	ASD, developmental delay (DD)	Find the preferences of the children for appearances and functionalities of the robots	Free play	7.8 avg.	74 (11, 63)	Dabao XiaoE Mika	Humanoid	Main interaction
[53]	ASD, intellectual disability, Down syndrome	Analyze the behavior of the participants	Games	24–42	6 (5, 1)	Cozmo	Non-Humanoid	Main interaction
[54]	ASD, ADHD, delayed speech development (DSD)	Engagement level measuring, find behavioral patterns	Games	4–8	21 (3, 18)	NAO	Humanoid	Main interaction, researcher is present
[55]	ASD, ADHD	Apply a novel robot behavior	Imitation games	3–5 6–12	7 (0, 7) 8 (0, 8)	NAO	Humanoid	Main interaction, researcher is present

3.3. Cerebral Palsy

This section summarizes (Table 3) the studies that included children with cerebral palsy or focused on treating or improving the mobility of children with cerebral palsy.

The studies in [56,57] focused on improving the children's mobility, both by performing body exercises with the robot (for example, performing specific movements, kicking a ball, or sitting and standing). Study [56] included six participants aged between four and nine years old, while in [57] only two male children participated, ages 9 and 13 years old. The experiments in [56] were executed using KineTron robot, and [57,58] with NAO. KineTron was chosen because of its ability to carry out precise movements with specified speed and force, providing feedback about position and tension and the ability to arrange complex movement patterns with the use of its special software RoboPlus. NAO was chosen for the same reasons as it includes position sensors at each joint, loudspeakers, sonars on the body, voice recognition and bumpers on its feet.

On the other hand, Ríos-Rincón et al. [59] focused on improving the children's playfulness by letting them play with the Lego Invention "Roverbot" robot [38]. This non-humanoid robot was selected mainly because, as mentioned above, they aimed to improve the children's playfulness and not their mobility or motor skills. This study included one female and three male participants between the ages of five and nine years old. The playfulness of the children was scored based on Rasch analysis using Facets. All of the data points in the intervention phase fell above the extended celeration line demonstrating, according to Bloom's criterion, which change during the intervention was statistically significant (p-value < 0.05). The effect size, calculated using the improvement rate difference (IRD), was moderate: 0.58 (58%) for one child and large: 1 (100%) for the other children. During intervention, all children had an increase in Control-self specifically the items decides, modifies, initiates and transitions. The fit statistics of the playfulness data indicated that 87% of the data was within acceptable limits of the Rasch model. Additionally, mothers' rating of play performance and satisfaction with performance on the COPM increased for all children during the intervention and some carry-over effects were perceived by mothers after the intervention. Most (81%) COPM scores improved more than two units during the intervention.

The usage of Lego Invention robots in [59] had many advantages, although they are not 100% accurate in their movements. Some children were momentarily disappointed when the robot did not go in the exact expected direction, similar to previous research. Children expressed frustration when the infrared signal did not reach the robot sensor in some sessions. A robot wheel and the robot scoop fell off in some sessions. Moreover, the authors mentioned that the robot seemed to misinterpret children with speech impairments.

Table 3. Quantitative information of the examined studies with cerebral palsy.

Ref.	Objectives	Interaction	Age Range (Years)	Participants Total (Female, Male)	Robot Name	Robot Type	Robot Role
[56]	Neurophysiological rehabilitation	Exercises	4–9	6 (-, -)	KineTron	Humanoid	Main interaction, therapist present
[57]	Improve mobility	Exercises	9–13	2 (0, 2)	NAO	Humanoid	Main interaction
[59]	Improve playfulness	Training sessions	5–9	4 (1, 3)	Lego Invention "Roverbot"	Non-Humanoid	Main interaction, child with mother

3.4. Other Impairments

Table 4 shows the information for each study that is not categorized to the previous discussed cases. Moreover, these studies are discussed hereafter.

3.4.1. Attention Deficit Hyperactivity Disorder (ADHD)

A single study [60] was conducted with children with only ADHD and it seems that it was carried out to observe the effects of the interaction of children with the robot. The study focused on collaborative learning (learn about the history of Japan) with the robot while the teachers that were present observed the interaction. Ifbot [61], which was used in this study, is a non-humanoid robot. The design of the robot is itself conversational, which can be used to support learning and promotes effective learning, with a limited number of expressions and arm and body movements. Additionally, the robot was controlled with the Wizard of Oz method during the interaction by one of the teachers. Three children participated, which is a small sample size and without any reference to their age and gender. Lastly, the results of the interaction were evaluated by the total time of the interaction in each case (with and without the robot), for two different learning sessions. Specifically, the learning time (min:sec) without the robot was 15:28 and 12:49 for each session and with the robot was 18:05 and 13:45, the running time (number of times the children get up and run) without the robot was 6 and 5 and with the robot was 7 and 9, and the average break time (min:sec) during the sessions without the robot was 0:49 and 1:52 and with the robot was 0:37 and 1:18.

3.4.2. Hearing Impairments

The conducted search in the literature found only one study that focused on children with hearing impairments. This study [62] focused on teaching the children sign language through two different sign games. In this game, after learning the signs from a multiple-choice test at two different levels (beginner and advanced), the children could choose one of the available robots (Robovie R3 [63] and Nao) to play with. Those two robots were chosen due to their degrees of freedom (29 and 25, respectively) and their fingers in their hands (five and three, respectively). The participating children were 31 in total (16 female and 15 male) and aged between seven and 16 years old. Ten of those children were advanced sign users and the others were beginner level sign users.

As a result, children of different levels of hearing impairment and sign language information were motivated to play with the applications. The children of beginner level preferred to play with the NAO robot first (12 children played their first game with NAO and nine with R3). However, their average error rates were smaller in the games played with R3 than NAO in the first games (average error rate with R3 = 2.8; NAO = 4.7), and total error in both games (R3 = 3.1; NAO = 4.3). Lastly, there was a case of a signed word ("table") where the children noted that the robots, mostly in the case of NAO, did not correctly sign it because R3 has more distinguishable hands and fingers.

3.4.3. Down Syndrome

Two studies that included children with Down syndrome were found in the literature [64,65]. None of the studies seem to have specific therapeutic aims for the children, although there may have been some positive results from those interactions. The studies focused on comparing the robots they used or investigated their effects on the children. In both cases, the interactions between the robot and the children included play scenarios with specific objectives or a free play scenario where the children were left to play freely with the robot.

The NAO robot and Lego Mindstorm KRAZ3 (humanoid and non-humanoid, respectively) were deployed in [64]. The two robots were used for two weeks for eight sessions each. Generally, during the tasks, the children were asked to move the robots in different ways (buttons or verbally) in particular directions, inside a maze, or in other kinds of conditions. NAO was chosen because it can be programmed to pick out specific inputs and respond appropriately, it can change its posture from standing down to standing up, can dance, talk and respond to sounds and pictures, and simple questions can be asked to it either verbally or with a tablet. On the other hand, the Lego Mindstorm was chosen because it can be controlled to move in different directions, detect colors, and be controlled with an infrared remote and generally because it was designed for educational purposes. Study [65] was similar to the first study, where they compared a humanoid (Kaspar [66]) and non-humanoid (Iromec [67]) robot through play scenarios. The scenarios that the children played were: "turn-taking", "move the robot" and an imitation scenario. Iromec robot was used because it can move in space, detect obstacles, has a digital touch screen on top of it with graphical interface elements, can engage in different play scenarios and can be configured in different ways and equipped with extra features. Kaspar was used because its size is similar to that of a child (as its torso and legs were taken from a child-sized shop mannequin), it can execute different play behaviors, can express simple and complex emotions and can be controlled remotely or operated semi-autonomously. The number of participants in both studies was low. In [64], one female and three males were included between the ages of 10 and 16 years old, and in [65], there was only one eight-year-old girl.

As far as the results are concerned, ref. [64] showed that three out of four participants had a higher percentage engagement with the Lego Mindstorm robot than with the NAO robot. In the fourth participant, there was no difference in percentage engagement between the two robots. In terms of percentage errors, there was no difference between the two robots in all four participants. Means for the percentage of engagement for each participant were: (1) NAO: 93.52, Lego: 96.12; (2) NAO: 94.11, Lego: 94.59; (3) NAO: 90.71, Lego: 95.45; and (4) NAO: 79.66, Lego: 91.50. The means for the percentage of error for each participant were: (1) NAO: 17.02, Lego: 20.25; (2) NAO: 25.60, Lego: 14.69; (3) NAO: 13.69, Lego: 19.23; and (4) NAO: 13.78, Lego: 12.29. For [65], the results seem to indicate that the child was more interactive with the experimenter and the robot during the sessions with Kaspar, since in most behavioral categories the rates per minute were higher while playing with Kaspar. The only behavioral category that showed a significant difference in favor of the Iromec platform was "touching the robot".

Lastly, for study [64], a limited range of learning objectives was also included; although the humanoid NAO robot is capable of a wide variety of functions when compared to the non-humanoid Lego Mindstorm, learning objectives were limited to those that could be carried out with both robots. There was also a difference between the two robots in the way they were controlled. The NAO robot was controlled using the tablet, whilst the Lego Mindstorm robot had its own remote control. Pupils found it easier to use the tablet than the remote control.

3.4.4. Oncological Disorders

During the search, one case [68] that included children with oncological disorders (acute myeloid leukemia, relapsed acute lymphoblastic leukemia, brain tumor, T-cell lymphoma, etc.) was found. The study aimed to increase the motivation of the children in participating in exercises. It is well-known that it is very difficult to motivate children with oncological disorders, and for this reason, gross motor exercises were carried out with and without a human/robot and with and without music.

The robot that was used was ZORA [69], which is a NAO robot launched and programmed by the Belgian company QBMT. ZORA was used because it already had dances preprogrammed by QBMT and was able to insert other sets of exercises or music through the 'composer' function that was available.

The number of participating children was 14, aging between three and 15 years old, with five being female and nine male. As mentioned above, they had varying oncological disorders, from leukemia to brain tumors.

Although children with oncological disorders are not motivated, the application of the robot, with the combination of music, for dance exercises had positive outcomes. The motivation of the children was assessed using three measures based on the Fun Toolkit (Smileyometer, Again score and Fun Sorter). From the results, it seems that having a humanoid robot instructor to deliver and help with the physical activity program (instead of a human) appeared to increase the children's initial motivation to participate.

3.4.5. Neuro-Developmental Disorder (NDD)

In a single study [70], the increase of the engagement of 11 participants aged between 25 and 42 years old, in a storytelling intervention scenario with the ELE pet-like robot, was investigated. The results were encouraging since 80% of the participants scored higher in the sessions, revealing that the ELE non-humanoid robot was able to engage more with all the subjects than a human speaker. It is worth noting that the ELE robot was able to attract the attention of the adults, although it is very cheap and with low interaction capabilities of the social robot.

Table 4. Quantitative information of the examined studies with miscellaneous impairments.

Ref.	Impairment	Objectives	Interaction	Age Range (Years)	Participants Total (Female, Male)	Robot Name	Robot Type	Robot Role
[60]	ADHD	Observe effects of the interaction	Collaborative learning	-	3 (-, -)	Ifbot	Non-Humanoid	Wizard of Oz, main interaction
[62]	Hearing impairments	Sign language teaching	Sign game	7–16	27 (16, 11)	Robovie R3, NAO	Humanoid	Main interaction
[64]	Down syndrome	Compare the two robots	Play scenarios	10–16	4 (1, 3)	NAO, Lego Mindstorms KRAZ3	Humanoid, Non-Humanoid	Support the learning
[65]	Down syndrome	Investigate effects of robots	Play scenarios	8	1 (1, 0)	Iromec, Kaspar	Non-Humanoid, humanoid	Main interaction, experimenter interacting

Table 4. Cont.

Ref.	Impairment	Objectives	Interaction	Age Range (Years)	Participants Total (Female, Male)	Robot Name	Robot Type	Robot Role
[68]	Oncological disorders	Increase motivation of children to perform exercises	Gross motor exercises	3–15	14 (5, 9)	ZORA (NAO)	Humanoid	Main interaction
[70]	NDD	Increase engagement	Storytelling	25–42	11 (-, -)	ELE	Non-Humanoid	Main interaction

3.5. Challenges

Based on the material presented in the previous sections, it is concluded that there is a strong effort to implement social robots in each category of impairment. The main research outcomes as well as the new challenges that emerged from these researches are summarized in Table 5.

Table 5. Main reported outcomes and challenges of some of the examined studies.

Reference	Impairment	Outcomes	Challenges
[25]	ASD	Sessions positively affected their walking, speaking and handwriting; autism severity and parental stress decreased, social skills increased and stereotyped behaviors improved.	A small number of participants and no control group, children were not mature enough, potential effects of other classes, heterogeneous autism severity on children, unpredicted behaviors during sessions, engineering and technical issues, the small number of sessions.
[34]	ASD	The use of the NAO robot showed significant improvement in several aspects of learning behaviors, confirming the confidence level for the techniques used.	Not reported.
[35]	ASD	Reduction in anxiety and increase in compliance with instructions.	Not reported.
[36]	ASD	Distrust task: the independent-sample Welch t-test showed a significant difference in overall distrust performance between the ASD (M = 7.70, SD = 2.62) and TD groups (M = 9.35, SD = 0.67. TD children were more likely than children with ASD to distrust the robot who offered incorrect information. Deception task: the overall performance analysis of the deception task also found a significant difference in the overall deception performance between the ASD (M = 6.70, SD = 3.64) and TD (M = 9.55, SD = 1.19) groups, indicating that TD children were more likely to deceive the robot than children with ASD.	Did not use a within-subject design to compare the same participants with human and robot conditions. Although there is no significant difference in the mean ages between the two ASD groups, the age difference of six months could still represent different neurodevelopmental patterns in children, which could affect their interactions with robots and humans. The anthropomorphic thinking for the human condition was not investigated; thus, it is not clear whether the interaction progress would affect children's anthropomorphic thinking answers. To study the regional difference of the performance of this study, and to replicate these findings in more cities and counties.
[37]	Multiple disabilities	The results obtained show that children can adapt quickly to the robot, and in the case of phonemic area, an immediate improvement. Helped to address the educational, cognitive, physical and social needs of the children, engaging youth with disabilities in a robotics program.	Three main improvements were identified for this study, based on its challenges: (1) to scale the research and to repeat it in more sites, (2) to increase the number of female children and (3) to generalize the designed experiments to children with other disabilities, since the authors realized that STEM learning for children with various disabilities may have different meanings and is an area worthy of further exploration.

Table 5. Cont.

Reference	Impairment	Outcomes	Challenges
[39]	Multiple disabilities	Children were engaged in the activity from the very beginning of the session.	The appearance and behaviors did not evoke an agent with its inner state and intentionality. Issues are mainly related to the functional aspect of the visual interface, design of the physical appearance of the robot and its faces.
[40]	Multiple disabilities	Helped to address the educational, cognitive, physical and social needs of the children.	The research was conducted at only one site. The girls were under-represented in the program.
[41]	Multiple disabilities	"No response" count decreases and flattens out with improvement. The "correct response" count consistently increases. These counts are consistent with the increase of total directives over time. The results for subject 3 are inconclusive. Another subject made considerable progress according to the SLP and SPED teacher.	Not reported.
[42]	Multiple disabilities	The Wilcoxon signed-rank test showed that for the group as a whole, ratings were significantly higher when working with the robot.	There was a small amount of bias that may have influenced the teachers' ratings. There were more people present in the classroom than when working with the robot and there was also the researcher and a camera.
[43]	Multiple disabilities	No positive changes for the Sensory developmental area were recorded. The motor developmental area was the only one that did not report any negative changes.	To extend this preliminary study.
[44]	Multiple disabilities	Some children had the highest increase on the variable "communication with Teo", while others had a high decrease. For four children, there was an increase in some variables, while there was a strong decrease in two children. The variable "manipulation of Teo" had a decrease for all children except for two of them. Additionally, the variables "externalization of needs", "positive emotions" and "negative emotions" showed a positive trend in the second session in both groups of children.	Causality relationships are hard to measure.
[45]	Multiple disabilities	Improvements in distinguishing the cards and overall behavior.	Not reported.
[46]	Multiple disabilities	The mean score of IPPA before the sessions was 11.8, and the mean score after the sessions was 8.8.	Not reported.
[47]	Multiple disabilities	Analysis of the data from the pre- and post-test questionnaires; all items were compared with each other in order to evaluate possible improvements in the developmental target areas.	The ability to speak and understand the language was vital for the children. Study data are preliminary.
[48]	Multiple disabilities	The three students became more confident and willing to engage in conversation after interacting with the robot over a period of time.	Not reported.
[49]	Multiple disabilities	They confirmed the lasting positive change by gross observation.	One boy did not like the big eyes or the slight drive noise.

Table 5. Cont.

Reference	Impairment	Outcomes	Challenges
[50]	Multiple disabilities	All groups in this experiment improved their knowledge and skills between the pre-test and the post-test. The interaction with the robot was more efficient in improving functional knowledge and skills. Students' IQ levels showed an improvement.	Not reported.
[51]	Multiple disabilities	Children successful at the end of the therapy. Two children with profound ID did not benefit from robot-assisted therapy. All children increased the time spent imitating the robot.	The results of this study only indicate the underlying potential of research in this field.
[56]	Cerebral palsy	All children liked the sessions with the Rehabilitation Robot. The children wanted him to be present during their other sessions.	Not reported.
[57]	Cerebral palsy	The robot misinterprets children with the speech impediment.	Not reported.
[59]	Cerebral palsy	Scoring based on Rasch analysis. During intervention, all children had an increase in self-control, specifically the items decides, modifies, initiates and transitions.	The Lego Invention robot is not 100% accurate in its movements.
[60]	ADHD	Learning time (min:sec): without robot: 15:28, 12:49; with robot: 18:05, 13:45. Running time: without robot: 6 and 5 times; with robot: 7 and 9 times.	Not reported.
[62]	Hearing impairments	The children of beginner's level preferred to play with NAO first. Their average error rates are smaller in the games played with R3 than NAO in the first games, and total error in both games.	The robots, due to their hands, did not correctly sign one of the words.
[64]	Down syndrome	Participants had a higher percentage of engagement with the Lego Mindstorm than with the NAO. In the fourth participant, there was no difference in percentage engagement between the two robots. In terms of percentage errors, there was no difference between the two robots in all four participants.	The learning objectives were limited to those that could be carried out with both robots.
[65]	Down syndrome	The child was more interactive with the experimenter and the robot during the sessions with the Kaspar robot.	Not reported.
[68]	Oncological disorders	The motivation was assessed using three measures based on the Fun Toolkit.	Not reported.

4. Robots—Taxonomy

An in-depth study of the published research efforts to integrate social robots into special education has highlighted the wide variety of social robots that have been developed and tested in a highly diverse set of experiments with children with various impairments. The need for the most useful social robots has led the market to design and produce a wide range of social robots with varying features (Tables 6 and 7). Among other things, this has highlighted the need for a customized methodology for developing [71] and selecting [72] social robots for specific applications.

In this section, an attempt is made to record the various types of social robots that have been applied in special education, with the ultimate goal of concluding the suitability of each type of robot for each category of impairments.

4.1. NAO Robot

A significant number (46%, N = 47) of studies used the NAO robot and it seems that in almost all the cases, NAO was used to help children with ASD. In other examples, it was also used to help children with multiple disabilities (from which most cases were with at least one of the disabilities being ASD), intellectual disabilities, Down syndrome, cerebral palsy, oncological disorders, physical disabilities and hearing impairments. In most cases, a humanoid robot is required as during the interaction between the robot and the child, the child had to imitate the robot's movements to improve its joint attention skills, mobility, or carry out other kinds of body exercises. This makes the choice of NAO robot more suitable as the movements can be programmed easily, with the help of its desktop program and its degrees of freedom to move. In addition to movement exercises, it was also used in cases of learning sessions and social interactions, where the children interacted by talking to each other.

4.2. Kaspar Robot

Kaspar, the second most popular social root (6%, N = 6), was used in studies that focused on children with ASD, Down syndrome and multiple disabilities (from which one was also ASD). Kaspar's humanoid body and features seem to help more children with ASD. In some of the studies, Kaspar was used with the intention of exploring and measuring its potentials in the improvement of children's general behavior by playing games and participating in play scenarios.

4.3. Lego Mindstorms

Different kinds of robots can be built with the Lego Mindstorms (the third most popular social root, used in five studies (4.85%) used this kind of robot) set. In most cases, the particular set was used to build robots that were applied to studies with children with diverse disabilities, such as ASD, multiple disabilities, cerebral palsy, Down syndrome, developmental disorder and other movement disabilities. Due to its design, the robot can be either a non-humanoid (a vehicle) or a humanoid robot. The interactions of the studies that this robot was used in vary. In some studies, the robot was used in training, learning, or working sessions, workshops and play sessions. This indicates that the robot, or the building set in general, can be used to build a robot for different kinds of interactions. In addition to that, a study conducted workshops with the particular set, in which the children had to build a robot using the set. As a result, children with movement impairments were also able to improve their mobility by building a robot with the help of other teachers participating.

In all cases, the robot was the main interaction of the child, with the exception of one, in which it was supporting the learning of the child; in other cases, the child was not alone during the interaction, with the researcher being present, or in one case, where the child was accommodated with their mother.

4.4. iRobiQ Robot

The iRobiQ robot was used in studies including children with ASD (or in one case, PDD-NOS). It seems that the design of the robot is mostly targeted to children with ASD impairment and the robot itself to be used in the context of interactions that aim to improve the communication and syntactic skills, or other skills that are closely related to those. In most cases, the robot was used as a tool to assist the teachers during the interaction between them and the children, by providing instructions or other assistive cues to the children. Additionally, it was used [73] to teach attention, communication and social skills to children with ASD by playing a card game and providing assistance and feedback during the game.

It is a non-humanoid robot with a display that was used to play the card game, through which it provided the feedback in combination with its head.

4.5. Iromec Robot

Iromec robot was mostly used in studies where the children had multiple disabilities, Down syndrome or ASD. Iromec is a non-humanoid robot with a visual interface that can show the robot's expressions and a body interface with the main purpose of driving the interaction and stimulating specific actions. For these reasons, it was mainly used in the context of interactions where the children played with the robot or participated in play scenarios/sessions.

The children that participated in these studies and interacted with the Iromec robot were younger than 11 years old. This means that this particular robot, combined with interactions that focus on games or play scenarios, is more applicable to this age.

4.6. Alice Robot

Alice is a humanoid robot that looks like a young girl (Table 5). Alice was used in three studies [74–76] (2.94% of the examined publications) with children with ASD, during which it played a game with the children to improve their imitation and joint attention skills. During the interactions, the particular robot was controlled and teleoperated using a Microsoft Kinect and with Haptic PhantomOmni.

4.7. Probo Robot

Probo is a humanoid robot with a safe and huggable design. This robot was used only in studies [77–79] with children with ASD. Its appearance is that of a stuffed imaginary animal providing soft touch and acting as a social interface by employing social cues and communication modalities. In one case, it was used to improve the social skills of the children by participating with each child in a social story.

4.8. KiliRo Robot

KiliRo is a parrot robot, which was used only in studies [80,81] with children with ASD. In those studies, KiliRo was used to lower the stress levels of the children or to improve the interaction of the teacher with the child by essentially making the child more relaxed or by assisting them. This indicates that this kind of robot (zoomorphic), or at least the particular one, can be used as a relaxing tool for the children. The usual interaction is a learning activity that aimed to improve the children's learning abilities, as an assistance tool or as the main interaction media.

4.9. Zeno Robot

Zeno is a humanoid robot that resembles a small boy. This robot was used in two studies [82,83] as a social mediator and as an assistant in game scenarios with children with ASD. The main target of using this robot was to improve the eye contact, joint attention, symbolic play, and basic emotion recognition of the children.

4.10. Miscellaneous Robots

Aibo robot, which is a dog robot, was used in an explorative study [84] for children with ASD that aimed to check if the specific robot engaged the children more into the activities. The interactions were interactive sessions with the robot, during which the children played or interacted with the robot while the experimenter was watching them or asking some questions.

Rero is a humanoid social robot [31] used to establish a child–robot interaction based on five interaction modules designed for children with ASD. This robot is reconfigurable and can be programmed to execute various interaction scenarios. Its mobility along with the attractive appearance make this robot suitable to increase the engagement of the children during the interventions.

Cozmo is a very cute non-humanoid robot that has the form of a small truck (Table 6). It is mainly used for children's companion and entertainment since it can be programmed to dance, sneeze, or play several games. In the study [53], adults with multiple impairments interacted with Cozmo while playing games, with the robot analyzing the behavior of the participants.

Paro is a non-humanoid (pet-like) social robot with the appearance of a baby seal. This social robot was used as a therapeutic tool in [49,85] for children with multiple impairments, by improving the children's cognitive skills through game/play sessions or free interactions.

MiRo is also a non-humanoid (pet-like) social robot, which has the form of a small dog. It is autonomous and is characterized by a brain-like control system. In [35], MiRo interacted with children with ASD, which helped them to reduce their anxiety and increased their compliance with game instructions.

CommU is a humanoid robot capable of initiating and maintaining conversations with ASD-impaired children [27]. It can move its head, eyes and body to reproduce human-like expressions during the conversation.

Astro was used in one study [30] with children with ASD for therapeutic purposes and was part of larger system architecture. Astro is a non-humanoid robot that was controlled by one researcher whilst another controlled its social behavior (speech and facial expressions) during the therapeutic sessions with the children. Moreover, a restricted-perception WoZ methodology was also applied. According to the researchers, this robot was used because it can socially interact with the children and is fully autonomous during therapy sessions.

The QTrobot was used in [86] that included children with ASD. This robot is a child-sized humanoid robot, with an expressive social appearance and a screen that allows the presentation of animated faces. QTrobot was used in the study as an interview partner to the child, during which it told a story, then asked some questions and lastly played an imitation game.

InMoov is a humanoid social robot designed [33] for interacting with ASD-impaired children. This is the first open-source 3D printed social robot [87], which anyone can print at home, subject to 3D printer availability. The main advantage of this robot is it is modular and adaptive nature, which permits it to be modified according to the needs of the study.

Ifbot is a non-humanoid robot able to communicate with humans verbally and non-verbally, with facial expression emotions. It is equipped with the appropriate hardware to execute computer vision algorithms such as object recognition, tracking etc. In [60], Ifbot was used to promote collaborative learning between children with ADHD.

Keepon is a non-humanoid robot that was used [88] as a tool to give feedback to children with ASD during their learning tasks with the teachers. An operator gave the feedback of the robot manually.

FACE is an android that includes the FACET, which is a complete therapy infrastructure based on the integration of the HIPOP (Human Interaction Pervasive Observation Platform). This humanoid robot, which has the appearance of a female human, interacted with children with ASD in order to improve their social capabilities through psychologist-driven interactions. During the interactions, the robot was performing expressions with its face and then the children had to label and imitate them, and at a later stage, the children were free to play and observe the robot [89].

Kinetron is a humanoid robot that was used in a study with children with cerebral palsy [56]. In this study, the robot was used in the context of games that aimed to rehabilitate the children's neurophysiology. KineTron was chosen because of its ability to perform precise movements with specified speed and force, providing feedback about position and tension and the ability to arrange complex movement patterns with the use of its special software RoboPlus.

Pleo is a socially expressive dinosaur robot that was designed to express emotions and attentions using body movement and vocalizations that are easily recognizable. It was used [90] to elicit social interaction and host of social perception reasoning to children with ASD, during a triadic interaction with the child and a teacher.

Queball is a robotic ball that is designed with the following feature categories: play, rough-and-tumble play, cognitive potential enhanced by movement and physical well-being. For these reasons, the robot was used in the study [91] as a therapeutic tool for children with ASD by engaging them in social interaction and physical, fun, learning and communication play.

Although Robovie R3 was used [62] in a part of the study, its humanoid characteristics made the children with hearing impairments better understand the signs it was showing, in comparison to the NAO robot that showed the same, during the sign language game they played. This was due to its 29 degrees of freedom and five independent fingers in its hands, combined with its expressive face.

SPELTRA (Speech and Language Therapy Robotic Assistant) was used [39] in speech exercises with children with multiple impairments. SPELTRA is a robotic system focused on providing support in speech therapy, with the main function of interacting with children through educational exercises and relational activities. It can also indirectly assist during the therapists in tasks.

Teo, a non-humanoid robot, was used [44] mainly to investigate its potential with children with ASD, Down syndrome, intellectual disabilities, Prader–Willi syndrome, psychosis and multiple disabilities. The children were left to play freely with the robot while the therapist was present.

Troy is a humanoid robot with only the upper torso, and has the size of an average four-year-old child. Troy was used [92] to examine the effects of its intervention on the challenging or tantrum behaviors of children with ASD, by letting it communicate with them.

In the following Tables 6 and 7, the appearance of some popular social robots along with their main characteristics are presented, respectively.

Table 6. Appearance of some of the most popular social robots used in special education.

Table 6. *Cont.*

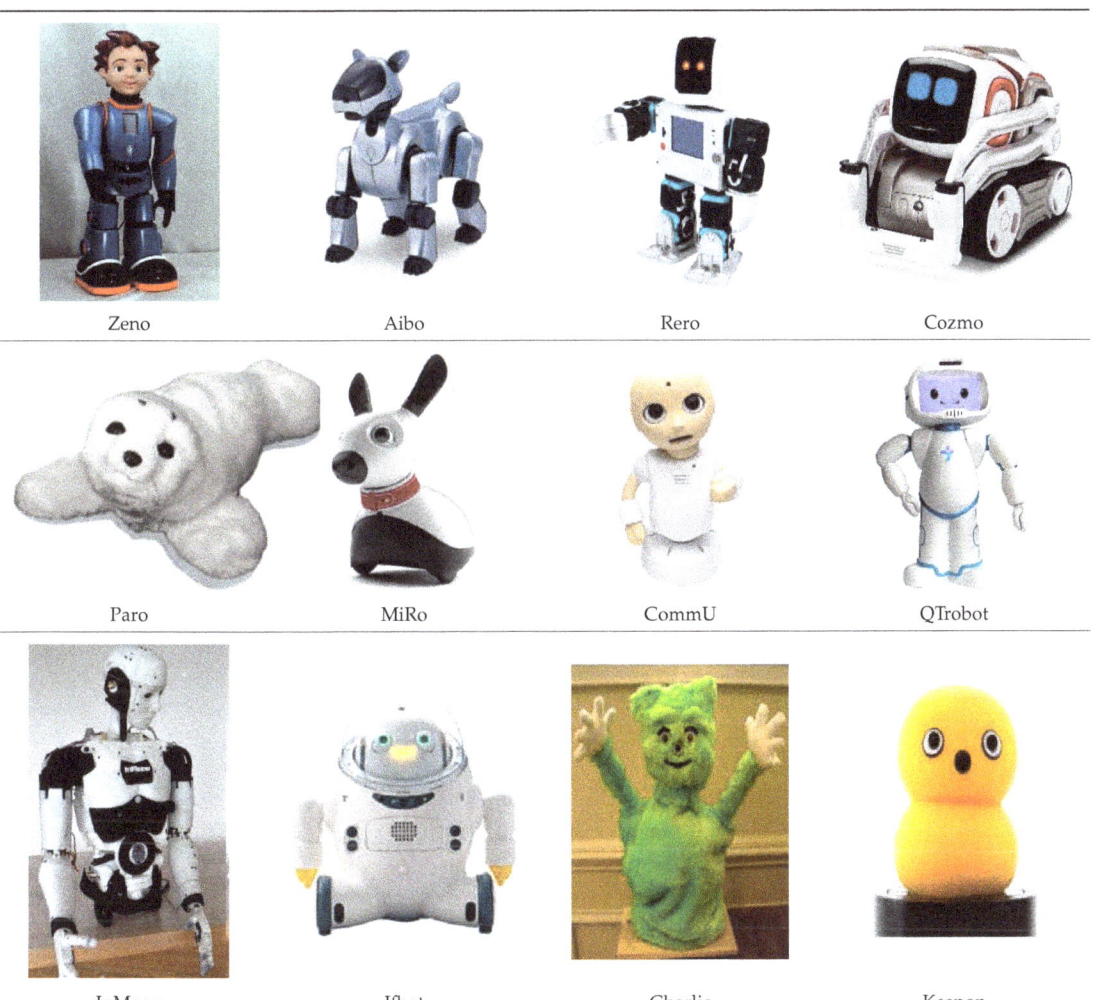

Table 7. Main characteristics of the commonly used social robots.

Robot Name	Robot Type	Ref.	Impairments	Robot Role	Interaction
NAO	Humanoid	[25,26,28,29,34–36,41,42,46,48,50,51,54,55,57,62,64,68,75,77,85,93–109]	ASD, multiple impairments, cerebral palsy, hearing impairments, oncological disorders	Proactive companion, assistive intervention tool, social mediator, therapeutic assistant	Imitation, therapeutic games, free play sessions, teaching joint attention, learning sessions
Kaspar	Humanoid	[32,47,65,110–112]	ASD, multiple impairments, Down syndrome	Game partner	Unconstrained interaction, tactile interaction through tactile play scenarios, games

Table 7. Cont.

Robot Name	Robot Type	Ref.	Impairments	Robot Role	Interaction
Lego Mind-storms	Non-Humanoid Humanoid	[37,45,59,113,113]	Multiple impairments, cerebral palsy	Main interaction	Working sessions, workshops (program robot to solve problems), games
iRobiQ	Humanoid	[73,114–116]	ASD, multiple impairments	Main interaction	Story intervention, social interaction
Iromec	Non-Humanoid	[40,43,47,65,117]	ASD, multiple impairments, Down syndrome	Companion and teacher assistant	Play scenarios, triadic interaction, imitation
Alice	Humanoid	[74–76]	ASD	Game partner	Game, triadic interaction
Probo	Humanoid (pet-like)	[77–79]	ASD	Main interaction	Storytelling, game
KiliRo	Non-Humanoid (pet-like)	[80,81]	ASD	Lower stress levels of the children, improve the interaction of the teacher	Pronouncing letters and dancing, free interaction, learning activities
Zeno	Humanoid	[82,83]	ASD	Social mediator, assistant	recognize emotions in a game scenario, stimulus-reinforcement
Aibo	Non-Humanoid (pet-like)	[84]	ASD	Main interaction	Interactive and therapy sessions
Rero	Humanoid	[31]	ASD	Main interaction	Interaction modules
Cozmo	Non-Humanoid	[53]	Multiple impairments	Main interaction	Games
Paro	Non-Humanoid (pet-like)	[49,85]	Multiple impairments	Main interaction	Free interaction
MiRo	Non-Humanoid (pet-like)	[35]	ASD	Main interaction	Mixed play activities
CommU	Humanoid	[27]	ASD	Main interaction	Conversations
Astro	Non-Humanoid	[30]	ASD	Main interaction	Therapy sessions
QTrobot	Humanoid	[86]	ASD	Interview partner	Storytelling, ask questions, imitation games
InMoov	Humanoid	[33]	ASD	Teacher assistant	Sign language learning
Ifbot	Non-Humanoid	[60]	ADHD	Collaborative learning	Wizard of Oz, main interaction
Keepon	Non-humanoid (pet-like)	[88]	ASD	Gives feedback to the children	Learning/reversal learning task
FACE	Humanoid (Android)	[89]	ASD	Treatment assistive tool	Imitation games
Kinetron	Humanoid	[56]	Cerebral palsy	Rehabilitation, precise movements with specified speed and force.	Games
Pleo	Non-humanoid (pet-like)	[90]	ASD	Elicit social interaction and host of social perception reasoning to children	Triadic interaction with the child and a teacher

Table 7. *Cont.*

Robot Name	Robot Type	Ref.	Impairments	Robot Role	Interaction
Queball	Non-humanoid	[91]	ASD	Therapeutic tool	Social interaction, play
Robovie R3	Humanoid	[62]	Hearing impairments	Teacher assistant	Sign language learning
SPELTRA	Non-humanoid	[39]	Multiple impairments	Main interaction	Speech exercises
Teo	Non-humanoid	[44]	Multiple impairments, Down syndrome	Main interaction	Free play
Troy	Humanoid	[92]	ASD	Treatment assistive tool	Social communication

5. Discussion

In the previous sections, the research attempts for the integration of social robots in the special education of children in the period 2008 to 2020 were recorded and presented in detail. The purpose of this analysis is to investigate the answers to the four questions that were initially posed as the main objectives of this systematic review.

In particular, the statistical analysis of papers published both chronologically and geographically indicates a growing research interest of the scientific community to apply social robots in the education of children and adults with impairments. Figure 3 shows Europe leading the effort to integrate social robots into special education, followed by the U.S.A. The need for the inclusion of these individuals into modern societies as equal members of them requires the acceleration of this integration world-wide. It seems that the rapid development of technology and artificial intelligence can help in this direction, through the development of more and more autonomous and intelligent social robots (Table 6).

In addition, another evidence that proves the high degree of integration of social robots in special education is the wide variety of impairments (Figure 6) of children who participated in interaction sessions with social robots. Although most of the publications are about groups of people with ASD, which was to be expected, the variety of different impairments that have been the subject of a study of the application of social robots is surprising. In all these cases, and although most studies have yielded encouraging results, it is a common finding that this road is very long.

Regarding the third question to be investigated, about the suitability of social robots in specific impairments, based on the analysis that was carried out, it appears that specific characteristics of robots are very useful for specific impairments. For example, the NAO robot, which is the most equipped robot of all, is preferred for educating children with ASD, which are cases that are more complex. In addition, in children with hearing problems, robots with five fingers are suggested for the teaching of sign language, e.g., Robovie R3, or InMoov. Apart from the type of impairment, another factor that determines the suitability of a robot is the age of the children involved. Thus, for young children, pet-like robots (Parot, Aibo, Pleo, etc.) prove to be more suitable due to their more playful appearance. However, a targeted study is required to identify the desired technical characteristics of the robots for each impairment, in order to select the most suitable robot in each case. It is worth mentioning that most robots on the market have been developed mainly for the education, entertainment and companionship of the children of typical education who are the largest population and not for the children of special education. Therefore, the design of robots aimed at children in special education is an unexplored field, in the direction of which more efforts are expected in the near future.

As far as the intelligence level of the social robots involving in special education is concerned, it is deduced that it does not differ from that of the typical education. Usually, the scientists follow the path taken by the pioneer Marvin Minsky [118], based on which several small and less intelligent parts build intelligence. In this context, face detection, face recognition, speech recognition, emotional recognition, visual behavioral analysis, visual tracking, etc. algorithms [119] are used to build intelligence in social robots that enable them to interact with children more naturally. However, it is worth mentioning that the needs for intelligent interaction of the robot with children in special education are particularly high, due to the particular behavior of children, e.g., in the expression of emotions. Therefore, the design of intelligent algorithms and/or the adaptation of existing algorithms to the specifics of each category of impairments is considered of paramount importance.

Although all the research papers studied in this work have reached positive conclusions about the use of social robots, in most cases, the authors have reported the challenges (Table 5) that need to be addressed in the future, because of the weaknesses of their methodologies. In conclusion, one could say that the biggest challenge that researchers have to deal with is conducting a large-scale study of the effect of social robots on special education, with large groups of children. It is worth mentioning that out of the total number of publications, the number of participants was 11.29 on average, while only six studies involved more than 20 children, with the study in [52] showing the highest number of participants equal to 74. At the same time, there is reduced participation in the researches of females, since, on average, 2.69 females participate in the sessions compared to 8.5 males, while in 10% of cases no girls participated at all. The small number of participants in combination with the lack of a control group are often factors that reduce the statistical accuracy of the studies and the reliability of their results. In addition, due attention has not yet been paid to the long-term effect of social robots on special education, through follow-up sessions, to study the maturation factor of the effects that children have on their interaction with social robots.

Finally, another area of significant challenges is the study of the intervention methodologies proposed in the various works. In this field, there is an inconsistency between the methodologies for developing intervention scenarios, resulting in not very convincing conclusions. Future work should be directed to compare the proposed intervention methods and interaction scenarios so that the conclusions drawn are more reliable.

6. Conclusions

In this work, the research activity of the period 2008 to 2020 regarding the application of social robots in special education was presented systematically. The study focused on four distinct directions: (1) the investigation of the degree of integration of social robots in the training of special education individuals, (2) the assessment of the scope of application of social robots in different impairments, (3) the search for different types of social robots and their appropriateness by category of impairments and (4) the emergence of challenges that need to be addressed in order for social robots to make a significant contribution to the social integration of people with impairments.

The present study quantified the satisfactory degree of integration of social robots in special education as well as the wide range of applications of social robots in a variety of impairments. A large number of different social robots used in special education were also identified, but it was found that most of them were not designed for the specific needs of special education individuals. The challenges highlighted through this study are mainly focused on the small size of the groups of children participating in the sessions, the low participation rate of girls, the lack of control group and follow up sessions, and the finding that the design of intervention scenarios should be executed with clear objectives so that the interpretation of the results leads to safe conclusions. This set of challenges should be the subject of future research in this field, towards the use of existing knowledge for the more effective integration of social robots in special education.

Author Contributions: Conceptualization, G.A.P.; methodology, G.A.P.; investigation, G.A.P., G.K.S. C.I.P.; resources, E.V., V.-A.N., M.T.P.; data curation, G.K.S., C.I.P., E.V.; writing—original draft preparation, G.A.P., G.K.S., V.H.; writing—review and editing, G.A.P., V.G.K. and M.T.P.; visualization, N.D. and V.-A.N.; supervision, G.A.P.; project administration, G.A.P.; funding acquisition, V.G.K. and G.A.P. All authors have read and agreed to the published version of the manuscript.

Funding: This research has been co-financed by the European Union and Greek national funds through the Operational Program Competitiveness, Entrepreneurship and Innovation, under the call RESEARCH—CREATE—INNOVATE (project code: T1EDK-00929).

Conflicts of Interest: The authors declare no conflict of interest.

References

1. Lasi, H.; Fettke, P.; Kemper, H.-G.; Feld, T.; Hoffmann, M. Industry 4.0. *Bus. Inf. Syst. Eng.* **2014**, *6*, 239–242. [CrossRef]
2. Fukuyama, M. Society 5.0: Aiming for a new human-centered society. *Jpn. Spotlight* **2018**, *27*, 47–50.
3. Breazeal, C. Toward sociable robots. *Robot. Autonom. Syst.* **2003**, *42*, 167–175. [CrossRef]
4. Lin, C.-Y.; Cheng, L.-C.; Huang, C.-C.; Chuang, L.-W.; Teng, W.-C.; Kuo, C.-H.; Gu, H.-Y.; Chung, K.-L.; Fahn, C.-S. Versatile humanoid robots for theatrical performances. *Int. J. Adv. Robot. Syst.* **2013**, *10*, 7. [CrossRef]
5. Katevas, K.; Healey, P.G.; Harris, M.T. Robot comedy lab: Experimenting with the social dynamics of live performance. *Front. Psychol.* **2015**, *6*, 1253. [CrossRef] [PubMed]
6. Lytridis, C.; Bazinas, C.; Kaburlasos, V.G.; Vassileva-Aleksandrova, V.; Youssfi, M.; Mestari, M.; Ferelis, V.; Jaki, A. Social robots as cyber-physical actors in entertainment and education. In Proceedings of the 2019 International Conference on Software, Telecommunications and Computer Networks (SoftCOM), Split, Croatia, 19–21 September 2019; pp. 1–6.
7. Fazekas, G.; Horvath, M.; Toth, A. A novel robot training system designed to supplement upper limb physiotherapy of patients with spastic hemiparesis. *Int. J. Rehab. Res.* **2006**, *29*, 251–254. [CrossRef]
8. Kachouie, R.; Sedighadeli, S.; Khosla, R.; Chu, M.-T. Socially assistive robots in elderly care: A mixed-method systematic literature review. *Int. J. Hum. Comput. Interact.* **2014**, *30*, 369–393. [CrossRef]
9. Savela, N.; Turja, T.; Oksanen, A. Social acceptance of robots in different occupational fields: A systematic literature review. *Int. J. Soc. Robot.* **2018**, *10*, 493–502. [CrossRef]
10. Lytridis, C.; Bazinas, C.; Sidiropoulos, G.; Papakostas, G.A.; Kaburlasos, V.G.; Nikopoulou, V.-A.; Holeva, V.; Evangeliou, A. Distance special education delivery by social robots. *Electronics* **2020**, *9*, 1034. [CrossRef]
11. Belpaeme, T.; Kennedy, J.; Ramachandran, A.; Scassellati, B.; Tanaka, F. Social robots for education: A review. *Sci. Robot.* **2018**, *3*, eaat5954. [CrossRef]
12. Kostova, S.; Dimitrova, M.; Kaburlasos, V.; Vrochidou, E.; Papakostas, G.; Pachidis, T.; Saeva, S.; Bonković, M.; Kružić, S.; Marasović, T.; et al. Identifying needs of robotic and technological solutions for the classroom. In Proceedings of the 2018 26th International Conference on Software, Telecommunications and Computer Networks (SoftCOM), Split, Croatia, 13–15 September 2018; pp. 1–6.
13. Musić, J.; Bonković, M.; Kružić, S.; Marasović, T.; Papić, V.; Kostova, S.; Dimitrova, M.; Saeva, S.; Zamfirov, M.; Kaburlasos, V.; et al. Robotics and information technologies in education: Four countries from Alpe-Adria-Danube region survey. *Int. J. Technol. Des. Educ.* **2020**. [CrossRef]
14. Lytridis, C.; Bazinas, C.; Papakostas, G.A.; Kaburlasos, V. On measuring engagement level during child-robot interaction in education. In Proceedings of the Robotics in Education, Online. 30 September–3 October 2020.
15. Sidiropoulos, G.K.; Papakostas, G.A.; Lytridis, C.; Bazinas, C.; Kaburlasos, V.G.; Kourampa, E.; Karageorgiou, E. Measuring engagement level in child-robot interaction using machine learning based data analysis. In Proceedings of the 2020 International Conference on Data Analytics for Business and Industry: Way Towards a Sustainable Economy (ICDABI), Online. 26–27 October 2020; pp. 1–5.
16. Sano, A.; Hernandez, J.; Deprey, J.; Eckhardt, M.; Goodwin, M.S.; Picard, R.W. Multimodal annotation tool for challenging behaviors in people with autism spectrum disorders. In Proceedings of the ACM Conference on Ubiquitous Computing; Association for Computing Machinery, New York, NY, USA, 21–26 September 2012; pp. 737–740.
17. Dong, W.; Lepri, B.; Cappelletti, A.; Pentland, A.S.; Pianesi, F.; Zancanaro, M. Using the influence model to recognize functional roles in meetings. In Proceedings of the 9th international Conference on Multimodal Interfaces—Association for Computing Machinery, New York, NY, USA, 9–13 November 2007; pp. 271–278.
18. Mubin, O.; Stevens, C.J.; Shahid, S.; Mahmud, A.A.; Dong, J.-J. A review of the applicability of robots in education. *Technol. Educ. Learn.* **2013**, *1*. [CrossRef]
19. Ismail, L.I.; Verhoeven, T.; Dambre, J.; Wyffels, F. Leveraging robotics research for children with autism: A review. *Int. J. Soc. Robot.* **2019**, *11*, 389–410. [CrossRef]
20. Papakostas, G.; Sidiropoulos, G.; Bella, M.; Kaburlasos, V. Social robots in special education: Current status and future challenges. *Proc. JSME Annu. Conf. Robot. Mechatron.* **2018**, *2018*, 1P1–A15. [CrossRef]
21. Kitchenham, B. *Procedures for Performing Systematic Reviews*; Keele University: Keele, UK, 2004; p. 33.
22. Khan, K.S. *Undertaking Systematic Reviews of Research on Effectiveness CRD's Guidance for Those Carrying Out or Commissioning Reviews*; NHS Centre for Reviews and Dissemination: York, UK, 2001; ISBN 978-1-900640-20-6.
23. Scopus. Available online: https://www.scopus.com (accessed on 22 June 2020).
24. Maenner, M.J. Prevalence of autism spectrum disorder among children aged 8 years—Autism and developmental disabilities monitoring network, 11 Sites, United States, 2016. *MMWR Surveill. Summ.* **2020**, *69*. [CrossRef] [PubMed]
25. Taheri, A.; Meghdari, A.; Alemi, M.; Pouretemad, H. Teaching music to children with autism: A social robotics challenge. *Sci. Iran.* **2019**, *26*, 40–58. [CrossRef]

26. Cao, H.-L.; Esteban, P.G.; Bartlett, M.; Baxter, P.; Belpaeme, T.; Billing, E.; Cai, H.; Coeckelbergh, M.; Costescu, C.; David, D.; et al. Robot-enhanced therapy: Development and validation of supervised autonomous robotic system for autism spectrum disorders therapy. *IEEE Robot. Automat. Mag.* **2019**, *26*, 49–58. [CrossRef]
27. Shimaya, J.; Yoshikawa, Y.; Kumazaki, H.; Matsumoto, Y.; Miyao, M.; Ishiguro, H. Communication support via a tele-operated robot for easier talking: Case/laboratory study of individuals with/without autism spectrum disorder. *Int. J. Soc. Robot.* **2019**, *11*, 171–184. [CrossRef]
28. Ali, S.; Mehmood, F.; Dancey, D.; Ayaz, Y.; Khan, M.J.; Naseer, N.; Amadeu, R.D.C.; Sadia, H.; Nawaz, R. An adaptive multi-robot therapy for improving joint attention and imitation of ASD children. *IEEE Access* **2019**, *7*, 81808–81825. [CrossRef]
29. Ali, S.; Mehmood, F.; Ayaz, Y.; Asgher, U.; Khan, M.J. Effect of different visual stimuli on joint attention of ASD children using NAO robot. In Proceedings of the Advances in Neuroergonomics and Cognitive Engineering, Washington, DC, USA, 24–28 July 2019; Volume 953, pp. 490–499, ISBN 978-3-030-20472-3.
30. Melo, F.S.; Sardinha, A.; Belo, D.; Couto, M.; Faria, M.; Farias, A.; Gamboa, H.; Jesus, C.; Kinarullathil, M.; Lima, P. Project INSIDE: Towards autonomous semi-unstructured human-robot social interaction in autism therapy. *Artif. Intell. Med.* **2019**, *96*, 198–216. [CrossRef] [PubMed]
31. Ishak, N.I.; Yusof, H.M.; Ramlee, M.R.H.; Sidek, S.N.; Rusli, N. Modules of interaction for ASD children using rero robot (Humanoid). In Proceedings of the 2019 7th International Conference on Mechatronics Engineering (ICOM), Putrajaya, Malaysia, 30–31 October 2019; pp. 1–6.
32. Wood, L.J.; Robins, B.; Lakatos, G.; Syrdal, D.S.; Zaraki, A.; Dautenhahn, K. Developing a protocol and experimental setup for using a humanoid robot to assist children with autism to develop visual perspective taking skills. *Paladyn J. Behav. Robot.* **2019**, *10*, 167–179. [CrossRef]
33. Axelsson, M.; Racca, M.; Weir, D.; Kyrki, V. A participatory design process of a robotic tutor of assistive sign language for children with autism. In Proceedings of the 28th IEEE International Conference on Robot and Human Interactive Communication (RO-MAN), New Delhi, India, 14–18 October 2019; pp. 1–8.
34. Qidwai, U.; Kashem, S.B.A.; Conor, O. Humanoid robot as a teacher's assistant: Helping children with autism to learn social and academic skills. *J. Intell. Robot. Syst.* **2020**, *98*, 759–770. [CrossRef]
35. Di Nuovo, A.; Bamforth, J.; Conti, D.; Sage, K.; Ibbotson, R.; Clegg, J.; Westaway, A.; Arnold, K. An explorative study on robotics for supporting children with autism spectrum disorder during clinical procedures. In Proceedings of the Companion of the 2020 ACM/IEEE International Conference on Human-Robot Interaction, Cambridge, UK, 23–26 March 2020; pp. 189–191.
36. Zhang, Y.; Song, W.; Tan, Z.; Zhu, H.; Wang, Y.; Lam, C.M.; Weng, Y.; Hoi, S.P.; Lu, H.; Man Chan, B.S.; et al. Could social robots facilitate children with autism spectrum disorders in learning distrust and deception? *Comput. Hum. Behav.* **2019**, *98*, 140–149. [CrossRef]
37. Lindsay, S.; Hounsell, K.G. Adapting a robotics program to enhance participation and interest in STEM among children with disabilities: A pilot study. *Disab. Rehab. Assist. Technol.* **2017**, *12*, 694–704. [CrossRef]
38. LEGO Education. Available online: https://education.lego.com/en-us/products (accessed on 22 June 2020).
39. Robles-Bykbaev, V.; Ochoa-Guaraca, M.; Carpio-Moreta, M.; Pulla-Sánchez, D.; Serpa-Andrade, L.; López-Nores, M.; García-Duque, J. Robotic assistant for support in speech therapy for children with cerebral palsy. In Proceedings of the 2016 IEEE International Autumn Meeting on Power, Electronics and Computing (ROPEC), Zihuatanejo, Mexico, 9–11 November 2016; pp. 1–6.
40. Marti, P.; Giusti, L. A robot companion for inclusive games: A user-centred design perspective. In Proceedings of the IEEE International Conference on Robotics and Automation, Anchorage, AK, USA, 3–8 May 2010; pp. 4348–4353.
41. Lewis, L.; Charron, N.; Clamp, C.; Craig, M. Co-robot therapy to foster social skills in special need learners: Three pilot studies. In *Methodologies and Intelligent Systems for Technology Enhanced Learning*; Springer: Berlin/Heidelberg, Germany, 2016; pp. 131–139.
42. Hedgecock, J.; Standen, P.J.; Beer, C.; Brown, D.; Stewart, D.S. Evaluating the role of a humanoid robot to support learning in children with profound and multiple disabilities. *J. Assist. Technol.* **2014**, *8*, 111–123. [CrossRef]
43. Marti, P.; Iacono, I. Learning through play with a robot companion. *Everyday Technol. Indep. Care* **2011**, *29*, 526–533.
44. Bonarini, A.; Clasadonte, F.; Garzotto, F.; Gelsomini, M.; Romero, M. Playful interaction with Teo, a mobile robot for children with neurodevelopmental disorders. In Proceedings of the 7th International Conference on Software Development and Technologies for Enhancing Accessibility and Fighting Info-Exclusion—Association for Computing Machinery, Vila Real, Portugal, 1–3 December 2016; pp. 223–231.
45. Costa, S.; Santos, C.; Soares, F.; Ferreira, M.; Moreira, F. Promoting interaction amongst autistic adolescents using robots. In Proceedings of the Annual International Conference of the IEEE Engineering in Medicine and Biology, Buenos Aires, Argentina, 31 August–4 September 2010; pp. 3856–3859.
46. Van den Heuvel, R.J.; Lexis, M.A.; de Witte, L.P. Robot ZORA in rehabilitation and special education for children with severe Physical disabilities: A pilot study. *Int. J. Rehab. Res.* **2017**, *40*, 353. [CrossRef]
47. Iacono, I.; Lehmann, H.; Marti, P.; Robins, B.; Dautenhahn, K. Robots as social mediators for children with autism—A preliminary analysis comparing two different robotic platforms. In Proceedings of the IEEE International Conference on Development and Learning (ICDL), Frankfurt, Germany, 24–27 August 2011; Volume 2, pp. 1–6.

48. Silvera-Tawil, D.; Bradford, D.; Roberts-Yates, C. Talk to me: The role of human-robot interaction in improving verbal communication skills in students with autism or intellectual disability. In Proceedings of the 27th IEEE International Symposium on Robot and Human Interactive Communication (RO-MAN), Naples, Italy, 31 August–4 September 2018; pp. 1–6.
49. Nakadoi, Y. Usefulness of animal type robot assisted therapy for autism spectrum disorder in the child and adolescent psychiatric ward. In *Proceedings of the JSAI International Symposium on Artificial Intelligence*; Springer: Berlin/Heidelberg, Germany, 2015; pp. 478–482.
50. Park, E.; Kwon, S.J. I can teach them: The ability of robot instructors to cognitive disabled children. *J. Psychol. Educ. Res.* **2016**, *24*, 101–114.
51. Conti, D.; Trubia, G.; Buono, S.; Di Nuovo, S.; Di Nuovo, A. Evaluation of a robot-assisted therapy for children with autism and intellectual disability. In *Proceedings of the Annual Conference Towards Autonomous Robotic Systems*; Springer: Berlin/Heidelberg, Germany, 2018; pp. 405–415.
52. Wan, G.; Deng, F.; Jiang, Z.; Lin, S.; Zhao, C.; Liu, B.; Chen, G.; Chen, S.; Cai, X.; Wang, H.; et al. Attention shifting during child—Robot interaction: A preliminary clinical study for children with autism spectrum disorder. *Front. Inf. Technol. Electron. Eng.* **2019**, *20*, 374–387. [CrossRef]
53. Balasuriya, S.S.; Sitbon, L.; Brereton, M.; Koplick, S. How can social robots spark collaboration and engagement among people with intellectual disability? In Proceedings of the 31st Australian Conference on Human-Computer-Interaction, Fremantle, WA, Australia, 2–5 December 2019; pp. 209–220.
54. Zhanatkyzy, A.; Telisheva, Z.; Turarova, A.; Zhexenova, Z.; Sandygulova, A. Quantitative results of robot-assisted therapy for children with autism, ADHD and delayed speech development. In Proceedings of the Companion of the 2020 ACM/IEEE International Conference on Human-Robot Interaction, Cambridge, UK, 23–26 March 2020; pp. 541–542.
55. Rakhymbayeva, N.; Seitkazina, N.; Turabayev, D.; Pak, A.; Sandygulova, A. A long-term study of robot-assisted therapy for children with severe autism and ADHD. In Proceedings of the Companion of the 2020 ACM/IEEE International Conference on Human-Robot Interaction, Cambridge, UK, 23–26 March 2020; pp. 401–402.
56. Kozyavkin, V.; Kachmar, O.; Ablikova, I. Humanoid social robots in the rehabilitation of children with cerebral palsy. In Proceedings of the 8th International Conference on Pervasive Computing Technologies for Healthcare, Oldenburg, Germany, 20–23 May 2014; pp. 430–431.
57. Rahman, R.A.A.; Hanapiah, F.A.; Basri, H.H.; Malik, N.A.; Yussof, H. Use of humanoid robot in children with cerebral palsy: The ups and downs in clinical experience. *Procedia Comput. Sci.* **2015**, *76*, 394–399. [CrossRef]
58. BIOLOID Premium Kit. Available online: https://www.generationrobots.com/en/401066-bioloid-premium-kit-robotis.html (accessed on 22 June 2020).
59. Ríos-Rincón, A.M.; Adams, K.; Magill-Evans, J.; Cook, A. Playfulness in children with limited motor abilities when using a robot. *Phys. Occupat. Ther. Pediatr.* **2016**, *36*, 232–246. [CrossRef] [PubMed]
60. Jimenez, F.; Yoshikawa, T.; Furuhashi, T.; Kanoh, M.; Nakamura, T. Effects of collaborative learning between educational-support robots and children who potential symptoms of a development disability. In Proceedings of the 2016 Joint 8th International Conference on Soft Computing and Intelligent Systems (SCIS) and 17th International Symposium on Advanced Intelligent Systems (ISIS), Sapporo, Japan, 25–28 August 2016; pp. 266–270.
61. Kato, S.; Ohshiro, S.; Itoh, H.; Kimura, K. Development of a communication robot Ifbot. In Proceedings of the IEEE International Conference on Robotics and Automation, New Orleans, LA, USA, 26 April–1 May 2004; Volume 1, pp. 697–702.
62. Özkul, A.; Köse, H.; Yorganci, R.; Ince, G. Robostar: An interaction game with humanoid robots for learning sign language. In Proceedings of the 2014 IEEE International Conference on Robotics and Biomimetics (ROBIO 2014), Bali, Indonesia, 5–10 December 2014; pp. 522–527.
63. Vstone. Available online: http://www.vstone.co.jp/english/ (accessed on 22 June 2020).
64. Aslam, S.; Standen, P.J.; Shopland, N.; Burton, A.; Brown, D. A comparison of humanoid and non-humanoid robots in supporting the learning of pupils with severe intellectual disabilities. In Proceedings of the 2016 International Conference on Interactive Technologies and Games (ITAG), Nottingham, UK, 26–27 October 2016; pp. 7–12.
65. Lehmann, H.; Iacono, I.; Dautenhahn, K.; Marti, P.; Robins, B. Robot companions for children with down syndrome: A case study. *Interact. Stud.* **2014**, *15*, 99–112. [CrossRef]
66. Kaspar the Social Robot. Available online: https://www.herts.ac.uk/kaspar/the-social-robot (accessed on 22 June 2020).
67. IROMEC. Available online: https://www.roboticstoday.com/projects/iromec (accessed on 22 June 2020).
68. Meyns, P.; van der Spank, J.; Capiau, H.; De Cock, L.; Van Steirteghem, E.; Van der Looven, R.; Van Waelvelde, H. Do a humanoid robot and music increase the motivation to perform physical activity? A quasi-experimental cohort in typical developing children and preliminary findings in hospitalized children in neutropenia. *Int. J. Hum. Comput. Stud.* **2019**, *122*, 90–102. [CrossRef]
69. Nao—Zorabots. Available online: https://zorarobotics.be/robots/nao (accessed on 22 June 2020).
70. Fisicaro, D.; Pozzi, F.; Gelsomini, M.; Garzotto, F. Engaging persons with neuro-developmental disorder with a plush social robot. In Proceedings of the 14th ACM/IEEE International Conference on Human-Robot Interaction (HRI), Daegu, Korea, 11–14 March 2019; pp. 610–611.
71. Belpaeme, T.; Vogt, P.; Van den Berghe, R.; Bergmann, K.; Göksun, T.; De Haas, M.; Kanero, J.; Kennedy, J.; Küntay, A.C.; Oudgenoeg-Paz, O. Guidelines for designing social robots as second language tutors. *Int. J. Soc. Robot.* **2018**, *10*, 325–341. [CrossRef] [PubMed]

72. Papakostas, G.A.; Strolis, A.K.; Panagiotopoulos, F.; Aitsidis, C.N. Social robot selection: A case study in education. In Proceedings of the 26th International Conference on Software, Telecommunications and Computer Networks (SoftCOM), Supetar, Croatia, 13–15 September 2018; pp. 1–4.
73. Jordan, K.; King, M.; Hellersteth, S.; Wirén, A.; Mulligan, H. Feasibility of using a humanoid robot for enhancing attention and social skills in adolescents with autism spectrum disorder. *Int. J. Rehab. Res.* **2013**, *36*, 221–227. [CrossRef]
74. Taheri, A.R.; Alemi, M.; Meghdari, A.; Pour Etemad, H.R.; Basiri, N.M. Social robots as assistants for autism therapy in Iran: Research in progress. In Proceedings of the Second RSI/ISM International Conference on Robotics and Mechatronics (ICRoM), Tehran, Iran, 15–17 October 2014; pp. 760–766.
75. Taheri, A.; Meghdari, A.; Alemi, M.; Pouretemad, H. Human-robot interaction in autism treatment: A case study on three pairs of autistic children as twins, siblings, and classmates. *Int. J. Soc. Robot.* **2018**, *10*, 93–113. [CrossRef]
76. Ghorbandaei Pour, A.; Taheri, A.; Alemi, M.; Meghdari, A. Human-robot facial expression reciprocal interaction platform: Case studies on children with autism. *Int. J. Soc. Robot.* **2018**, *10*, 179–198. [CrossRef]
77. Pop, C.A.; Simut, R.; Pintea, S.; Saldien, J.; Rusu, A.; David, D.; Vanderfaeillie, J.; Lefeber, D.; Vanderborght, B. Can the social robot probo help children with autism to identify situation-based emotions? A series of single case experiments. *Int. J. Hum. Robot.* **2013**, *10*, 1350025. [CrossRef]
78. Simut, R.E.; Vanderfaeillie, J.; Peca, A.; Van de Perre, G.; Vanderborght, B. Children with autism spectrum disorders make a fruit salad with probo, the social robot: An interaction study. *J. Autism Dev. Disord.* **2016**, *46*, 113–126. [CrossRef] [PubMed]
79. Vanderborght, B.; Simut, R.; Saldien, J.; Pop, C.; Rusu, A.S.; Pintea, S.; Lefeber, D.; David, D.O. Using the social robot probo as a social story telling agent for children with ASD. *Interact. Stud.* **2012**, *13*, 348–372. [CrossRef]
80. Bharatharaj, J.; Huang, L.; Al-Jumaily, A.; Elara, M.R.; Krägeloh, C. Investigating the effects of robot-assisted therapy among children with autism spectrum disorder using bio-markers. In Proceedings of the IOP Conference Series: Materials Science and Engineering, Busan, Korea, 25–27 August 2017; Volume 234, pp. 1–7.
81. Bharatharaj, J.; Huang, L.; Krägeloh, C.; Elara, M.R.; Al-Jumaily, A. Social engagement of children with autism spectrum disorder in interaction with a parrot-inspired therapeutic robot. *Procedia Comput. Sci.* **2018**, *133*, 368–376. [CrossRef]
82. Palestra, G.; Varni, G.; Chetouani, M.; Esposito, F. A multimodal and multilevel system for robotics treatment of autism in children. In *Proceedings of the International Workshop on Social Learning and Multimodal Interaction for Designing Artificial Agents—DAA '16*; ACM Press: Tokyo, Japan, 2016; pp. 1–6.
83. Silva, V.; Soares, F.; Esteves, J.S.; Pereira, A.P. Building a hybrid approach for a game scenario using a tangible interface in human robot interaction. In *Serious Games*; Göbel, S., Garcia-Agundez, A., Tregel, T., Ma, M., Baalsrud Hauge, J., Oliveira, M., Marsh, T., Caserman, P., Eds.; Lecture Notes in Computer Science; Springer International Publishing: Cham, Switzerland, 2018; Volume 11243, pp. 241–247, ISBN 978-3-030-02761-2.
84. Stanton, C.M.; Kahn, P.H.; Severson, R.L.; Ruckert, J.H.; Gill, B.T. Robotic animals might aid in the social development of children with autism. In *Proceedings of the 3rd ACM/IEEE International Conference on Human-Robot Interaction (HRI)*; ACM Press: New York, NY, USA, 2008; pp. 271–278.
85. Alhaddad, A.Y.; Javed, H.; Connor, O.; Banire, B.; Al Thani, D.; Cabibihan, J.-J. Robotic trains as an educational and therapeutic tool for autism spectrum disorder intervention. In *Robotics in Education*; Lepuschitz, W., Merdan, M., Koppensteiner, G., Balogh, R., Obdržálek, D., Eds.; Advances in Intelligent Systems and Computing; Springer International Publishing: Cham, Switzeralnd, 2019; Volume 829, pp. 249–262, ISBN 978-3-319-97084-4.
86. Costa, A.P.; Charpiot, L.; Lera, F.R.; Ziafati, P.; Nazarikhorram, A.; Van Der Torre, L.; Steffgen, G. More attention and less repetitive and stereotyped behaviors using a robot with children with autism. In Proceedings of the 27th IEEE International Symposium on Robot and Human Interactive Communication (RO-MAN), Nanjing, China, 27–31 August 2018; pp. 534–539.
87. InMoov—Open-Source 3D Printed Life-Size Robot. Available online: https://inmoov.fr/ (accessed on 28 April 2021).
88. Costescu, C.A.; Vanderborght, B.; David, D.O. Reversal learning task in children with autism spectrum disorder: A robot-based approach. *J. Autism Dev. Disord.* **2015**, *45*, 3715–3725. [CrossRef]
89. Mazzei, D.; Greco, A.; Lazzeri, N.; Zaraki, A.; Lanatà, A.; Igliozzi, R.; Mancini, A.; Stoppa, F.; Scilingo, E.P.; Muratori, F. Robotic social therapy on children with autism: Preliminary evaluation through multi-parametric analysis. In Proceedings of the International Conference on Privacy, Security, Risk and Trust and 2012 International Confernece on Social Computing, Amsterdam, The Netherlands, 3–5 September 2012; pp. 766–771.
90. Kim, E.S.; Berkovits, L.D.; Bernier, E.P.; Leyzberg, D.; Shic, F.; Paul, R.; Scassellati, B. Social robots as embedded reinforcers of social behavior in children with autism. *J. Autism Dev. Disord.* **2013**, *43*, 1038–1049. [CrossRef]
91. Salter, T.; Davey, N.; Michaud, F. Designing & developing QueBall, a robotic device for autism therapy. In Proceedings of the 23rd IEEE International Symposium on Robot and Human Interactive Communication, Edinburgh, UK, 25–29 September 2014; pp. 574–579.
92. Whitmer, T. Incorporating a Robot in Intervention with Children with ASD: The Effect on Tantrum Behaviors. Master's Thesis, Brigham Young University, Provo, UT, USA, 2015.
93. Srinivasan, S.M.; Kaur, M.; Park, I.K.; Gifford, T.D.; Marsh, K.L.; Bhat, A.N. The effects of rhythm and robotic interventions on the imitation/praxis, interpersonal synchrony, and motor performance of children with autism spectrum disorder (ASD): A pilot randomized controlled trial. *Autism Res. Treat.* **2015**, *2015*, 1–18. [CrossRef] [PubMed]

94. So, W.-C.; Wong, M.K.-Y.; Lam, C.K.-Y.; Lam, W.-Y.; Chui, A.T.-F.; Lee, T.-L.; Ng, H.-M.; Chan, C.-H.; Fok, D.C.-W. Using a social robot to teach gestural recognition and production in children with autism spectrum disorders. *Disabil. Rehab. Assist. Technol.* **2018**, *13*, 527–539. [CrossRef]
95. Hirokawa, M.; Funahashi, A.; Itoh, Y.; Suzuki, K. Adaptive behavior acquisition of a robot based on affective feedback and improvised teleoperation. *IEEE Trans. Cogn. Dev. Syst.* **2019**, *11*, 405–413. [CrossRef]
96. Mavadati, S.M.; Feng, H.; Salvador, M.; Silver, S.; Gutierrez, A.; Mahoor, M.H. Robot-based therapeutic protocol for training children with autism. In Proceedings of the 25th IEEE International Symposium on Robot and Human Interactive Communication (RO-MAN), New York, NY, USA, 26–31 August 2016; pp. 855–860.
97. Nie, G.; Zheng, Z.; Johnson, J.; Swanson, A.R.; Weitlauf, A.S.; Warren, Z.E.; Sarkar, N. Predicting response to joint attention performance in human-human interaction based on human-robot interaction for young children with autism spectrum disorder. In Proceedings of the 27th IEEE International Symposium on Robot and Human Interactive Communication (RO-MAN), Nanjing, China, 31 August–4 September 2018; pp. 1–4.
98. Shamsuddin, S.; Yussof, H.; Ismail, L.I.; Mohamed, S.; Hanapiah, F.A.; Zahari, N.I. Initial response in HRI—A case study on evaluation of child with autism spectrum disorders interacting with a humanoid Robot NAO. *Procedia Eng.* **2012**, *41*, 1448–1455. [CrossRef]
99. Manner, M.D. Identifying differences in social responsiveness among preschoolers interacting with or watching social robots. In Proceedings of the Twenty-Seventh International Joint Conference on Artificial Intelligence—International Joint Conferences on Artificial Intelligence Organization, Stockholm, Sweden, 13–19 July 2018; pp. 5777–5778.
100. Shamsuddin, S.; Yussof, H.; Ismail, L.I.; Mohamed, S.; Hanapiah, F.A.; Zahari, N.I. Humanoid robot NAO interacting with autistic children of moderately impaired intelligence to augment communication skills. *Procedia Eng.* **2012**, *41*, 1533–1538. [CrossRef]
101. Shamsuddin, S.; Yussof, H.; Miskam, A.; Hamid, M.A.C.; Malik, N.A.; Hashim, H.; Hanapiah, A.; Ismail, L.I. Humanoid robot NAO as HRI mediator to teach emotions using game-centered approach for children with autism. In Proceedings of the HRI 2013 Workshop on Applications for Emotional Robots, Tokyo, Japan, 3–6 March 2013.
102. Anzalone, S.M.; Tilmont, E.; Boucenna, S.; Xavier, J.; Jouen, A.-L.; Bodeau, N.; Maharatna, K.; Chetouani, M.; Cohen, D. How children with autism spectrum disorder behave and explore the 4-dimensional (spatial 3D+time) environment during a joint attention induction task with a robot. *Res. Autism Spect. Disord.* **2014**, *8*, 814–826. [CrossRef]
103. Greczek, J.; Kaszubski, E.; Atrash, A.; Mataric, M. Graded cueing feedback in robot-mediated imitation practice for children with autism spectrum disorders. In Proceedings of the 23rd IEEE International Symposium on Robot and Human Interactive Communication, Edinburgh, UK, 25–29 August 2014; pp. 561–566.
104. Desideri, L. Exploring the use of a humanoid robot to engage children with Autism Spectrum Disorder (ASD). *Harness. Power Technol. Improve Lives* **2017**. [CrossRef]
105. Alemi, M.; Basiri, N.M. Exploring social robots as a tool for special education to teach english to Iranian kids with autism. *Int. J. Robot. Theory Appl.* **2016**, *4*, 12.
106. Zheng, Z.; Zhao, H.; Swanson, A.R.; Weitlauf, A.S.; Warren, Z.E.; Sarkar, N. Design, development, and evaluation of a noninvasive autonomous robot-mediated joint attention intervention system for young children with ASD. *IEEE Trans. Hum. Mach. Syst.* **2018**, *48*, 125–135. [CrossRef] [PubMed]
107. Kaboski, J.R.; Diehl, J.J.; Beriont, J.; Crowell, C.R.; Villano, M.; Wier, K.; Tang, K. Brief report: A pilot summer robotics camp to reduce social anxiety and improve social/vocational skills in adolescents with ASD. *J. Autism Dev. Disord.* **2015**, *45*, 3862–3869. [CrossRef] [PubMed]
108. Warren, Z.E.; Zheng, Z.; Swanson, A.R.; Bekele, E.; Zhang, L.; Crittendon, J.A.; Weitlauf, A.F.; Sarkar, N. Can robotic interaction improve joint attention skills? *J. Autism Dev. Disord.* **2015**, *45*, 3726–3734. [CrossRef]
109. Anzalone, S.M.; Tanet, A.; Pallanca, O.; Cohen, D.; Chetouani, M. A Humanoid robot controlled by neurofeedback to reinforce attention in autism spectrum disorder. In Proceedings of the 3rd Italian Workshop on Artificial Intelligence and Robotics, Genova, Italy, 28–30 November 2016.
110. Wainer, J.; Dautenhahn, K.; Robins, B.; Amirabdollahian, F. Collaborating with kaspar: Using an autonomous humanoid robot to foster cooperative dyadic play among children with autism. In Proceedings of the 10th IEEE-RAS International Conference on Humanoid Robots, Nashville, TN, USA, 6–8 December 2010; pp. 631–638.
111. Wood, L.J.; Robins, B.; Lakatos, G.; Syrdal, D.S.; Zaraki, A.; Dautenhahn, K. Piloting scenarios for children with autism to learn about visual perspective taking. In *Towards Autonomous Robotic Systems*; Giuliani, M., Assaf, T., Giannaccini, M.E., Eds.; Lecture Notes in Computer Science; Springer International Publishing: Cham, Switzerland, 2018; Volume 10965, pp. 260–270, ISBN 978-3-319-96727-1.
112. Robins, B.; Amirabdollahian, F.; Ji, Z.; Dautenhahn, K. Tactile interaction with a humanoid robot for children with autism: A case study analysis involving user requirements and results of an initial implementation. In Proceedings of the 19th International Symposium in Robot and Human Interactive Communication, Viareggio, Italy, 12–15 September 2010; pp. 704–711.
113. Conti, D.; Di Nuovo, A.; Trubia, G.; Buono, S.; Di Nuovo, S. Adapting robot-assisted therapy of children with autism and different levels of intellectual disability: A preliminary study. In Proceedings of the Companion of the 2018 ACM/IEEE International Conference on Human-Robot Interaction, Chicago, IL, USA, 5–8 March 2018; pp. 91–92.

114. Yun, S.-S.; Park, S.-K.; Choi, J. A robotic treatment approach to promote social interaction skills for children with autism spectrum disorders. In Proceedings of the 23rd IEEE International Symposium on Robot and Human Interactive Communication, Edinburgh, UK, 25–29 August 2014; pp. 130–134.
115. Han, B.Y.; Yim, D.; Kim, Y.T.; Lee, S.J.; Hong, K.H. The effect of a story intervention on the syntactic skills of children with autism spectrum disorders by using an educational humanoid robot. *Commun. Sci. Disord.* **2016**, *21*, 244–261. [CrossRef]
116. Jeon, K.H.; Yeon, S.J.; Kim, Y.T.; Song, S.; Kim, J. Robot-based augmentative and alternative communication for nonverbal children with communication disorders. In Proceedings of the ACM International Joint Conference on Pervasive and Ubiquitous Computing—UbiComp '14 Adjunct, Seattle, WA, USA, 13–17 September 2014; pp. 853–859.
117. Pennazio, V. Social robotics to help children with autism in their interactions through imitation. *Res. Educ. Media* **2017**, *9*, 10–16. [CrossRef]
118. Minsky, M. *Society of Mind*; Simon and Schuster: New York, NY, USA, 1988; ISBN 978-0-671-65713-0.
119. Sidiropoulos, G.K.; Bazinas, C.; Lytridis, C.; Papakostas, G.A.; Kaburlasos, V.G.; Kechayas, P.; Kourampa, E.; Katsi, S.R.; Karatsioras, C. Synergy of intelligent algorithms for efficient child-robot interaction in special education: A feasibility study. In Proceedings of the Robotics in Education, Online. 30 September–3 October 2020; pp. 98–105.

Review

Computer Vision Meets Educational Robotics

Aphrodite Sophokleous [1], Panayiotis Christodoulou [1], Lefteris Doitsidis [2] and Savvas A. Chatzichristofis [1,*]

[1] Intelligent Systems Laboratory, Department of Computer Science, Neapolis University Pafos, 8042 Pafos, Cyprus; a.sofokleous@nup.ac.cy (A.S.); panayiotis.christodoulou@nup.ac.cy (P.C.)
[2] Intelligent Systems & Robotics Laboratory, School of Production Engineering & Management, Technical University of Crete, 73100 Chania, Greece; ldoitsidis@dpem.tuc.gr
* Correspondence: s.chatzichristofis@nup.ac.cy

Abstract: Educational robotics has gained a lot of attention in the past few years in K-12 education. Prior studies have shown enough shreds of evidence and highlight the benefits of educational robotics as being effective in providing impactful learning experiences. At the same time, today, the scientific subject of computer vision seems to dominate the field of robotics, leading to new and innovative ideas, solutions, and products. Several articles from the recent literature demonstrate how computer vision has also improved the general educational process. However, still, the number of articles that connect computer vision with educational robotics remains limited. This article aims to present a systematic mapping review, with three research questions, investigating the current status of educational robotics, focusing on the synergies and interdependencies with the field of computer vision. The systematic review outlines the research questions, presents the literature synthesis, and discusses findings across themes. More precisely, this study attempts to answer key questions related to the role, effectiveness and applicability of computer vision in educational robotics. After a detailed analysis, this paper focuses on a set of key articles. It analyzes the research methodology, the effectiveness and applicability of computer vision, the robot platform used, the related cost, the education level, and the educational area explored. Finally, the results observed are referred to as educational process benefits. The reviewed articles suggest that computer vision contributes to educational robotics learning outcomes enhancing the learning procedure. To the best of our knowledge, this is the first systematic approach that revises the educational robotics domain by considering computer vision as a key element.

Keywords: educational robotics; computer vision; educational tool

1. Introduction

In recent decades, education has been transformed and transitioned beyond the traditional learning process methods and is now enriched with procedures that make use of technological, mainly Information Communication Technology (I.C.T.), related tools. Many researchers studied the convergence of I.C.T. in education while highlighting the growing and successful incorporation between I.C.T. applications and teaching [1]. They provided clear explanations about the significance of its I.C.T. role, identifying the opportunities offered to teachers and students [2], resulting in a more useful and exciting learning process.

Over the years, rapid growth in robotics has been reported, improving a lot of developments in many fields, such as navigation and path planning [3,4], search and rescue applications [5], industrial applications [6], and entertainment. Considering the impact of the field, robots would inevitably be adapted for educational purposes also. Educational robotics is a field of study that aims to improve the learning experience through the creation, implementation, improvement, and validation of pedagogical activities [7–9]. Learning theory principles, constructivism and constructionism [10], are particularly bearing for the field of educational exploitation of robotics. According to Piaget, learning results from interaction with the environment lead to new learning experiences [7,11]. In [12], another study is presented. Authors report the benefits of the Internet of things (IoT) adoption in education, including increased interactivity, personalized learning, efficient classroom management, and better student monitoring. In [13], the integration of computer vision in tandem with IoT in education is also discussed.

The importance of Science, Technology Engineering, and Mathematics (STEM) and, therefore, educational robotics as a core part of it has been identified as a key tool towards digitizing education, involving students in learning activities, and developing their skills project-based learning through robotics. In this context, in recent years, many research programs have emerged related to educational robotics. Among them, the 'Educational Robotics for ER4STEM (STEM)' which has a concept the three important pillars of constructionism: (i) engaging students with powerful ideas, (ii) building on personal interests, and (iii) learning through making (or presenting ideas with tangible artifacts). Edubots is an ongoing Erasmus+ Knowledge Alliance project aiming to improve results and raise attainment levels in European higher education. The 'Science with robotics' project is another Erasmus+ Knowledge Alliance project which provides teachers with the necessary training to go one step further and introduce robotics to work with content from different areas. The CODESKILLS4ROBOTICS project, also funded by Erasmus+, aims to design an innovative program that aims to introduce coding and robotics' to primary school students. The direct target group is children aged 9–12 years old, emphasizing children with fewer opportunities who will learn how to code. Furthermore, of course, these are just a small indicative sample of the research projects that have been funded and helped the evolution, adoption, and spread of educational robotics.

The increased importance of educational robotics for the academic and educational communities has been identified in [14]. The authors in [15] define the educational robotics term according to the three main fields involved: (1) education, (2) robotics, and (3) human–computer interaction and conclude that educational robotics '... is a field of study that aims to improve the learning experience of people through the creation, implementation, improvement, and validation of pedagogical activities, tools (e.g., guidelines and templates) and technologies, where robots play an active role, and pedagogical methods inform each decision...'.

The authors in [7] reassess the definition of educational robotics, using a bibliometric map, as an '... an essential branch of educational technology implemented by activities designed using the theory of constructionism focused on the development of computational thinking skills, collaborative learning, and project-based learning...'. Various definitions are also presented in [16,17]. In [16], educational robotics is described as a '... research field that aims to promote active engage learning through the artifacts students, create the phenomena and simulate...' while, in [17] educational robotics is defined as '...the application of robots and robotics activities in teaching and learning...'.

According to the literature, there are various ways where educational robotics can be applied in the learning process: (i) as a learning and teaching tool, during the pedagogical method or an educational practice where robotics are used as another I.C.T. tool in the hands of teachers; (ii) as a cognitive, educational object, where robotics is just another subject with its curriculum, and the student learns and understands among others the concept of robotics, the technical knowledge on how it works, how it is programmed and how it can be managed; (iii) as social robots where they interact naturally with humans and behave in a way that is comfortable for humans [15] and finally; (iv) as a valuable tool that can help students in developing cognitive and social skills during their K-12 education [18]. Independent of how educational robotics is integrated into the learning process, they aim to fulfill certain learning outcomes, as formally defined and outlined in [7]. These help to:

- Improve problem-solving skills by helping the student understand difficult concepts more easily, research, and conduct decisions.
- Increase self-efficacy: The machine's natural handling promotes experimentation, discovery, and rejection and, consequently, enhances the student's self-confidence

because the student feels that he controls the machine. This also strengthens the students' critical thinking.
- Improve computational thinking: Students acquire algorithmic thinking to break down a large problem into smaller ones and then solve it. Students learn how to focus on important information and reject irrelevant ones.
- Increase creativity by learning with play-transmitting knowledge in a more playful form. Learning turns into a fun activity and becomes more attractive and interesting for the student.
- Increase motivation as educational robotics enables students to engage and persist at a particular activity.
- Improve collaboration as the team spirit and the cooperation between the students are promoted.

Currently, there is a broad range of robots for serving different requirements and age groups among students [19] ready to be used during the educational process. Although educational robotics and computer vision, as different fields, may be part of the educational process in K-12 education until recently, no one has ever investigated how they jointly may support the educational robotics area. This concern has risen since computer vision, one of the key tools used by the research community in robotics has significantly contributed to adopting various robots in different applications and introducing them as mainstream devices.

To fully understand the importance of computer vision in education and specifically in educational robotics, it is deemed necessary to define computer vision. According to the literature, there are many definitions of computer vision. In [20], it is defined as the '... science that studies means on how to provide to a computer the ability to 'see'...' computer vision uses cameras to analyze or understand scenes in the real world [21] and allows computers to capture, interpret, process the visually perceivable objects, and understand the captured digital images and react suitably. Moreover, during recording light on a video camera, computer vision can be defined as the scientific field that extracts information from digital images that can eventually lead to a decision or execution of an action. Computer vision deals with how computers can acquire high-level knowledge from digital content.

Nowadays, the number of personal, medical, scientific, and social networking images uploaded on the Internet is growing exponentially. Computer vision is essential because we need computers to understand the images' content, describe the real-world that humans see in one or more images, and reconstruct its properties, such as shape, illumination, and color distributions [22]. Moreover, as distance learning and online classrooms require good quality of both image and streaming video, recent advances in computer vision and algorithms have made considerable potential improvements [20]. An endless list of fast-growing and advanced computer vision applications is being used today in a wide variety of real-world applications, including sports, health and medicine, agriculture and farming, autonomous driving, social distance, people counting, and so on.

One of the essential educational principles for both educators and students is how knowledge is constructed. According to the sociology of education based on the individual's uniqueness, everyone learns differently [23]. The authors in [24] present computer vision to improve learning and knowledge acquisition. Teaching methods can be enhanced through computer vision tasks by analyzing the students' interest level, body posture, eye movement, and behavior. Subsequently, teachers can immediately react by modifying their teaching methods to harvest more attention from students, maximize their interest, and design lectures that are easier to understand [13]. In addition, computer vision in education can maximize students' academic output by offering customized learning experiences based on students' strengths and weaknesses. Moreover, it can improve students' and teachers' relationships, especially for students with learning difficulties. Between 2014 and 2020, 111,100 articles with the keyword 'computer vision in education' have been published. Figure 1 depicts the upward trend of research in this field.

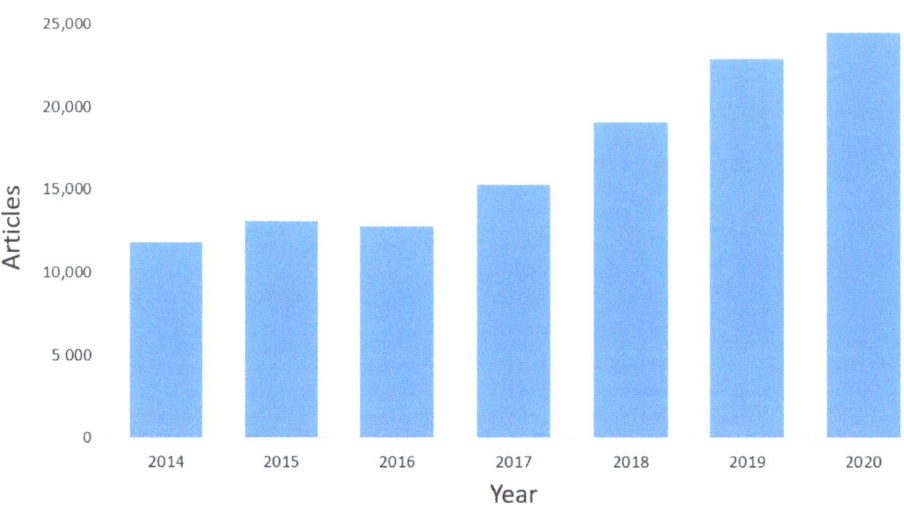

Figure 1. Articles per year reporting in computer vision in education.

Motivation

Despite the recent research attention on applying computer vision in education, there is still a limited amount of works focusing on educational robotics' applications. This paper revisits the articles that adopt computer vision mechanisms and technologies on educational robotic tasks, highlighting the impact of combining these two scientific fields. This work's primary focus is, to provide a systematic review, shaping an overview of computer vision and educational robotics' current research. The article aims to investigate how computer vision enhances and supports the educational robotics' impact. It examines the role of computer vision in educational robotics and the benefits of using computer vision in K-12 education. Moreover, it checks how easy and affordable it is to integrate computer vision and educational robotics in K-12 education. Finally, this study identifies and determines computer vision's role in the learning procedure and how it improves students' interest and performance in K-12 education. Overall, this study attempts to answer key questions related to the role, effectiveness and applicability of computer vision in educational robotics.

The rest of the paper is organized as follows. Section 2 firstly outlines the adopted research methodology and the process of collecting relevant research papers and then presents the gathered papers' results. Section 3 analyses and summarizes the study's outcomes, and provides answers to the research questions examined in this work. Section 4 concludes the article.

2. Research Methodology

A systematic mapping study suggested by Preferred Reporting Items for Systematic Reviews and Meta-Analyses (PRISMA) [25] was selected as the research methodology for this study. As depicted in Figure 2, the systematic mapping procedure aims to provide an overview of a research area, identify if research evidence exists, and quantify the amount of evidence. In order to accomplish our goal we follow the systematic review process described by [8,9,26,27]. The systematic review outcomes will help us identify and map research areas related to computer vision and educational robotics and possible research gaps.

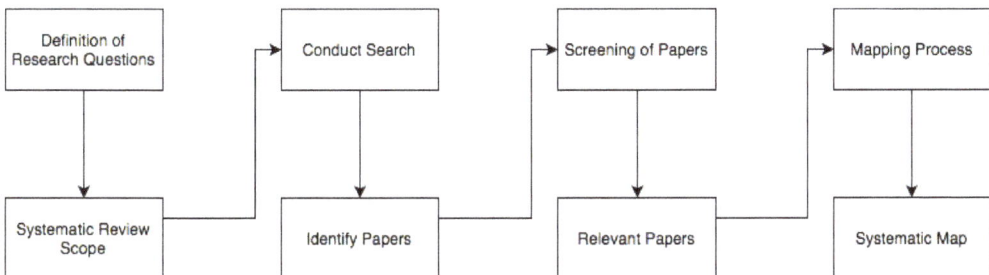

Figure 2. The systematic mapping process.

2.1. Definition of Research Questions

The first stage of the systematic mapping process is the definition of the research questions. As the primary goal of this systematic review is to identify the synergies and interdependence between computer vision and educational robotics, we developed a bibliometric map that helped us define this study's research questions.

The bibliometric map, presented in Figure 3, was constructed considering two criteria as reference points, computer vision and educational robotics. A set of related keywords to the critical criteria are represented on a 2-Dimensional plane. On a bibliometric map, the keywords that co-occur are linked together through a line that has a length proportional to the co-occurrences; this outlines the similarity (link strength) between the terms. The distances that may exist between the various keywords on the map compromise indicators of dissimilarity. As it can be observed from Figure 3, the map constructs a triangle of three main classes: (1) computer vision, (2) robotics, and (3) educational robots. Each of the classes mentioned above creates various keywords which are analyzed further below.

Near the computer vision class, we can observe several other keywords, including robots, object recognition, image processing, speech recognition, and other visual serving terms that mainly compose the definition of computer vision. The educational robots class is related to deep learning, convolutional neural networks, learning systems, virtual reality, deep neural networks, artificial intelligence, intelligent robot, and robot learning. The conjunction between computer vision and educational robots' classes raises questions about how computer vision is linked with educational robots and how it can aid the overall educational process. The third broader class of robotics, consists of the following keywords curricula, cost, object detection, and cameras.

Another aspect that can be observed from the bibliometric map analysis is that near the educational robotics class which is the result of the robotics and educational robots classes, there are additional keywords like teaching, students, robot programming, image processing, object recognition, and education. This raises new questions concerning (1) How educational robots use image processing or object recognition to enhance the teaching process, and (2) What benefits do students receive from educational robots.

Finally, it is worth mentioning that on the one hand, social robots as well as humanoid robots are close to the educational robots and educational robotics classes, respectively. On the other hand, the keywords human–computer interaction and human–robot interaction are close to the computer vision class. This observation concludes that most robotics platforms that adapt computer vision mechanisms are humanoid social models. This observation was also taken into consideration during the formation of the research questions below.

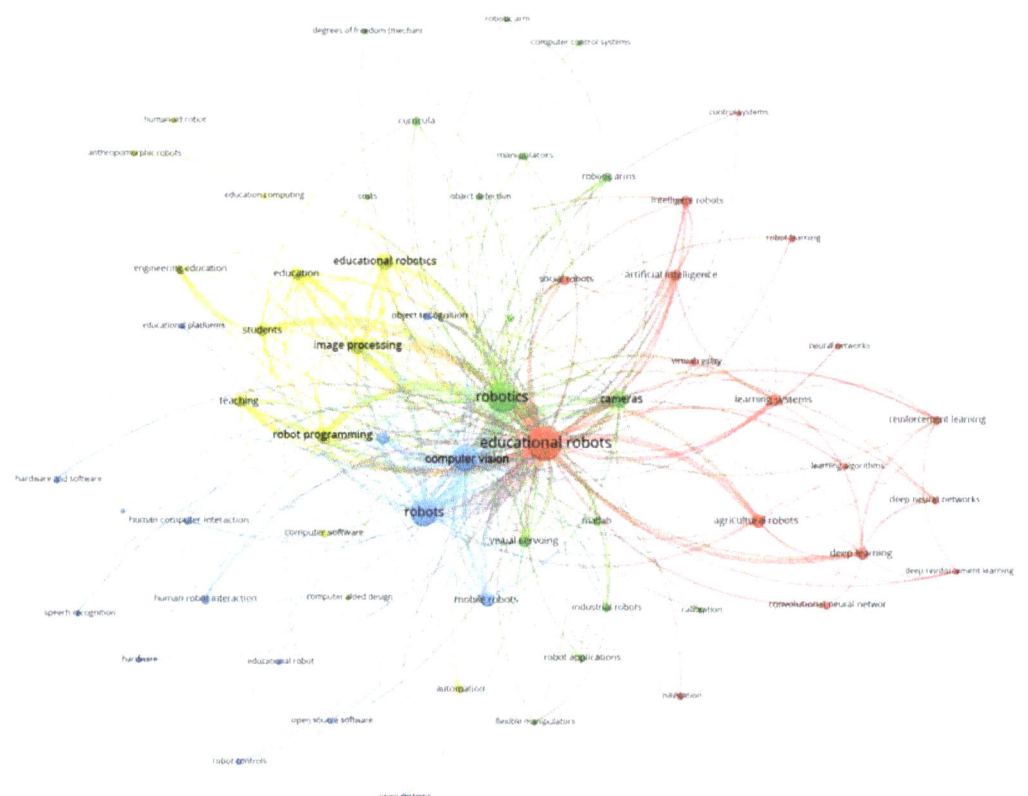

Figure 3. Overview of $Q1$ index term bibliometric map based on Scopus data.

The observations above and questions were used to set up the main research questions which guided us through the systematic review. These are the following:

- RQ1: What is the role of computer vision in educational robotics?
  The first research question helps the reader identify the current research that has been conducted on computer vision in educational robotics and attempts to provide answers on how computer vision can be used during the learning process.
- RQ2: How computer vision benefits educational robotics' expected learning outcomes in K-12 education?
  The second research question revisits educational robotics' expected learning outcomes and investigates how computer vision benefits K-12 education.
- RQ3: How affordable and feasible is the integration of solutions that combine educational robotics and computer vision in K-12 instructional activities?
  The third research question aims to reveal if the integration of computer vision and educational robotics activities in education can be adopted from a cost–benefit perspective. The same research question investigates also the ease of access and the availability of tools.

2.2. Search Approach

A detailed search protocol was established to identify all scientific papers of interest for our study. Our goal was to reduce, if not eliminate, the possibility of researcher bias. Before finalizing the appropriate search keywords for this study, we conducted pilot searches and tested possible keywords. We concluded in using the following query Q_1 as the search terms:

$Q_1=$

('image processing' **OR** 'camera' **OR** 'computer vision')

AND

('robotics in education' **OR** 'educational robotics' **OR** 'educational robots' **OR** 'robotics learning' **OR** 'robotics teaching')

We extracted high-quality peer-reviewed papers published in various conferences and journals related to the research topic. For paper retrieval, we used the following scientific databases (1) IEEE Xplore, (2) ACM Digital Library, (3) Springer Link, and (4) ScienceDirect.

2.3. Screening of Relevant Papers

Utilizing the Q_1 query, we retrieved 370 related papers. The yearly distribution of the papers, from 2014 to 2020, is presented in Figure 4. Given that many of those papers were not implicitly related to the research questions, we needed to assess them for actual relevance.

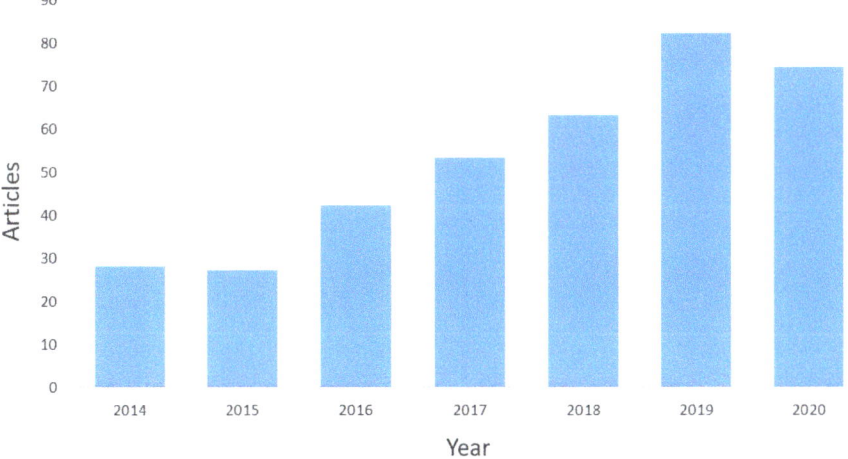

Figure 4. Articles per year reporting in computer vision in educational robotics.

Since our primary focus is on papers that use computer vision in educational robotics from pre-schools to secondary education, we identified a set of inclusion and exclusion criteria to shortlist the papers used to answer our research questions.

Inclusion Criteria (I.C.):
- I.C.1: Articles that present the use of computer vision in schools along with experimental outcomes.
- I.C.2: Articles that outline computer vision as an educational tool from pre-schools to the high school context.
- I.C.3: Articles that present computer vision as an assistive tool to support the educational process from pre-school to the high school context.

Exclusion Criteria (E.C.):
- E.C.1: Articles that did not mention the use of computer vision in educational robotics.

- E.C.2: Articles that outline the positive effects of computer vision in education, but they do not provide experimental results.
- E.C.3: Articles that are related to higher education.
- E.C.4: Articles that mention the use of robotics in education without utilizing computer vision techniques.
- E.C.5: Theses or books or annual reports.
- E.C.6: Articles that describe teachers' efforts on educational robotics.
- E.C.7: Articles that were not written in English.
- E.C.8: Articles published before 2014.

2.4. Mapping Process

Based on the Inclusion and Exclusion Criteria defined during the screening of relevant papers, our initial set of 370 articles was reduced to 21 articles. In total, 176 articles were excluded because they were focusing on computer vision tasks (object recognition, image segmentation, color recognition, and convolutional neural networks) in other scientific fields such as Engineering, Medicine, etc., and not in educational robotics. Furthermore, 50 of the articles were removed as they used robotics in education but did not utilize any computer vision techniques. Subsequently, 39 articles were excluded as they do not show any experimental results to support their study and 31 papers were removed since they describe computer vision or education robotics in higher education. Apart from that, 30 articles were excluded because they were published as thesis, books, or annual reports and 4 papers were removed as they outlined teachers' efforts in robotics education. Finally, 9 were excluded as they were not written in English.

To sum up, the final list consists of 21 papers published from 2014 until 2020 which present the use of computer vision as an educational or assistive tool that supports the educational process from pre-school to the secondary school context (K-12 education).

The mapping process stage is divided into two steps. During the first step, we read the abstract and identified keywords that reflected the paper's contribution. During the second step, we firstly developed a higher level of understanding based on the identified keywords. We used those keywords to form the various categories, and finally, we read the selected papers. We were continuously updating the categories or creating new ones if an article was revealing something new. This process resulted in forming a systematic map of clusters that took into consideration all relevant papers.

3. Analyzing the Literature

This section analyses the systematic review results and answers the three research questions identified and highlighted during the systematic mapping process.

3.1. What Is the Role of Computer Vision in Educational Robotics?

The first research question helps us identify the current research that has been conducted on computer vision in educational robotics and tries to provide answers on how computer vision can be used during the learning process.

The authors in [28] present the use of a robotic educational system that exploits advanced computer vision capabilities to detect written characters. The histogram of oriented gradients (also known as HOG) is used as a low-lever descriptor of the characters' detection stage. The proposed system aims to help new alphabet learners, mainly young children, write alphabet characters correctly. The system was benefiting from advanced computer vision algorithms to detect written characters. While interacting with the robot, children are led to a point where they want to write clear enough to make the robot understand their handwriting or write fast to meet the robot's requirements.

In a more sophisticated setup, Wu et al. in [29] introduced a robotic educational system combined with an object recognition technology that provides innovative second language learning services for pre-school children in China. The kid places physical objects into recognizable areas for an interactive operation. An avatar guides them in English to touch, drag, click, and press to interact with various objects. The presented system consists of three main components: a projector that casts images and items on the flat surface with which the child interacts, a Kinect that takes pictures of things on a fixed area to realize object recognition and finger tracking, and the main controller that receives the captured object of the camera and identifies and controls the content of the projector playback. The object recognition uses the SURF algorithm provided by OpenCV to obtain SURF features from the database.

Subsequently, authors in [30], demonstrated a prototype for a robotic language tutor that uses various computer vision techniques for behavior analysis, face recognition methods for guessing the user's age, object and speech recognition modules, and synthesis tools to emulate a human-to-human interaction. For this purpose, the authors used the state-of-the-art architecture GoogLeNet for object recognition and deep-convolutional neural networks for classifying age and gender trained using the Caffe framework [31]. The teaching process is adjusted according to the user's age estimation. Initially, communication between the robot and the user starts, and then object detection is being used to enable the communication of the object's name in the user's language. It is worth noting that this article does not involve any tangible device, but it was chosen to be included in the analysis since the authors classify it as a robotic educational tutor.

Moreover, Kusumota et al. [32], adapts a Cozmo mobile robot for educational purposes. The Cozmo robot utilizes computer vision using the Google Cloud Vision API. The robot receives images through web requests and returns a set of textual image characteristics. The robot was developed to run educational functions and games that include mathematical operations, spelling, directions, and question functions. In the proposed paper, various procedures for educational purposes were implemented on a web server for a more friendly user interface. More specifically, the first function tested with the students' was the drawing shapes function and Cozmo was programmed to draw a circle and a square shape. The second function tried was the sum function. When a student was finding the right answer, Cozmo played a happy animation. The last function tested was spelling. Students' had to spell their names, and when they were making mistakes, Cozmo was playing the sad animation.

The educational benefits of computer vision in educational robotics are also analyzed in [33]. In [33], the authors introduce the MonitoRE system to create an interactive educational environment for teaching robotic. MonitoRE helps students during the teaching-learning process through the web camera by conducting computer vision tasks. The image processing is done with the support of the OpenCV Computational Vision library and is used to complete different activities, like rescue activity, divided into multiple degrees of difficulty. An object is placed in a predetermined location, and then it needs to be rescued by the robot using color and object recognition.

In addition, an educational robotic system for preschoolers' cognition education based on the NAO platform is presented in [34]. The robot's model uses a fast object recognition mechanism which utilizes region proposal networks [35] and convolutional neural networks. The robot's core aims to automatically generate visual questions and answers based on the recognition results, including pronunciation, spelling, story, learning cards, and other related resources to serve as a learning trainer and partner. More specifically, objects in the real-world are detected, and a set of learning materials associated with the objects is presented to the learners. For example, when a cat is detected, the robot will teach learners to pronounce the word 'cat' in different languages, and more related pictures will be presented to the learners. For geometrical thinking training, an automatic questioning-and-answering section that implements voice interaction between learners and robots is employed to engage learners' thinking.

As observed in the articles' analysis, computer vision in educational robotics is also applied in special education. In [36], the authors introduce the use of humanoid robots, such as NAO, in special education, with emphasis on children diagnosed with autism spectrum conditions. The robots' primary goal is to encourage and improve imitation and social-communication skills of the child by taking advantage of computer vision algorithms' capabilities. Thus, the NAO's visual system employs a localized version of the color, and edge directivity descriptor [37] and a bag of visual words model in its recognition tasks to implement simple imitation games for the therapist's objectives. Moreover, Amanatiadis et al. in [38], extended the previous studies in special education using humanoid robots by adding multi-robot game sessions therapies with two children. Computer vision algorithms based on color features and the robot operating system for inter-process and multi-robot communication were used. Children face two NAOs, the NAO1 that demonstrates a game like 'Rock-Paper-Scissors' and NAO2 which asks the children to participate. Additionally, a humanoid NAO Robot outlined by the authors in [39] was also used in therapy sessions from children with Down Syndrome. In order to deal with image processing purposes, OpenCV, a computerized visionary library, was used by the authors. In [39], the robot's purpose was to teach children how to recognize various colors using the camera by mentioning a toy's color every time they showed a humanoid NAO figure. Since then, efficient tools such as tactile and precision sensors, cameras, microphones, and voice synthesizers were used to take advantage of the capabilities of NAO because humanoid robots can attract children's attention.

A recent study demonstrates that children's interaction and communication are enhanced through computer vision mechanisms. The authors in [40] proposed, once again, using a NAO robot, a platform for teaching geometric figures and colors to children in nursery age. Children hear various color or shape names and touch the different colors or shapes on the board during the activities. Then the NAO, using computer vision mechanisms, checks what the children have chosen and either correct or reward them. In addition, another work that uses open-source robotics to support the synergistic learning of computational thinking and STEM, with an emphasis on computer science, is introduced in [41]. In the proposed work, students used a robotics learning platform that combined the physical and algorithmic aspects of model building and problem-solving through computer vision algorithms' for shape and color detection, object tracking, or face detection.

Moreover, the study presented in [42] outlines a social NAO robot that interacts with a child while its playing until the child becomes 'Happy'. The NAO robot includes a fuzzy rule-based system and sensor signals processed by Computational Intelligence and Machine Learning algorithms. In [42], the authors proposed a feedback control that compares a resultant sentence caused by crowd-computing techniques to a computer-vision-induced sentence in driving a linguistic controller. Sentences have to be correct such as 'Give the toy to an older child,' 'Give the toy to a child of the opposite gender,' 'Change Toy', etc. The 'Happy' feeling is succeeded while the child plays a game with the robot to recognize their age, expressions, and gender by conducting computer vision tasks.

The ChildBot outlined in [43] presents a different study that uses multiple robots' platforms for educational purposes. ChildBot includes several modules such as audio-visual active speaker localization, object tracking, visual activity recognition, and distant speech recognition. The integrated visual system classifies the encoded features that result from Vector of Locally Aggregated Descriptors (VLAD) by employing linear support vector machines and perceives various events during the interaction, such as children's speech and activities, children's locations in the room, and tracking of objects, and asks them to complete different tasks-games. For example, the robot requests a child to perform a gesture that usually denotes a meaning and then asks the child to confirm the recognition. Another task is the Pantomime; the child can use their whole body to mimic an activity and interact extensively with the robot. Both the robot and the child repeatedly swap the mime's roles. After a child's reaction, the robot also expresses the same feeling using its body and face.

All the aforementioned studies adopt computer vision mechanisms to enhance the educational robotics-based learning procedure strictly. Other studies engage computer vision as assistive technology to stimulate the students' interest. Of course, several approaches combine the twofold nature of computer vision in educational robotics resulting in efficient solutions that significantly enhance the educational process.

In [44], 38 children in the ages of 10–11 were separated into two groups to solve various mathematical concepts taught (arithmetic). Group 1 performed the teacher's activities, and Group 2 performed the activities with the teacher and a robot teaching-assistant. By comparing the results of both groups, Group 2 scored better than Group 1 in all questions. In addition, experiments outlined that even not all children like mathematics, when they were learning mathematics with a robot's help, they enjoyed the lesson. Finally, most of the children in Group 2 believe that the NAO robot helped them understand the course more easily, and they all stated that they would like to have a robot-assistant in their classroom. In the previous paper, the robot's computer vision acted as a mediator to co-teach and aided the education process. The authors in [11] introduce multimodal NAO robots for learning purposes in the classroom when teaching various courses such as Danish, English, ethics, programming, and technology. Pupils mainly used the robot's text-to-speech and gesture features. The use of such robots benefits pupils' experience in both academic and technological teaching. In [11], the NAO's camera helped assistive tasks, but not in teaching.

Furthermore, the authors in [45] presented a study with 46 Iranian female students in the age of 12, who study junior English, divided into two groups. The main objective of the study was to investigate vocabulary learning through interaction with a human teacher assisted by a humanoid robot. The first group consists of 30 students who use an intelligent robotics-assisted language learning tool, known as RALL. The second group contains 16 students who do not have access to the RALL system. The RALL system consists of a NAO robot with voice command/recognition and computer vision capability, providing an opportunity for discussion, and prompt students to think of the word or concept. The paper concludes that the RALL group achieved higher scores on both the post-test and the delayed post-test.

In [46], the authors present the capability of young students to interact and communicate with a NAO robot in an autonomous way and in a teleoperated way (when someone controls the robot). Communication exists in three ways: speech, vision, and gesture. For the visual module, a combination of techniques to detect and recognize the chosen objects was selected. More precisely, the VOCUS2 system for segmentation and background noise extraction was used; then, SURF features extraction and the bag-of-words method were utilized and, finally, trained with multiple Support Vector Machines. Experiments were performed randomly by assigning 82 students aged between 7 and 11 to interact with the robot.

Educational ROS Robot Platform (EUROPA) [47], is an open-source robotic platform focused on STEM teaching that can be applied in physics, mathematics, and computer science courses. EUROPA's hardware consists of a Raspberry Pi3 B+ while its software infrastructure is based on the Robot Operating System (ROS) that covers a range of applications, from basic educational robotics to advanced applications, such as vision and mapping. Vision is performed by extracting color features from the camera's images using the OpenCV library. The vision's goal is to use the camera as a color sensor and direct EUROPA to follow a yellow line painted on the floor. In addition, through video activities, children can teleoperate the robot from their computer keyboard. Projects like the EUROPA aim to provide students with real-world STEM examples and a better understanding of notions that they have already been taught.

Subsequently, the authors in [48] employ a Bee-bot robot in pre-school education to provide immediate, personalized feedback and recommendations to young children while performing a series of programming-related activities. The proposed system uses an intelligent fuzzy-rule-based system and computer vision techniques to monitor the activities and interact with the participants. These activities are related to algorithmic thinking and sequencing. Participants were divided into three groups: the first one that used a computer graphical interface, the second which provided the instruction directly to the tangible robot, and the third group that adopted a hybrid approach composed of the Bee-bot and the proposed computer vision platform. Participants were receiving instructions through simple stories such as . . . 'robot has to go to school starting from her house assist it by giving her the correct instructions to take the shortest path and not be late'. . . or . . . 'After school, the robot must visit the grandmother's house to have lunch with her. However, they must be cautious, avoid the factories as they are hazardous places for a young robot', and interacting with the robot.

The contribution of computer vision in teaching STEM is also highlighted in the following articles. The PiBot project, described in [49], was developed to improve robotics' teaching in secondary education. PiBot is an open low-cost robotic platform with computer vision capabilities used in the classroom to train pre-university students during STEM education. Image processing is performed using the OpenCV library, a standard in the computer vision community. The activities of PiBot cover programming, robotics, and technology.

The work outlined by the authors in [50] describes a robot platform that aims to help the student learn how to code using a more exciting methodology that makes the student more interactive in solving problems. The robot uses a single camera complemented with the following computer vision algorithms (a) a field detection algorithm, (b) a robot position and orientation detection, and (c) a robot neighborhood extraction and labeling algorithm. Students deal with algorithms that help the robot to prevent obstacles to reach the goal point.

In summary, based on the literature, computer vision can enhance educational robotics activities and learning procedures, following two different learning mechanisms. On the one hand, several papers proposed specially designed computer vision tasks to enhance the learning process. In this category, computer vision undertakes, for example, to recognize shapes or patterns, to monitor the robot's movement, and to supervise the participant's choices and decisions. In these cases, computer vision is referred to as a primary factor in the educational process.

In some other cases, however, computer vision participates as a support activity. The combination of computer vision and educational robotics techniques helps present the course or the traditional activities differently from the teaching chair's stereotype, stimulating the student's interest. In these cases, we consider that computer vision operates as an assistive technology. Table 1 summarizes whether the relevant computer vision activity serves either as a primary factor or as an assistive technology.

Table 1. Classifying computer vision as a primary educational tool or as an assistive technology.

	Primary Educational Tool	Assistive Technology
Altin et al. (2014)	•	
Wu et al. (2019)	•	
Madhyastha (2016)	•	
Kusumota et al. (2018)	•	
Rios et al. (2017)	•	
He et al. (2017)	•	
Amanatiadis et al. (2017)		•
Amanatiadis et al. (2020)		•
Jimenez et al. (2019)		•
Olvera et al. (2019)		•
Darrah et al. (2018)	•	
Kaburlasos et al. (2018)		•

Table 1. *Cont.*

	Primary Educational Tool	Assistive Technology
Efthymiou et al. (2020)	●	
Vrochidou et al. (2018)		●
Majgaard et al. (2015)		●
Alemi et al. (2014)		●
Tozadore et al. (2017)	●	●
Karalekas et al. (2020)	●	●
Evripidou et al. (2021)	●	●
Vega et al. (2018)	●	●
Park and Lenskiy (2014)	●	●

As observed by the analysis of articles in this section, computer vision tasks are used as educational tools to help and support both, students and educators. Overall, these 21 papers under the first research question analysis indicated that incorporating computer vision tasks as an education tool in educational robots is valuable for students to build knowledge better and enhance their academic success and/or professional skills. Besides that, the combination of humanoid robots and computer vision helps students increase their interest, enhance their communication skills, and improve their social abilities. As summarized in Table 2 and Figure 5, the topics and areas of interest vary. Computational thinking/programming as well as the playing/interacting with robots are on top positions while STEM and language teaching follow.

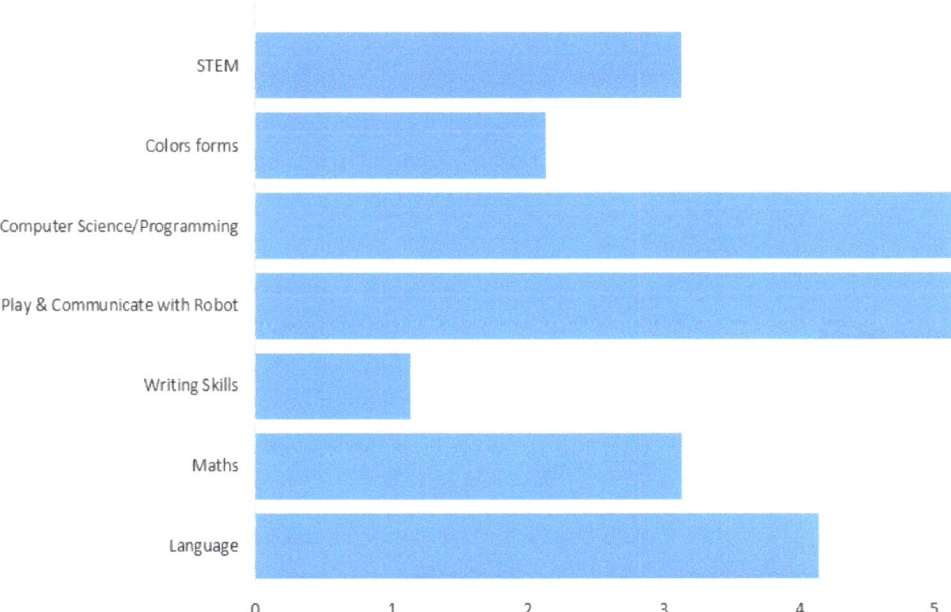

Figure 5. Areas of interest of the articles analyzed.

3.2. How Computer Vision Benefits Educational Robotics' Expected Learning Outcomes in K-12 Education?

The second research question aims to extract the benefits of using computer vision in K-12 education by examining the evidence reported in other research studies. The enhanced capabilities of educational robots, comparing to traditional methods, are the main reason that robotic activities can improve the teaching process. However, the empirical evidence of the impact of robots in education is considered limited in many cases [8]. Giving more intelligence to robots, is one of the future challenges in the design of robotics [51]. The following questions arise: Is computer vision one of the parameters that can help in this direction? Are the expected educational robotics outcomes, as described earlier, contributed through computer vision?

The study conducted in [28] presents how students can boost their learning skills when interacting with a proposed educational robotic system. In the proposed method, the children tried their best to make the robot understand their writing, and then the robot was either correcting or rewarding for their effort. The work conducted in [29] presents a robotics-based system that uses object recognition for teaching English to pre-school children in China. Outcomes showed that a computer vision robot could keep children's interest in learning while improving its efficiency. In both, the previous papers, self-efficacy and motivation skills are enhanced with computer vision.

The authors in [44], present how students are motivated by a robot's presence in the class. The study revealed that the robot's presence increases the engagement during the course, enhances the understanding of mathematical concepts, increases computational and logical thinking, and improves children's cognitive skills. Humanoid robot with computer vision contributes to the Computational thinking and motivation skills in educational robotics.

Moreover, the RALL platform proposed by the authors in [45], attempts to evaluate human robots' use and effectiveness in a game-based learning activity. Experimental outcomes present that RALL students' improvement can triple as they scored higher than non-RALL students. This demonstrates the effectiveness of the RALL system over traditional methods both in short-term and long-term learning. Creativity and problem-solving skills are supported by computer vision in the educational learning process.

According to [36], results suggest that robot-assisted treatment can improve children's behavior. The use of NAO social robots with imitation games can increase children's social and communication skills. Subsequently, the study demonstrated by the authors in [11] investigates how technology can support and enrich the learning process to help students learn more efficiently. Teachers highlighted robots' opportunities that can be used to support children's active experiments. Results show that pupils can quickly become self-propelled, and they can have an excellent academic discussion amongst them. Self-efficacy can be supported with computer vision, as in both articles robots were providing encouraging comments to the children. In addition, in Amanatiadis et al. [38] additional skills such as interaction skills, joint attention, and cognitive flexibility, team spirit, etc. can be enhanced as multi-robot collaborative games can assist children treatment and participation in a social environment with other children. It is worth noting that this is one of the two articles from the examined literature that directly impacts collaboration skills boosted through computer vision tasks.

The authors in [47] present the use of EUROPA robots for STEM teaching and highlight that students can better understand real-world problems. As authors mentioned within the paper, 'The students were acquainted with more advanced technological subjects and were motivated for independent learning and discovery. All students could follow, understand, and work on the EUROPA robots without any serious problems. Some of them were even willing to drill down to the robot's architecture'. Problem-solving and motivation skills are enhanced through computer vision tasks.

Moreover, the strategy proposed by the authors in [40] demonstrated how children could learn the geometrical shapes and colors correctly. Results present that game-like teaching is more attractive to children as they do not get bored. This demonstrates that problem-solving and creativity skills are enhanced with the use of computer vision tasks.

In addition, the authors in [49] outline STEM teaching to children in secondary schools using a PiBot robot as an educational tool supported by a camera. The proposed approach introduces to students computer vision and allows the creation of different exercises that combine vision and vision-based behaviors to practice. In [49], problem-solving skills are supported by computer vision tasks.

Experimental results demonstrated in [39] highlight that an interaction between a human–robot and a user can be achieved quickly. This can aid the children to gain knowledge through activities that use color recognition algorithms. According to the authors ... 'NAO can hold their attention a little bit longer so the kid can analyze, understand and learn what NAO is saying, increasing the ability to relate the names with the colors, not only those of the figures but the colors that the child sees around him'. Hence, the problem-solving skills are improved with the use of computer vision.

Furthermore, Ref. [41] presents an Open-Source Robotic system with an on-board camera that conducts essential computer vision functions such as shape and color detection. The robot is emphasized in STEM technology and, more specifically, in computer networks. Experimental results show that it can provide students with rich learning experiences. According to the authors, computational thinking and problem-solving skills are boosted through computer vision functions.

The following articles highlight the participant's interaction with humanoid social, creative robots benefiting through play-full environments supported by computer vision. Firstly, the work outline in [32] presents how students reacted when playing with a Cozmo robot. Students quickly understood how to interact with Cozmo, reported their impressions, and indicated that the proposed system could be a useful educational tool. During the drawing process, all students were focused only on Cozmo, so after the robot finished the drawing, the students showed a surprised reaction and applauded it. Secondly, the work conducted in [34] indicates that an educational robot system with contextual teaching characteristics that can mine knowledge from the real world can dramatically improve the enjoyment and engagement of robotic learning. The work presented in [42] outlines the interaction between a NAO robot and children when playing games. Experimental outcomes discussed in the paper are encouraging since the robot learns using crowd-computing feedback techniques. Besides the previous articles, in [46] young age children interacted excitingly with a NAO robot regardless of the method used (autonomous or teleoperated). Authors observe no significant difference between the conditions in the user's enjoyment and time response, and children lessen their perception of the robot's intelligence after learning more about the teleoperation. However, most children (80%) said that they preferred to interact with an autonomous robot. The above articles' main findings indicated that creativity is enhanced using computer vision tasks in play-full games.

Subsequently, the experimental outcomes discussed in [43] present that through the integration of multiple robots, sensors, and modalities, and with the use of an unconstrained and autonomous child–robot system people can achieve a high level of understanding. In the previous work, children felt comfortable playing and communicating with robots, and they believe that robots can behave like humans. The authors reported very characteristically about the multi-party game 'Form a Farm': In case of a wrong guess, the robot reveals more characteristics of the animal (animal color, number of legs, animal class, e.g., mammals, reptiles). In case of correct identification of the animals, the robot asks the children to properly place the animal in a farm with some distinct segmented areas which appears in a touch screen in front of them, aiming to entertain, educate, but also establish a natural interaction between all parties. Experimental results showed that most children (27/31) stated that they like playing with the robots, while 22 enjoyed the play since robots understood both their movements and speech. During the games, computer vision tasks supported all the tasks mentioned above to create a proper framework for multi-modal communication between children and robots, as it happens between humans. According to the play-full learning environment created by educational, social robots, creativity educational robotics learning outcome is supported by computer vision task. Furthermore, the collaboration learning outcome can be enhanced with computer vision, as mentioned before, since, through interactive games, students communicated and worked together as a team to win the robots.

Furthermore, authors in [50] outline the educational environment's improvement and students' engagement in the learning process by utilizing a hamster robot platform and computer vision algorithms. Using this combination, students were motivated and passionate about programming, and their creativity skills were improved. As mentioned in this paper, creativity, motivation, and computational thinking are enhanced by computer vision tasks as students' firstly extract the robot's position and orientation and then label the obstacles close to the robot. This information is employed to help children make decisions about the robot's future movements.

In [30], authors present a prototype language tutor robot that teaches new words in French and Spanish. Authors reported that the use of various techniques in Machine learning, computer vision, and Speech Processing has helped build a reasonably robust robot tutor which attempts to mimic a human teacher. Experimental results show that participants were overall satisfied by how the robot teaches. The participants evaluated different criteria, including comfort level of communication, the fluidity of the interaction, robustness of individual components, quality of overall experience, and user-friendliness with the robot. The average score from the participants was around 8/10. Furthermore, the participants share their opinions on certain qualities that human teachers have which may be hard to be replaced entirely with a score of 6.7. The MonitoRE system reported by the authors in [33] presents that students feel motivated and demonstrate more interest in educational robotics which considers the practicality in computer vision tasks. More precisely, authors reported ... 'students felt more motivated, demonstrating interest in using monitored task environments because it eases the understanding of the difficulties the moving robot faces in completing the activities, assisting students in the teaching-learning process'. In a sample of 46 users, 93% said that they found it interesting and enjoyed the experience, 86% noted that they were satisfied with the usability of the proposed system and the established scenarios, 95% considered the correction of the proposed efficient design, and 84% reported that they had obtained a learning return with the proposed approach. By analyzing both previous papers, we concluded that motivation skills are improved with computer vision.

The results obtained in [48] present that participants can increase their algorithmic/programming thinking skills while developing a positive attitude towards programming. Outcome results show that the hybrid group has rated its experience satisfaction high and requires less average time to complete the exercises than students who attended the entire course and other students who completed all activities. Motivation and self-efficacy skills are boosted with computer vision as children received encouraging messages from the robot. Moreover, computational thinking and problem-solving skills are also enhanced through the robot's advice to children.

Overall, under the spectrum of the second research question, the literature highlights that the implementation of computer vision techniques and tasks in educational robotics appears to benefit the overall teaching/educational process. Based on the observations analyzed in detail earlier, computer vision tasks increase students' interest in learning and motivate them to search for something new. Moreover, the formation of appropriate computer vision tasks into traditional education robotics activities improves the participants' social and communication skills and helps them better understand and then solve real-world problems.

More precisely, computer vision efficacy on the six expected learning outcomes of educational robotics are highlighted for each relevant paper and are summarized in Table 2. Furthermore, the hypothesis about humanoid and Social robots relationship with computer vision in educational robotics extracted from the 'computer vision in educational robotics' index related terms from the bibliographic map (Figure 3) is confirmed since 60% of robotics platform argue this assessment as can be seen in Table 3.

Table 2. Correlating the expected learning outcomes of educational robotics with computer vision.

	Problem Solving Skills	Self Efficacy	Computat. Thinking	Creativity	Motivation	Collaborat.
Altin et al. (2014)		•			•	
Wu et al. (2019)		•			•	
Madhyastha (2016)					•	
Kusumota et al. (2018)				•		
Rios et al. (2017)					•	
He et al. (2017)				•		
Amanatiadis et al. (2017)		•				
Amanatiadis et al. (2020)		•				•
Jimenez et al. (2019)	•					
Olvera et al. (2018)	•			•		
Darrah et al. (2018)	•		•			
Kaburlasos et al. (2018)				•		
Efthymiou et al. (2020)				•		•
Vrochidou et al. (2018)			•			
Majgaard et al. (2015)		•				
Alemi et al. (2014)	•			•	•	
Tozadore et al. (2017)				•		
Karalekas et al. (2020)	•				•	
Evripidou et al. (2021)	•	•	•		•	
Vega et al. (2018)	•					
Park and Lenskiy (2014)			•	•	•	

Table 3. Summarizing the context of related literature.

Paper	Age/Level	Area Explored/Topic(s)	Computer Vision	Robot Used
Altin et al. (2014)	Young children	Writing Skills	Image Processing	NAO
Wu et al. (2019)	Pre-school children	English as a second language	Object Recognition	Kinect, Projector, PC
Madhyastha (2016)	From 14+ ages	French or Spanish	Image Processing Object Recognition	A prototype robot language tutor
Kusumota et al. (2018)	Elementary Children	Mathematical operations, spelling, directions, and questions functions	Image and Textual Processing	Cozmo
Rios et al. (2017)	Secondary School	Teaching Robotics	Color and Image processing	MonitoRE
He et al. (2017)	Pre-school children	Metacognition tutoring and geometrical thinking training the pronunciation of the vocabulary in both Chinese and English	Image processing Object Recognition	NAO
Amanatiadis et al. (2017)	Children diagnosed with Autism Spectrum Condition (ASC)	Social communication and interaction skills, joint attention, response inhibition	Color Recognition and Image Processing	NAO
Amanatiadis et al. (2020)	ASC	Social communication and interaction skills, joint attention, response inhibition	Color Recognition and Image Processing	2 NAOs
Jimenez et al. (2019)	Children diagnosed with Syndrome Down	Colors Forms	Color Recognition	NAO
Olvera et al. (2018)	Pre-school, 3 and 4 years	Geometric Forms and Colors	Object and Color Recognition	NAO
Darrah et al. (2018)	Secondary Children	learning of computational thinking and STEM, with an emphasis on Computer Science concepts	Shape and Color detection	Open-Source Robotics
Kaburlasos et al. (2018)	From 5 to 14 years old	Play and Communicate with Robots	Image Processing and Pattern Recognition	NAO
Efthymiou et al. (2020)	Elementary, 6 to 11 years	Play and Communicate with Robots	Image Processing Object recognition, Distance Speech Recognition	ChildBot (NAO, Furhat, Zeno)
Vrochidou et al. (2018)	K12 system (ages 16–17)	Mathematics	Camera Presenting	NAO

Table 3. *Cont.*

Paper	Age/Level	Area Explored/Topic(s)	Computer Vision	Robot Used
Majgaard et al. (2015)	Between 11 and 16 years old	Programming, language learning, ethics, technology and mathematics	Camera Presenting	NAO
Alemi et al. (2014)	Children at the age of 12	English Vocabulary	Camera Presenting	NAO
Tozadore et al. (2017)	Elementary Between 7 and 11 years	Interact with robot	Camera Presenting/ object recognition	NAO
Karalekas et al. (2020)	K12 system (ages 15–17)	STEM Teaching in sciences, engineering and programming	Using camera for watching and as a color sensor	EUROPA
Evripidou et al. (2021)	Pre-school children	Programming/algorithmic thinking	Camera Presenting/ Fuzzy system	Bee-bot
Vega et al. (2018)	Pre-university children in secondary schools	STEM Teaching	Color Recognition, Visualisation through camera	PiBot
Park and Lenskiy (2014)	Secondary School	Language Programming	Camera with computer vision algorithms	Hamster robot

3.3. How Affordable and Feasible Is the Integration of Solutions That Combine Educational Robotics and Computer Vision in K-12 Instructional Activities?

The third research question aims to present if the integration of computer vision in education can be applied from a cost–benefit perspective and robot models' availability.

Educational robotic platforms are available in a wide range and vary in cost, parts, and complexity [51]. To provide thorough answers to the third research question, we investigated the following aspects: (i) the design specifications and how complex it is to build a robot? Furthermore, (ii) what is the cost of the various types of robots' outlined in the literature?

Initially, based on the data summarized in Table 3, 60% of relevant papers uses NAO in educational activities. NAO is an up-and-coming robotic system with tremendous potential that incorporates computer vision to affect the learning process, as presented during the analysis of the second research question. However, it is still not affordable to educators as its cost is too high [51].

According to [47], the Europa robot model significantly cheaper compared to NAO. The overall cost of EUROPA robot is estimated less that 120 euros. EUROPA is 'a two-wheel, inexpensive differential drive robot with a manipulator' easy to be integrated into the educational learning process. EUROPA is adequately scalable and flexible to fit into different educational levels and curricula, and it allows introductory or advanced-level programming, depending on educational level. In addition, the authors in [41] present an attractive alternative solution to the most expensive kits commercially available that can aid the instruction of multiple STEM + computer science related topics. This study's proposed approach aims to increase computational thinking strategies among high school computer science course students.

The work conducted in [50] outlines a low-cost implementation based on a sensor simulation to test their proposed computer vision algorithm. Authors claim that the selected hamster robot development platform is inexpensive compared to others (around 150 euro). Moreover, [30] describes a low-cost robot language tutor with interaction capabilities that can be personalized. At a broad system level, the main components used in this prototype robot include a microphone to capture speech, a camera that moves in different directions and captures frames, and of course, a processing unit.

The proposed system developed and presented in [29] which is still in an early stage of development, explores new teaching methods for pre-school children. It consists of three components that can be easily procured, a projector, a Kinect, and a computer system, making it possible to be applied in a school. The task environment recommended by the authors in [33] is composed of artificial landmarks, including the mobile robot, and allows the monitoring system to identify and evaluate the overlap of colors and shapes established in the environment. In this way, teachers and students can use any educational robotic kit during the learning process, depending on the cost efficacy.

Furthermore, the study conducted in [32] presents the development and implementation of an educational platform for the Cozmo mobile robot. As the authors mentioned, the proposed educational tool is a low-cost solution (around 150 euro) that can be applied in the education environment, providing teachers the ability to create and run their scripts. In [49], the authors claim that the PiBot platform is a low cost (under 180 euros) solution for supporting STEM teaching which makes it affordable for most schools and students. Apart from the price, the robot hardware can be easily assembled using a 3D printer that follows the Do It Yourself (D.I.Y.) philosophy. As mentioned by the authors, the 3D PiBot model and all the developed plugins are. The Bee-pot is an easy to use, low-cost educational platforms (around 75 euro) that can be integrated into pre-schools to support the learning procedure. Childbot as mentioned by [43], combines three different robotic platforms (NAO, Furhat and Zeno), available in the market but their integration into the educational process climbs to their high cost (about 39,000 euro).

To sum up, as analyzed in this subsection, the final research question instigated that most of the robotic platforms presented in this study are applicable to be integrated into the educational process. In this study, it can be observed that Robotic models are available in a wide range, consist of a low-cost solution, and can be quickly developed in K-12 education. More precisely, 60% of Robotics model in relevant articles adopt the humanoid social robot NAO as presented in Table 3. NAO is a very promising robot capability, according to the literature, but its high cost (about 13,000 euro), may be seen as an obstacle to its integration into the educational process.

4. Conclusions

To highlight the synergies and the intersections between educational robotics and computer vision and demonstrate how the combination of these disciplines impact K-12 education, this paper maps all relevant research studies using a systematic mapping process.

This study aims to present how robotics autonomy gained through computer vision supports educational robotics by examining three significant factors. Firstly, to identify the role of computer vision in educational robotics. Secondly, to determine the benefits of computer vision in educational robotics, and thirdly investigate how efficient it is to apply computer vision in K-12 education. After a systematic search in online bibliographic databases using keyword searching and a snowballing approach, we extracted and analyzed 21 primary articles from the recent literature.

Based on the performed analysis, computer vision-related tasks in educational robotics demonstrate high potential in teaching assistance. Children's gain in learning is significant as determined by the selected articles' outcomes analysis. In the comparison groups, it was found that in those who were assisted with the computer vision procedures, the participants demonstrated more interest in the educational process, learned the concepts they taught more easily, spent less time completing their work, and generally were very satisfied with the way of teaching. The results highlighted that the most common use of computer vision in educational robotics is as a primary factor for teaching while, a limited number of studies (only 3) presented computer vision as an assistive tool only. Regarding the discussion in all relevant articles, the results were positive about computer vision tasks' effectiveness to support the learning process. The research claimed the increase in academic achievement from pre-school to secondary schools and special education in different subjects area and skills, as summarized in Figure 5.

Moreover, through relevant articles, computer vision correlation with the six expected learning outcomes of educational robotics was presented, and the results are summed up in Table 2. It is noteworthy that 'Creativity', 'Motivation', and 'Problem-Solving Skills' are considered the most common learning outcomes supported by computer vision activities involving educational robotics, with 'Self-Efficacy' and 'Computational Thinking' to follow. The 'Collaboration' learning outcome appears with two degrees of participation; the articles' analysis has shown that the interactive game's use in the learning process involves all students to cooperate and develop a team spirit to succeed in a mission or to win. Future research directions in this area are needed to create an educational process that supports this outcome. One example of this direction is computer vision analysis of students' behavior and interaction during group tasks on how they communicate, teach others, and how comfortable they are with fellow students. Later, it enhances peer-to-peer interaction between students as per their comfort levels.

Besides, computer vision integration in schools depends on the robot model's availability and the cost factor. From the relevant article's analysis, we found that all the robot models presented in this study can easily enhance the educational process, and they are available for K-12 education. However, 60% of the documents used the humanoid and social NAO robot, recognizing its many potentials, without considering the high integration cost.

To sum up, computer vision-related tasks in educational robotics are considered useful tools for the learning process. The convergence of computer vision and educational robotics is still in the incipient phase. It is worth exploring ways in which such technology can mutually benefit the students involved in the education process to develop the proposed outcomes skills by making learning more effective, garner more attention from them, maximize their interest, customizing courses and materials as per their understanding capabilities, and most importantly, fun.

According to the different perspective observed by the systematic analysis, the essential factors that influence educational robotics enhanced with computer vision tasks in K-12 education effectiveness, include usability and availability of appropriate learning activities and content (knowledge area to be explored), children age group, robot models to be used and cost parameter. Possible applications to be designed must consider the robot as communication mediators to support group learning, interacting with the robot in a playful environment, the children can respond with high motivational levels and creativity, focus on children interests and weakness could improve self-efficacy, and helps to problem-solving and computational thinking skills. Further researchers would help develop more applications (design new or modify current robotic activities) to use computer vision in educational robotics.

Author Contributions: Conceptualization, A.S. and S.A.C.; methodology, A.S.; validation, A.S, P.C. and L.D.; formal analysis, A.S., L.D. and P.C.; investigation, A.S.; writing—original draft preparation, A.S. and P.C.; writing—review and editing, A.S., P.C., L.D. and S.A.C.; visualization, S.A.C.; supervision, S.A.C. and L.D. All authors have read and agreed to the published version of the manuscript.

Funding: This research received no external funding.

Data Availability Statement: The data presented in this study are available on request from the corresponding author.

Conflicts of Interest: The authors declare no conflict of interest.

References

1. Goswami, S.; Uddin, M.S.; Islam, M.R. Implementation of Active Learning for ICT Education in Schools. *Int. J. Innov. Sci. Res. Technol.* **2020**, *5*, 455–459. [CrossRef]
2. Hegedus, S.; Moreno-Armella, L. Information and communication technology (ICT) affordances in mathematics education. *Encycl. Math. Educ.* **2020**, 380–384. [CrossRef]
3. Qi, Y.; Pan, Z.; Zhang, S.; van den Hengel, A.; Wu, Q. Object-and-Action Aware Model for Visual Language Navigation. *arXiv* **2020**, arXiv:2007.14626.
4. Hong, Y.; Wu, Q.; Qi, Y.; Rodriguez-Opazo, C.; Gould, S. A Recurrent Vision-and-Language BERT for Navigation. *arXiv* **2020**, arXiv:2011.13922.
5. Scaramuzza, D.; Achtelik, M.; Doitsidis, L.; Fraundorfer, F.; Kosmatopoulos, E.B.; Martinelli, A.; Achtelik, M.W.; Chli, M.; Chatzichristofis, S.A.; Kneip, L.; et al. Vision-Controlled Micro Flying Robots: From System Design to Autonomous Navigation and Mapping in GPS-Denied Environments. *IEEE Robot. Autom. Mag.* **2014**, *21*, 26–40. [CrossRef]
6. Kouskouridas, R.; Amanatiadis, A.; Chatzichristofis, S.A.; Gasteratos, A. What, Where and How? Introducing pose manifolds for industrial object manipulation. *Expert Syst. Appl.* **2015**, *42*, 8123–8133. [CrossRef]
7. Evripidou, S.; Georgiou, K.; Doitsidis, L.; Amanatiadis, A.A.; Zinonos, Z.; Chatzichristofis, S.A. Educational Robotics: Platforms, Competitions and Expected Learning Outcomes. *IEEE Access* **2020**, *8*, 219534–219562. [CrossRef]
8. Benitti, F.B.V. Exploring the educational potential of robotics in schools: A systematic review. *Comput. Educ.* **2012**, *58*, 978–988. [CrossRef]
9. Toh, L.P.E.; Causo, A.; Tzuo, P.W.; Chen, I.M.; Yeo, S.H. A review on the use of robots in education and young children. *J. Educ. Technol. Soc.* **2016**, *19*, 148–163.
10. Piaget, J. Part I: Cognitive development in children: Piaget development and learning. In *J. Res. Sci. Teach.* **1964**, *2*, 176–186. [CrossRef]
11. Majgaard, G. Multimodal robots as educational tools in primary and lower secondary education. In Proceedings of the International Conferences Interfaces and Human Computer Interaction, Las Palmas de Gran Canaria, Spain, 22–24 July 2015; pp. 27–34.
12. Shoikova, E.; Nikolov, R.; Kovatcheva, E. Conceptualizing of Smart Education. *Electrotech. Electron. E+ E* **2017**, *52*.
13. Savov, T.; Terzieva, V.; Todorova, K. Computer Vision and Internet of Things: Attention System in Educational Context. In Proceedings of the 19th International Conference on Computer Systems and Technologies, Ruse, Bulgaria, 13–14 September 2018; pp. 171–177.

14. Zhong, B.; Xia, L. A systematic review on exploring the potential of educational robotics in mathematics education. *Int. J. Sci. Math. Educ.* **2020**, *18*, 79–101. [CrossRef]
15. Angel-Fernandez, J.M.; Vincze, M. Towards a definition of educational robotics. In Proceedings of the Austrian Robotics Workshop, Innsbruck, Austria, 17–18 May 2018; p. 37.
16. Gabriele, L.; Tavernise, A.; Bertacchini, F. Active learning in a robotics laboratory with university students. In *Increasing Student Engagement and Retention Using Immersive Interfaces: Virtual Worlds, Gaming, and Simulation*; Emerald Group Publishing Limited: West Yorkshire, UK, 2012.
17. Misirli, A.; Komis, V. Robotics and programming concepts in Early Childhood Education: A conceptual framework for designing educational scenarios. In *Research on e-Learning and ICT in Education*; Springer: New York, NY, USA, 2014; pp. 99–118.
18. Alimisis, D. Educational robotics: Open questions and new challenges. *Themes Sci. Technol. Educ.* **2013**, *6*, 63–71.
19. Mubin, O.; Stevens, C.; Shahid, S.; Mahmud, A.; Jian-Jie, D. A Review of the Applicability of Robots in Education. Available online: http://roila.org/wp-content/uploads/2013/07/209-0015.pdf (accessed on 1 January 2013).
20. Jin, L.; Tan, F.; Jiang, S. Generative Adversarial Network Technologies and Applications in Computer Vision. *Comput. Intell. Neurosci.* **2020**, *2020*, 1459107. [CrossRef]
21. Klette, R. *Concise Computer Vision*; Springer: Cham, Switzerland, 2014.
22. Szeliski, R. *Computer Vision: Algorithms and Applications*; Springer Science & Business Media: Cham, Switzerland, 2010.
23. Boronski, T.; Hassan, N. *Sociology of Education*; SAGE Publications Limited: London, UK, 2020.
24. Bebis, G.; Egbert, D.; Shah, M. Review of computer vision education. *IEEE Trans. Educ.* **2003**, *46*, 2–21. [CrossRef]
25. Moher, D.; Liberati, A.; Tetzlaff, J.; Altman, D.G.; Group, P.; PRISMA Group. Preferred reporting items for systematic reviews and meta-analyses: the PRISMA statement. *PLoS Med.* **2009**, *6*, e1000097. [CrossRef]
26. Petersen, K.; Feldt, R.; Mujtaba, S.; Mattsson, M. Systematic mapping studies in software engineering. In Proceedings of the 12th International Conference on Evaluation and Assessment in Software Engineering (EASE), Bari, Italy, 26–27 June 2008; pp. 1–10.
27. Yli-Huumo, J.; Ko, D.; Choi, S.; Park, S.; Smolander, K. Where is current research on blockchain technology?—A systematic review. *PLoS ONE* **2016**, *11*, e0163477. [CrossRef]
28. Altin, H.; Aabloo, A.; Anbarjafari, G. New era for educational robotics: Replacing teachers with a robotic system to teach alphabet writing. In Proceedings of the 4th International Workshop Teaching Robotics, Teaching with Robotics & 5th International Conference Robotics in Education, Padova, Italy, 18 July 2014; pp. 164–166.
29. Wu, Q.; Wang, S.; Cao, J.; He, B.; Yu, C.; Zheng, J. Object recognition-based second language learning educational robot system for chinese preschool children. *IEEE Access* **2019**, *7*, 7301–7312. [CrossRef]
30. Madhyastha, M.; Jayagopi, D.B. A low cost personalised robot language tutor with perceptual and interaction capabilities. In Proceedings of the 2016 IEEE Annual India Conference (INDICON), Bangalore, India, 16–18 December 2016; pp. 1–5.
31. Jia, Y.; Shelhamer, E.; Donahue, J.; Karayev, S.; Long, J.; Girshick, R.; Guadarrama, S.; Darrell, T. Caffe: Convolutional architecture for fast feature embedding. In Proceedings of the 22nd ACM international conference on Multimedia, Mountain View, CA, USA, 18–19 June 2014; pp. 675–678.
32. Kusumota, V.; Aroca, R.; Martins, F. An Open Source Framework for Educational Applications Using Cozmo Mobile Robot. In Proceedings of the 2018 Latin American Robotic Symposium, 2018 Brazilian Symposium on Robotics (SBR) and 2018 Workshop on Robotics in Education (WRE), João Pessoa, Brazil, 6–10 November 2018; pp. 569–576.
33. Rios, M.L.; Netto, J.F.d.M.; Almeida, T.O. Computational vision applied to the monitoring of mobile robots in educational robotic scenarios. In Proceedings of the 2017 IEEE Frontiers in Education Conference (FIE), Indianapolis, IN, USA, 18–21 October 2017; pp. 1–7.
34. He, B.; Xia, M.; Yu, X.; Jian, P.; Meng, H.; Chen, Z. An educational robot system of visual question answering for preschoolers. In Proceedings of the 2017 2nd International Conference on Robotics and Automation Engineering (ICRAE), Shanghai, China, 29–31 December 2017; pp. 441–445.
35. Ren, S.; He, K.; Girshick, R.; Sun, J. Faster r-cnn: Towards real-time object detection with region proposal networks. *arXiv* **2015**, arXiv:1506.01497.
36. Amanatiadis, A.; Kaburlasos, V.G.; Dardani, C.; Chatzichristofis, S.A. Interactive social robots in special education. In Proceedings of the 2017 IEEE 7th International Conference on Consumer Electronics-Berlin (ICCE-Berlin), Berlin, Germany, 3–6 September 2017; pp. 126–129.
37. Chatzichristofis, S.A.; Boutalis, Y.S. CEDD: Color and Edge Directivity Descriptor: A Compact Descriptor for Image Indexing and Retrieval. In *Computer Vision Systems, Proceedings of the 6th International Conference, ICVS 2008, Santorini, Greece, 12–15 May 2008*; Lecture Notes in Computer Science; Gasteratos, A., Vincze, M., Tsotsos, J.K., Eds.; Springer: Berlin/Heidelberg, Germany, 2008; Volume 5008, pp. 312–322. [CrossRef]
38. Amanatiadis, A.; Kaburlasos, V.G.; Dardani, C.; Chatzichristofis, S.A.; Mitropoulos, A. Social robots in special education: Creating dynamic interactions for optimal experience. *IEEE Consum. Electron. Mag.* **2020**, *9*, 39–45. [CrossRef]
39. Jiménez, M.; Ochoa, A.; Escobedo, D.; Estrada, R.; Martinez, E.; Maciel, R.; Larios, V. Recognition of Colors through Use of a Humanoid Nao Robot in Therapies for Children with Down Syndrome in a Smart City. *Res. Comput. Sci.* **2019**, *148*, 239–252. [CrossRef]
40. Olvera, D.; Escalona, U.; Sossa, H. Teaching Basic Concepts: Geometric Forms and Colors on a NAO Robot Platform. *Res. Comput. Sci.* **2019**, *148*, 323–333. [CrossRef]

41. Darrah, T.; Hutchins, N.; Biswas, G. Design and development of a low-cost open-source robotics education platform. In Proceedings of the 50th International Symposium on Robotics (ISR 2018), Munich, Germany, 20–21 June 2018; pp. 1–4.
42. Kaburlasos, V.; Bazinas, C.; Siavalas, G.; Papakostas, G. Linguistic social robot control by crowd-computing feedback. In Proceedings of the JSME annual Conference on Robotics and Mechatronics (Robomec), Kyushu, Japan, 2–5 June 2018; p. 1A1-B13.
43. Efthymiou, N.; Filntisis, P.P.; Koutras, P.; Tsiami, A.; Hadfield, J.; Potamianos, G.; Maragos, P. ChildBot: Multi-Robot Perception and Interaction with Children. *arXiv* **2020**, arXiv:2008.12818.
44. Vrochidou, E.; Najoua, A.; Lytridis, C.; Salonidis, M.; Ferelis, V.; Papakostas, G.A. Social robot NAO as a self-regulating didactic mediator: A case study of teaching/learning numeracy. In Proceedings of the 2018 26th International Conference on Software, Telecommunications and Computer Networks (SoftCOM), Split, Croatia, 13–15 September 2018; pp. 1–5.
45. Alemi, M.; Meghdari, A.; Ghazisaedy, M. Employing humanoid robots for teaching English language in Iranian junior high-schools. *Int. J. Humanoid Robot.* **2014**, *11*, 1450022. [CrossRef]
46. Tozadore, D.; Pinto, A.; Romero, R.; Trovato, G. Wizard of oz vs. autonomous: Children's perception changes according to robot's operation condition. In Proceedings of the 2017 26th IEEE International Symposium on Robot and Human Interactive Communication (RO-MAN), Lisbon, Portugal, 28 August–1 September 2017; pp. 664–669.
47. Karalekas, G.; Vologiannidis, S.; Kalomiros, J. EUROPA: A Case Study for Teaching Sensors, Data Acquisition and Robotics via a ROS-Based Educational Robot. *Sensors* **2020**, *20*, 2469. [CrossRef] [PubMed]
48. Salomi, E.; Amanatiadis, A.; Christodoulou, K.; Chatzichristofis, S.A. Introducing Algorithmic Thinking and Sequencing using Tangible Robots. *IEEE Trans. Learn. Technol.* **2021**. [CrossRef]
49. Vega, J.; Cañas, J.M. PiBot: An open low-cost robotic platform with camera for STEM education. *Electronics* **2018**, *7*, 430. [CrossRef]
50. Park, J.S.; Lenskiy, A. Mobile robot platform for improving experience of learning programming languages. *J. Autom. Control Eng.* **2014**, *2*, 265–269. [CrossRef]
51. Pachidis, T.; Vrochidou, E.; Kaburlasos, V.; Kostova, S.; Bonković, M.; Papić, V. Social robotics in education: State-of-the-art and directions. In Proceedings of the International Conference on Robotics in Alpe-Adria Danube Region, Patras, Greece, 6–8 June 2018; Springer: Cham, Switzerland, 2018; pp. 689–700.

Review

Robotics in Education: A Scientific Mapping of the Literature in Web of Science

Jesús López-Belmonte [1], Adrián Segura-Robles [2,*], Antonio-José Moreno-Guerrero [1] and María-Elena Parra-González [2]

[1] Department of Didactics and School Organization, University of Granada, 51001 Ceuta, Spain; jesuslopez@ugr.es (J.L.-B.); ajmoreno@ugr.es (A.-J.M.-G.)
[2] Department of Research Methods and Diagnosis in Education, University of Granada, 51001 Ceuta, Spain; elenaparra@ugr.es
* Correspondence: adrianseg@ugr.es

Citation: López-Belmonte, J.; Segura-Robles, A.; Moreno-Guerrero, A.-J.; Parra-González, M.-E. Robotics in Education: A Scientific Mapping of the Literature in Web of Science. *Electronics* **2021**, *10*, 291. https://doi.org/10.3390/electronics10030291

Academic Editors: Savvas A. Chatzichristofis and Zinon Zinonos
Received: 20 December 2020
Accepted: 22 January 2021
Published: 26 January 2021

Publisher's Note: MDPI stays neutral with regard to jurisdictional claims in published maps and institutional affiliations.

Copyright: © 2021 by the authors. Licensee MDPI, Basel, Switzerland. This article is an open access article distributed under the terms and conditions of the Creative Commons Attribution (CC BY) license (https://creativecommons.org/licenses/by/4.0/).

Abstract: The technological revolution has created new educational opportunities. Today, robotics is one of the most modern systems to be introduced in educational settings. The main objective of this research was to analyze the evolution of the "robotics" concept in the educational field while having, as a reference point, the reported literature in the Web of Science (WoS). The methodology applied in this research was bibliometrics, which we used to analyze the structural and dynamic development of the concept. The collection of WoS studies on robotics in education began in 1975. Its evolution has been irregular, reaching peak production in 2019. Although the focus was on collecting studies with educational knowledge areas, other knowledge areas were also present, such as engineering and computing. It was found that the types of manuscript most commonly used to present scientific results in this area are proceedings papers. The country with the highest level of production in this field of study is the United States. The results confirm the potential of this type of study in the scientific field. The importance of this technology in the training of future surgeons and in the results they produce in their own learning was also detected.

Keywords: robotics; education; Web of Science; bibliometric

1. Introduction

Today's society is involved in a technological revolution that started in the early 20th century [1]. This revolution has occurred in the diverse fields in which society is divided, from business, social, and health fields to the educational field. In other words, this technological explosion has deeply changed the way we interact, cure diseases, and learn [2].

Focusing on the educational field, information technologies have led to a significant, though sometimes slow, change in all current teaching and learning processes [3]. This technological revolution in education has not always been related to a direct improvement of current teaching and learning processes [4]. In this regard, the incorporation of different technological tools in any educational process must be related to an improvement of the pedagogical process. As never before, teachers cannot be oblivious to this transformation and should be willing to introduce new tools to help students develop creative, collaborative, and active learning [5].

Today, there are many methodologies that can help teachers to transform their daily teaching, such as active methodologies [6], but there are also new tools and devices that allow us to approach the most complex aspects of existing technologies in the educational field, such as robotics [7,8].

Robotics have taken on a special interest in today's education, and the number of educational programs introducing this aspect into their curriculum has grown in recent years, especially in developed countries [9]. The advantages and potential of introducing these systems in education were detected by several authors more than 20 years ago [10]. Among the most relevant advantages of this type of system, we found its direct bond with the improvement of learning [11], the development of specific cognitive skills [12], or the learning of complex scientific concepts [13].

The use of robotics in education can be considered from two well-distinguished perspectives. On the one hand, the perspective related to the programming of devices or software and, on the other, that which is associated to the assembly and operation of devices or hardware [14]. This difference is decisive for posing our activities within the classroom, which must be adapted, as with any technology, depending on the needs of the students [15]. Though most robotics educational applications focus exclusively on programming or in subjects directly related to technology [16], the truth is that they can be applied to a much wider range of subjects, such as mathematics, languages, music, or art [17].

Robotics in education can be seen as an underlying branch of robotics [18], which focuses on training students in the development, design, and construction of robots [19]. To do this, students must generate robots by building the robot itself and establishing its capabilities through software [20].

It can be said that the main purpose of educational robotics is to teach students to design and create a programmable robot [21] capable of performing various actions, including moving, responding to environmental stimuli, or communicating through sound, light, or images [22–24]. In addition, the application of robotics in the educational field involves other associated factors in the education of students [25], including contributing to the development of logical thinking, psychomotor skills, and spatial perception of students [26], promoting student autonomy through the development of their own projects [27] and the active involvement of students in the teaching and learning process [28], promoting creativity, research, and understanding oriented toward the computer world [29], generating students' problem-solving skills [30], encouraging the development of students' digital competence [31], associating it with other pedagogical methods, such as project learning, collaborative learning, or cooperative learning [32], and encouraging functional learning given that it generates resources that can be applied in the social environment [33]. Therefore, it can be said that robotics in education generates a series of advantages [34], including learning to work in a team [35], increasing self-confidence [36], promoting entrepreneurship [37], developing skills [38], identifying and taking an interest in other disciplines [39], increasing concentration [40], increasing creativity [41], and promoting curiosity and increasing interest in mathematics [42].

A widely used branch of education for robotics is science, technology, engineering, arts, and mathematics (STEAM) education for training based in these subject areas [43]. The usual approach when implementing robotics in education is to provide students with robotics kits [44]. Such a kit should have materials adapted to their age and abilities [45]. A kit for students aged 6–10 years should not contain the same materials as a kit for students aged 16–18 years [46]. There are a number of computer resources that allow robotics to be applied in education, including Scratch, Wedo 2.0, Lego Boost, Makey Makey, Arduino, and Microbit [47–50]. The application that is used depends on the purpose and capacity of the learners [51].

It is important to keep in mind that robotics in education can be presented from several perspectives [52–55]: learning robotics, where students learn to design, build, and program a robot; learning with robotics, where robots are tools that serve to promote student learning; and robots for education, where the robot is the main tool for the learning process. This last option is related to telepresence in the educational sphere, where robots are used to develop distance learning [56].

The truth is that robotics in the educational field does not form part of the curriculum today [57]. This is developed through specific methods during teaching and learning processes or through extracurricular activities [58]. For robotics to be an integrated part of education systems, a number of aspects must be considered, which may make its inclusion in schools difficult [59]. These include its high cost [60], the need to train teachers in the use of technological resources [61], students' own digital competence [62], and the need for the pedagogical training of teachers [63].

Knowing how the term "robotics" has evolved within the educational scientific literature is therefore a valuable resource for many teachers and researchers. Having a detailed view of its evolution allows us to focus efforts, as teachers and researchers, in specific fields, learn how studies on the subject have advanced, and even detect the rise of new and future research niches.

2. Justification and Objectives

This work arises from the projection that robotics has potential in today's different learning spaces [64–67]. For this reason, this study analyzed the term "robotics" in education (ROBEDU) from a bibliometric aspect of scientific production [68]. Bibliometry is considered a method of scientific analysis focused on publications on a state of the art. This methodology contributes to revealing to the scientific community, and to all interested readers, the progress and significance of a certain topic or concept throughout history. For this, a series of variables or bibliometric indicators used in the indexing of each study (year, authors, keywords, journal, countries, language, and source of origin being among the most prominent) are taken into account. Therefore, bibliometrics is beneficial as a research methodology as it reveals the journey made by a certain topic [69]. Another fundamental aspect is the selection of an impact database in order to carry out a pertinent and in-depth study from which interesting results can be obtained, allowing conclusions to be reached and relevant prospects to be considered. In this case, the selected database for the documentary report is the Web of Science (WoS), which is considered to be one of the most relevant databases in the field of social sciences, of which education is a part of it [70].

In this particular research, an innovative research process has been used. It is about the analysis of documentary performance and the scientific mapping of the literature concerning these concepts. For effective development of the study, the guidelines and models established by experts in this type of research have been followed. This allowed the development of the study to follow an investigative structure for the analysis as well as for the presentation of the data validated by experts [71,72].

The purpose of this work was based on the analysis of the evolution of ROBEDU in WoS publications, that is, from when this subject appeared in the scientific literature, its evolution over time, and the concepts to which it is linked. All this is due to a deep analysis of the publications on ROBEDU where the conceptual connections established between the different studies were extracted. This allowed the establishment of not only what has been done so far but also of future trends on this state of the art. As far as our knowledge reaches, and after leading a search in the expert literature, no study analyzing the concept of robotics at a documentary level using these techniques has been reported. In providing a knowledge base, this study will contribute to a reduction in the gap found in the impact literature and to the future work of other researchers. Therefore, this research is positioned under an exploratory and a novel nature. Likewise, this work aims to present to the scientific community the implications and future trends [73] of this educational technology.

Based on all the above, the objectives formulated in this study were to (1) know the documentary performance of ROBEDU in WoS, (2) establish the scientific evolution of ROBEDU in WoS, (3) find the most significant thematics of ROBEDU in WoS, and (4) trace the most influential authors of ROBEDU in WoS.

3. Materials and Methods

3.1. Research Design

Bibliometrics was established as the research methodology to achieve the objectives of this study. This methodology quantifies and evaluates scientific documents in detail [74,75]. We developed a research design that allows several actions such as searching, recording, analyzing, and predicting the literature on the state of the art [76]. The proposed design is based on a coword analysis [77] and on the analysis of the h, g, hg, and q^2 indices [78]. Each of the different analytical processes to be carried out allow the preparation of maps that integrate nodes on the performance and location of various terminological subdomains and the evolution of the themes over time [79] of ROBEDU in WoS.

3.2. Procedure

Taking impact studies as the reference [80–82], the document analysis process was set in several actions. The first action was focused on the selection of the database to be analyzed. In this case, WoS was chosen, as it is a database with recognized worldwide prestige. The second action was based on the delimitation of concepts. In this case, the concept "robotics" was chosen, as it was the most significant term for this study. The third action focused on the creation of a precise search equation. In this case it was "robotic*" in [TITLE] in the categories of "Education Educational Research", "Education Scientific Disciplines", "Psychology Educational", and "Education Special". Finally, the fourth action focused on applying this equation in the main WoS collection, which contains several indices (SCI-EXPANDED, SSCI, A and HCI, CPCI-S, CPCI-SSH, BKCI-S, BKCI-SSH, ESCI, CCR-EXPANDED, and IC).

These performances yielded a total of 1037 publications. To improve the literary reporting process, different criteria for both exclusion and inclusion were defined [83]. The exclusion criteria focused on removing the publications of the year 2020, since the year had not yet finished, as it could lead to a bias in the research if it was included ($n = 100$). Repeated or poorly indexed documents in WoS were also suppressed ($n = 9$). This reduced the documentary sample to 926 publications. Figure 1 shows a flow diagram that collects the actions carried out with the PRISMA protocol.

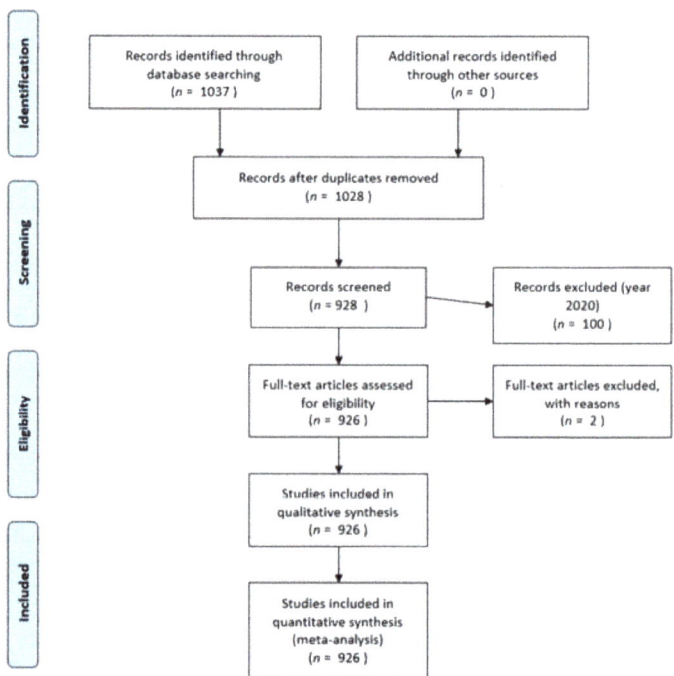

Figure 1. Flowchart according to the PRISMA declaration.

On the other hand, different inclusion criteria, taken from the expert literature, were established [84,85] to optimally represent scientific production and performance: year of publication (all production); language (x ≥ 7); areas of knowledge (x ≥ 140); type of documents (x ≥ 10); institutions (x ≥ 15); authors (x ≥ 15); sources of origin (x ≥ 40); country (x ≥ 35); and the four most cited documents (x ≥ 109).

3.3. Data Analysis

To carry out the analytical process of the literature, various programs were used. Specifically, the Analyze Results and Creation Citation Report were used as tools to define the year, authorship, country, type of document, institution, language, media, and most cited documents. In addition, SciMAT was used to carry out all necessary actions to accomplish the structural and dynamic development at the longitudinal level of the scientific documents and to execute the analysis of cowords. For efficient use of the programs, the premises established in preceding studies were followed [86,87].

As postulated by experts [88], the analysis of cowords was carried out in four processes:

- Recognition: In this process, the keywords (*n* = 1969) of the different publications were analyzed. Next, the co-occurrence node maps were designed. In addition, a normalized network of cowords was developed. Likewise, the most relevant keywords were determined (*n* = 1863). This process concluded with the delimitation of the most prominent topics and terms by means of a clustering algorithm [89].
- Reproduction: In this process, the thematic networks and strategic diagrams articulated in four sections were designed. The upper right section shapes the relevant and motor themes. The upper left section reflects the deep-rooted, isolated issues. The lower left section represents issues in disappearance or in projection. The lower right section reflects the underdeveloped and cross-cutting themes. This process considers the principles of density (network internal strength) and centrality (connection degree between networks) [90].
- Determination: In this process, the reported documental volume was classified in three time periods based on the principle of equality of publications in each interval [91]. The periods were as follows: P1 = 1975–2012, P2 = 2013–2016, and P3 = 2017–2019. The strength of association between these periods arises from the number of keywords in common. For the authors' analysis, a single period, covering all existing production, was considered (PX = 1975–2019).
- Performance: In this process, various production indicators linked to the inclusion criteria were defined [92,93] (Table 1).

Table 1. Production indicators and inclusion criteria.

Configuration	Values
Analysis unit	Keywords authors, keywords WoS
Frequency threshold	Keywords: P_1 = (2), P_2 = (2), P_3 = (2) Authors: P_X = (3)
Network type	Co-occurrence
Co-occurrence union value threshold	Keywords: P_1 = (1), P_2 = (2), P_3 = (2) Authors: P_X = (2)
Normalization measure	Equivalence index: eij = cij2/Root (ci–cj)
Clustering algorithm	Maximum size: 9; Minimum size: 3
Evolutionary measure	Jaccard index
Overlapping measure	Inclusion rate

4. Results

4.1. Performance and Scientific Production

The production volume of ROBEDU in WoS was 926 manuscripts. The first documents compiled in this database go back to 1975. From that date to 2019, the evolution of this topic was uneven. From 1975 to 1998, production was not continuous, with leaps of years in scientific production. From 2000 to 2010, scientific production was constant but irregular in terms of production volume, which did not exceed 50 products per year. From 2011 onwards, production increased considerably, although unsteadily. From 2011 to 2013, production increased. From 2014 to 2015, the production trend decreased and then increased. This increase in production continued into 2016 and beyond, with a small break in 2018 (Figure 2).

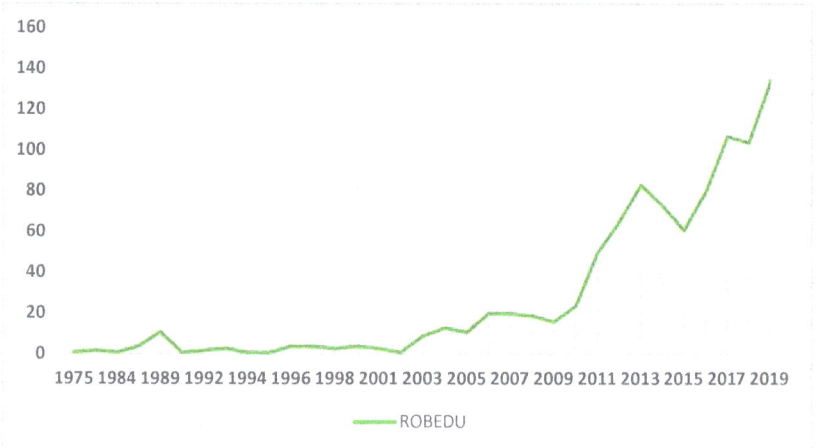

Figure 2. Evolution of scientific production.

The manuscripts that deal with ROBEDU were written mainly in English, which accounted for more than 95% of the production. Spanish and Portuguese also appeared but in a very low volume (Table 2).

Table 2. Scientific language used.

Language	n
English	888
Spanish	35
Portuguese	8

There were two knowledge areas that stood out in the ROBEDU field of study. These were "Education Educational Research" and "Education Scientific Disciplines". The other areas, with lower production levels, were focused on the knowledge areas of engineering and computer science (Table 3).

Table 3. Areas of knowledge.

Area of Knowledge	n
Education Educational Research	590
Education Scientific Disciplines	539
Engineering Multidisciplinary	177
Engineering Electrical Electronic	151
Computer Science Interdisciplinary Applications	145

The volume of manuscripts generated in conference communications stood out considerably, being higher than the other types of documents. The high production volume of existing research articles was also significant (Table 4).

Table 4. Types of document.

Document Type	n
Proceedings paper	563
Article	345
Book chapter	35
Editorial material	17

There were no major differences between the various institutions worldwide in ROBEDU's scientific production. The University System of Georgia had the highest volume of production (Table 5).

Table 5. Institutions.

Institution	n
University System of Georgia	22
Tufts University	19
State University System of Florida	16
Carnegie Mellon University	15

As with the institutions, no author stood out above the rest in terms of production volume. Interestingly, several authors had the same volume of scientific production (Table 6).

Table 6. Most prolific authors.

Author	n
Adamchuk, V.I.	16
Barker, B.S.	16
Bers, M.U.	16
Grandgenett, N.	16
Nugent, G.	16

In accordance with the type of manuscript, the main source of production was conference proceedings. Among the magazines with the most production, Advances in Intelligent Systems and Computing stood out (Table 7).

Table 7. Source of provenance.

Source Title	n
ASEE Annual Conference Exposition	79
Frontiers in Education Conference	62
Advances in Intelligent Systems and Computing	46
INTED Proceedings	41
IEEE Transactions on Education	40

The country with the largest volume of production was the United States. Spain followed with a much smaller volume of production (Table 8).

Table 8. Country.

Country	n
USA	351
Spain	105
Italy	39
Brazil	35

The most cited manuscripts, mainly research articles, present a high volume of citations. The most cited manuscript, almost doubling its successor, is [94]. This work includes a systematic review on the application of robotics in educational centers. The main findings focus on the virtues of this educational technology to improve the learning process, but with caution, since studies have appeared in which there were no improvements. It also offers a series of implications for educators and professionals in this field of knowledge. It is followed by [95] with 190 citations. This study focuses on revealing the findings achieved after the application of a project that combines robotics with programming in students no more than 4 years old. The main results focus on the improvements produced in the interest and in the learning capacity on topics concerning robotics, its programming and, as a consequence, computational thinking. It is followed by [96] with 128 citations. In this research, we tried to verify the improvement of the performance of adolescent students through robotics. The students were divided into a control and experimental group. Prepost tests were performed. The findings reflect that students who received a teaching and learning process through robotics obtained better scores than those who did not use it. The fourth most cited article was [97] with 109 citations. In this work, a hybrid learning experience was carried out in higher education, combining the face-to-face plane with virtuality through content management platforms of a robotic nature. The findings reached determine the demonstrated effectiveness in both learning and performance of university students (Table 9).

Table 9. Most cited articles.

Reference	Citations
[94]	328
[95]	190
[96]	128
[97]	109

4.2. Structural and Thematic Development

The evolution of keywords in adjacent periods showed a medium-low percentage of coincidence. Between the first period (1975–2011) and the second period (2013–2016), the percentage of coincidence was 28%, and, between the second period (2013–2016) and the third period (2017–2019), the percentage of coincidence was 30%. This indicates that the scientific community is establishing common research bases, though at a low volume. The coincidence percentages show the appearance of new research trends in the ROBEDU field of study (Figure 3).

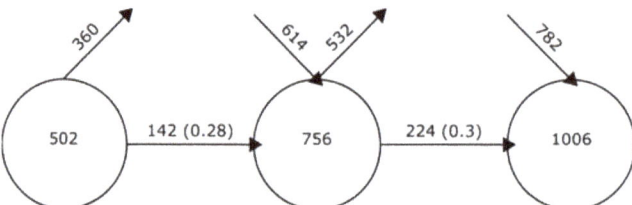

Figure 3. Continuity of keywords between adjacent intervals.

Academic performance offers information on the bibliometric values of the thematics resulting from the coword analysis. In the first period (1975–2011), the thematic "education" has the highest bibliometric values. In the second period (2013–2016), the two most prominent thematics have similar bibliometric values. They are "science" and "education". In the third period (2017–2019), there are also two prominent thematics with similar bibliometric values. In this case, the two thematics are "programming" and "computational-thinking" (Table 10).

Table 10. Thematic performance in robotics in education (ROBEDU).

Denomination	Works	Index h	Index g	Index hg	Index q2	Citations
Interval 1975–2012						
Physics	3	2	2	2	12.08	86
Engineering	8	3	4	3.46	4024	23
Programming	11	4	7	5.29	9.38	83
Educational-robotics	8	3	5	3.87	4.58	99
Design	5	5	5	5	8.06	106
Education	8	7	8	7.48	9.9	186
Robotics-education	5	2	2	2	5.1	16
Remote-laboratory	3	3	3	3	10.82	151
Hands-on	2	1	2	1.41	3.32	12
Partnerships	2	1	2	1.41	5.2	28
Online-learning	2	0	0	0	0	0
Gender	2	2	2	2	13.93	103
Interval 2013–2016						
Denomination	Works	Index h	Index g	Index hg	Index q2	Citations
Joint-attention	3	3	3	3	8.12	64
Simulation	7	5	5	5	8.06	60
Science	14	9	11	9.95	12.37	390
Education	29	9	18	12.73	13.08	335
Educational-robotics	10	2	7	3.74	9.27	57
Programming	7	5	5	5	10	317
Mobile-robots	7	2	2	2	2.45	8
Learning-curve	5	2	3	2.45	6.16	38
Project-based-learning	4	2	3	2.45	3.46	11
Teamwork	6	1	1	1	1	1
Mechatronics	3	3	3	3	5.74	47
Interval 2017–2019						
Denomination	Works	Index h	Index g	Index hg	Index q2	Citations
Outcomes	8	4	8	5.66	10.2	88
Performance	10	3	4	3.46	4.24	29
Programming	58	7	12	9.17	11.22	185
Technology	10	3	7	4.58	7.35	51
Computational-thinking	32	7	13	9.54	11.53	180
Robotic-surgery	7	4	6	4.9	5.66	37
Robots	7	2	3	2.45	4.24	16
School	7	3	6	4.24	3.46	37
Students	5	2	4	2.83	6	26
Computer-science-education	4	0	0	0	0	0
Gender-differences	4	2	4	2.83	6	28

The strategic thematic diagrams, categorized according to the h-index, mark the value and relevance of the various thematics in a set time period. The diagrams are presented on a Cartesian axis. In this case, the y-axis shows density and the x-axis shows centrality. Density represents the external relationship of the thematics, while centrality represents the internal relationship. The evolution of the research on robotics in the educational field is represented in Figure 4.

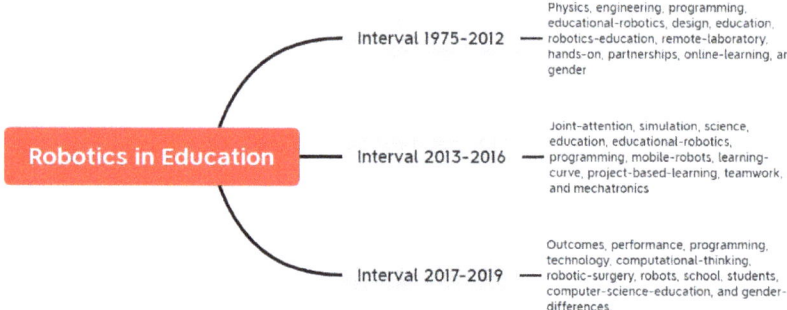

Figure 4. Synoptic representation of the evolution of robotics in education in the lines of research.

The data represented in Figure 5 indicate that in the first period (1975–2012) the motor thematics were "physics", which is related to "sensors", "robotic-assisted-teaching", "interactive-learning-environments", "camera", "laboratories", "learning-environments", "skills", and "intelligent-tutoring-systems"; and "engineering", which is related to "computer-science", "mathematics", "nasa", "competition", "technology", "stem", "science", and "outreach". In this period, the most relevant studies were concerned with physics, focused on engineering studies, where active teaching methods based on robotics were applied.

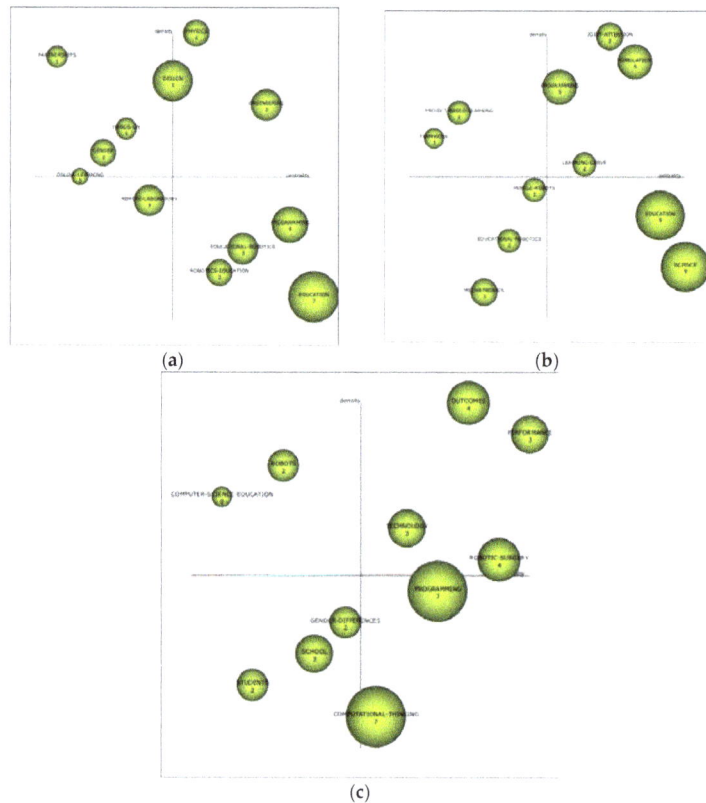

Figure 5. Strategic diagrams by ROBEDU h-index: (**a**) interval 1975–2012; (**b**) interval 2013–2016; and (**c**) interval 2017–2019.

In the second period (2013–2016), the main thematics were "programming", which is related to "early-childhood", "concept-mapping", "prekindergarten", "engineering", and "early-childhood-education"; "joint-attention", which is related to "imitation", "motor", "music-therapy", "behavior", "young-children", "autism", "individuals", and "rhythm"; "simulation", which is related to "resident-training", "robotic-training", "robotic-prostatectomy", "surgery", "face", "performance", "robotic-surgery", and "radical-prostatectomy"; and "learning-curve", which is related to "validation", "surgical-education", "experience", and "simulator". In this period, the focus of studies on robotics in education expanded. In this case, the use of robotics was addressed in various educational stages, in the attention of students with special educational needs, and, above all, in the educational field to carry out simulations.

In the third period (2017–2019), the motor thematics were "outcomes", which is related to "residency-training", "resection", "surgical-education", "learning-curve", and "minimally-invasive"; "performance", which is related to "self-efficacy", "validation", "surgery-simulator", "computer-simulation", "expert", "virtual-reality", "stereotypes", and "girl"; "technology", which is related to "teaching/learning-strategies", "perception", "needs", "attitudes", and "choice"; "experience", which is related to "science" and "elementary-education"; and "robotic-surgery", which is related to "robotic-training", "curriculum", "simulation", "simulator", "tool", "impact", and "resident-training". In this period, the line of research established in the previous period was maintained, with added aspects such as simulation, self-efficacy, science, and stereotypes in the use of robotics. In addition, in this period, we must highlight the themes "student", "school", and "gender-differences", which given their position in the diagram can be considered as the future motor thematics of the ROBEDU field of study.

4.3. Thematic Evolution of Terms

The thematic evolution represents the connection between the various themes generated between adjacent periods. This connection can be of two types: conceptual and non-conceptual. The conceptual connection occurs when the two themes represented have a third theme in common. The non-conceptual connection occurs when the connection between themes occurs only through keywords. The conceptual connection is presented with solid lines, and the non-conceptual connection is presented with a broken line. Another feature to bear in mind is the line thickness. The thicker the line is, the more themes or keywords concur between them. This type of connection represents the value and level of coincidences existing in a field of study.

The data shown in Figure 6 indicate several aspects. Firstly, there is no conceptual gap, as the topic "programming" appears in all periods. Secondly, although the topic "programming" appears in all periods, it cannot be considered to be setting an established and solid line of research in the ROBEDU field of study. In this case, there is no consolidated line in all three periods, though the one established by "educational-robotics–educational-robotics–computational-thinking" may slightly stand out. What can certainly be said is that some strong research lines are starting to be generated, made visible from the second period. This is the case of "simulation–robotic-surgery", "education–programming", "science–technology", "science–school", and "science–student". Finally, it can be observed that there are not many connections between themes from adjacent periods; nevertheless, conceptual rather than non-conceptual connections predominate. This shows that there are not many shared lines of research.

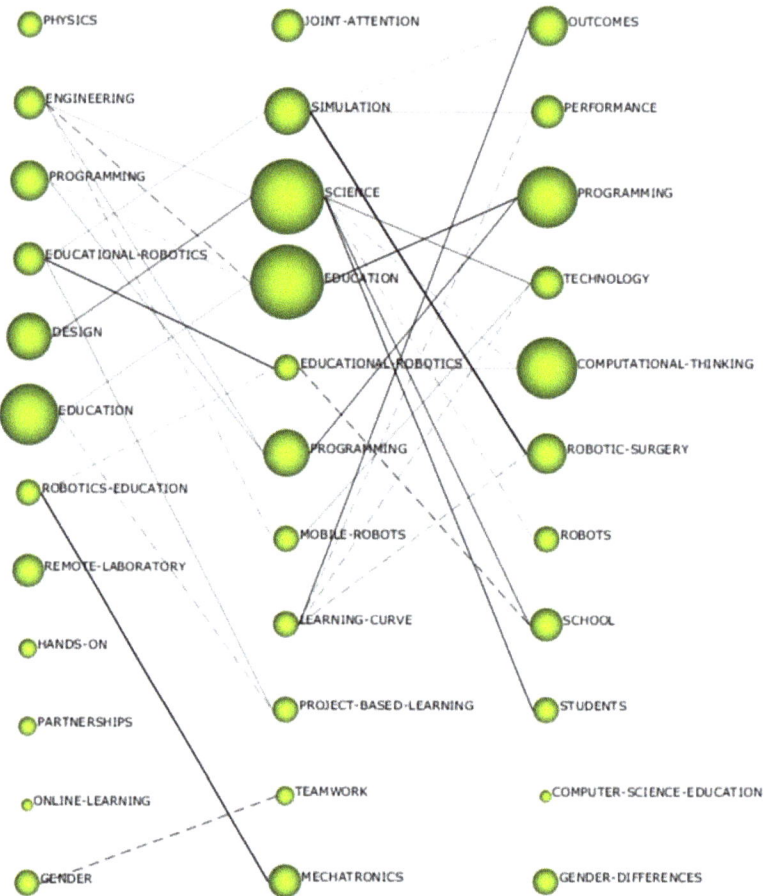

Figure 6. Thematic evolution by h-index.

4.4. Authors with the Highest Relevance Index

Regarding the authors, Figure 7 shows that the most relevant are Candelas, F.A., Rihtarsic, D., and Loreto-Gómez, G. In addition, Hamner, E. and Sutinen, E. must be taken into account due to their location in the diagram, which places them as relevant authors in this field of study.

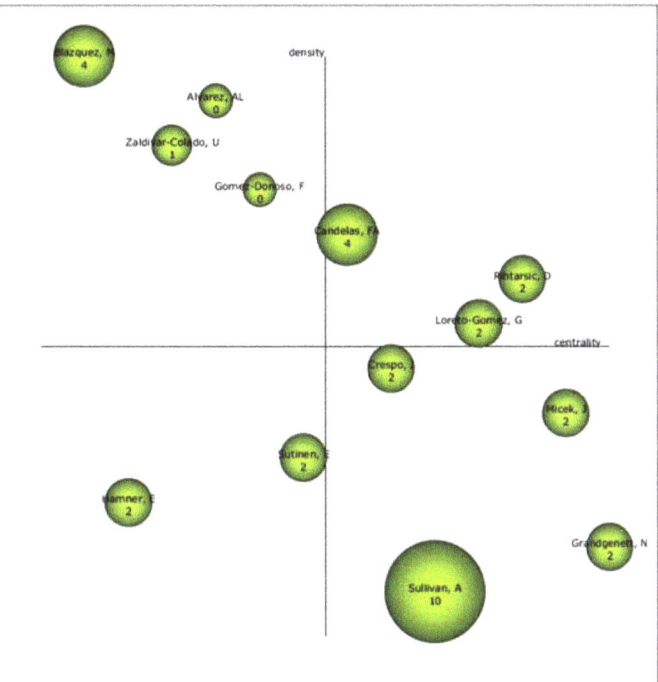

Figure 7. Strategic author diagram of the entire production.

5. Discussion and Conclusions

Technology has changed the way we interact and learn [1]. Therefore, teachers should include its use in their pedagogical practice as one more element so that students can learn in a collaborative and active manner [5]. There is a variety of hardware and software that allows the implementation of robotics in the teaching and learning process. As analyzed in other studies, robotics has not yet been implemented in a concrete way in education systems. However, due to the potential it offers for the academic development of students, it will probably be included in the not-too-distant future as a specific subject in various education systems [25–41,47–50].

Regarding the performance analysis and scientific production on robotics in education, the first publication appeared in 1975. The evolution of the volume of production has been uneven, showing an irregular production from 1975 to 1998. There was a low production of documents between 1975 and 2010. However, scientific production increased from 2010 to 2019, with 2019 having the highest production peak with respect to the thematic.

The most used language for publishing in this field of study is English. Two purely educational publication areas stand out, although engineering and computer science areas also appear in the top positions. One of the most prolific institutions in terms of the thematic is the University System of Georgia; however, other institutions have a similar volume of production. As for the country, the United States is the largest producer of documents.

The types of documents produced are mostly proceedings papers. This indicates that the bases of the investigations are not settled at the time in the form of articles, perhaps showing new lines and trends in the investigation. Regarding the source of production, the minute number of books stands out (matching with the data obtained for the types of documents). The most productive journal in the ROBEDU field of study is *Advances in Intelligent Systems and Computing*. As for the authors, several stand out as the highest producers, with the volume of production being nearly the same among the first places. The most prominent relevant authors are Candelas, F.A., Rihtarsic, D., and Loreto-Gómez,

G. According to production and evolution, the authors that will probably be relevant in the future are Hamner, E. and Sutinen, E. With regard to citations, the manuscripts on ROBEDU have a considerable volume of citations, among which the most cited manuscript is that of [42] with 328 citations. In relation to the topics of these works, the most cited manuscript's topic is about the benefits of this educational technology to improve the learning process [94], and practical implications for teachers and professionals. The second most cited work's topic [95] is about the findings of applying robotics with programming on early stages of education. The third topic or work most cited [96] is about verifying the improvement of the performance of adolescent students through robotics. Additionally, finally, the fourth most cited article [97] is about a hybrid learning experience, which was carried out in higher education, combining the face-to-face plane with virtuality through content management platforms of a robotic nature.

On the other hand, in terms of structural and thematic development, the keyword coincidence level between adjacent periods is medium-low. This denotes a lack of established or fixed lines of investigation over time. Academic performance displays changes between the examined periods, moving from focusing on the educational field in general to focusing on science and on programming actions and computational thinking. This corroborates the keyword coincidence, demonstrating that there is no line of investigation established over time.

As for the strategic diagrams, they indicate that during the period between 1975 and 2012, the most relevant investigations pointed toward physics, focused on engineering studies, where active teaching methods based on robotics were applied. Later, in the period between 2013 and 2016, the focus of studies about robotics in education widened. In this case, the use of robotics is addressed in different educational stages, in the attention of students with special educational needs, and especially in the educational field for carrying out simulations. Then, in the period between 2017 and 2019, the line of research previously established is maintained, adding aspects such as simulation, self-efficacy, science, and stereotypes in the use of robotics. In the future, the field of study may focus on the students themselves, schools, and gender differences.

The thematic evolution of terms indicates three main aspects. Firstly, there is no conceptual gap and, therefore, no line of research is recognized in the three periods; however, "educational-robotics–educational-robotics–computational-thinking" is slightly highlighted. Secondly, strong lines of research are observed from the second period onwards, highlighting "simulation–robotic-surgery", "education–programming", "science–technology", "science–school", and "science–student". Finally, there are not many connections between themes from adjacent periods, with the conceptual rather than the non-conceptual connections prevailing. This proves that there are not many shared research lines.

As this study has shown, the field of robotics in education has had an increase and consequent upswing in recent years, especially in 2019. Several parameters have shown that no lines of research have been established over time, but, at the same time, there are clues that, recently, the interest in the subject has been increasing. This opens a field of work for researchers on the thematic of robotics and education, which has expanded over recent years in the field of simulation and self-efficacy.

Regarding future prospects, this study shows the potential that the latest studies on the subject have, showing experts, whether researchers and/or teachers, the next path of research on the subject. In addition, a clear systematic review of the robotics and education aspects of recent research in the scientific literature can be carried out.

About the limitations of this study, it should be highlighted that the year 2020 was not included, since the year had not yet finished and the data would therefore not be real. Furthermore, future research could include a coword analysis on topics associated with the study topic.

With regard to the educational implications of this study, based on the analysis carried out, teachers would have the documents on the thematic of robotics and education at their disposal and the relevance that they have had and still have in the educational field. Proof of this is the finding of the use of robotics in various educational stages, in foregrounds particularly, and specifically in the attention of students with special educational needs, in the educational field to carry out simulations, and in self-efficacy with the use of robotics. Given the importance it has for the scientific community in general and teachers in particular, this study paves the way for new lines of work for both teachers and researchers.

Author Contributions: J.L.-B.: Methodology, formal analysis, investigation, writing—original draft preparation, writing—review and editing, visualization, and supervision. A.S.-R.: Conceptualization, formal analysis, investigation, writing—original draft preparation, writing—review and editing, and visualization. A.-J.M.-G.: Software, formal analysis, investigation, data curation, writing—original draft preparation, writing—review and editing, and visualization. M.-E.P.-G.: Formal analysis, investigation, writing—original draft preparation, writing—review and editing, and visualization. All authors have read and agreed to the published version of the manuscript.

Funding: This research received no external funding.

Conflicts of Interest: The authors declare no conflict of interest.

References

1. Baller, S.; Dutta, S.; Lanvin, B. *Global Information Technology Report 2016*; Ouranos: Geneva, Switzerland, 2016.
2. Bardakci, S.; Ünver, T.K. Preservice ICT teachers' technology metaphors in the margin of technological determinism. *Educ. Inf. Technol.* **2019**, *25*, 905–925. [CrossRef]
3. Pavel, A.; Fruth, A.; Neacsu, M. ICT and E-Learning—Catalysts for Innovation and Quality in Higher Education. *Procedia Econ. Financ.* **2015**, *23*, 704–711. [CrossRef]
4. Pandolfini, V. Exploring the Impact of ICTs in Education: Controversies and Challenges. *Ital. J. Sociol. Educ.* **2016**, *8*, 28–53. [CrossRef]
5. Chen, C.-L.; Wu, C.-C.; Chen, C.-L.; Cheng-Chih, W. Students' behavioral intention to use and achievements in ICT-Integrated mathematics remedial instruction: Case study of a calculus course. *Comput. Educ.* **2020**, *145*, 103740. [CrossRef]
6. Segura-Robles, A.; Fuentes-Cabrera, A.; Parra-González, M.E.; López-Belmonte, J. Effects on Personal Factors Through Flipped Learning and Gamification as Combined Methodologies in Secondary Education. *Front. Psychol.* **2020**, *11*, 1103. [CrossRef]
7. Scaradozzi, D.; Screpanti, L.; Cesaretti, L. Towards a Definition of Educational Robotics: A Classification of Tools, Experiences and Assessments. In *Smart Learning with Educational Robotics: Using Robots to Scaffold Learning Outcomes*; Daniela, L., Ed.; Springer International Publishing: Cham, Switzerland, 2019; pp. 63–92.
8. Marín-Marín, J.-A.; Costa, R.S.; Moreno-Guerrero, A.-J.; López-Belmonte, J. Makey Makey as an Interactive Robotic Tool for High School Students' Learning in Multicultural Contexts. *Educ. Sci.* **2020**, *10*, 239. [CrossRef]
9. Miller, D.P.; Nourbakhsh, I. Robotics for Education. In *Springer Handbook of Robotics*; Siciliano, B., Khatib, O., Eds.; Springer International Publishing: Cham, Switzerland, 2016; pp. 2115–2134.
10. Papert, S. *Mindstorms: Children, Computers, and Powerful Ideas*; Basic Books, Inc.: New York, NY, USA, 2020.
11. Kubilinskiene, S.; Zilinskiene, I.; Dagiene, V.; Sinkevičius, V. Applying Robotics in School Education: A Systematic Review. *BJMC* **2017**, *5*, 50–69. [CrossRef]
12. Sullivan, F.R. Robotics and science literacy: Thinking skills, science process skills and systems understanding. *J. Res. Sci. Teach.* **2008**, *45*, 373–394. [CrossRef]
13. Williams, D.C.; Ma, Y.; Prejean, L.; Ford, M.J.; Lai, G. Acquisition of Physics Content Knowledge and Scientific Inquiry Skills in a Robotics Summer Camp. *J. Res. Technol. Educ.* **2007**, *40*, 201–216. [CrossRef]
14. Vargheese, M.G.; Education, M.T.; Suresh, M.J. *Beginner Robotics: Robotic Mechanics—With Lego Mindstorms: Volume 2*; CreateSpace Independent Publishing Platform: Scotts Valley, CA, USA, 2013; ISBN 978-1-4820-9038-3.
15. Ferreira, E.; Silva, M.J.; da Cruz Valente, B. Collaborative uses of ICT in education: Practices and representations of preservice elementary school teachers. In Proceedings of the 2018 International Symposium on Computers in Education (SIIE), Jerez, Spain, 19–21 September 2018; pp. 1–6.
16. Qureshi, M.; Syed, R. The Impact of Robotics on Employment and Motivation of Employees in the Service Sector, with Special Reference to Health Care. *Saf. Health Work* **2014**, *5*, 198–202. [CrossRef]
17. Marín-Marín, J.A.; Soler-Costa, R.; Moreno-Guerrero, A.J.; López-Belmonte, J. Effectiveness of Diet Habits and Active Life in Vocational Training for Higher Technician in Dietetics: Contrast between the Traditional Method and the Digital Resources. *Nutrients* **2020**, *12*, 3475. [CrossRef] [PubMed]
18. Sáez, J.M.; Buceta, R.; De Lara, S. Introducing robotics and block programming in elementary education. *RIED* **2021**, *24*, 95–113. [CrossRef]
19. Ruíz, F.; Zapatera, A.; Montes, N. Curriculum analysis and design, implementation, and validation of a STEAM project through educational robotics in primary education. *Comput. Appl. Eng. Educ.* **2020**, 1–15. [CrossRef]
20. Schina, D.; Esteve-González, V.; Usart, M.; Lizaro-Cantabrana, J.L.; Gisbert, M. The Integration of Sustainable Development Goals in Educational Robotics: A Teacher Education Experience. *Sustainability* **2020**, *12*, 85. [CrossRef]
21. Canas, J.M.; Perdices, E.; García-Pérez, L.; Fernández-Conde, J. A ROS-Based Open Tool for Intelligent Robotics Education. *Appl. Sci.* **2020**, *10*, 7419. [CrossRef]

22. Yilmaz, E.; Koc, M. The consequences of robotics programming education on computational thinking skills: An intervention of the Young Engineer's Workshop (YEW). *Comput. Appl. Eng. Educ.* **2020**, 1–18. [CrossRef]
23. Chen, C.H.; Yang, C.K.; Huang, K.; Yao, K.C. Augmented reality and competition in robotics education: Effects on 21st century competencies, group collaboration and learning motivation. *J. Comput. Assist. Learn.* **2020**, *36*, 1052–10662. [CrossRef]
24. Zhong, B.C.; Zheng, J.J.; Zhan, Z.H. An exploration of combining virtual and physical robots in robotics education. *Interact. Learn. Environ.* **2020**, 1–13. [CrossRef]
25. Tang, A.L.L.; Tung, V.W.S.; Cheng, T.O. Teachers' perceptions of the potential use of educational robotics in management education. *Interact. Learn. Environ.* **2020**, 1–12. [CrossRef]
26. Alemi, M.; Taheri, A.; Shariati, A.; Meghdari, A. Social Robotics, Education, and Religion in the Islamic World: An Iranian Perspective. *Sci. Eng. Ethics* **2020**, *26*, 2709–2734. [CrossRef]
27. Caballero-González, Y.A.; García-Valcarcel, A. Learning with Robotics in Primary Education? A Means of Stimulating Computational Thinking. *Educ. Knowl. Soc.* **2020**, *21*, 1–10. [CrossRef]
28. Turan, S.; Aydogdu, F. Effect of coding and robotic education on pre-school children's skills of scientific process. *Educ. Inf. Technol.* **2020**, *25*, 4353–4363. [CrossRef]
29. Naik, R.; Mandal, I. Robotic simulation experience in undergraduate medical education: A perspective. *J. Robot. Surg.* **2020**, *14*, 793–794. [CrossRef] [PubMed]
30. Zhong, B.C.; Li, T.T. Can Pair Learning Improve Students' Troubleshooting Performance in Robotics Education? *J. Educ. Comput. Res.* **2020**, *58*, 220–249. [CrossRef]
31. Gorjup, G.; Liarokapis, M. A Low-Cost, Open-Source, Robotic Airship for Education and Research. *IEEE Access* **2020**, *8*, 70713–70721. [CrossRef]
32. Chootongchai, S.; Songkram, N.; Piromsopa, K. Dimensions of robotic education quality: Teachers' perspectives as teaching assistants in Thai elementary schools. *Educ. Inf. Technol.* **2019**, 1–21. [CrossRef]
33. Vega, J.; Canas, J.M. Open Vision System for Low-Cost Robotics Education. *Electronics* **2019**, *8*, 1295. [CrossRef]
34. Díaz-Lauzurica, B.; Moreno-Salinas, D. Computational Thinking and Robotics: A Teaching Experience in Compulsory Secondary Education with Students with High Degree of Apathy and Demotivation. *Sustainability* **2019**, *11*, 5109. [CrossRef]
35. Gaudiello, I.; Zibetti, E. Educational Robotics in Science Education: Why and how. *Enfance* **2019**, *3*, 309–332. [CrossRef]
36. Ospennikova, E.; Ershov, M.; Iljin, I. Educational Robotics as an Inovative Educational Technology. *Procedia Soc. Behav. Sci.* **2015**, *214*, 18–26. [CrossRef]
37. Blackley, S.; Howell, J. The Next Chapter in the STEM Education Narrative: Using Robotics to Support Programming and Coding. *Australas. J. Teach. Educ.* **2019**, *44*, 51–64. [CrossRef]
38. García-Valcarcel, A.; Caballero-González, Y.A. Robotics to develop computational thinking in early Childhood Education. *Comunicar* **2019**, *27*, 63–72. [CrossRef]
39. Parent, S.; Iatauro, S. Global Robotics Competition Meets Inclusive Education: The Exceptional Journey of Five Resilient Students. *Learn. Landsc.* **2019**, *12*, 29–32. [CrossRef]
40. Moreno-Guerrero, A.J.; Rodríguez, C.; Ramos, M.; Sola, J.M. Secondary Education students' interest and motivation towards using Aurasma in Physical Education classes. *Retos* **2020**, *38*, 333–340. [CrossRef]
41. Yi, H. Robotics and kinetic design for underrepresented minority (URM) students in building education: Challenges and opportunities. *Comput. Appl. Eng. Educ.* **2019**, *27*, 351–370. [CrossRef]
42. Hsieh, S.J. Development and Evaluation of Remote Virtual Teach Pendant for Industrial Robotics Education. *Int. J. Eng. Educ.* **2019**, *35*, 1816–1826.
43. Hinojo-Lucena, F.J.; Dúo-Terrón, P.; Ramos, M.; Rodríguez-Jiménez, C.; Moreno-Guerrero, A.J. Scientific Performance and Mapping of the Term STEM in Education on the Web of Science. *Sustainability* **2020**, *12*, 2279. [CrossRef]
44. Vivas, L.; Sáez, J.M. Integration of educational robotics in Primary Education. *RELATEC* **2019**, *18*, 107–129. [CrossRef]
45. Vega, J.; Canas, J.M. PiBot: An Open Low-Cost Robotic Platform with Camera for STEM Education. *Electronics* **2018**, *7*, 430. [CrossRef]
46. Moreno-Guerrero, A.J.; Alonso, S.; Ramos, M.; Campos-Soto, N.; Gómez, G. Augmented Reality as a Resource for Improving Learning in the Physical Education Classroom. *Int. J. Environ. Res. Public Health* **2020**, *17*, 3637. [CrossRef]
47. Fonseca, N.M.; Freitas, E.D.C. Computer applications for education on industrial robotic systems. *Comput. Appl. Eng. Educ.* **2018**, *26*, 1186–1194. [CrossRef]
48. Morze, N.V.; Gladun, M.A.; Dziuba, S.M. Formation of key and subject competences of students by robotics kits of Stem-Education. *Inf. Technol. Learn. Tools* **2018**, *65*, 37–52. [CrossRef]
49. Esposito, J.M. The State of Robotics Education Proposed Goals for Positively Transforming Robotics Education at Postsecondary Institutions. *IEEE Robot. Autom. Mag.* **2017**, *24*, 157–164. [CrossRef]
50. Merkouris, A.; Chorianopoulos, K.; Kameas, A. Teaching Programming in Secondary Education through Embodied Computing Platforms: Robotics and Wearables. *ACM Trans. Comput. Educ.* **2017**, *17*, 1–22. [CrossRef]
51. López, J.A.; López-Belmonte, J.; Moreno-Guerrero, A.J.; Pozo, S. Effectiveness of Innovate Educational Practices with Flipped Learning and Remote Sensing in Earth and Environmental Sciences—An Exploratory Case Study. *Remote Sens.* **2020**, *12*, 897. [CrossRef]
52. Galimullina, E.Z.; Ljbimova, E.M.; Sharafeeva, L.R. Introduction of the robotics in education of children and youth. *Turk. Online J. Des. Art Commun.* **2017**, *7*, 738–744. [CrossRef]
53. Viegas, J.V.; Villalba, K.O. Education and Educative Robotics. *RED* **2017**, *54*, 1–13. [CrossRef]

54. Salgarayeva, G.I.; Bazarbayeva, A. STEAM system in Education and Robotics. *News Natl. Acad. Sci. Repub. Kazakhstan* **2017**, *2*, 81–86.
55. Deniz, C.; Cakir, M. A novel designed interactive training platform for industrial robot offline programming and robotics education. *Int. J. Robot. Autom.* **2017**, *32*, 665–672. [CrossRef]
56. Zalewski, J.; González, F. Evolution in the Education of Software Engineers: Online Course on Cyberphysical Systems with Remote Access to Robotic Devices. *Int. J. Online Eng.* **2017**, *13*, 133–146. [CrossRef]
57. Kanbul, S.; Uzunboylu, H. Importance of Coding Education and Robotic Applications for Achieving 21st-Century Skills in North Cyprus. *Int. J. Emerg. Technol. Learn.* **2017**, *12*, 130–140. [CrossRef]
58. Vitale, G.; Bonarini, A.; Matteucci, M.; Bascetta, L. Toward Vocational Robotics an Experience in Post-Secondary School Education and Job Training Through Robotics. *IEEE Robot. Autom. Mag.* **2016**, *23*, 73–81. [CrossRef]
59. Takacs, A.; Eigner, G.; Kovacs, L.; Rudas, J.J.; Haidegger, T. Teacher's Kit Development, Usability, and Communities of Modular Robotic Kits for Classroom Education. *IEEE Robot. Autom. Mag.* **2016**, *23*, 30–39. [CrossRef]
60. Wallace, M.L.; Freitas, W.M. Resources for Underwater Robotics Education. *J. Ext.* **2016**, *54*, 1–3.
61. Mester, G. Massive open online courses in education of robotics. *Interdiscip. Descr. Complex Syst.* **2016**, *14*, 182–187. [CrossRef]
62. Núñez, A.J. Robotics Education Done Right: Robotics Expansion (TM), A STEAM Based Curricula. *Contemp. Trends Issues Sci. Educ.* **2016**, *44*, 169–185. [CrossRef]
63. Sánchez, E.; Cózar, R.; González-Calero, J.A. Robotics in the teaching of knowledge and interaction with the environment. A formative study in Early Childhood Education. *RIFOP* **2019**, *94*, 11–28.
64. Arís, N.; Orcos, L. Educational robotics in the stage of secondary education: Empirical study on motivation and STEM skills. *Educ. Sci.* **2019**, *9*, 73. [CrossRef]
65. Zhong, B.; Xia, L. A systematic review on exploring the potential of educational robotics in mathematics education. *Int. J. Sci. Math. Educ.* **2020**, *18*, 79–101. [CrossRef]
66. Tan, P.J.B.; Hsu, M.H. Designing a system for English evaluation and teaching devices: A PZB and TAM model analysis. *Eurasia J. Math. Sci. Technol. Educ.* **2018**, *14*, 2107–2119. [CrossRef]
67. Tan, P.J.B. An empirical study of how the learning attitudes of college students toward English e-tutoring websites affect site sustainability. *Sustainability* **2019**, *11*, 1748. [CrossRef]
68. Segura-Robles, A.; Moreno-Guerrero, A.J.; Parra-González, E.; López-Belmonte, J. Review of Research Trends in Learning and the Internet in Higher Education. *Soc. Sci.* **2020**, *9*, 101. [CrossRef]
69. Ellegaard, O.; Wallin, J.A. The bibliometric analysis of scholarly production: How great is the impact? *Scientometrics* **2015**, *105*, 1809–1831. [CrossRef] [PubMed]
70. Carmona-Serrano, N.; López-Belmonte, J.; López-Núñez, J.-A.; Moreno-Guerrero, A.-J. Trends in autism research in the field of education in Web of Science: A bibliometric study. *Brain Sci.* **2020**, *10*, 1018. [CrossRef] [PubMed]
71. López-Belmonte, J.; Moreno-Guerrero, A.J.; López-Núñez, J.A.; Pozo-Sánchez, S. Analysis of the Productive, Structural, and Dynamic Development of Augmented Reality in Higher Education Research on the Web of Science. *Appl. Sci.* **2019**, *9*, 5306. [CrossRef]
72. Cobo, M.J.; López, A.G.; Herrera, E.; Herrera, F. Science mapping software tools: Review, analysis, and cooperative study among tools. *J. Am. Soc. Inf. Sci. Technol.* **2011**, *62*, 1382–1402. [CrossRef]
73. Rodríguez-García, A.M.; López-Belmonte, J.; Agreda-Montoro, M.; Moreno-Guerrero, A.J. Productive, Structural and Dynamic Study of the Concept of Sustainability in the Educational Field. *Sustainability* **2019**, *11*, 5813. [CrossRef]
74. Leung, X.Y.; Sun, J.; Bai, B. Bibliometrics of social media research: A co-citation and co-word analysis. *Int. J. Hosp. Manag.* **2017**, *66*, 35–45. [CrossRef]
75. López-Belmonte, J.; Parra-González, M.E.; Segura-Robles, A.; Pozo-Sánchez, S. Scientific Mapping of Gamification in Web of Science. *Eur. J. Investig. Healthpsychol. Educ.* **2020**, *10*, 832–847. [CrossRef]
76. Martínez, M.A.; Cobo, M.J.; Herrera, M.; Herrera, E. Analyzing the scientific evolution of social work using science mapping. *Res. Soc. Work Pract.* **2015**, *25*, 257–277. [CrossRef]
77. Carmona-Serrano, N.; Moreno-Guerrero, A.-J.; Marín-Marín, J.-A.; López-Belmonte, J. Evolution of the Autism Literature and the Influence of Parents: A Scientific Mapping in Web of Science. *Brain Sci.* **2021**, *11*, 74. [CrossRef]
78. Hirsch, J.E. An index to quantify an individual's scientific research output. *Proc. Natl. Acad. Sci. USA* **2005**, *102*, 16569–16572. [CrossRef] [PubMed]
79. Moreno-Guerrero, A.J.; Gómez-García, G.; López-Belmonte, J.; Rodríguez-Jiménez, C. Internet Addiction in the Web of Science Database: A Review of the Literature with Scientific Mapping. *Int. J. Environ. Res. Public Health* **2020**, *17*, 2753. [CrossRef]
80. López-Robles, J.R.; Otegi-Olaso, J.R.; Porto, I.; Cobo, M.J. 30 years of intelligence models in management and business: A bibliometric review. *Int. J. Inf. Manag.* **2019**, *48*, 22–38. [CrossRef]
81. López-Belmonte, J.; Marín-Marín, J.A.; Soler-Costa, R.; Moreno-Guerrero, A.J. Arduino Advances in Web of Science. A Scientific Mapping of Literary Production. *IEEE Access* **2020**, *8*, 128674–128682. [CrossRef]
82. Moral-Muñoz, J.A.; Herrera-Viedma, E.; Santisteban-Espejo, A.; Cobo, M.J. Software tools for conducting bibliometric analysis in science: An up-to-date review. *El Prof. De La Inf.* **2020**, *29*, e290103. [CrossRef]
83. Moreno-Guerrero, A.J.; López-Belmonte, J.; Marín-Marín, J.A.; Soler-Costa, R. Scientific development of educational artificial intelligence in Web of Science. *Future Internet* **2020**, *12*, 124. [CrossRef]

84. López-Núñez, J.A.; López-Belmonte, J.; Moreno-Guerrero, A.J.; Ramos, M.; Hinojo-Lucena, F.J. Education and Diet in the Scientific Literature: A Study of the Productive, Structural, and Dynamic Development in Web of Science. *Sustainability* **2020**, *12*, 4838. [CrossRef]
85. Moreno-Guerrero, A.J. Estudio bibliométrico de la producción científica en Web of Science: Formación Profesional y blended learning. *Píxel-Bit. Rev. De Medios Y Educ.* **2019**, *56*, 149–168. [CrossRef]
86. Montero-Díaz, J.; Cobo, M.J.; Gutiérrez-Salcedo, M.; Segado-Boj, F.; Herrera-Viedma, E. Mapeo científico de la Categoría «Comunicación» en WoS (1980-2013). *Comunicar* **2018**, *26*, 81–91. [CrossRef]
87. López-Belmonte, J.; Segura-Robles, A.; Moreno-Guerrero, A.-J.; Parra-González, M.-E. Projection of E-Learning in Higher Education: A Study of Its Scientific Production in Web of Science. *Eur. J. Investig. Healthpsychol. Educ.* **2021**, *11*, 3. [CrossRef]
88. Parra-González, M.; Segura-Robles, A.; Vicente-Bújez, M.; López-Belmonte, J. Production Analysis and Scientific Mapping on Active Methodologies in Web of Science. *Int. J. Emerg. Technol. Learn.* **2020**, *15*, 71–86. [CrossRef]
89. Herrera-Viedma, E.; López-Robles, J.R.; Guallar, J.; Cobo, M.J. Global trends in coronavirus research at the time of Covid-19: A general bibliometric approach and content analysis using SciMAT. *El Prof. De La Inf.* **2020**, *29*, e290103. [CrossRef]
90. Callon, M.; Courtial, J.P.; Laville, F. Co-word analysis as a tool for describing the network of interactions between basic and technological research: The case of polymer chemsitry. *Scientometrics* **1991**, *22*, 155–205. [CrossRef]
91. López-Belmonte, J.; Moreno-Guerrero, A.J.; López-Núñez, J.A.; Hinojo-Lucena, F.J. Augmented reality in education. A scientific mapping in Web of Science. *Interact. Learn. Environ.* **2020**, 1–15. [CrossRef]
92. López-Belmonte, J.; Segura-Robles, A.; Moreno-Guerrero, A.J.; Parra-González, E. Machine Learning and Big Data in the Impact Literature. A Bibliometric Review with Scientific Mapping in Web of Science. *Symmetry* **2020**, *12*, 495. [CrossRef]
93. Carmona-Serrano, N.; López-Belmonte, J.; Cuesta-Gómez, J.L.; Moreno-Guerrero, A.J. Documentary Analysis of the Scientific Literature on Autism and Technology in Web of Science. *Brain Sci.* **2020**, *10*, 985. [CrossRef]
94. Vavassoru, B.; Barreto, F. Exploring the educational potential of robotics in schools: A systematic review. *Comput. Educ.* **2012**, *58*, 978–988. [CrossRef]
95. Bers, M.U.; Flannery, L.; Kazakoff, E.R.; Sullivan, A. Computational thinking and tinkering: Exploration of an early childhood robotics curriculum. *Comput. Educ.* **2014**, *72*, 145–157. [CrossRef]
96. Barker, B.S.; Ansorge, J. Robotics as Means to Increase Achievement Scores in an Informal Learning Environment. *J. Res. Technol. Educ.* **2007**, *39*, 229–243. [CrossRef]
97. Jara, C.A.; Candelas, F.A.; Puente, S.T.; Torres, F. Hands-on experiences of undergraduate students in Automatics and Robotics using a virtual and remote laboratory. *Comput. Educ.* **2011**, *57*, 2451–2461. [CrossRef]

MDPI
St. Alban-Anlage 66
4052 Basel
Switzerland
Tel. +41 61 683 77 34
Fax +41 61 302 89 18
www.mdpi.com

Electronics Editorial Office
E-mail: electronics@mdpi.com
www.mdpi.com/journal/electronics

www.ingramcontent.com/pod-product-compliance
Lightning Source LLC
LaVergne TN
LVHW070458100526
838202LV00014B/1748